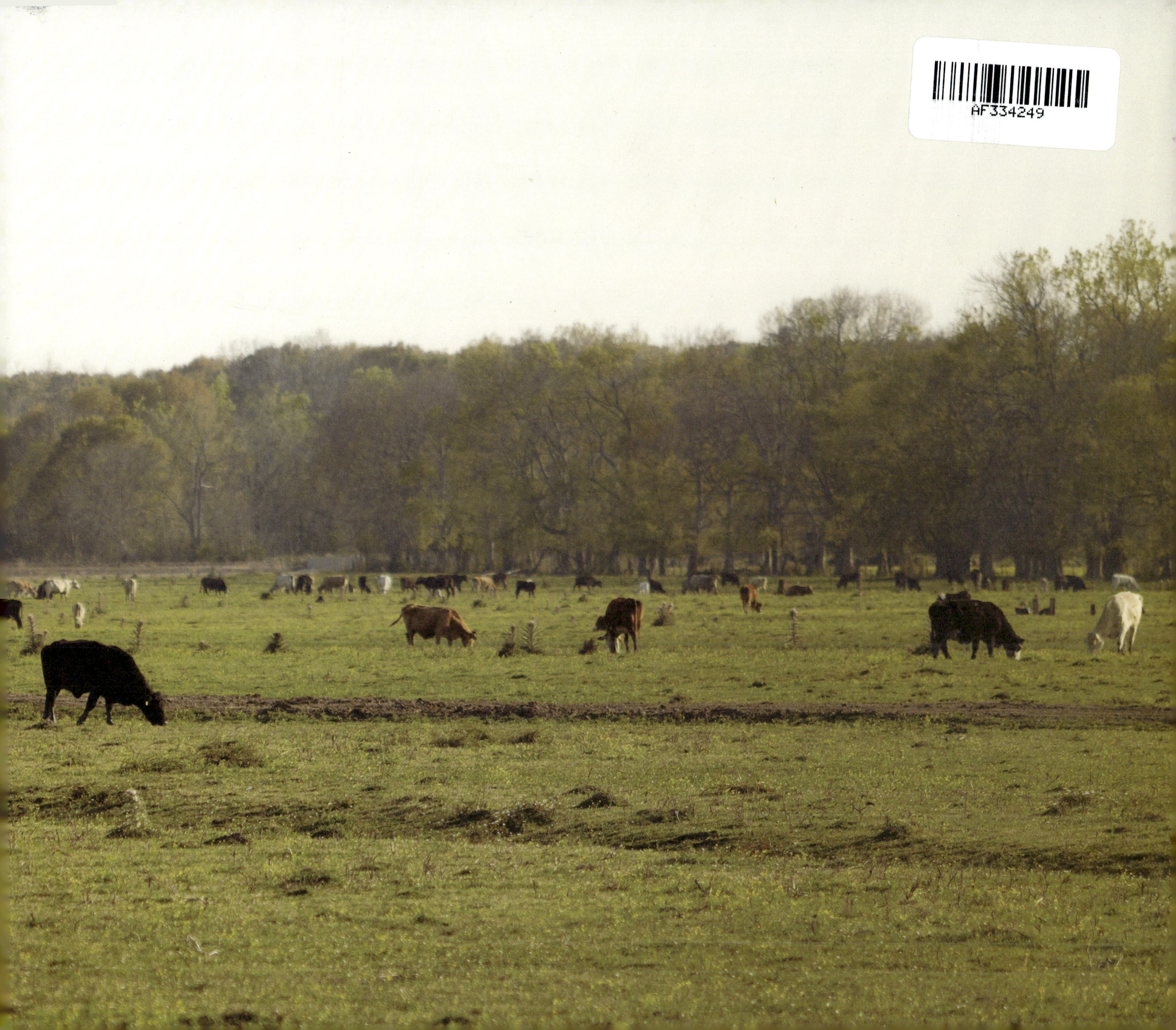

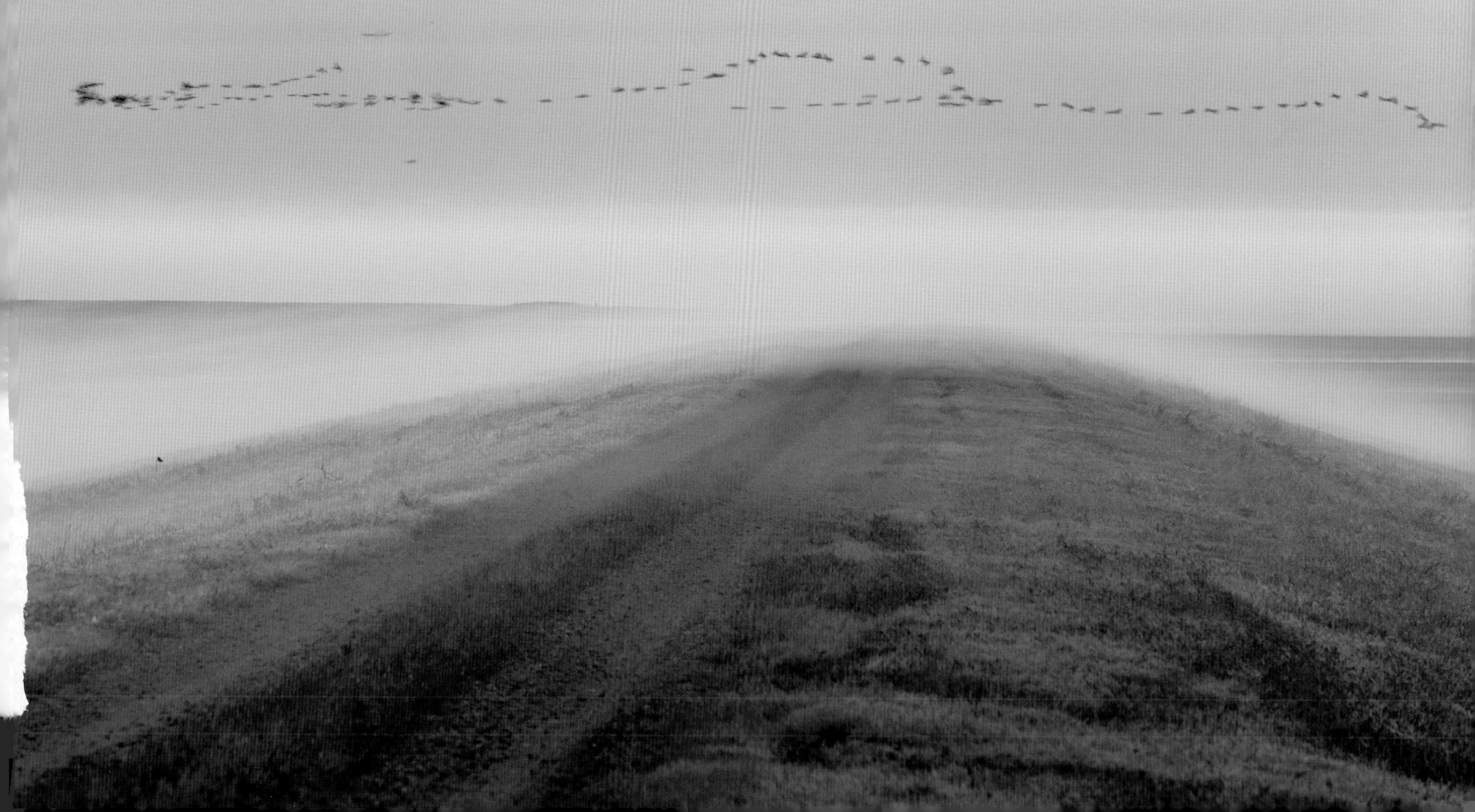

New Roads and Old Rivers

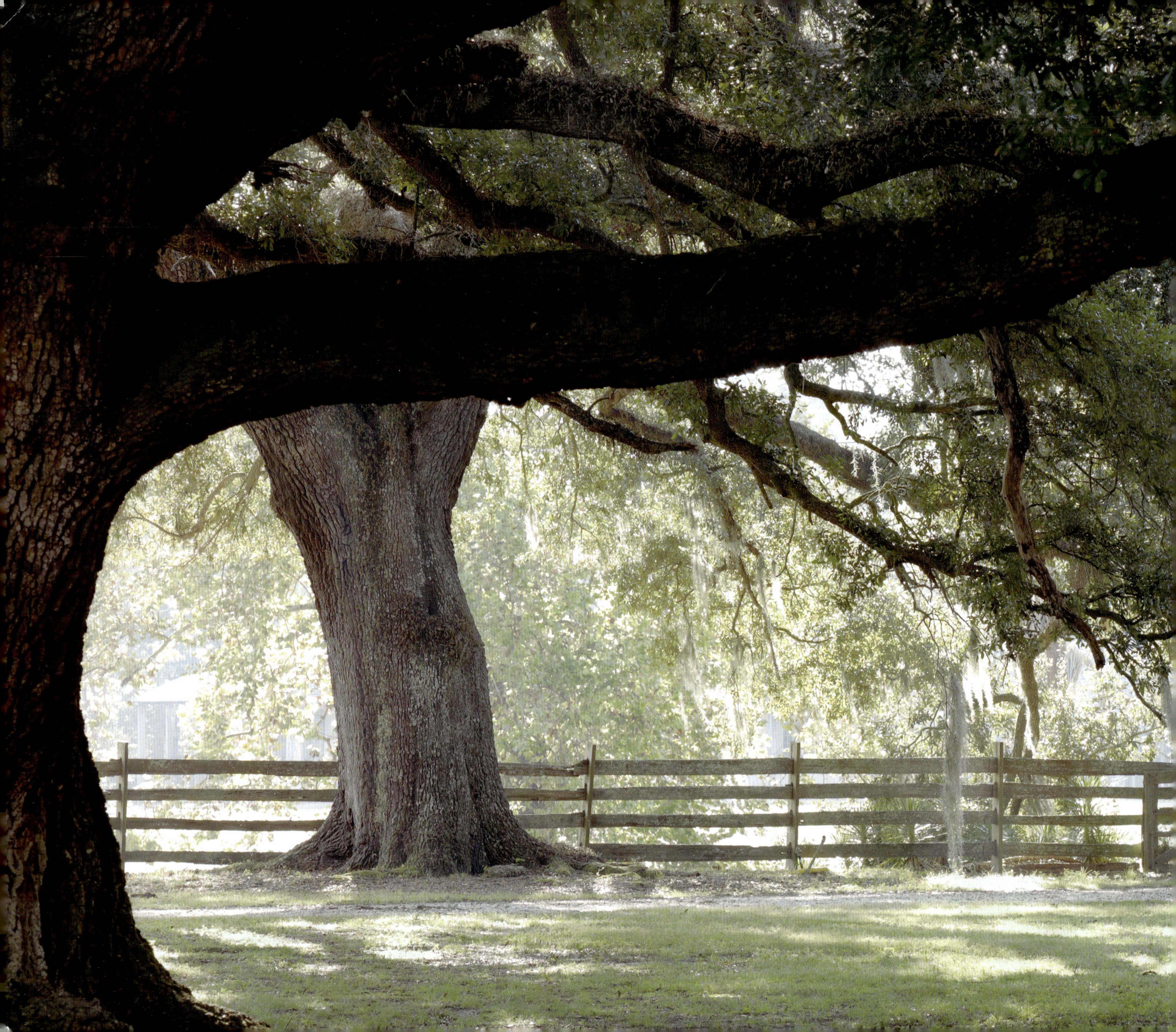

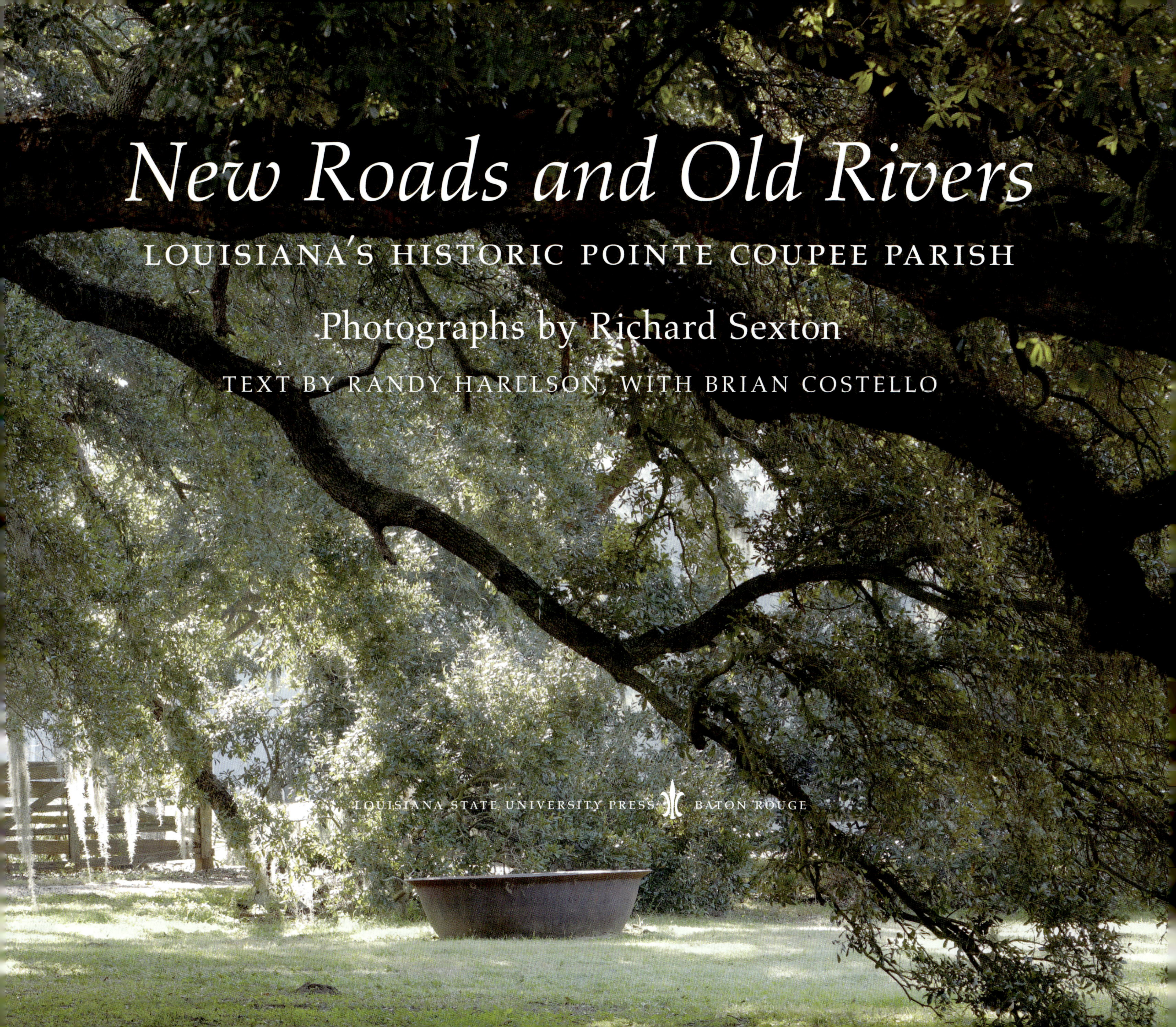

New Roads and Old Rivers

LOUISIANA'S HISTORIC POINTE COUPEE PARISH

Photographs by Richard Sexton

TEXT BY RANDY HARELSON, WITH BRIAN COSTELLO

LOUISIANA STATE UNIVERSITY PRESS · BATON ROUGE

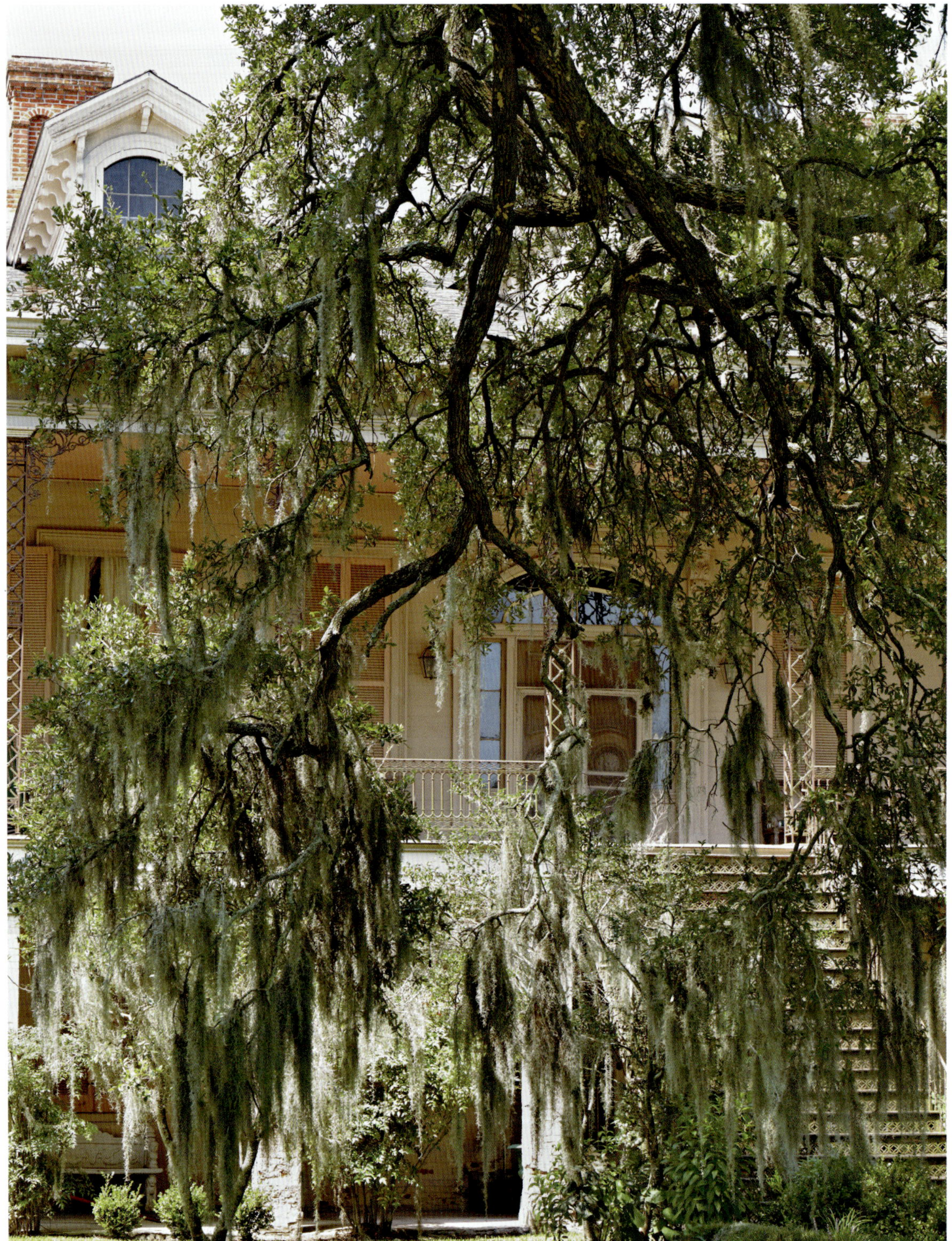

PUBLISHED BY LOUISIANA STATE UNIVERSITY PRESS
Copyright © 2012 by Louisiana State University Press
Photographs copyright © 2012 by Richard Sexton
All rights reserved
Manufactured in China
FIRST PRINTING

DESIGNER: *Mandy McDonald Scallan*
TYPEFACE: *Aldus*
PRINTER AND BINDER: *Everbest Printing Co. through
Four Colour Imports, Ltd., Louisville, Kentucky*

The authors and LSU Press gratefully acknowledge the assistance of the
Pointe Coupee Historical Society in publication of this book.

Library of Congress Cataloging-in-Publication Data
Sexton, Richard.
  New Roads and old rivers : Louisiana's historic Pointe Coupee Parish / photographs by Richard Sexton ; text by Randy Harelson, with Brian Costello.
    p. cm.
  Includes bibliographical references and index.
  ISBN 978-0-8071-4544-9 (cloth : alk. paper) — ISBN 978-0-8071-4545-6 (pdf) — ISBN 978-0-8071-4546-3 (epub) — ISBN 978-0-8071-4547-0 (mobi)
  1. Pointe Coupee Parish (La.) —Pictorial works. 2. Pointe Coupee Parish (La.) —History—Pictorial works. I. Harelson, Randy. II. Costello, Brian J. III. Title.
  F377.P55S49 2012
  976.3'454—dc23

                                        2011050923

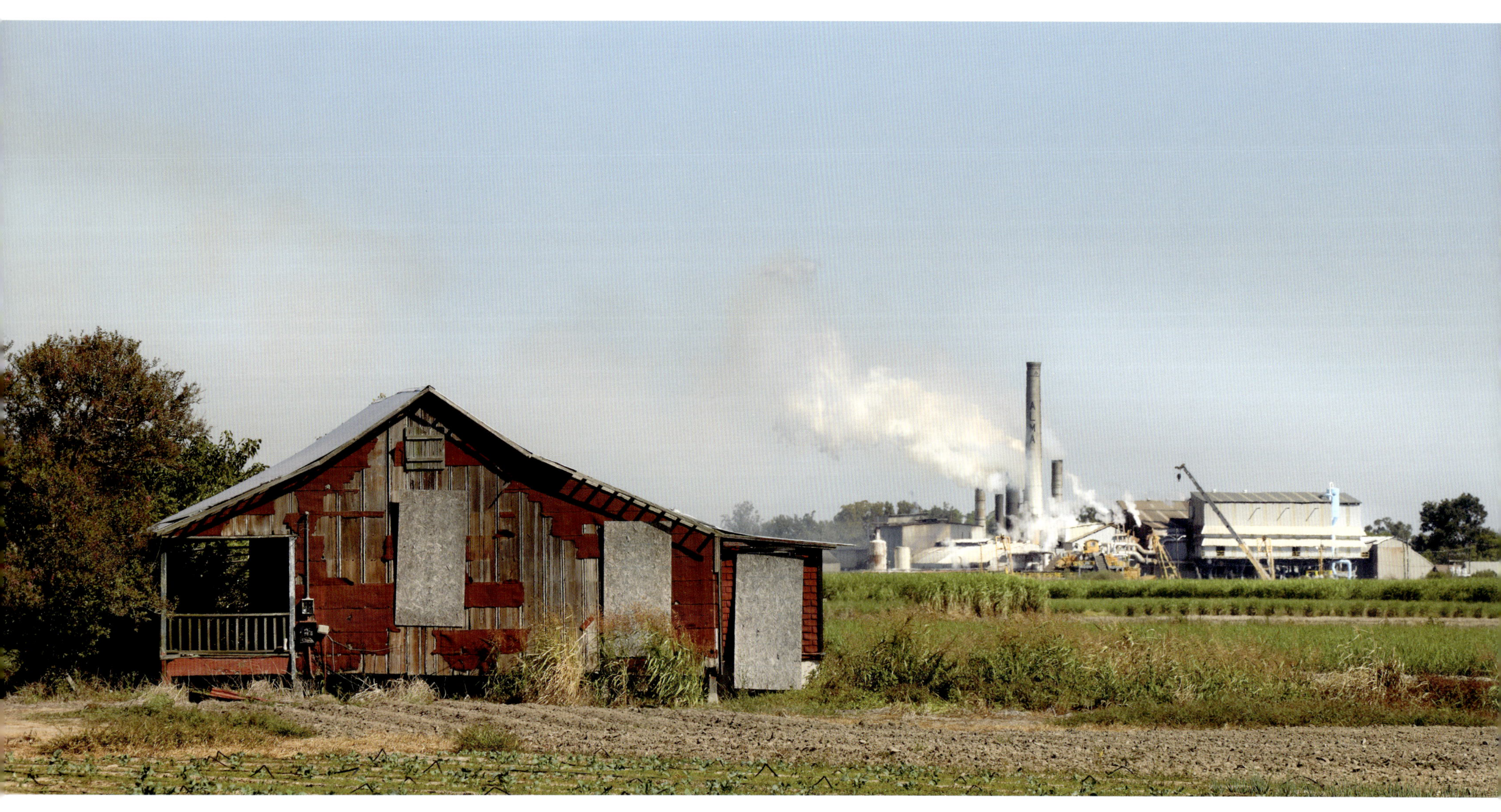

In all of us there is a hunger, marrow-deep, to know our heritage, to know who we are and where we have come from. Without this enriching knowledge, there is a hollow yearning. No matter what our attainments in life, there is still a vacuum, an emptiness, and the most disquieting loneliness.

—ALEX HALEY

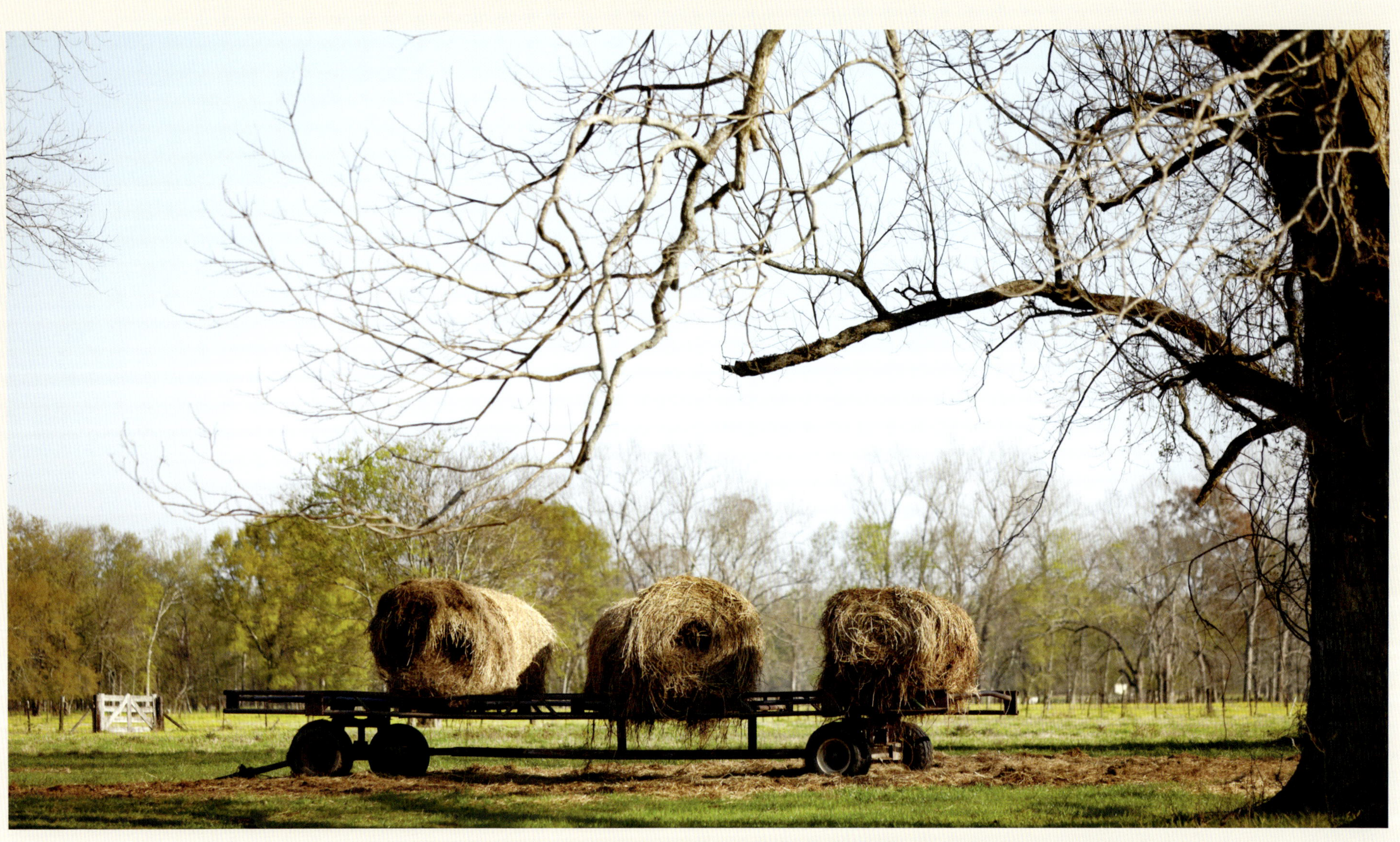

CONTENTS

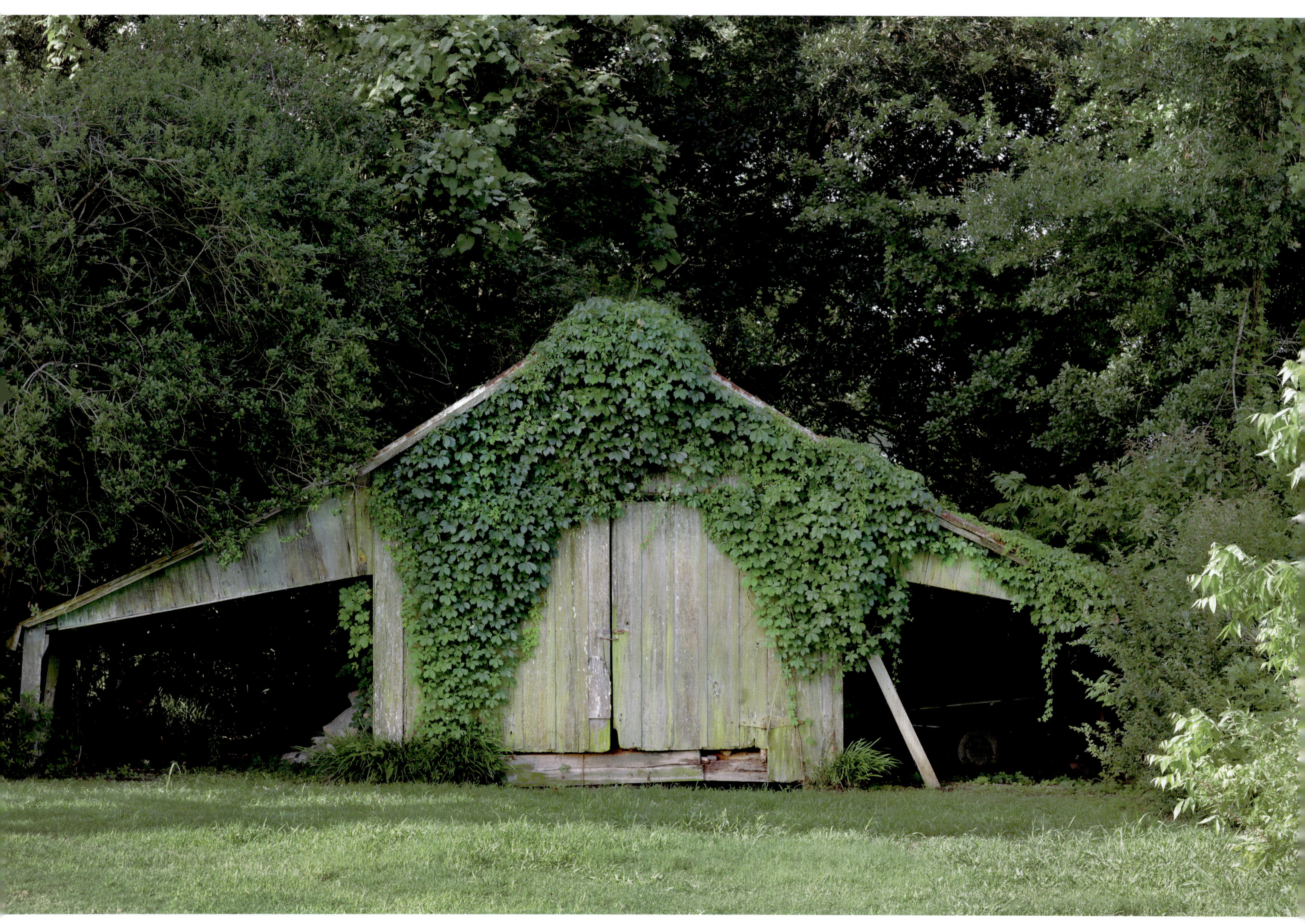

PREFACE

Timely yet timeless graphic essay, *New Roads and Old Rivers* captures through the striking photography of Richard Sexton and the insightful narration of Randy Harelson the history, traditions, and culture of a remarkable community created and sustained by the power of the Mississippi River and her daughter streams. Whether coming voluntarily and expectantly or against their own wishes throughout the past three centuries, the French, Spanish, African, Anglo-Saxon, Italian, and other peoples have each added threads to the rich tapestry of time and place that is Pointe Coupee Parish, Louisiana.

One of the oldest settlements in the Mississippi Valley, Pointe Coupee owes its existence and agricultural fecundity to the rich alluvium of the great rivers, yet at least eighteen times the Mississippi and Atchafalaya Rivers have flooded the land, seriously damaging or totally destroying man's best efforts. In addition to the floods, the people of Pointe Coupee have endured hurricanes, crop failures, epidemics, wartime invasion, and socioeconomic injustices, all the while remaining a viable, ever-evolving American community.

Vestiges of history and culture bear witness to Pointe Coupee's fascinating, though oftentimes challenging, past. Native American mounds, Creole cottages, mansions, hallowed churches and burial grounds, quaint towns and villages, fields of undulating sugarcane stalks and snowy cotton blossoms, volumes of time-worn documentary evidence, the sounds of the melodious local Creole dialect, a spicy indigenous cuisine, the *joie de vivre* of the state's second-oldest Mardi Gras celebration, the solemnity and joy of All Saints' Day and other holidays, *fêtes,* and feasts—all survive and thrive here as they have for generations.

Born and nurtured within a setting of ancient live oaks, gnarled cedars, and towering pecan trees, breathtaking vistas of river and bayou, primeval forest and vivid patchwork of farm and plantation, the people of Pointe Coupee embrace neighbor and visitor alike with a sincere and genteel hospitality that is, perhaps, the parish's greatest virtue. May the following images and text convey something of that virtue to each reader, whether scholar or photo enthusiast, local resident or friend abroad.

Devoted to the memory of the pioneers and their sacrifices, which make Pointe Coupee Parish, Louisiana, what it is today, I remain,

Brian J. Costello
Fausse Rivière, 2012

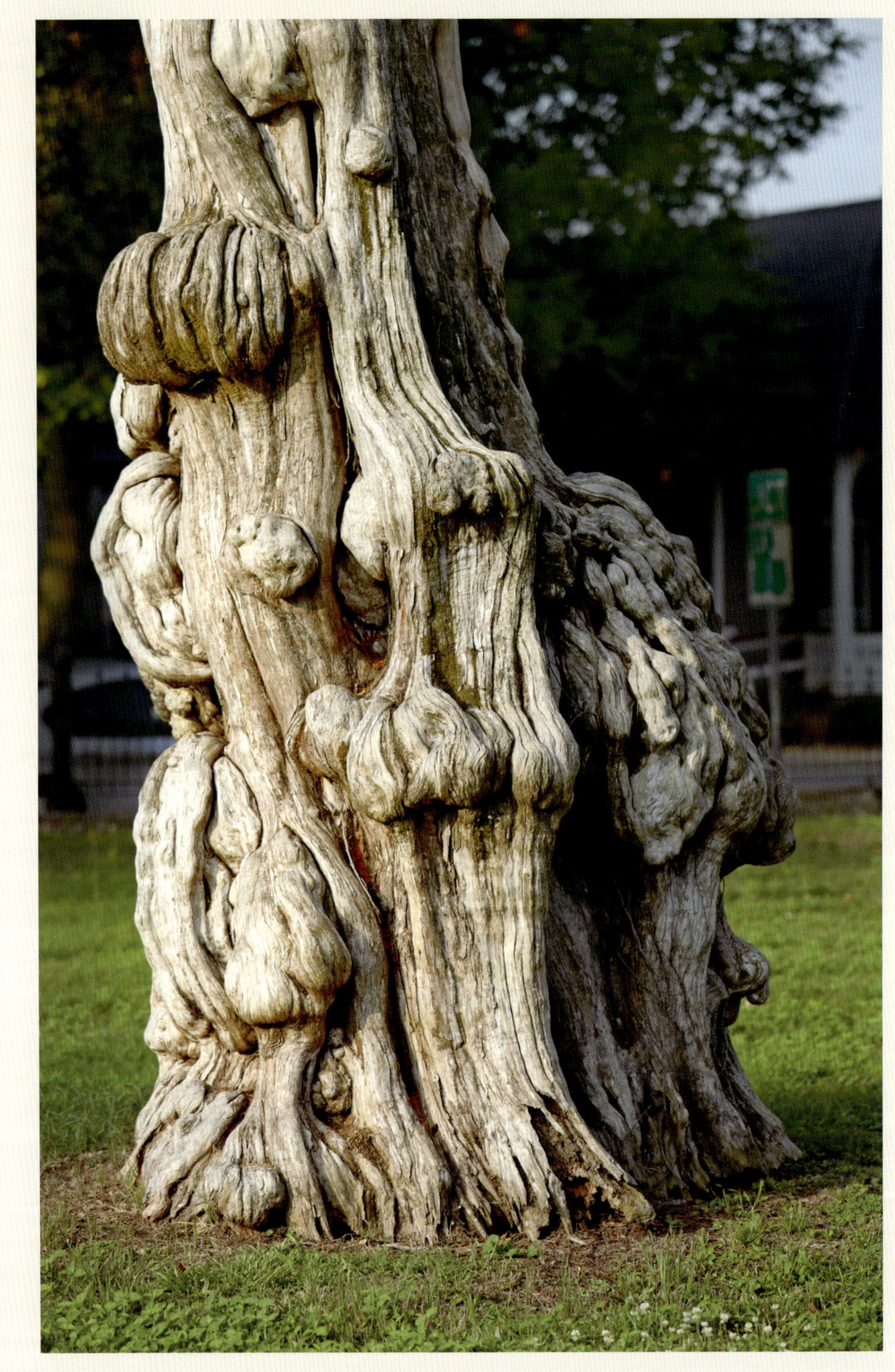

ACKNOWLEDGMENTS

I WOULD LIKE to begin by thanking my longtime friend and erstwhile collaborator, Randy Harelson, for inviting me to be a part of *New Roads and Old Rivers*. It has been a true pleasure working with Randy on this project. He and his partner Richard Gibbs were very gracious hosts, allowing me to stay in their charming guest cottage on LeJeune Street in the heart of New Roads. I looked forward to every photography session because of the idyllic stays in the shadow of the LeJeune House and gardens. I'd also like to thank Angélique Gardner of the Pointe Coupee Historical Society, who provided a great deal of logistical support for the photography sessions along with an equal amount of enthusiasm and energy for the project itself. I'd like to thank my studio manager, Jonathan Traviesa, who assisted me on some of the photo sessions and completed a number of sessions on his own when I was unavailable due to scheduling conflicts. Jonathan's photographic contributions help make *New Roads and Old Rivers* a better, more journalistically complete book. I owe a special debt of gratitude to all the homeowners who allowed me to photograph their houses. Without their help and cooperation this book would not be what it is. Finally, I'd like to thank all those residents of Pointe Coupee Parish that I had the pleasure of meeting and working with on this project. Everyone made me feel at home, and I'll always remember the back roads, plowed fields, proud homes, and, most of all, the wonderful people of Pointe Coupee Parish.

Richard Sexton

IN POINTE COUPEE CREOLE we say *byen mesi* instead of *merci bien*. Our way implies a more heartfelt thanks. So *byen mesi* to the people who believed in and generously supported our book project from its inception:

The H. T. Olinde Jr. Foundation and David and Jeanie Bondy;

NRG Energy, Inc.; Pointe Coupee Farm Bureau and Kenneth St. Romain, CLU, CHFC Agency Manager; Noelie Ewing and family; Dustin and Angélique Gardner; Mr. and Mrs. Andrew Grezaffi Sr. and family; and Mr. and Mrs. Michael H. James;

Alma Plantation, LLC; Bordelon Builders, LLC; Jimmy Duckworth and Shelley Ford; Dorothy Eglin; the O. B. Laurent Jr. Family; New Roads Lions Club; and Joanna Wurtele;

Keith and Julie Bergeron; James and Sarita Bouanchaud; Philip and Catherine Dabadie Boudreaux; David and Madeline Breidenbach; Jodie, Alexis, Mark, and Thomas Cotten; the families of Louis Curet and David M. James; Hosea Doucet III, M.D., and Mark Cassidy, M.D.; Cille and Curt Engemann; Lane Ewing; Mitch and Duggie Frey; Glenn E. Grezaffi; Dr. and Mrs. Jack Holden; Brent Labatut; Louise and Jim Laurent; Mr. and Mrs. James A. Laurent Jr.; Gerald and Shirley LeBlanc; Mr. and Mrs. J. B. Olinde; Angèle Parlange; Cary Saurage; Hunt Slonem; Ronnie Virgets and Lynne Jensen; Elizabeth Wilson; and Stuart and Betty Wooddy;

Joe and Nelda Beaud; Stu Braud; Kerry Callegan; Donald and Ann Cazayoux; Francis and Julia Cazayoux; Cathy Coates; Chrissy Lapeyre Gay; Della Graham; Fred and Alice Bondy Hill; Al and Verline Olinde; Brandon Parlange;

Richard and Suzanne Poole; Hurst and Nicki Samson; Wayne and Margaret Sciacca; Charles and Emily Smith; and Susan Tomlin and Raymond Tyler.

❧

For sharing their lives, homes, gardens, and businesses and allowing us to photograph, our sincere thanks to: Jeanie Andre; Todd Andre; Nelda Beaud; Steve Bergeron; Paul and Becky Berthier; "Miss Sarita" and Cootchie Bouanchaud; Karl and Natalie Bradberry; Miles Brashier; Stu Braud; Madeline and David Breidenbach; Melanie Bueche; Les Créoles de Pointe Coupée; Louis D. Curet; Hosea Doucet and Mark Cassidy; Colleen Caillet; Madeline Caillet; Kerry Callegan; Bettie Capps; Walter H. Claiborne III; Jodie and Suzanne Cotten; Sid Dreyfus; Father Greg Daigle; Jimmy Duckworth and Shelley Ford; Curt and Cille Engemann; Ernest and Dianne Gaines; Richard Gibbs; Charles and Jynell Glaser; Drew and LesAnne Grezaffi; Peggy Grezaffi; Mary Beth and George Guerin; Grace Hebert; Timothy and Jennifer Henry; Joseph and Catherine Hinckley; Jack and Pat Holden; Sis Hollensworth; Jeanne Curet James; Mike and Lisa James; Roger and Chad Jones; Father George Kontos; Jay and Julia Labatut; Faye LaCour; Cecilia and Donald LeBlanc; the family of Roland Landry; Mary Langlois; Father Lee; Bill and Maureen McGurk; Sam McVea; Ovide Miller; Andre and Virginia Monceret; Hilda Moore; Georgia and Buddy Morel; Glenn Morgan; Mr. and Mrs. J. K. Nicholson; Angèle, Brandon, and "Miss Lucy" Parlange; Gwin and Walter Parlange III; Camile Persica; Alfred and Malvina Pickett; Mitch Pinsonat; Gail Roberts and Rodney Schexnayder; Mitch and Susan Ruether; Beth and Joe Rougon; Kirk and Yvonne Rousset; Albin Saizan Jr.; Hunt Slonem; Cindy Steib; David Stewart; "Miss Margebelle" Stewart; Gary Sutton and Marc Becker; Charlotte Thomas; Suzanne Turner and Scott Purdin; Stuart and Betty Wooddy; and Joanna Wurtele.

For information, help, and kindness, we are grateful to Morris Bennet, Chris Russo Blackwood, Jennifer Cline, Mary Langlois Costello, General Stephen C. Dabadie, General Levi Dabadie, Cynthia G. Dupree, Mary Lee Eggart, Jude Grezaffi, Sara and Kevin Gummow, Jacqui Hale, General Russel Honoré, Elizabeth Holloway, Reverend Jeremy Jones, James "Big Brown" Joseph, George LaCour, Ovide and Tracy LaCour, Coleen Landry, Lauren Lee, Dr. Rob Mann, Cokie Roberts, Gale Roy, Ben Scherrer, Carolyn Steinmuller, Robert Valley, Rebecca Washington, and Jon Weil.

For a wonderful airplane flight over the parish, thanks to pilot Jason Amy; for a lovely afternoon boat ride on Old River, thanks to Kenny Bordelon; for meeting us before dawn to capture the ethereal beauty of the Morganza Spillway during the fall bird migration, thanks to Jacques LaCour; for welcoming us to Easter service at Old St. Mark Baptist Church, thanks to Reverend Dr. Lionel Davis, Mother Minnie Howard, Sister Brenda Franklin, and Brother Roosevelt Scott; for their hospitality and assistance regarding the St. Joseph's Day altar, thanks to Father Lee and Reta Ramagos of St. Ann, the San Giuseppe Altar Ladies, and also to David Breidenbach, who took the photograph of the St. Joseph altar; for her wonderful photograph of the winning Cub Scout Mardi Gras float, thanks to Grace Hebert; for giving us a last ride across the Atchafalaya on the now-defunct Melville Ferry (in his 1948 Chevrolet), thanks to Constable George Miller; for setting a lovely coffee with Alma sugar, thanks to Georgia Morel; for keeping the Pointe Coupee Museum open to visitors, thanks to Charlotte Gandy, Olinde "Toppy" Haag, KerriLyn Langlois, "Miss Winona" Sicard, Stu Braud, and the Pointe Coupee Parish Police Jury; for helping us find the DAR plaque at the courthouse and giving us an impromptu military history lesson, thanks to Sheriff Bud Torres; for their tireless leadership in preservation throughout Louisiana, thanks to Winnie Byrd and Sue Turner, and to Michael Wyatt of the Louisiana Trust; and for her wonderful pralines, thanks to Inez Toussaint.

For guiding the book project so carefully as they continued to execute many other duties, our devoted thanks to the Board of Directors of the Pointe Coupee Historical Society: Ann Bachmann, Philip Boudreaux, Stafford Chenevert, Lane Ewing, Dustin Gardner, Yvonne Jarvis, Randy Jarreau, Brent Labatut, Pat Laurent, Sheila Maciasz, Adele Robillard, H. F. "Buck" Tucker, and Sylvia O. Weigand.

Finally, big thank-yous to Lane Ewing, who believed in the project from the start; Noelie Ewing, who always kept the faith; Angélique Gardner, who joyfully added this book to her slate of responsibilities (and accomplishments); Richard Gibbs, who nourished us with his good home cooking and warm encouragement; Jonathan Traviesa, Richard Sexton's assistant, who took some of the photographs; and to our editors at LSU Press, Margaret Lovecraft and Catherine L. Kadair, who guided the book with sure and gentle hands.

Randy Harelson
Brian Costello

POINTE COUPEE TIMELINE

10,000 BC — Indians live in Pointe Coupee for thousands of years before Europeans "discover" the Mississippi River and begin settlement and colonization.

AD 700–1200 — Livonia Indian mounds are built by native people of the Coles Creek period.

1492 — Christopher Columbus discovers America. Lands first in the Bahamas, then Cuba and Hispaniola, the Caribbean island that is today Haiti and the Dominican Republic.

1541 — Hernando de Soto discovers the Mississippi River. His followers are believed to be the first Europeans in the Pointe Coupee area.

1673 — Jacques Marquette and Louis Joliet verify that the Mississippi River flows into the Gulf of Mexico.

1682 — LaSalle claims Louisiana territory. Names it "La Louisiane" for King Louis XIV of France.

1699 — Sieur d'Iberville with other French Canadians explores area of present-day Pointe Coupee.

1718 — New Orleans is founded.

1722 — False River: The Mississippi River completes its geological cut-off process and leaves behind an oxbow lake, giving rise to the place names *Pointe Coupée* (the cut-off point), *Fausse Rivière* (False River), and *L'Isle de la Fausse Rivière* (The Island of False River).

1726 — Census lists French settlers living in Pointe Coupee area.

1729 — Natchez Massacre: Natchez Indians kill 250 at Fort Rosalie, present-day Natchez; some settlers escape downriver to Pointe Coupee.

1729 — French military *poste* of Pointe Coupee is established on the Mississippi River.

1731 — Census lists African slaves living in Pointe Coupee area.

1738 — St. Francis of Pointe Coupee Church is established.

1754–1763 — French and Indian War

1755 — Acadian deportation: French citizens are expelled from Canada by the British government. About 2,000 Acadians make their way to Louisiana, mostly settling in southwestern Louisiana, now called Acadiana. The Louisiana government forbids their settlement in Pointe Coupee.

1756 — France cedes all lands east of the Mississippi River, except New Orleans, to England. Spain gives up East Florida and West Florida to England in return for Cuba.

1756–1763 — Seven Years' War in Canada and Europe

1762 — Treaty of Fontainebleau cedes Louisiana to Spain.

1768 — Julien Poydras arrives in Louisiana.

1775–1783 — American Revolutionary War

1776 — American Declaration of Independence
Spanish authorities open a royal road, from False River to the Mississippi. Local French call the route *chemin neuf*, the "new road" from which the town would take its name.

1777 — Governor Bernardo de Gálvez lends Louisiana aid to the American Revolution. Pointe Coupee militia serve with him.

1778 — France declares war against Britain. Forms alliance with American Revolutionary forces.

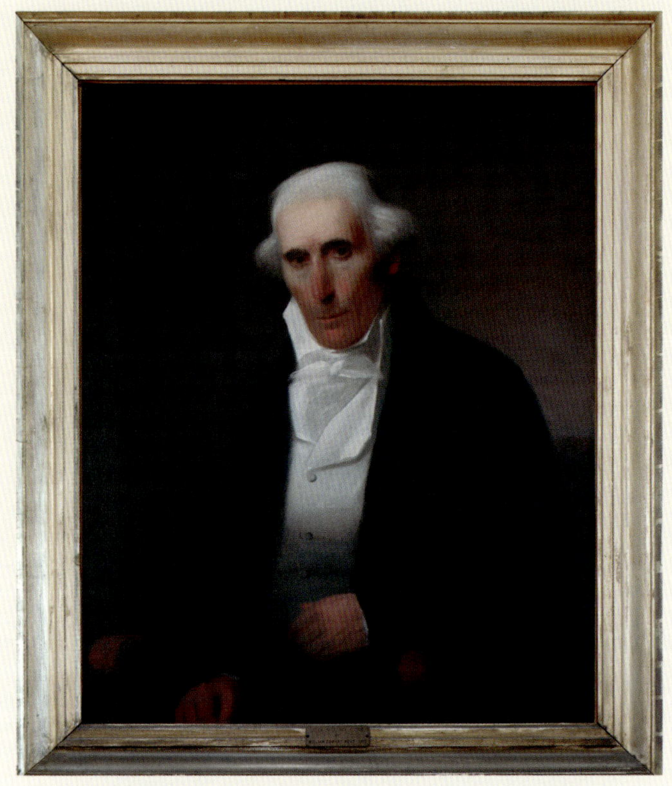

JULIEN POYDRAS (1746–1824) was one of Pointe Coupee's most illustrious citizens. He was born in France. A sailor in the French navy by the age of fourteen, he was captured by the British, and learned English and German while a prisoner. At seventeen he escaped on a West Indies merchant ship to Saint-Domingue (present-day Haiti), and made his way to New Orleans five years later.

With a good head for business and fluency in at least three languages, Poydras set about making money as a traveling merchant, selling goods to people in rural areas outside New Orleans and north to Natchez. A lifelong bachelor, Poydras purchased his first property in Pointe Coupee in 1775. Over time he became one of the state's major landowners, with successful farms and plantations in Pointe Coupee, West Baton Rouge, and St. Bernard Parishes.

A natural leader, Poydras became friends with William C. C. Claiborne, who served as governor of the Territory of Orleans from 1804 to 1812 and as governor of the state of Louisiana from 1812 to 1816. As delegate from the Territory of Orleans to the U.S. House of Representatives (1809–1811), Poydras argued successfully for Louisiana statehood. After Louisiana became a state in 1812, he served as senate president.

Poydras is often credited as Louisiana's first published poet, first banker, and founder of the first public schools in Louisiana (in Pointe Coupee Parish). He died at age seventy-eight.

Poydras Street in downtown New Orleans was named in his honor. Bequests in his will still support charitable organizations in New Orleans, West Baton Rouge, and Pointe Coupee. He is buried near False River in front of the Julien Poydras Museum and Arts Center in New Roads.

1783	Treaty of Paris signed by victorious United States and defeated Great Britain.
1787	Signing of U.S. Constitution
1789–1799	French Revolution
1791–1803	Haitian Revolution
1794	Eli Whitney patents the cotton gin.
1795	Etienne de Boré demonstrates successful process of crystallizing sugar.
1798	Julien Poydras entertains the Duc d'Orléans, who later becomes King Louis Philippe of France.
1800	Treaty of San Ildefonso secretly cedes Louisiana to France. Sugarcane first grown in Pointe Coupee.
1803	Louisiana Purchase: The United States purchases territory from France for $15 million. Wm. C. C. Claiborne becomes first territorial governor.
1805	Pointe Coupee is named one of Louisiana's twelve original counties.
1807	Pointe Coupee is one of nineteen Louisiana parishes established. (Today Louisiana has sixty-four parishes.)
1808	Public schools are established in Pointe Coupee, the first in Louisiana.
1811	Julien Poydras is elected president of the Louisiana convention on statehood. River steamboats begin operation on Mississippi.
1812	Louisiana is admitted to the United States as the eighteenth state, on April 30.

1815 Battle of New Orleans: Andrew Jackson routs the British; Pointe Coupeeans fight alongside "Old Hickory."

1817 Explosion of steamboat *Constitution* near Pointe Coupee.

1822 Catherine Depau, nicknamed *la fille Gougis* (Gougis's daughter), develops six-block area of her False River plantation, the genesis of the town of New Roads.

1823 Church of St. Mary's of False River is established.

1831 Lower Old River: Captain Henry Shreve cuts off Mississippi loop at north end of Pointe Coupee to expedite travel on the river.

1833 St. Peter African Methodist Episcopal Church is founded by slaves at Waterloo.
Poydras College opens as a boys' preparatory school on False River.

1835 Joseph Leblanc de Villeneuve seals the lower end of False River at Hermitage.

1842 State engineers seal the upper end of False River at Waterloo.
Parlange Lane is cut from False River to Bayou Grosse Tete, spurring development along Bayous Grosse Tete, Fordoche, and Maringouin.

1847 Raccourci–Old River: Old River (originally called Lake Lafayette) is cut off by state engineers to expedite travel on the Mississippi River.
Seat of parish government is moved from the Mississippi River to present-day New Roads.

1848 First courthouse is completed at New Roads.

1850 "Cotton is King and Sugar is Queen": Cotton and sugar are highly profitable in Pointe Coupee. Money and people flow into the parish.

1859 Immaculate Conception Church and its cemetery are established at Chenal.
St. Stephen's Episcopal Church is completed in Innis.

1861 Louisiana secedes from the Union.
American Civil War begins.
"Maryland, My Maryland" is written at Poydras College.

1863 Emancipation Proclamation is signed.
Siege of Port Hudson
Battle of Stirling Plantation near Bayou Fordoche

1865 Robert E. Lee surrenders at Appomattox , Virginia, on April 9. "Last surrender of Civil War" signed at El Dorado in Pointe Coupee, June 7.
Thirteenth Amendment is ratified, abolishing slavery.
St. Mary's Cemetery is established.

1868 Louisiana Constitution grants all adult males, black and white, the vote. (Women do not get the vote until 1920.)

1869 First free African American church, St. Paul Methodist Church, is established on the *Chemin Neuf*. Believed to be the first Protestant and first African American church in New Roads.

1870 *Robert E. Lee* vs. *Natchez*: Most famous steamboat race in history. This time Lee wins.

1875 New Roads is first incorporated.

1881 First Mardi Gras ball at New Roads. Directed by John Boudreau and held at the Duvernet Hotel.

1882 First railroad tracks are laid across southwestern Pointe Coupee Parish, linking New Orleans with Shreveport.
Worst flood in Louisiana history. New Roads' Main Street is flooded four feet deep.

1885 First telephone line in the parish is erected in Upper Pointe Coupee.

1886 Steamboat *J. M. White* explodes and burns at St. Maurice's Landing with great loss of life.

1891 First electric lights in Pointe Coupee at Alma and Oakland plantations.

1894 New Roads is incorporated under its current charter.

1895 Two feet of snow: Greatest snowfall on record in Pointe Coupee.

1898–1901 Spanish American War

1899 Zero degrees: Lowest temperature ever recorded in Pointe Coupee.
Texas & Pacific Railroad builds branch line through Pointe Coupee from Addis to Ferriday.

1902 Progressive League builds a pavilion, clubhouse, and bathhouse on False River.
New Roads Oil Mill & Manufacturing Company builds an

electric railway from False River to the mill up Community Street.

1904 First Methodist Episcopal Community Church is built on Pennsylvania Street in New Roads.

1904–1907 New St. Mary's church is built, tower not completed until 1929.

1906 New technology: New Roads town power plant is built, providing electricity and water. False River Telephone Line begins operations. New Roads Ice and Light Company opens.

1907 Father John Joseph Plantevigne, first African American priest from Pointe Coupee, is ordained in Baltimore.

1908 Morganza is incorporated.
4-H is established in Louisiana.

1910 First public library is established in New Roads by Adrienne Laurence Claiborne.
Bergeron Pecans is established.

1912 Flood: Worst disaster in Pointe Coupee history. Approximately 17,000 people are driven from their homes; at least 40 die.

1914–18 World War I

1917 Satterfield's Motor Car Company is established.

1920–29 General John Archer LeJeune, Pointe Coupee native, serves as U.S. Marine Corps commandant.

1922 Jimmy Boudreaux establishes the Community Center Carnival, known today as the "morning parade." Oldest Mardi Gras parade in Louisiana outside of New Orleans.

1923 The first Rosenwald School opens in New Roads.
St. Augustine Catholic Church is established in New Roads.

1924 Poydras High School is built.

1927 Great Mississippi Flood. One of the most destructive floods in U.S. history, with 75 percent of Pointe Coupee under water.

1928 Huey Long is elected governor of Louisiana.

1932 Second New Roads Mardi Gras parade, the "afternoon parade," is established.

1935 Huey P. Long is assassinated.

1939–1955 The Morganza Spillway is created.

1941–1945 World War II

1959 Livonia is incorporated.
The Long Hot Summer is partly filmed at Ramsey.

1962 Fordoche is incorporated.

1965 The Civil Rights Act is passed into law. The New Roads branch of the NAACP is chartered.

1969 Key scenes of *Easy Rider* are filmed in Morganza.

1971 *The Autobiography of Miss Jane Pittman*, by Ernest J. Gaines, is published.
Hospital Road opens. Will be developed as New Roads' second business district.
Celebration of Life music festival is held in McCrea; an estimated 50,000 attend.

1973 Lindy Claiborne Boggs, Pointe Coupee native, becomes Louisiana's first congresswoman after husband Congressman Hale Boggs is killed in a plane crash.

1976 Pointe Coupee Parish Museum is restored and opened to the public.

1978 Trina Olinde Scott is elected as New Roads' first female mayor.

1989 Sylvester Muckelroy is elected as New Roads' first African American mayor.

2005 Hurricane Katrina: 2,000 evacuees from New Orleans take refuge in Pointe Coupee.

2008 Hurricane Gustav: 91-mile-per-hour winds and 14 inches of rain.

2011 Audubon Bridge opens, linking New Roads with St. Francisville, Louisiana.

2012 Louisiana celebrates bicentennial of its statehood.

2020–22 Pointe Coupee tricentennial.

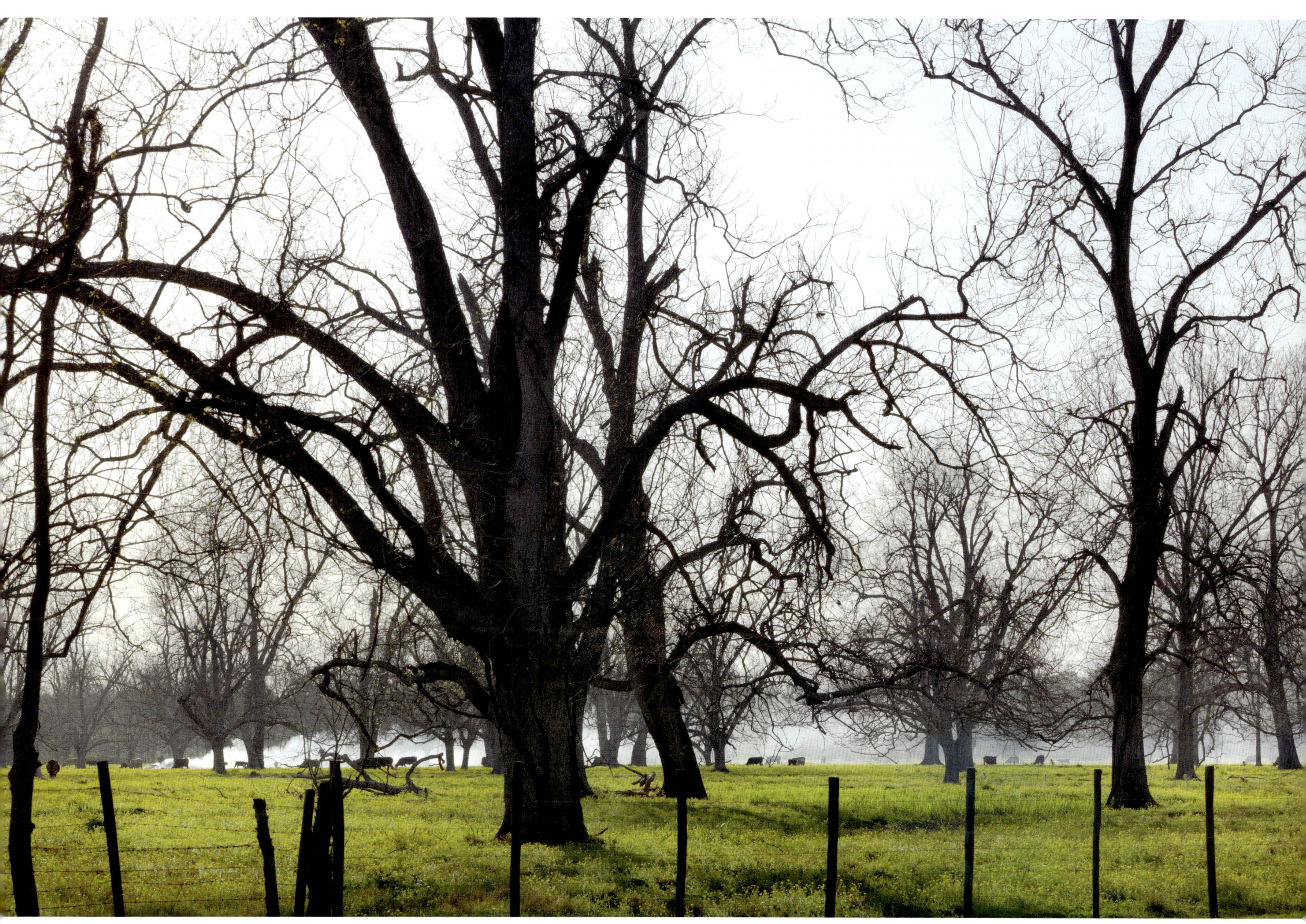

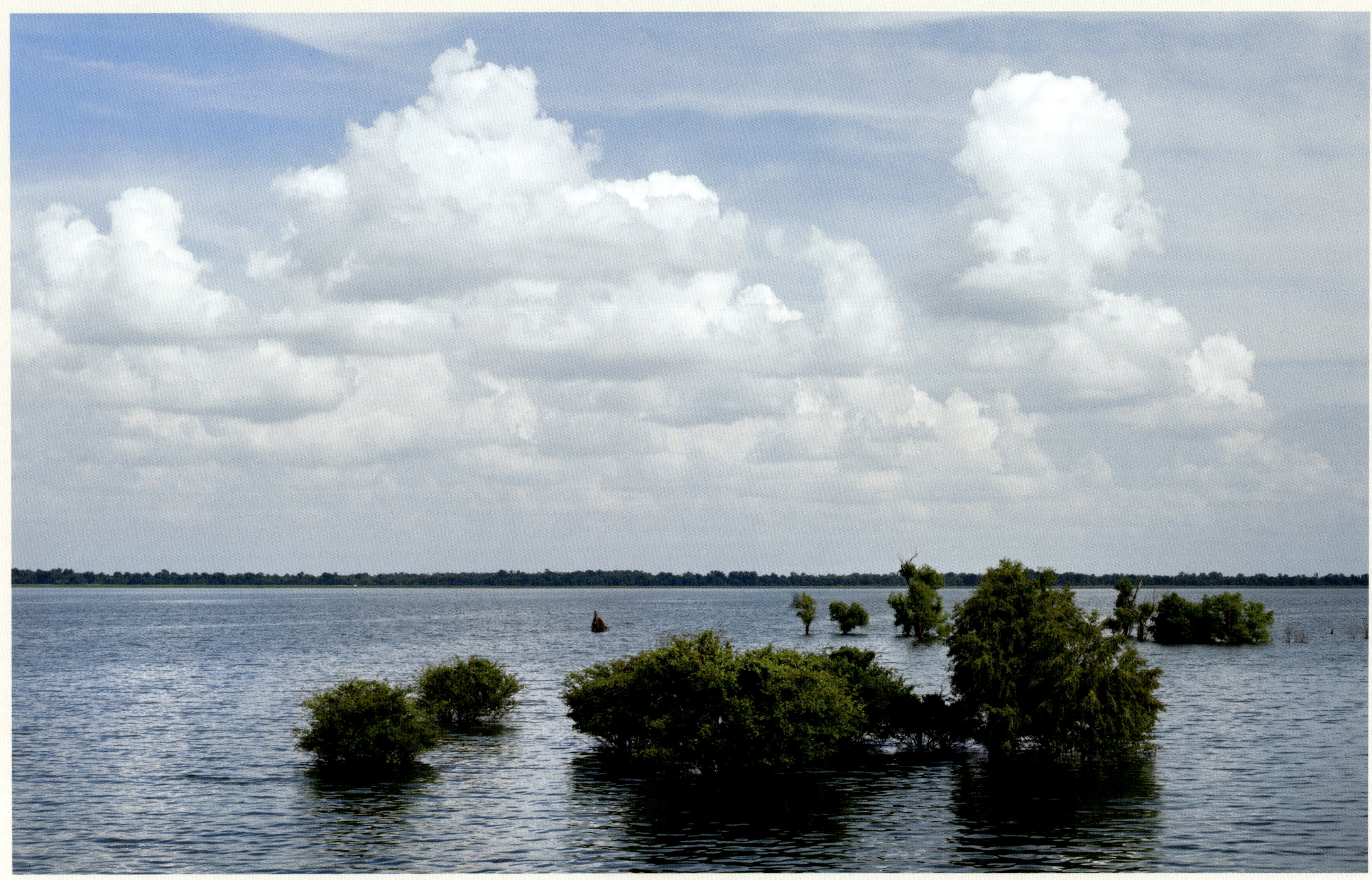

When the forebay of the Morganza Spillway is flooded, one can get a good idea of what Pointe Coupee and most of south Louisiana looked like before the levees were built. For thousands of years the Mississippi River has flooded annually with the spring rains and snowmelt farther north. Many of the bottomland trees withstand inundation by fresh water very well, remaining under water for weeks or even months at a time. Bald cypress and tupelo gum often grow in swamps with their roots underwater year round. Black willow, ash, water locust, red maple, and even oak trees can withstand weeks, sometimes months, of being waterlogged.

A PLACE CUT OFF

POINTE COUPEE is a parish created, bounded, and described by rivers: The Mississippi to its east, the Atchafalaya to its west, and Lower Old River (merging with the Red River) carving out its short northern boundary. Only the southern parish borders are drawn with the straight lines of a government survey.

American Indians called the Mississippi River the Father of Waters. Rainwater and snowmelt from most of North America (31 of the 49 continental U.S. states) drains into the Mississippi. For more than ten thousand years the river has brought sediment and nutrients from the North that have, through deposits made by annual flooding, created the rich soil and alluvial plains of south Louisiana.

Pointe Coupée is French for "the place of cut-off" and refers to a specific location on the Mississippi River. The place has been known by that name for almost three hundred years. Three separate oxbow bends (or loops) of the Mississippi have been cut off from the river during those three centuries in what is now Louisiana. The first one was *la Fausse Rivière* (False River), cut off through the natural power of the Mississippi around 1722. The second was at the very northern tip of the parish in what is known as the Three Rivers area, where the Red River emptied into the Mississippi and where the Atchafalaya began its own path to the Gulf of Mexico. In 1831 Captain Henry Shreve, for whom Shreveport is named, reengineered the river connections to improve transportation. This area is where the Old River control structures and locks are today. The third was Raccourci-Old River, cut off in 1847 by Louisiana state engineers again to increase efficiency of transportation on the Mississippi. Newly cut off, Old River was called Lake Lafayette in honor of the Revolutionary War hero the Marquis de Lafayette.

In *Life on the Mississippi,* Mark Twain tells a story of a riverboat that gets caught in one of Pointe Coupee's cutoffs at night, as the river is in the process of changing its course. The boat and its crew never get out, and to

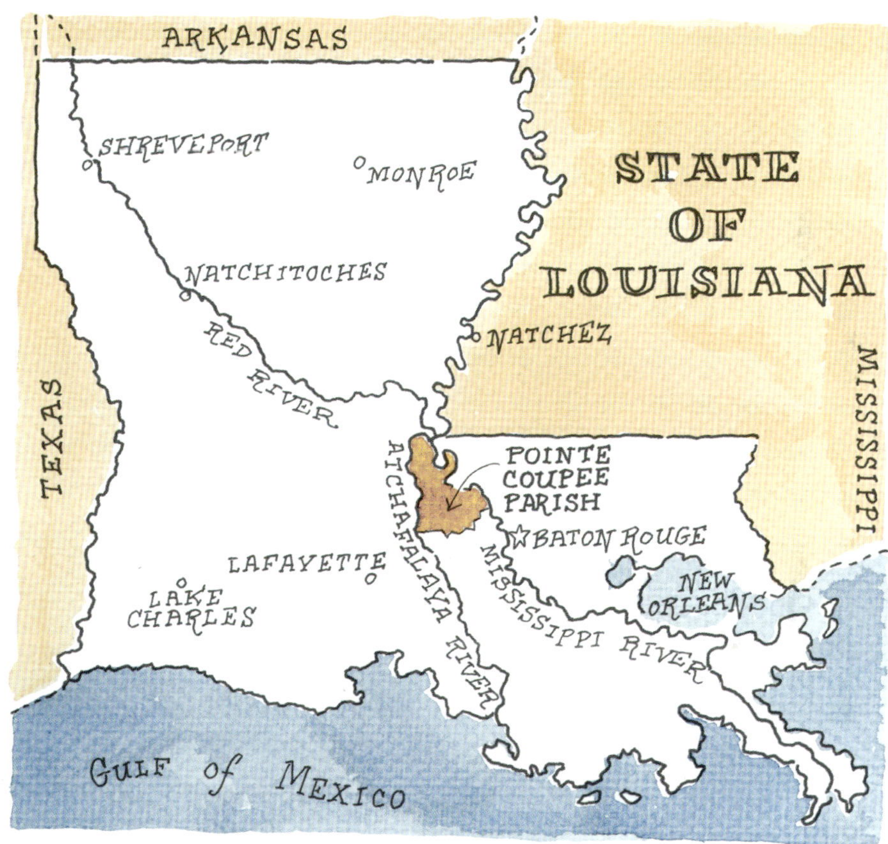

this day the dim lights of the ghostly riverboat can be seen on a misty night if you peer down the old channel. Pointe Coupee history is full of such stories: shipwrecks, explosions, murders, slave revolts, love affairs, infidelities, feuds, family dynasties, splendid wealth, reversals of fortune, selfless charity, underhanded self-serving—in other words, human stories. Many of these

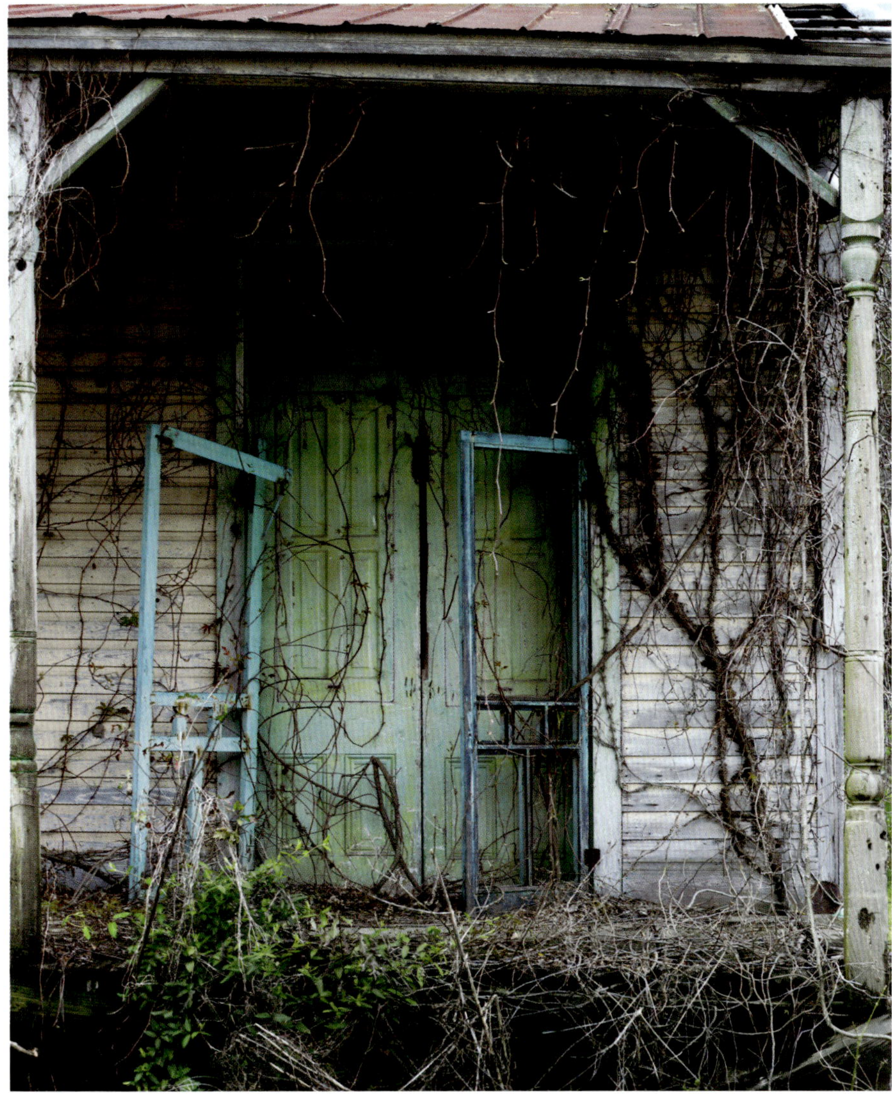

plain of Pointe Coupee and most of south Louisiana. The threat of flooding still raises old ghosts and the memory of sopping disasters in centuries past. In 2011 the Mississippi almost topped the levees with the highest water on record, the Morganza Spillway was opened, and Pointe Coupee residents worried until the river subsided.

Huge native pecan trees still stand in the woods and fields, although Hurricanes Andrew and Gustav toppled thousands of them. Most of the ancient bald cypress trees of the parish were felled by lumbermen in the eighteenth and nineteenth centuries, used to build many of the fine structures still standing. Some cypress lumber continues to be milled today, primarily for fine home building, furniture, and a specialty craftsman market. The cypress trees seen along the bayous now are almost all new growth, one hundred years old or less. Up until about a century ago, the waterways were the primary means of transport in the parish, and bayous were dredged and kept clean and free of obstruction. Live oaks still shade the great-great-great-great-grandchildren of the people who built their early houses near those oaks. And even before, those same trees may have provided shade for Indians and for European missionaries. Gorgeous old oak trees are found in every corner of Pointe Coupee, many listed on the Live Oak Society register, and a number of those are well over three hundred years old.

Sugarcane, cotton, soybeans, corn, wheat, and rice grow abundantly in Pointe Coupee fields, making the parish the most diverse in the state in agricultural production. Cattle graze freely. Rooted in agriculture, the parish is still home to farmers and those who work in accompanying industries. The way of life keeps a farmer's feet on the ground and his eyes on the world beyond the living room: plants and animals, soil, water, and weather.

Churches are imbedded in the small towns, villages, and the farm landscape of Pointe Coupee. In early days churches had to be within walking distance from homes, and even today some churches stand within a few hundred yards of each other. As in the past, some small churches open for worship only once a month, and share a pastor with other churches in the parish or even with a neighboring parish. These churches represent communities of families and friends who often share a common history and a strong sense of place.

An Indian mound in Livonia stands beside Bayou Grosse Tete as it has for a thousand years. Another mound in the same group was flattened with earthmoving equipment in the twentieth century. In the Great Flood of 1927 someone was buried in the top of the big mound until the waters subsided and the body could be moved to a cemetery. People still remember that story.

are based on fact; others have been embellished and belong more properly in parish folklore. Some have been written down, while others, too painful, are never told, or told only in families or among trusted friends. All are part of the tradition and history of Pointe Coupee.

What of the physical world of the past has survived and is still present in our twenty-first-century life? The mighty Mississippi still flows as it has for ten thousand years. For the past hundred however, it has been carefully channeled and contained to prevent the yearly deluge that created the flood-

A slave cabin stands behind River Lake plantation, but today the woods have grown up around it, hiding it almost entirely from view. If left untended, nature will reclaim it in short order.

Every year brings the relentless destruction of the relics of history. Hurricanes knock down trees, crush houses, and demolish old stores and post offices. People pull down old barns for their lumber. Trees grow up through the porches of houses long vacant and, left to grow there, eventually become living parts of the buildings, nearly inseparable. These buildings go back to nature; they become pieces of the earth itself like shards of pottery broken and discarded hundreds or even thousands of years ago that resurface in open ground with the turn of a shovel.

One of the remarkable things about Pointe Coupee Parish, however, is that the people have saved, protected, preserved, and maintained so much of their history. There are approximately seventy antebellum buildings left in the parish, structures built before the first rifle was fired in the American Civil War. An industry and an economy based on legal slavery came to an end with that war, America's only civil war and our most devastating in resulting loss of life. Yet, with all the changes that followed, families continued to get by, to build new businesses, new lives, new relationships, new values. Most of the big old buildings—houses, barns, sugar mills—too expensive to maintain, fell into disrepair or were lost to floods, storms, and fires.

Every historic structure we see today was saved from the usual fate by families and individuals who worked to put on a new roof and a new coat of paint, or to rebuild a crumbling foundation. The new technology of electrification actually destroyed many more antebellum homes in the twentieth century as faulty wiring hidden in walls started fires not seen until it was too late.

Any insurance man will tell you that a lived-in house is safer and will last longer than a vacant house. One aspect of the consistent, slow-moving economy of Pointe Coupee (the parish population has fluctuated around 21,000 people for a century) is that people have tended to stay in their family houses. A new roof is less expensive than a new house. In the villages and small towns of Pointe Coupee, sharecropper houses and slave cabins have been moved and sited on small lots side by side with Victorian cottages, Craftsman bungalows, and twentieth-century brick ranches. Old barns there when the land was divided into large farm tracts stand where they have always stood, too valuable for their storage capacity to be taken down.

Today, when many of the antebellum homes up and down the Great River Road have been opened to the public as museums, bed-and-breakfast inns, and pilgrimage destinations, Pointe Coupee plantation houses continue their lives as homes. Tourists drive by slowly and peer down an entry drive or across a field to get a sense of the heart still beating in one of the grand old places. Some are still owned by descendants of the builders or early owners. Others have been bought by people who just love old houses—their beauty, romance, and history.

All the people who live in the old houses of Pointe Coupee, who farm the ancient land, who garden and prune the trees, who care for the animals, who tell the old stories, who worship in the old churches, who bury their dead in the old cemeteries and clean the graves every year: they are the most important of all preservationists.

This book is organized to take you, the reader, on a road trip through historic Pointe Coupee Parish. Words and maps provide your transportation. Richard Sexton's photographs supply the view. With your imagination fueled, travel easily over new roads and old rivers, and back and forth through time as well.

Your trip begins at the Pointe Coupee Coast, where in the early 1700s European explorers and soldiers, Catholic missionaries and colonists, free people and slaves began settling the banks of the Mississippi River. From there, travel southeast along the Mississippi to the old Chenal and the oxbow lake False River; around the lake to the town of New Roads; and then north along the modern road LA-1 to Morganza. Cross the Morganza Spillway and continue to Upper Pointe, alongside Old River, and on to the Three Rivers area. From here, your northernmost destination, travel south along the Atchafalaya River, then along Bayou Fordoche, past the town of Fordoche, and to the town of Livonia. Finally, cross the Acadiana Trail (US-190, the only four-lane highway in the parish), head south toward the southern boundary of Pointe Coupee past El Dorado, where the final surrender of the Civil War was signed, to Valverda plantation home.

This tour follows the natural geography of the parish and also gives a sense of its history. After your armchair visit, consider taking a real road trip in your automobile or on your motorcycle, on your bicycle or on foot, to explore firsthand Louisiana's historic Pointe Coupee Parish.

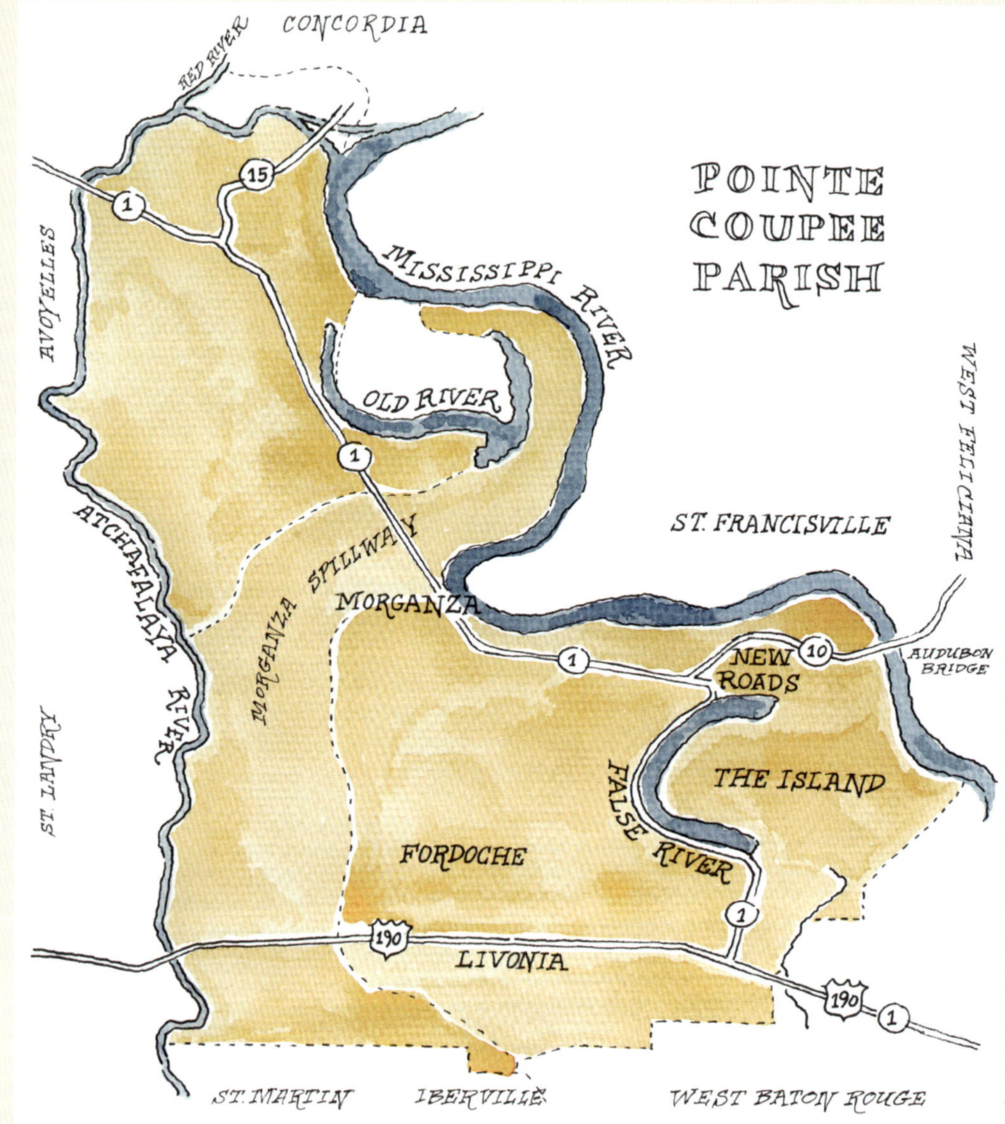

CHAPTER 1

The Pointe Coupee Road and the Mississippi River

THE POINTE COUPEE COAST

In the twists and turns of the Mississippi, there is a stretch of river about four miles long that travels pretty much due east. The bank of that part of the river was named *La Côte de la Pointe Coupée* (the Pointe Coupee Coast), and the road that follows the levee is the Pointe Coupee Road. French colonists, Capuchin missionaries, Canadian *coureurs du bois* (fur trappers), soldiers, and African slaves settled along the coast. The river itself has washed away most evidence of those early settlements, but the church dedicated to St. Francis in 1738 is still there.

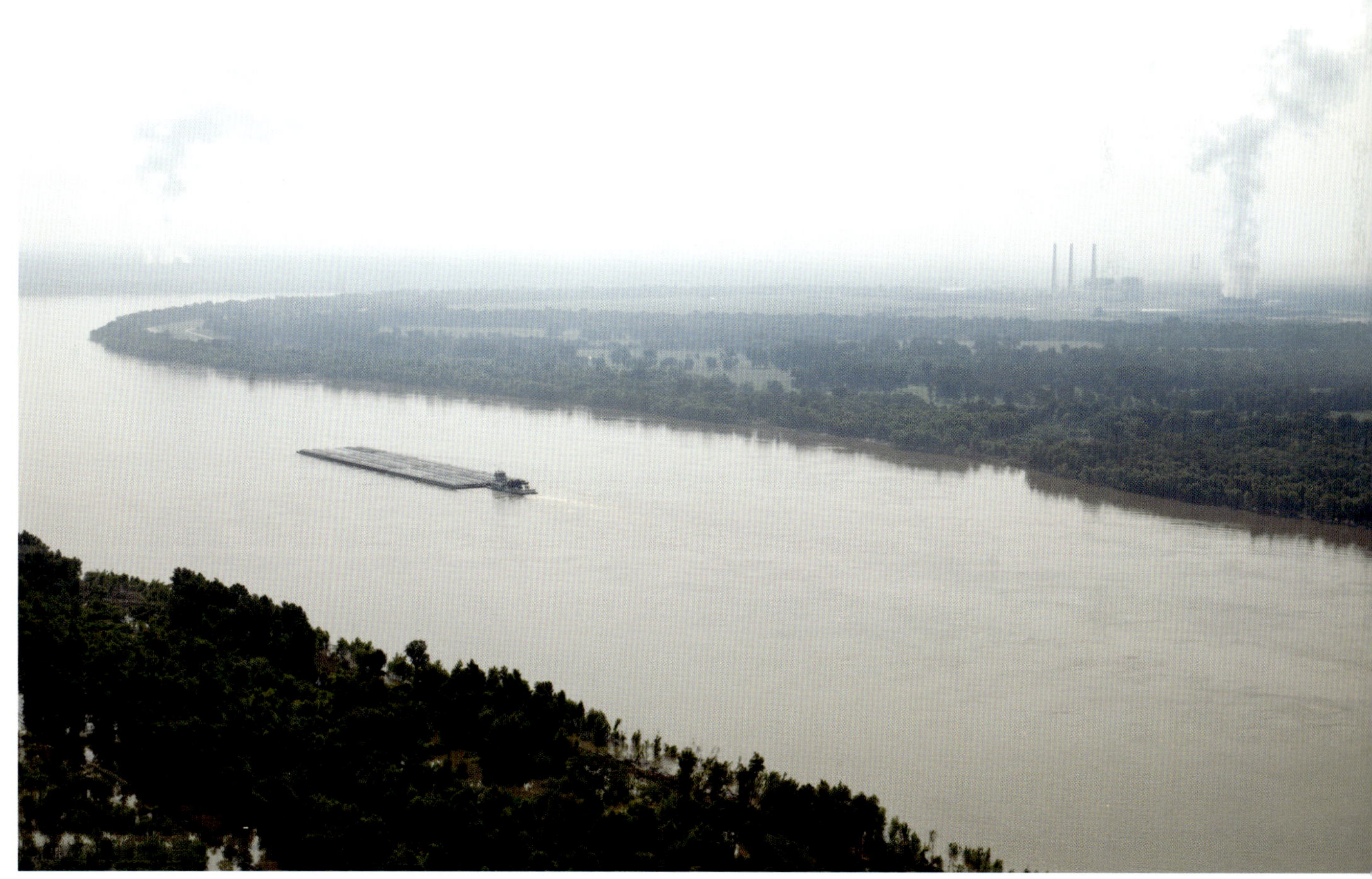

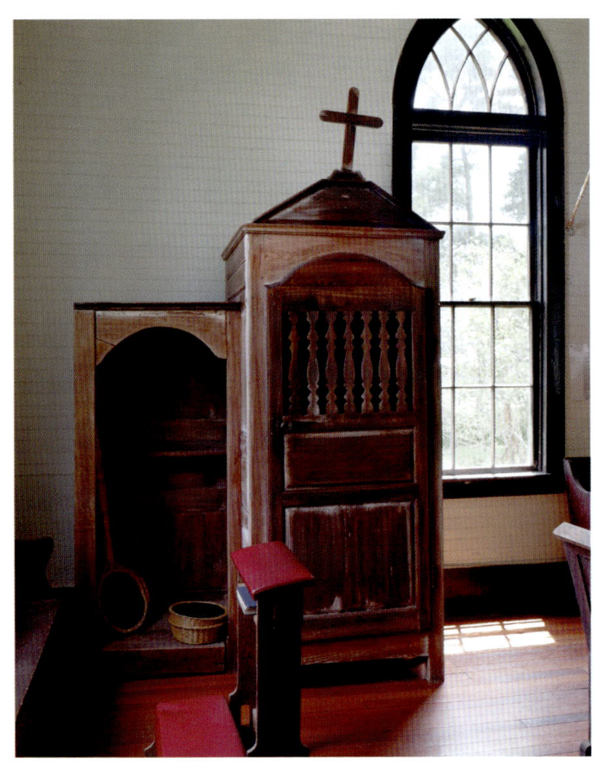

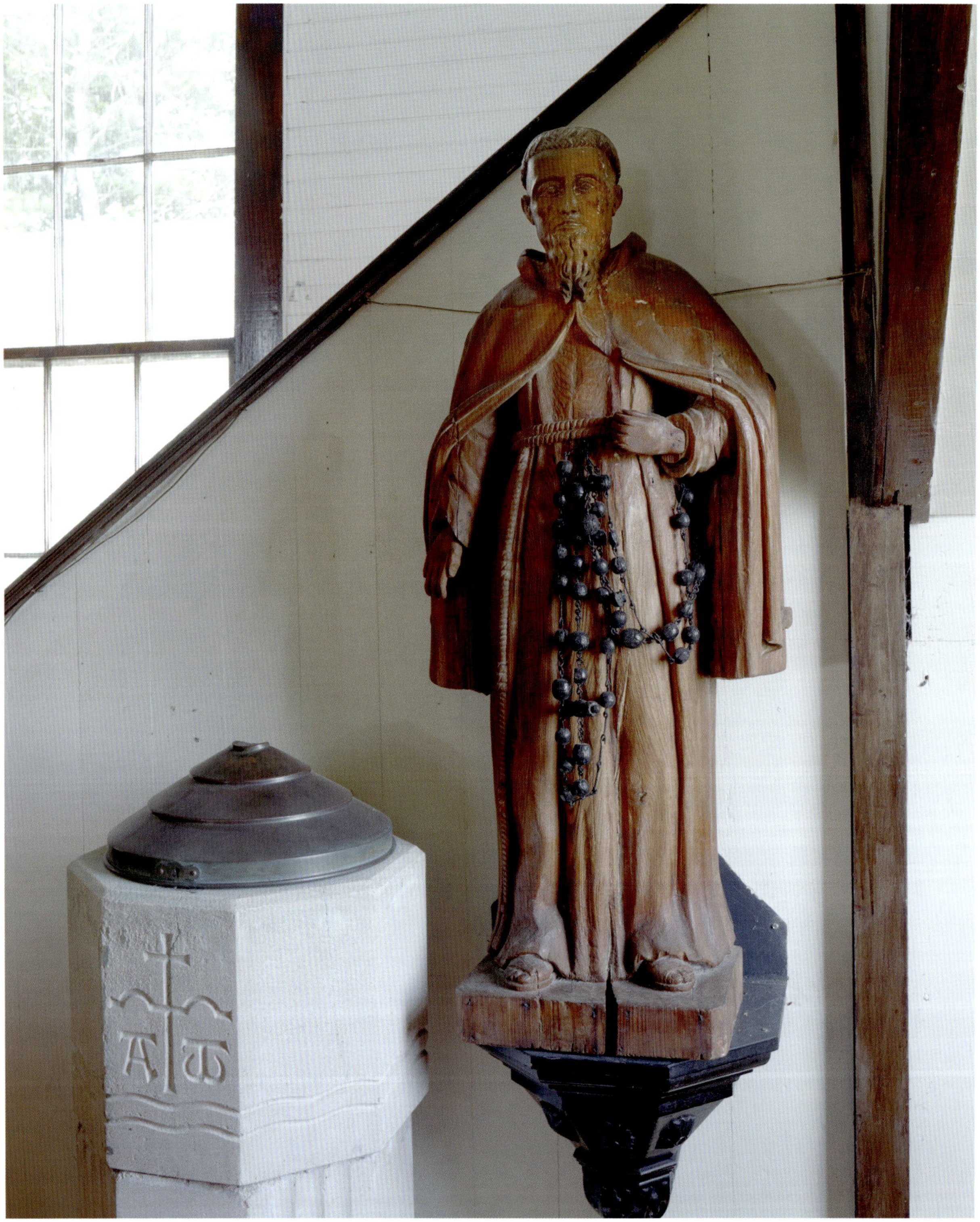

St. Francis of Assisi (1182–1226) is an Italian saint, named by his father for France, and much beloved by both French and Spanish Catholics. He is the founder of the Franciscan order of monks, the Order of Friars Minor or "Little Brothers." The missionaries who founded the church in Pointe Coupee and Bayou Sara were members of the Order of Friars Minor Capuchin.

St. Francis is well known as the patron saint of animals and of the environment. Little statues of St. Francis are often placed in gardens, not only in Louisiana but also around the world.

French Capuchins began their missionary work in the Pointe Coupee area in 1722. Sacramental records date from 1727. The Capuchins served native Tunica Indians and European settlers to the area on both sides of the Mississippi. (The town directly across the river from Pointe Coupee is called St. Francisville in memory of that early history.)

The Capuchins did not anticipate the power and ranging movement of the Mississippi River when they built the first church building and dedicated it in 1738. That church lasted little more than twenty years before a new church was built in 1760. The second church served its parish for 130 years. A model of the 1760 building is among the artifacts on display in the St. Francis Chapel today.

By 1890, once again the Mississippi River had moved its course closer and closer to the church, requiring the building of a new church in a new location, and the removal of the old cemetery. Graves were moved from the riverside to St. Mary Cemetery in New Roads, and the third St. Francis church was built several miles upriver. Mass is still offered weekly at St. Francis Chapel.

The confessional was moved from the old churches to St. Francis Chapel. Built entirely of cypress, it was probably made between 1738 and 1760.

An old wooden statue of St. Francis is believed to have been carved long ago by Tunica Indians, converts in the early Capuchin missionary era.

A bell struck with the date 1719 is believed to be one used in the first St. Francis church. The model of the 1760 church was made by James Stonaker, a St. Francis parishioner, using wood that came from the old building when it was taken down.

A statue of the beloved St. Francis of Assisi stands in a little niche above the front doors of the third church built in his honor on the Pointe Coupee Coast.

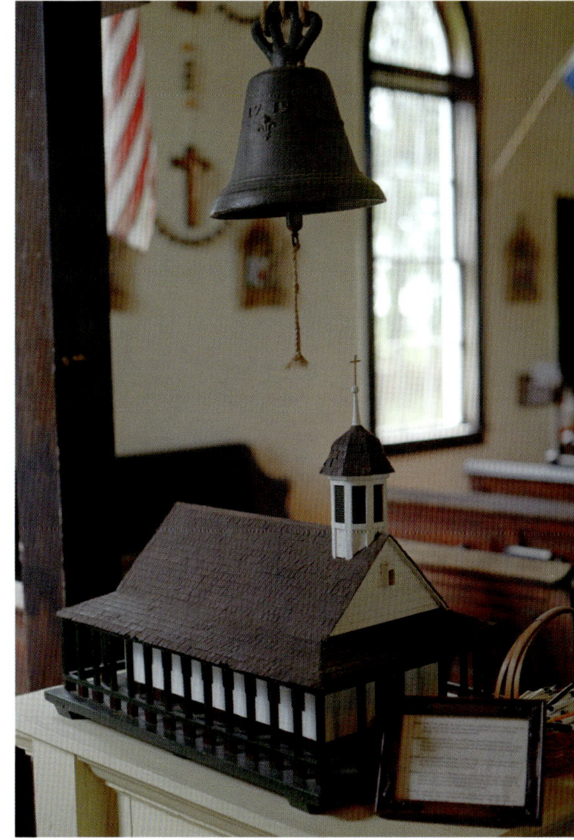

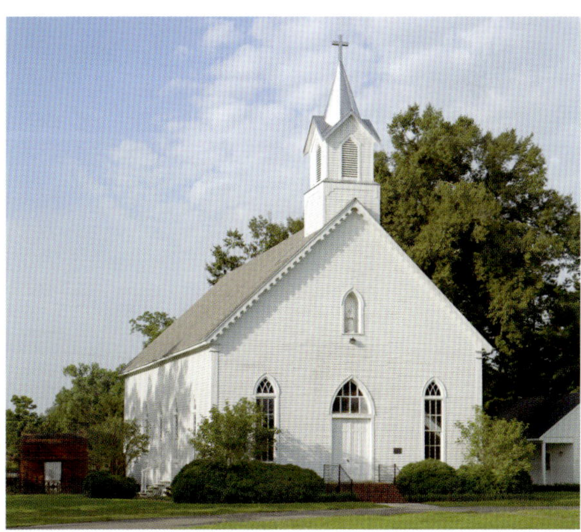

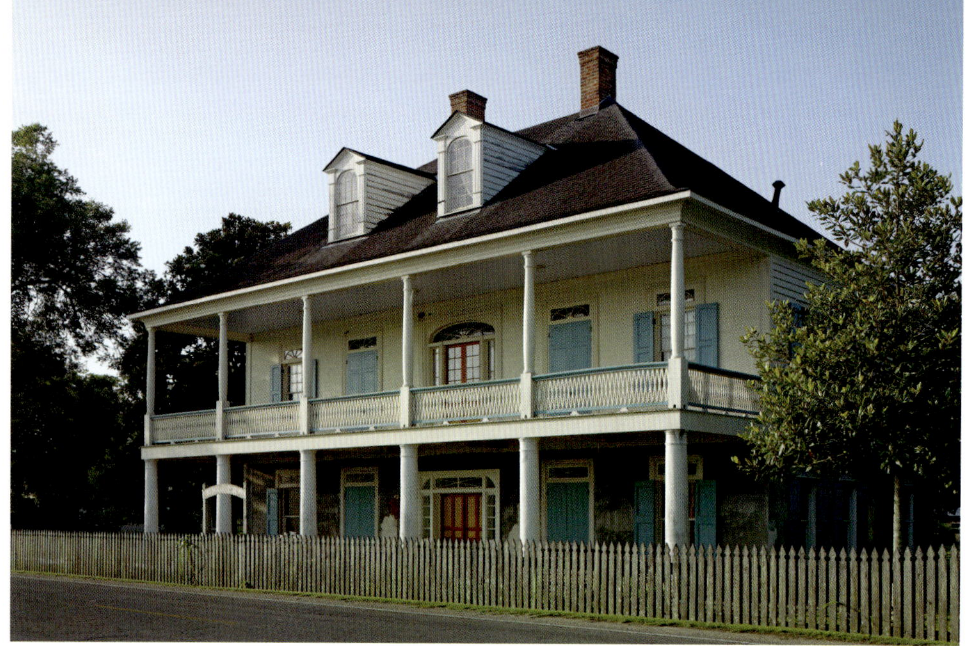

Labatut House sits just over the levee on the edge of the Mississippi River. Behind the house are the deep agricultural fields, the French long lots, which give Pointe Coupee its sense of immense space and openness.

When it was built around 1830, the lovely Labatut House sat far back from the Mississippi with an *allée* of live oaks leading from the river to the house. Over the years the course of the river moved closer and closer, taking the trees, and eventually requiring the protective levee and river road to transect the front yard of the house.

The second-floor loggia was enclosed in the twentieth century, so the stairs are now indoors.

The original cypress fanlight over the French doors from the loggia to the central hall is carved with a sunburst pattern.

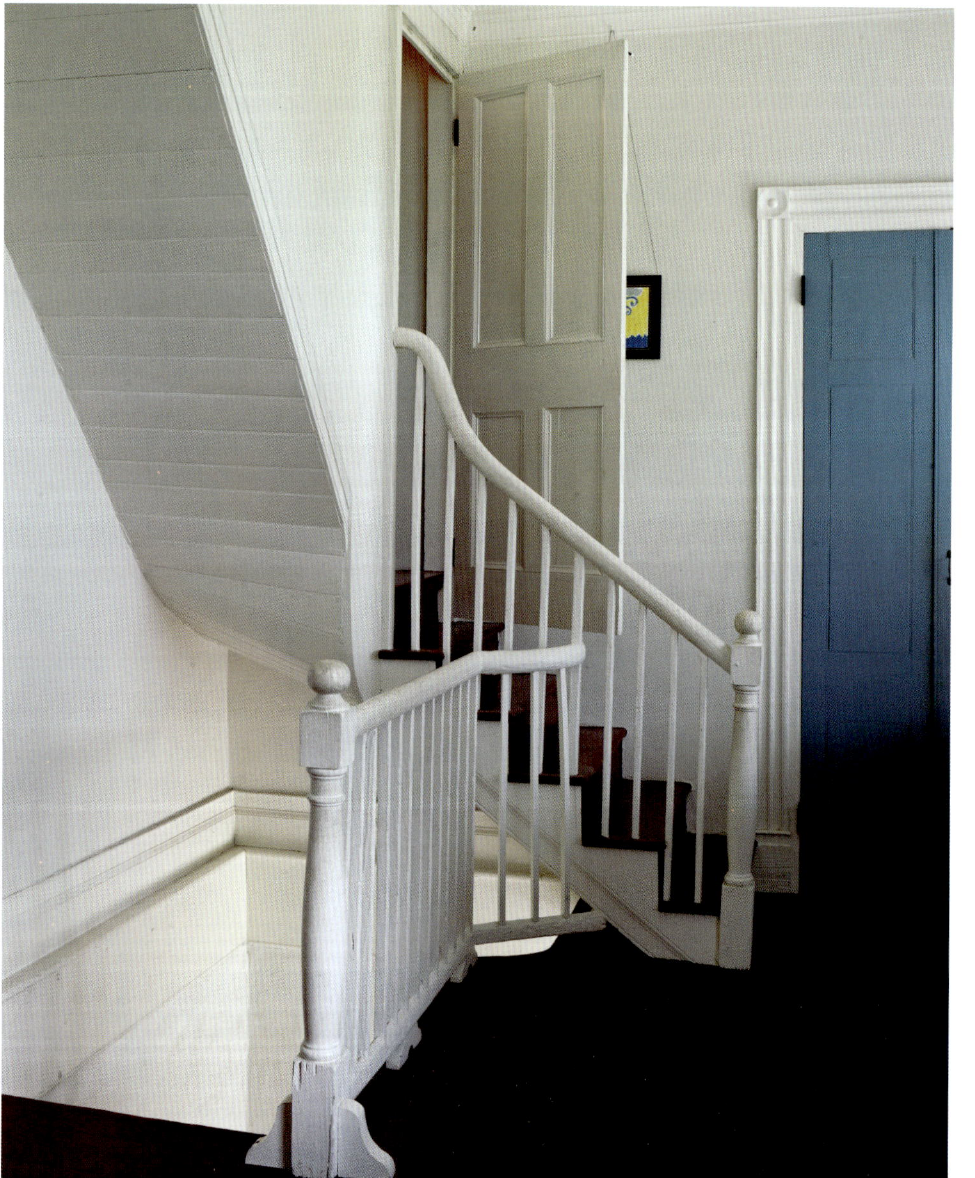

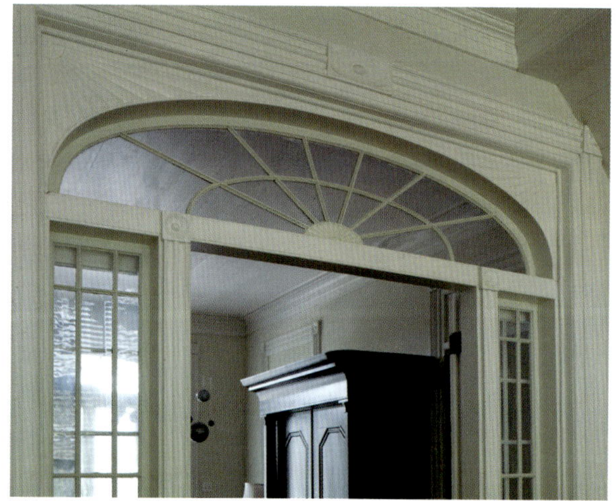

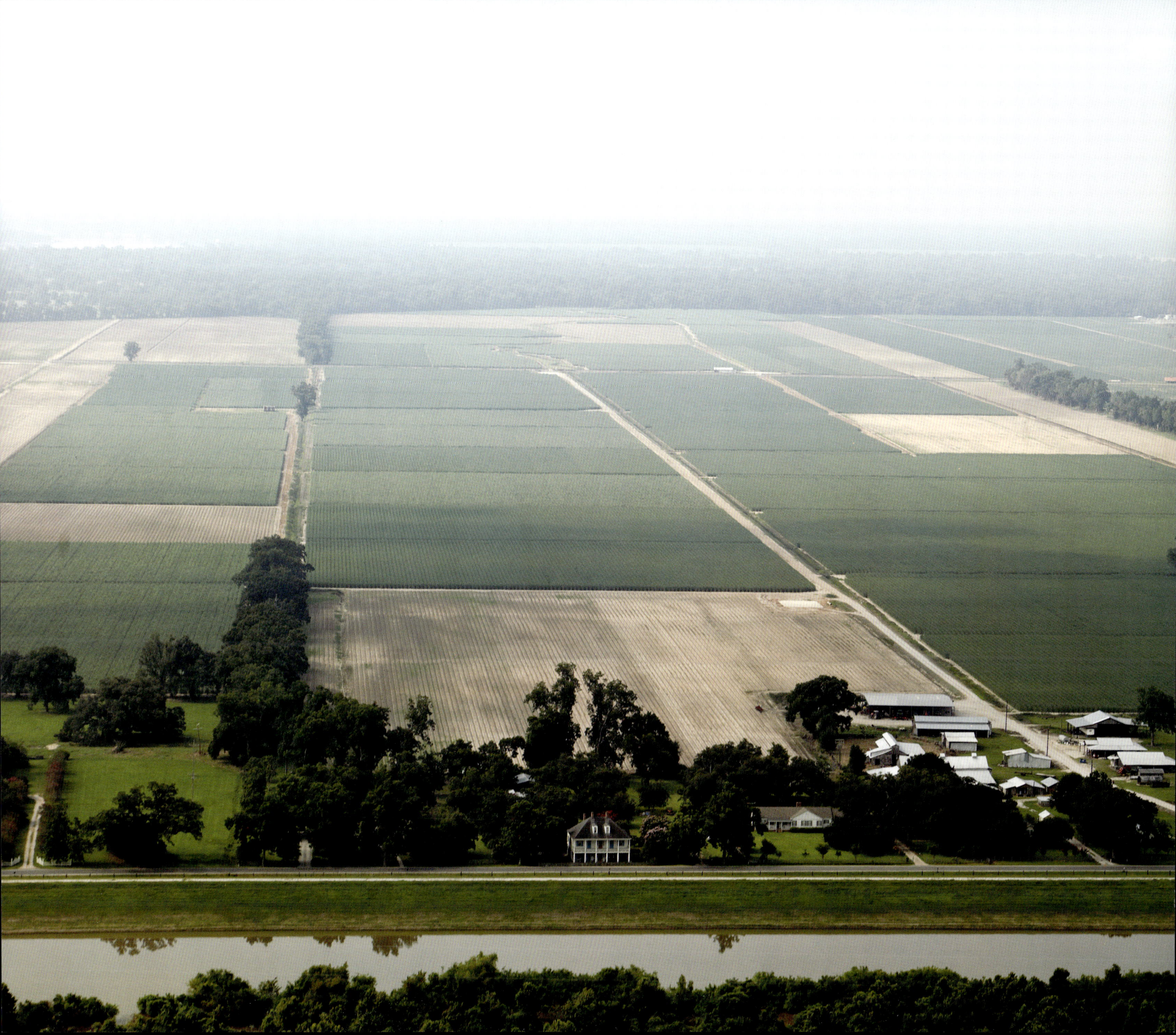

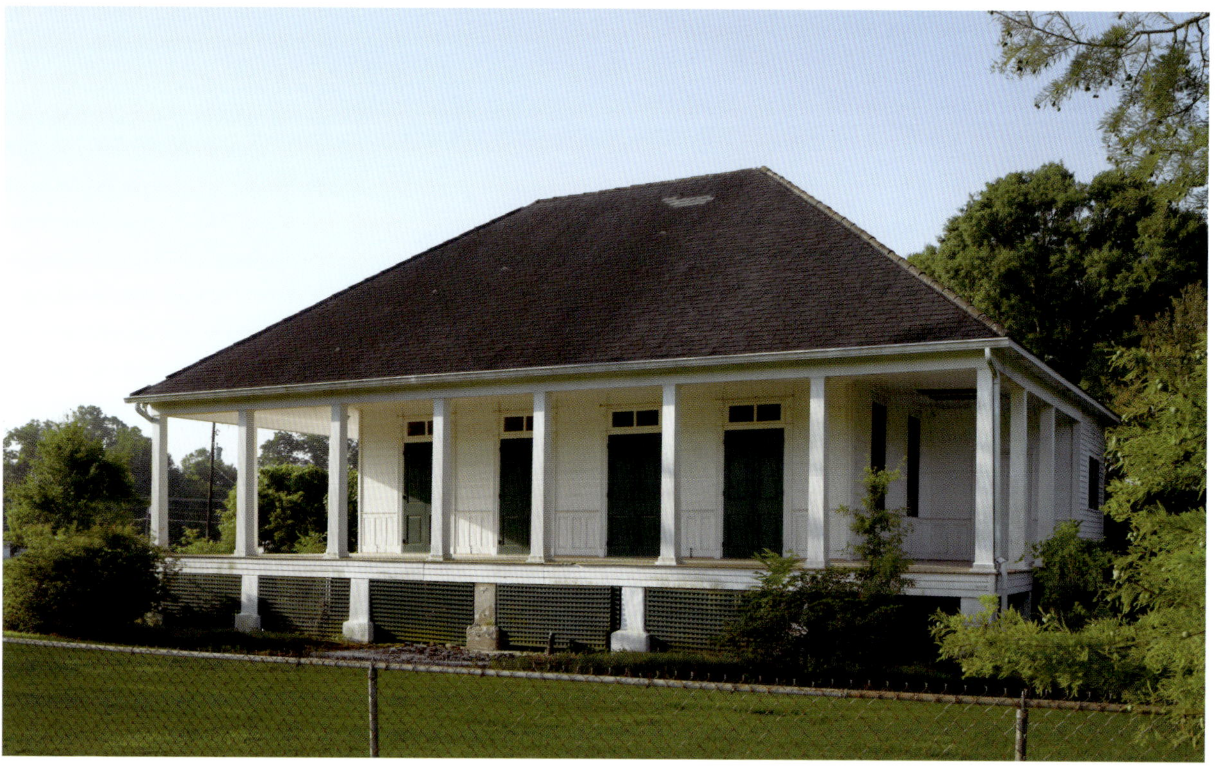

Joseph Tounoir (1780–1836) built a lovely home in 1825 on the Mississippi River. The house one sees today, close to the levee on the Pointe Coupee Road, originally was the upper floor of a Creole cottage raised upon a brick basement. The movement of the Mississippi and successive floods eventually undermined the brick foundation, so it was removed in the twentieth century.

In the attic of the Fannie Riche House one can see the so-called Norman truss, the Y-shape with center post, built to hold up steep early roofs in French settlements from Missouri to Louisiana.

The Fannie Riche House is known for its fine interior woodwork, all made of cypress. The house is currently undergoing restoration by owner Joanna Wurtele with the help of architect Glenn Morgan.

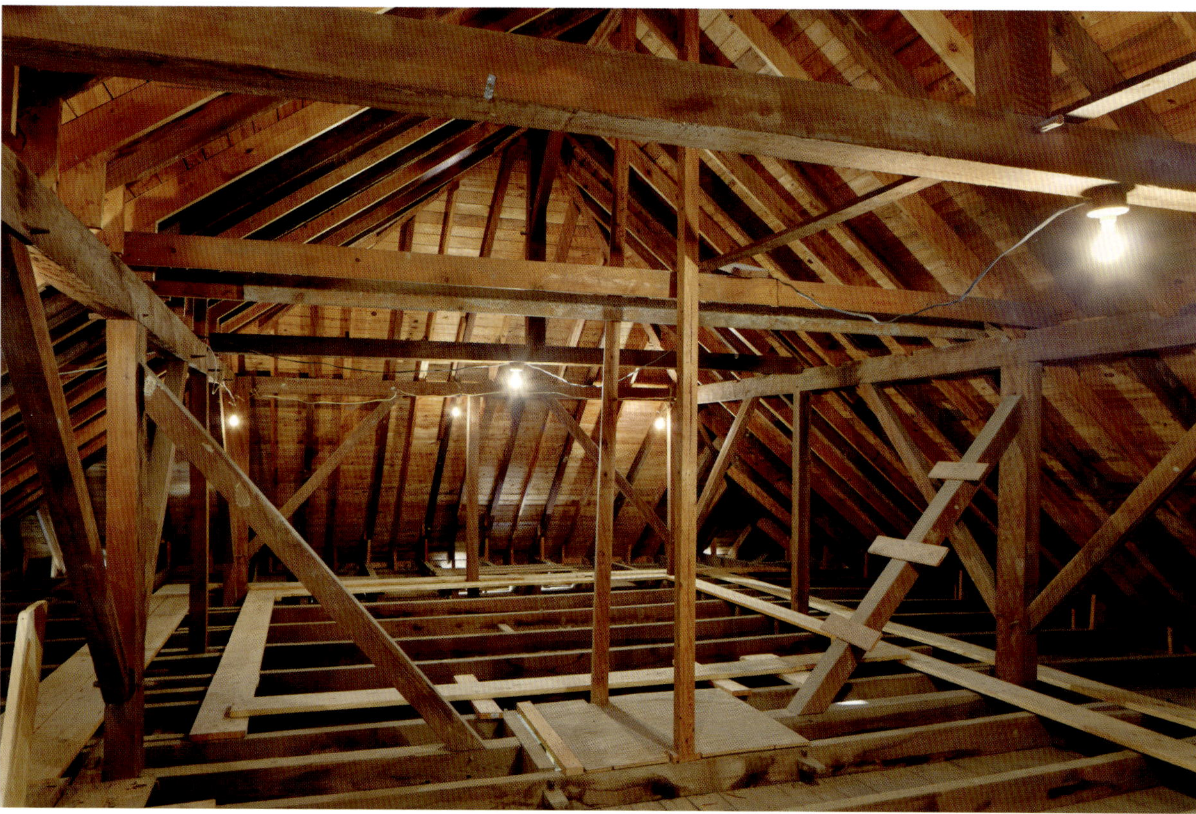

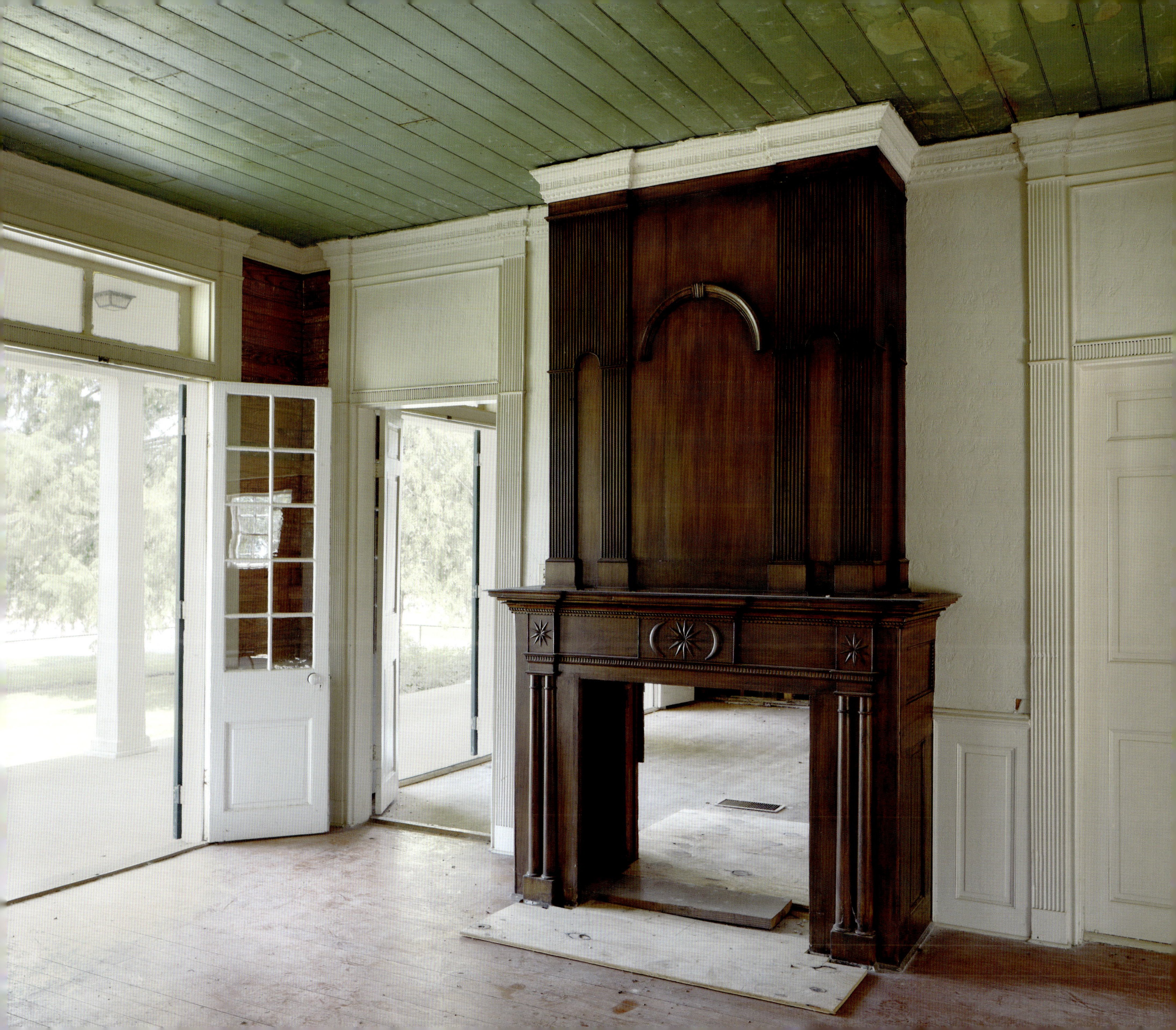

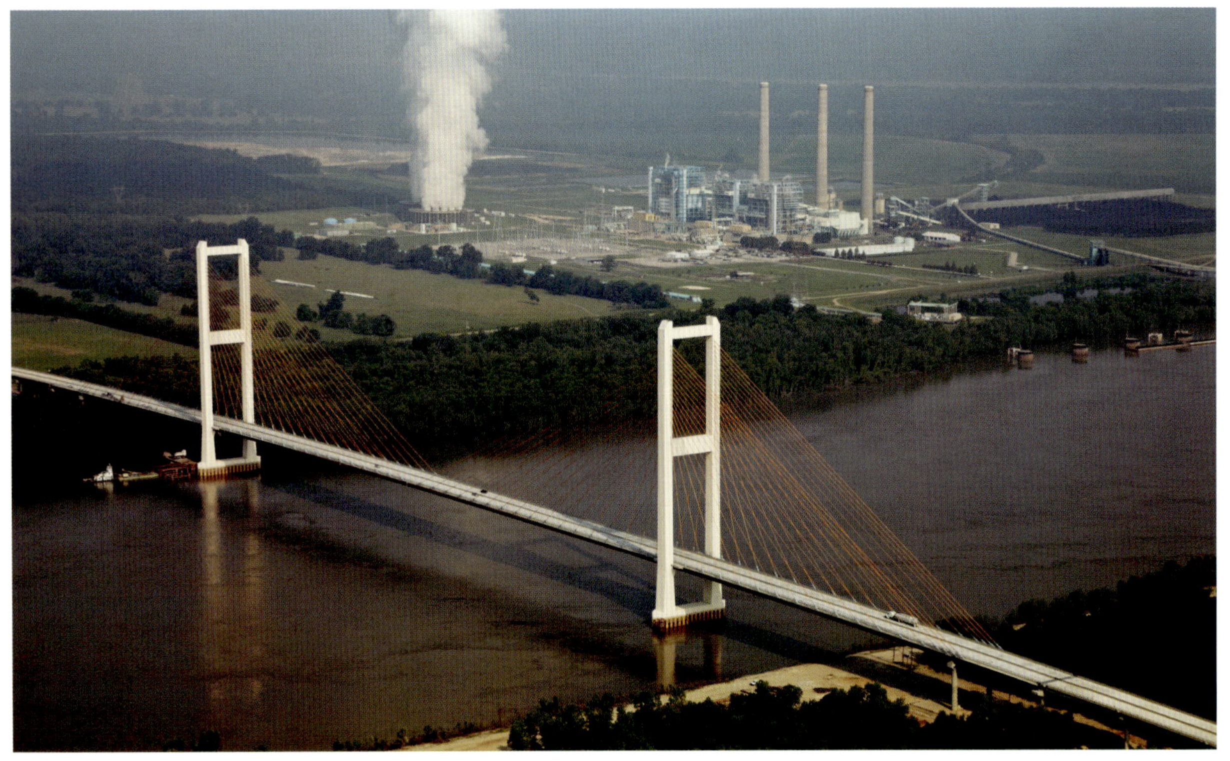

The John James Audubon Bridge, opened in 2011, has the longest cable-stayed span in the Western Hemisphere. It is almost 2½ miles in length. The bridge connects Pointe Coupee to West Feliciana Parish, and is part of the Zachary Taylor Parkway that extends from Poplarville, Mississippi, to Alexandria, Louisiana. Seen beyond the bridge is Pointe Coupee's Big Cajun II coal-fired power plant.

The bridge is named for John James Audubon (1785–1851), a Creole artist and naturalist born in Saint-Domingue (Haiti). Audubon became world-famous for painting the birds of America and producing a printed portfolio of those paintings. His prints are still prized today. Audubon lived at Oakley Plantation near St. Francisville in 1821, and created thirty-two of his bird paintings during his stay.

Ferry service between New Roads and St. Francisville closed in 2011 when the Audubon Bridge opened to traffic. Regular ferry service had connected the two sides of the Mississippi River for generations. As far back as the early 1700s, the Capuchin missionaries had traveled by boat between the two banks, and considered both sides as one place that they called *Pointe Coupée*.

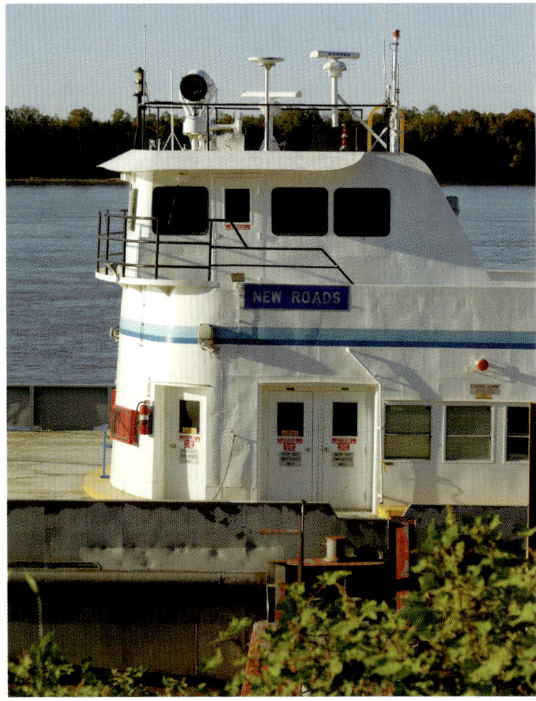

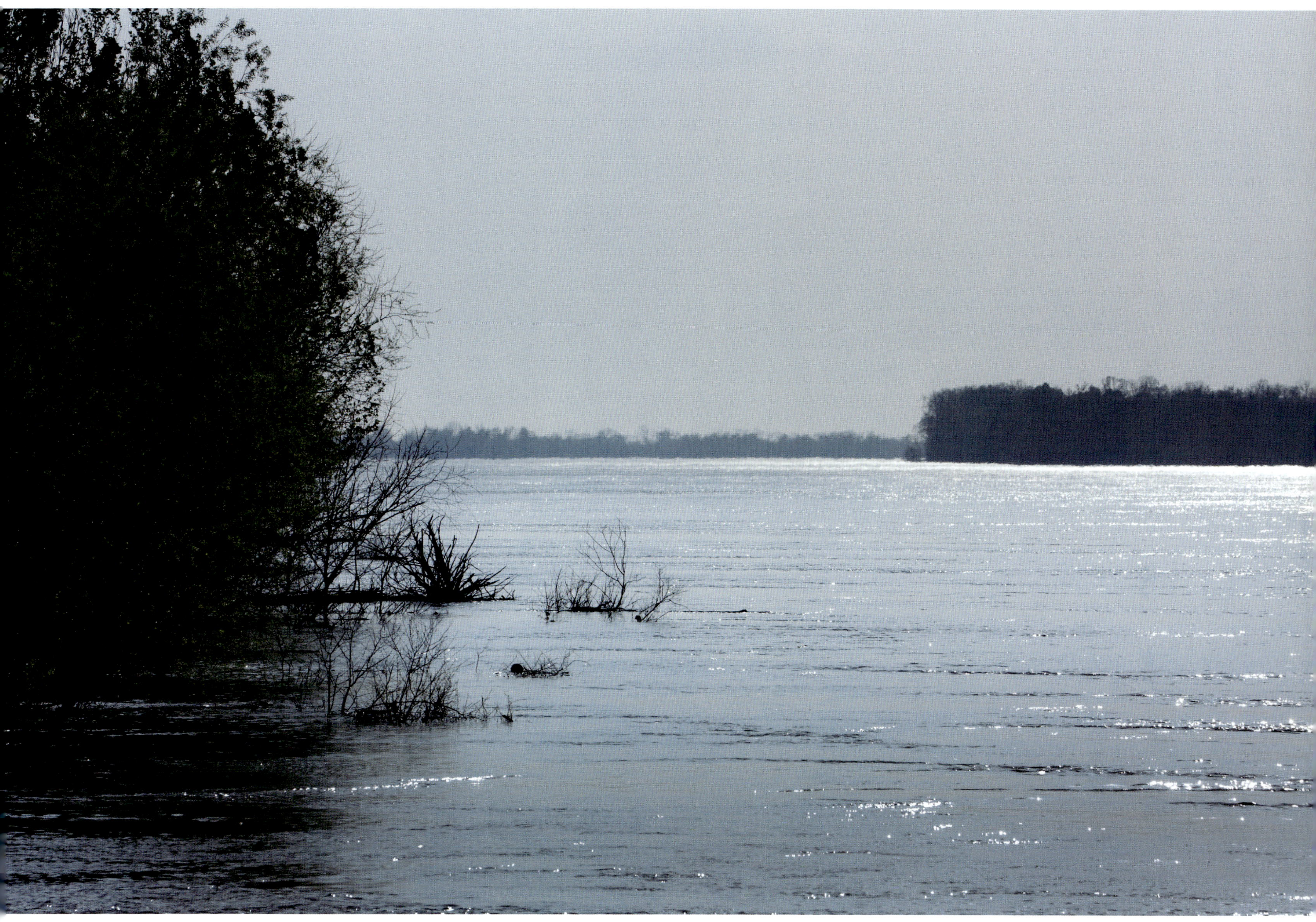

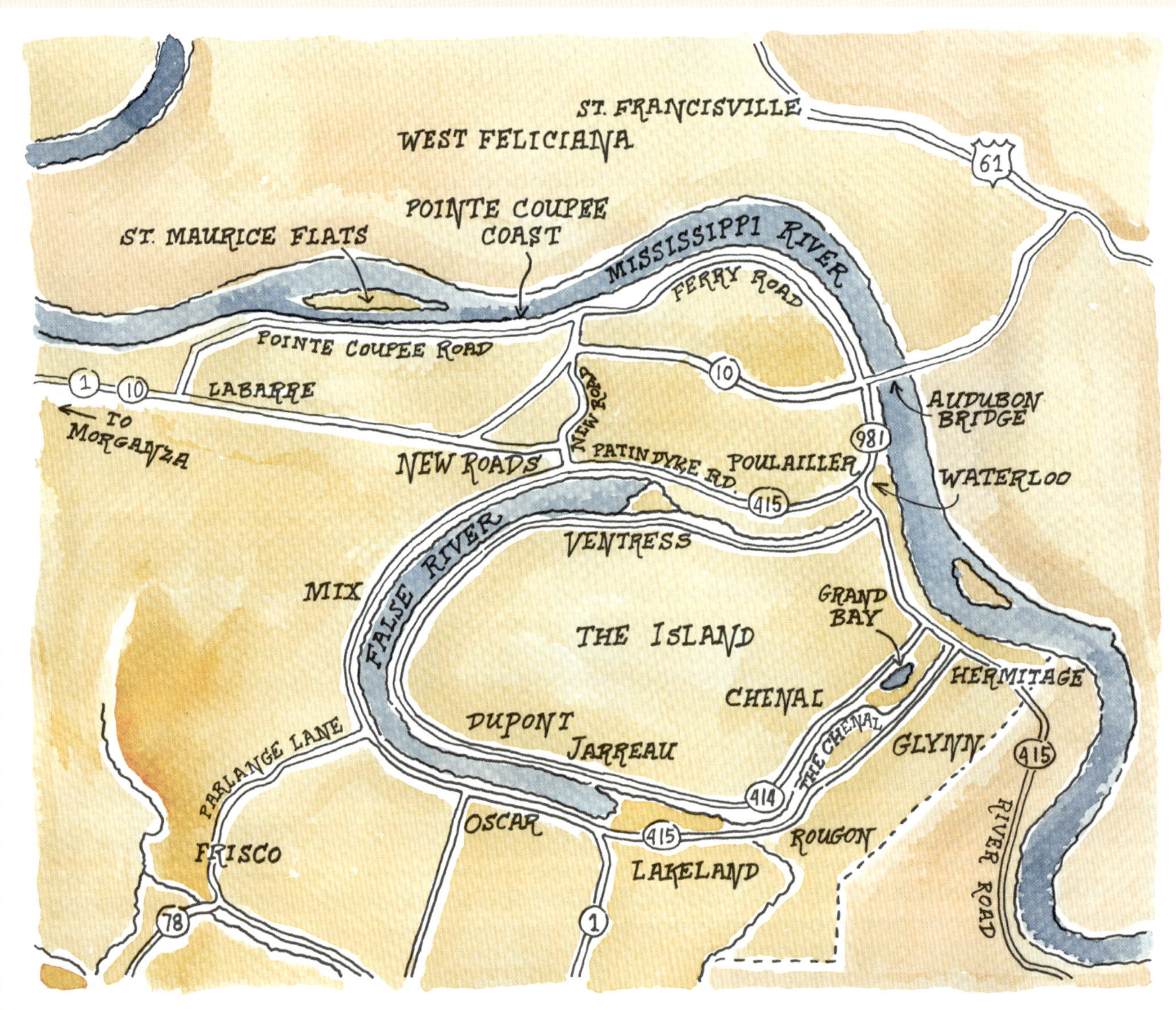

ST. FRANCISVILLE
WEST FELICIANA
61
POINTE COUPEE COAST
ST. MAURICE FLATS
MISSISSIPPI RIVER
FERRY ROAD
POINTE COUPEE ROAD
1
10
LABARRE
10
NEW ROAD
AUDUBON BRIDGE
TO MORGANZA
981
NEW ROADS
PATIN DYKE RD.
POULAILLER
WATERLOO
415
FALSE RIVER
VENTRESS
MIX
GRAND BAY
THE ISLAND
CHENAL
HERMITAGE
PARLANGE LANE
DUPONT
JARREAU
THE CHENAL
GLYNN
415
414
OSCAR
415
ROUGON
RIVER ROAD
FRISCO
LAKELAND
1
78

CHAPTER 2

Chenal Road and the Chenal

THE CHENAL

Looking down the peaceful waters of the Chenal, one may find it hard to believe that less than three hundred years ago this same riverbed was the main channel of the mighty Mississippi. The river makes exaggerated twists and turns as it wends its way toward the Gulf of Mexico. Sometimes one of these turns becomes very long and twists back on itself. Then the river might make a shortcut from the beginning of the loop across a short stretch of land directly to the end of the loop. When this happens, an oxbow lake is left behind. False River was created in just this way around 1722.

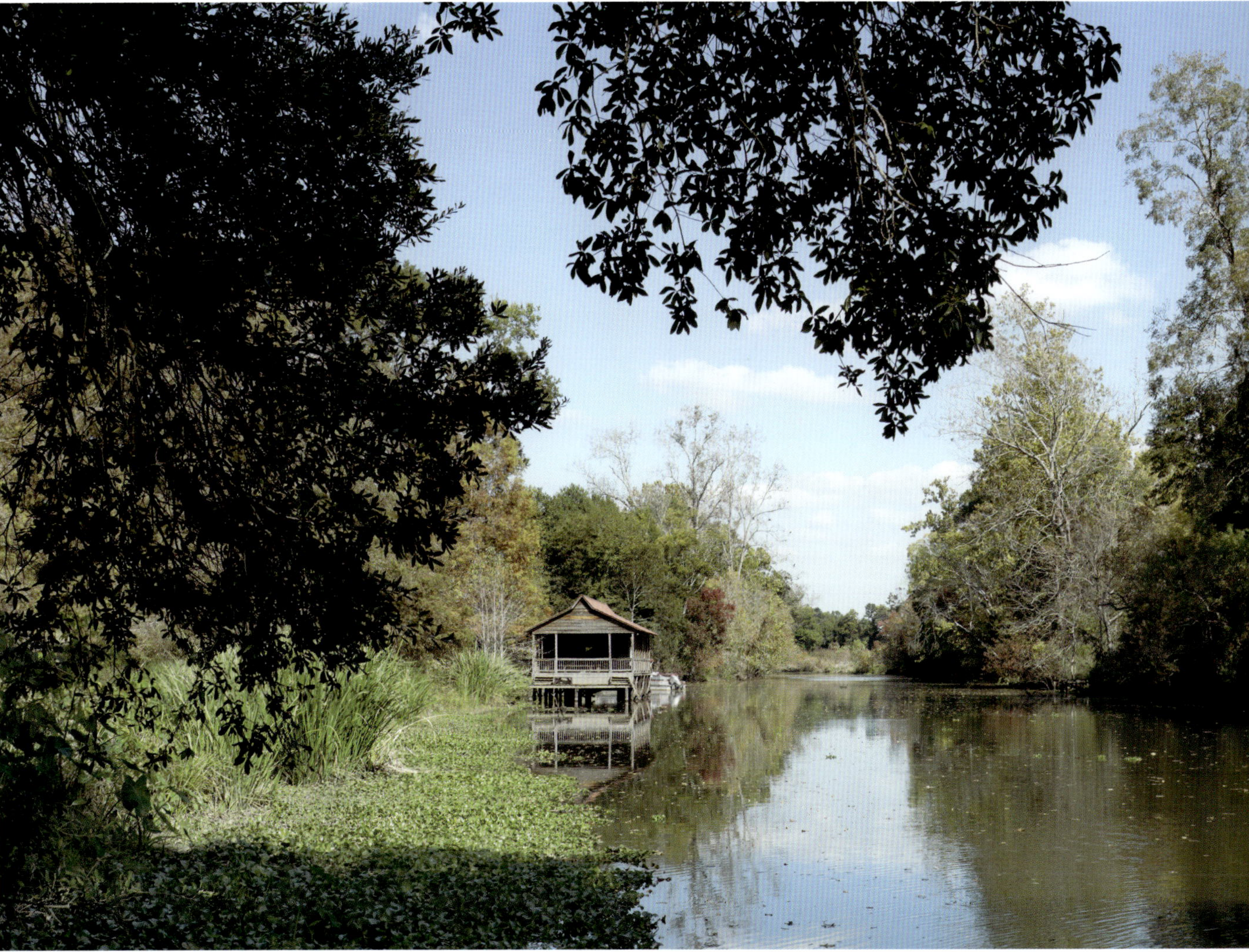

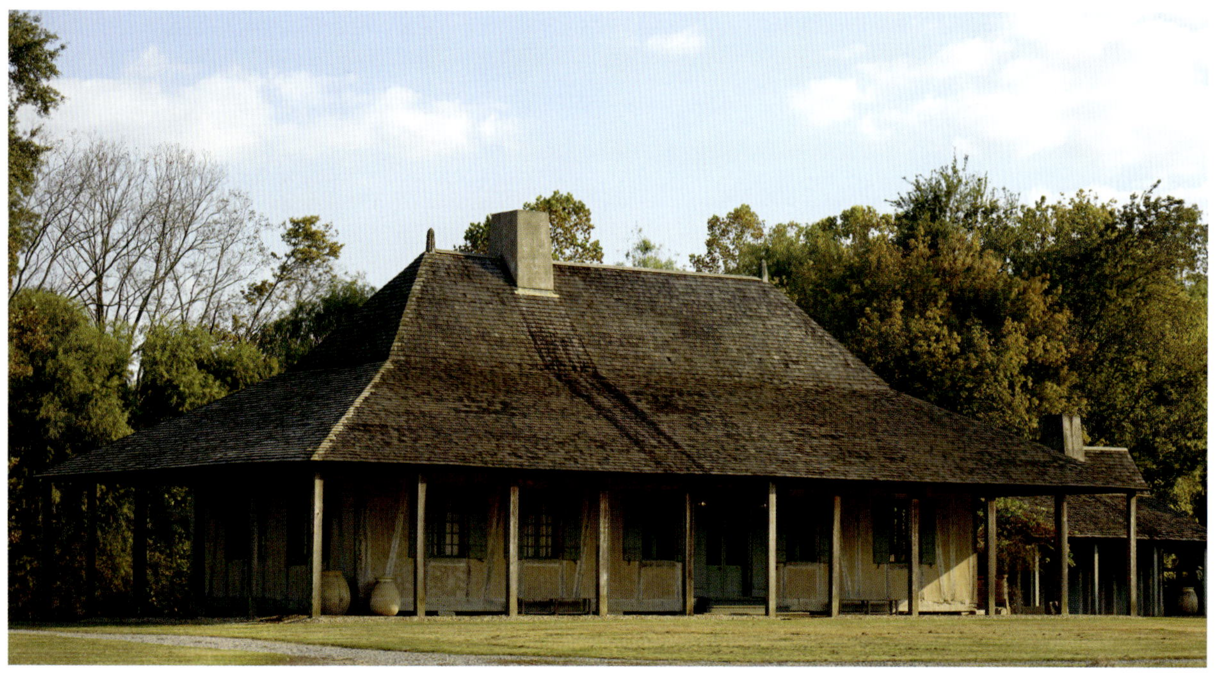

The LaCour House is one of the oldest surviving buildings in this parish. It is named for Frenchman Nicolas LaCour (1699–1761), who came to Pointe Coupee from Natchez, having fled the Indian Revolt of 1729. He and his family owned property at Pointe Coupee from 1731 through 1856. This venerable structure was moved to the banks of the Chenal and restored by Jack and Pat Holden in 1996.

An eighteenth-century *table à tréteau* (trestle table) is set with earthenware and pewter in the *chambre* (bedchamber) of the LaCour House. Next to the bed is a petite chair built before 1800 that was found elsewhere in Pointe Coupee.

In the huge *salle* (salon or parlor) of the LaCour House, massive molded ceiling joists and *colombage* (plaster between wood frame) are clearly seen. The upright timbers of the walls are filled in with *bousillage*, a mixture of mud, straw, and Spanish moss often used in early Louisiana buildings. Two long tables seat plenty of guests, young and old, at big family dinners. The refectory table to the left came from the Ursuline Convent in New Orleans.

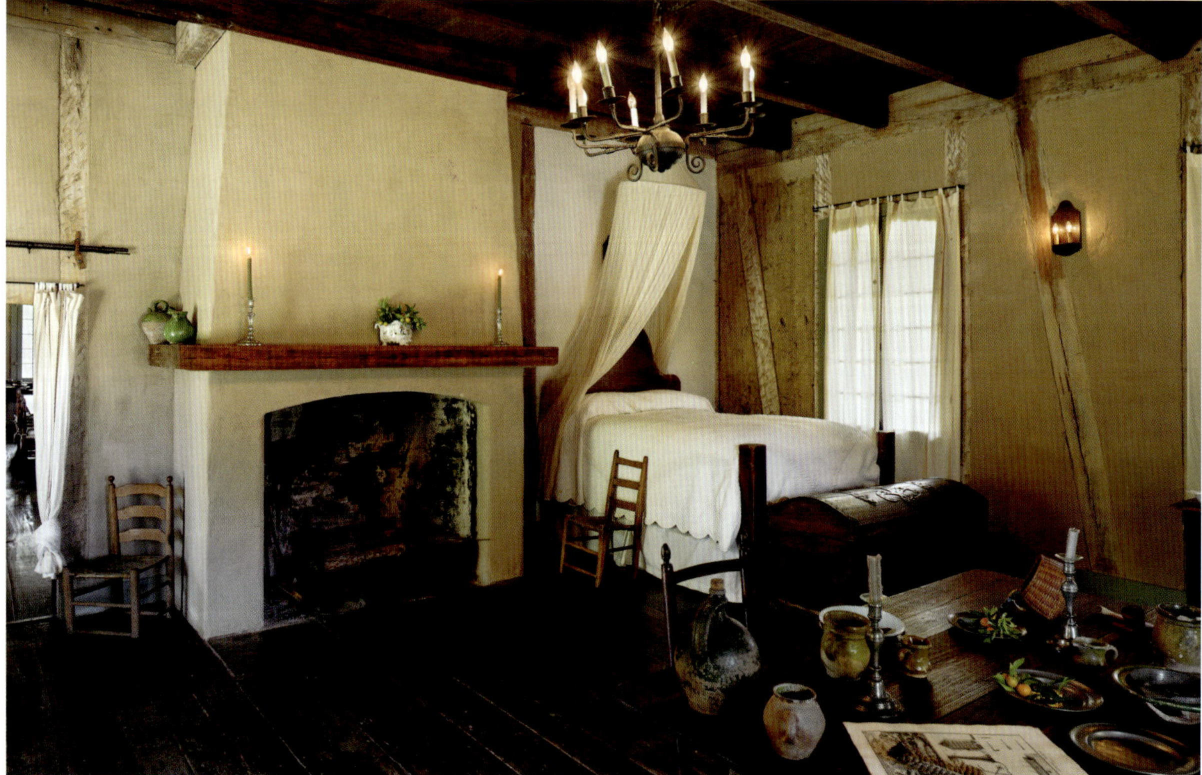

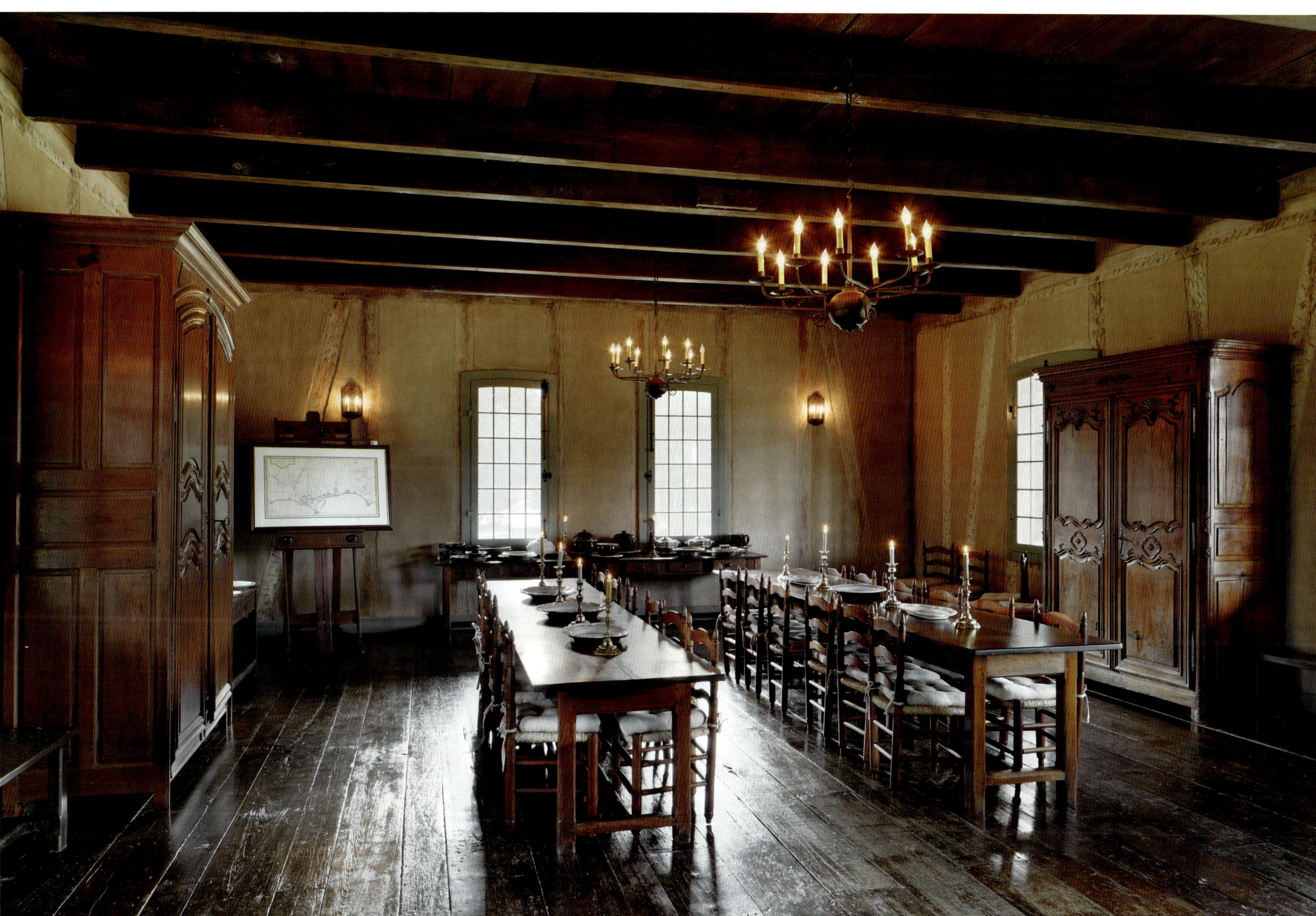

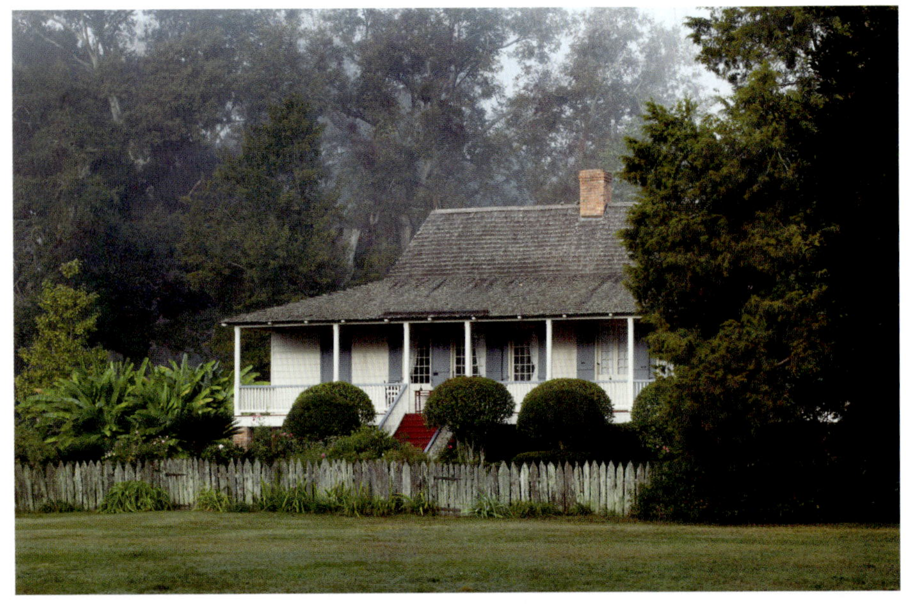
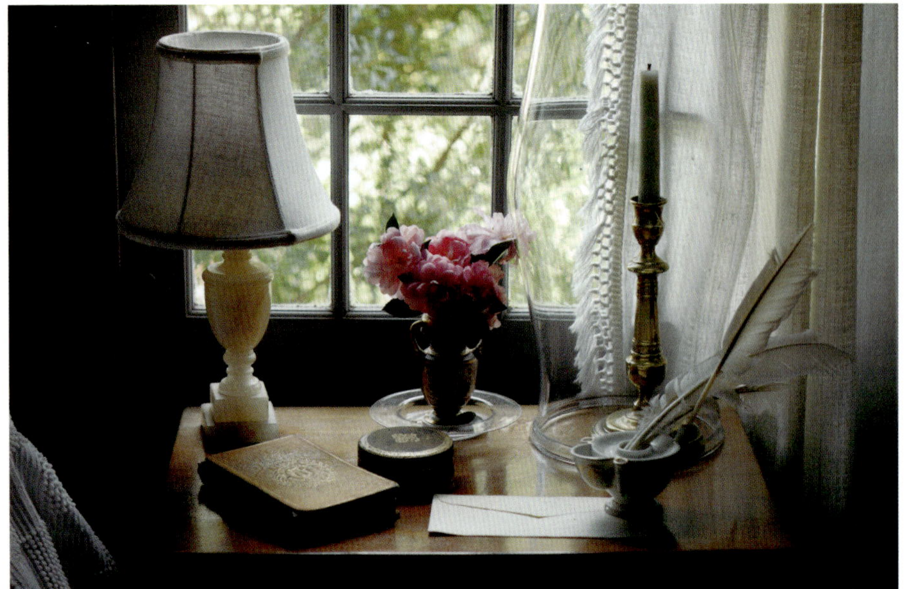
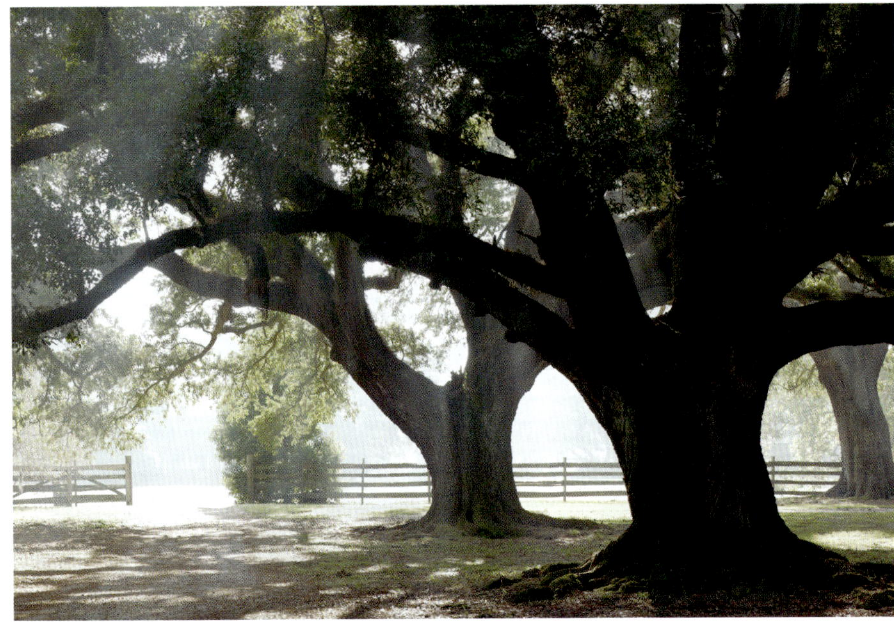
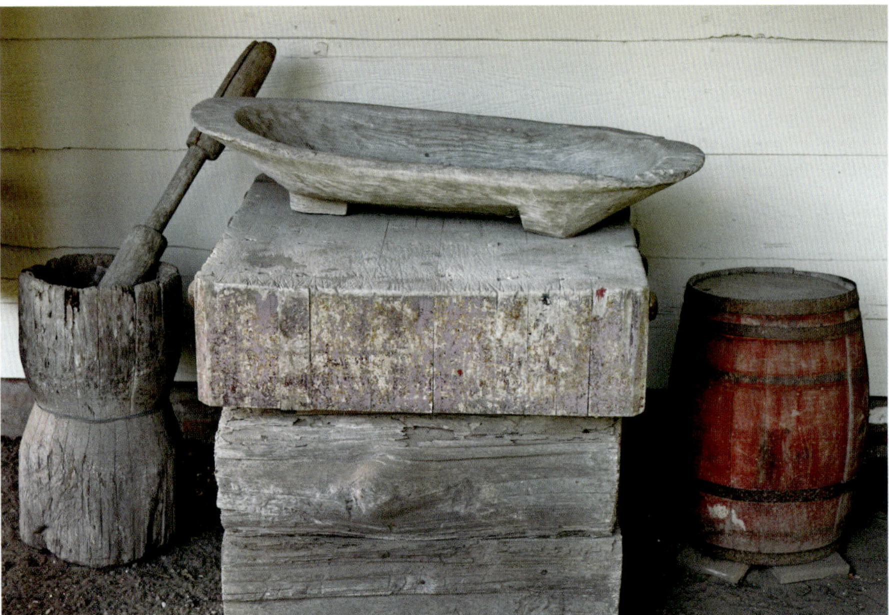

Before it was moved in the late twentieth century, the house known as *Maison Chenal* (Channel House) stood on a large plot of farmland now within the city limits of New Roads (at the corner of Major Parkway and False River Drive). Threatened with demolition, the house was purchased and moved by Jack and Pat Holden. The restoration that followed has been a labor of love.

The old oak trees were clearly arranged for a home site though no home remained on the property when Pat Holden found the land where she and her husband would move a number of historic buildings over the next forty years.

Pieux à travers (post-and-rail fences), as seen here, enclosed large pastures surrounding country homes in the nineteenth century. The vertical *pieux* fence with pickets enclosed smaller gardens near the home.

Pink sasanquas, picked from the garden and tucked into a little *Vieux Paris* urn, brighten a side table in Maison Chenal. Sasanquas are early-blooming camellias grown in Louisiana gardens since the 1820s.

An old dough bowl sits on a chopping block on wooden supports. The *pile et pilon* (mortar and pestle) to the left was used to grind corn, wheat, and other grains. The cypress barrel to the right served many purposes, including storage and transport.

Simple cotton curtains hang on iron rods as they probably did when Julien Poydras purchased Maison Chenal in 1808. In French style, five teacups sit on the wraparound mantelpiece. Ginger lilies fill the room with their sweet perfume.

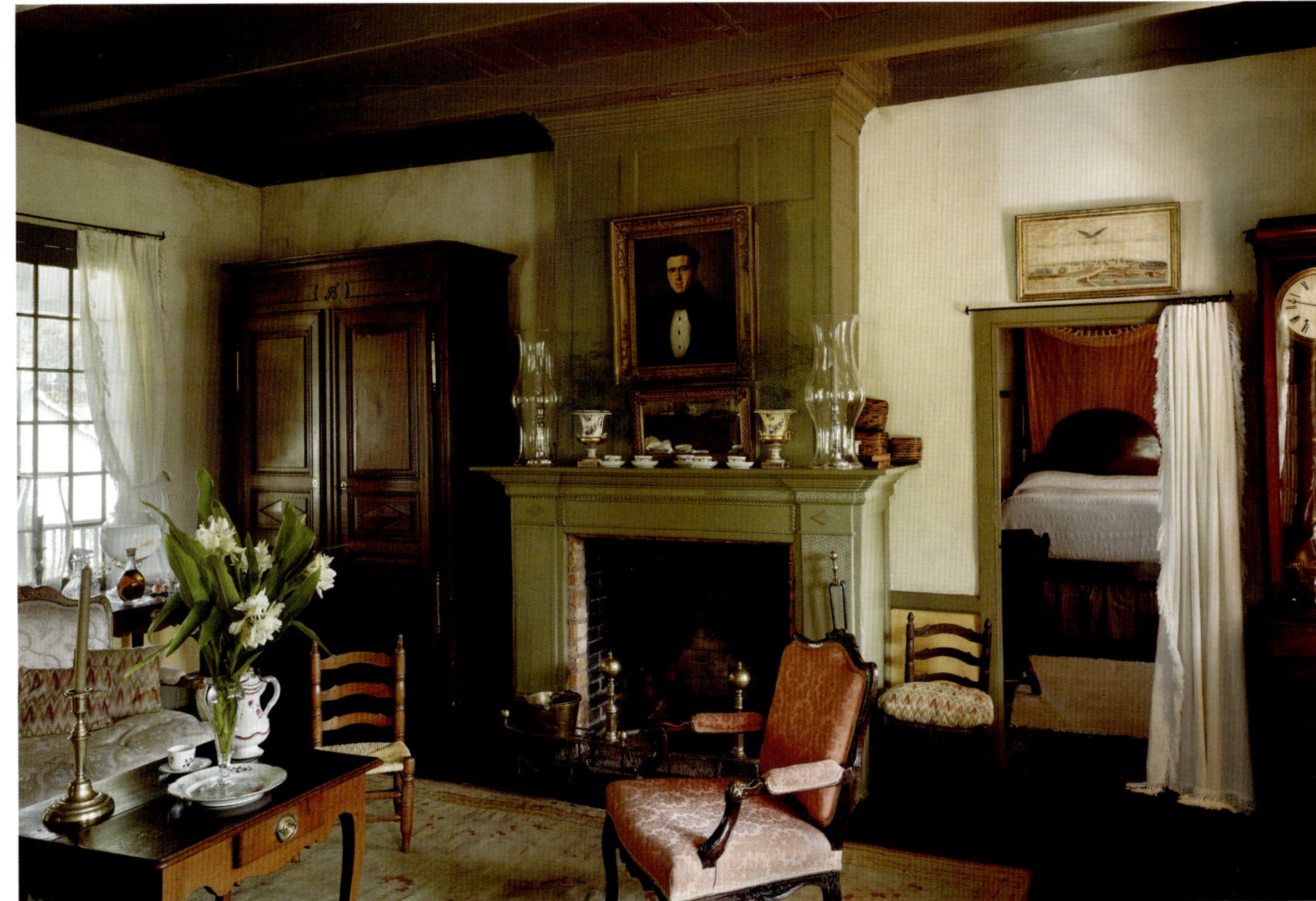

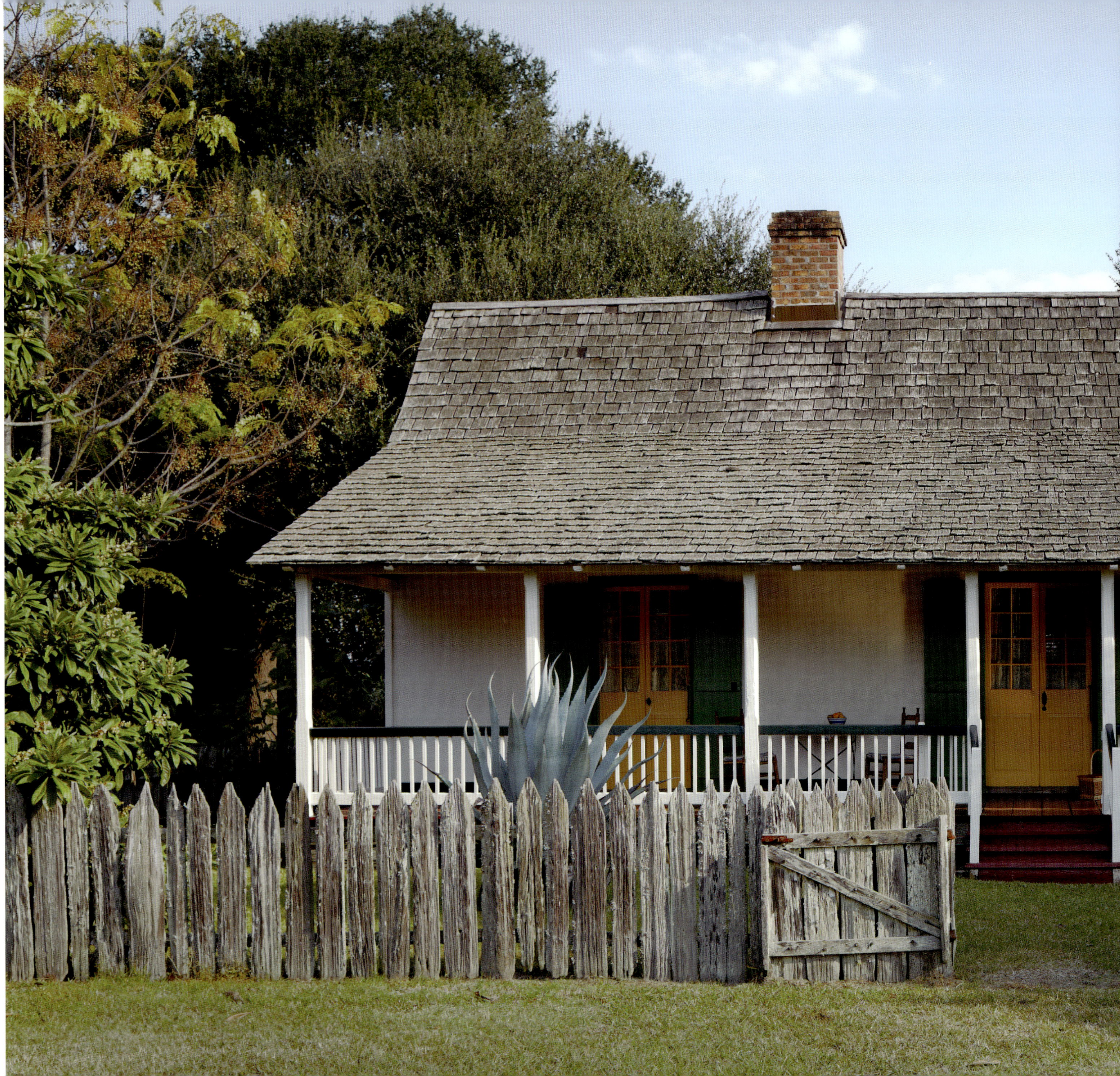

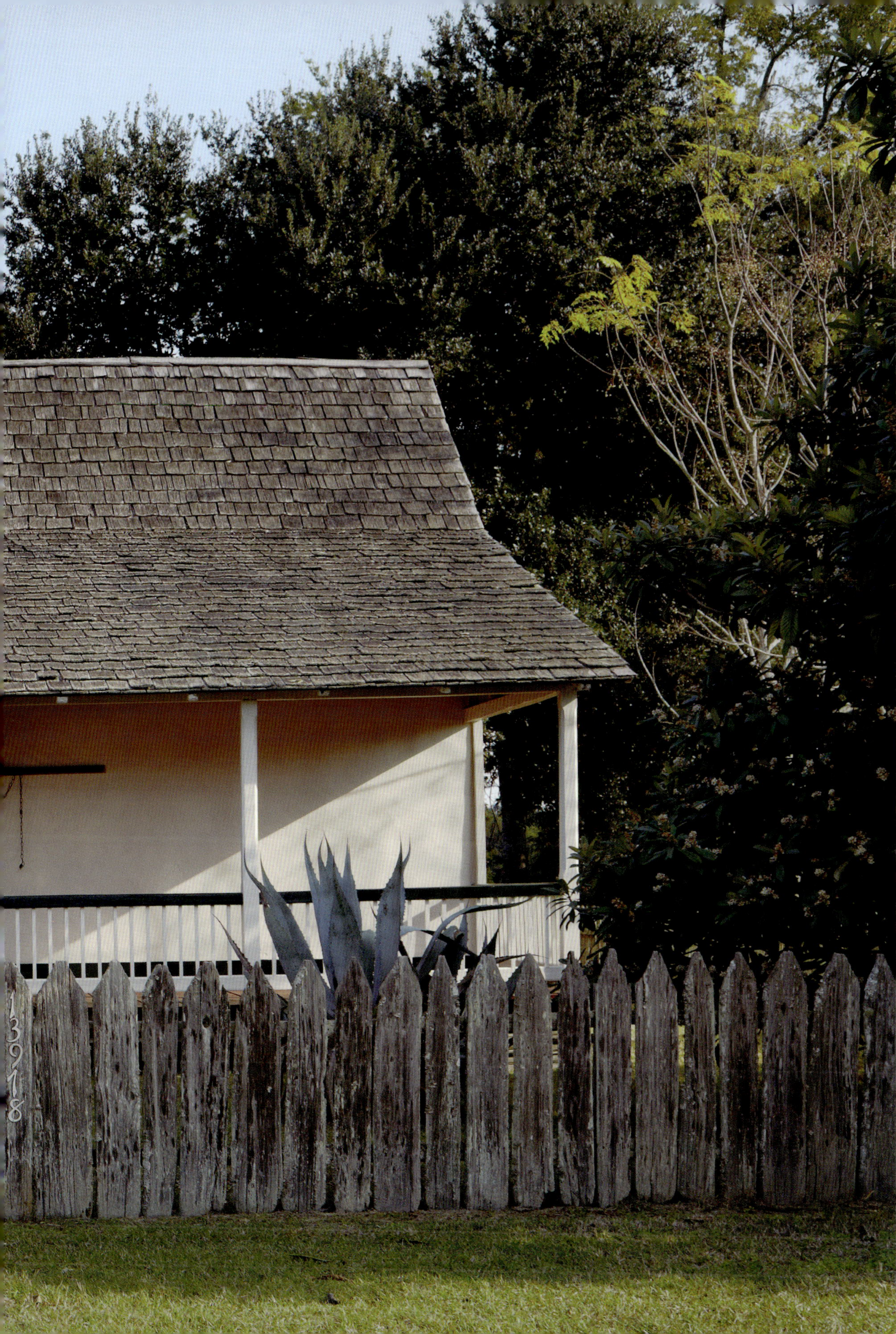

The front porch stretches fully across this classic Creole cottage. Paint scrapings indicate that red window sash and green shutters adorned this house long ago. Agave or century plants, popular in the 1800s, ornament the front yard. A line of old-fashioned chinaberry trees adds charm to the side of the house.

The broken-gable roof is characteristic of the classic cottage form in Pointe Coupee during the nineteenth century. Two centuries ago, almost every roof in the parish was sheathed in wood shingles or shakes.

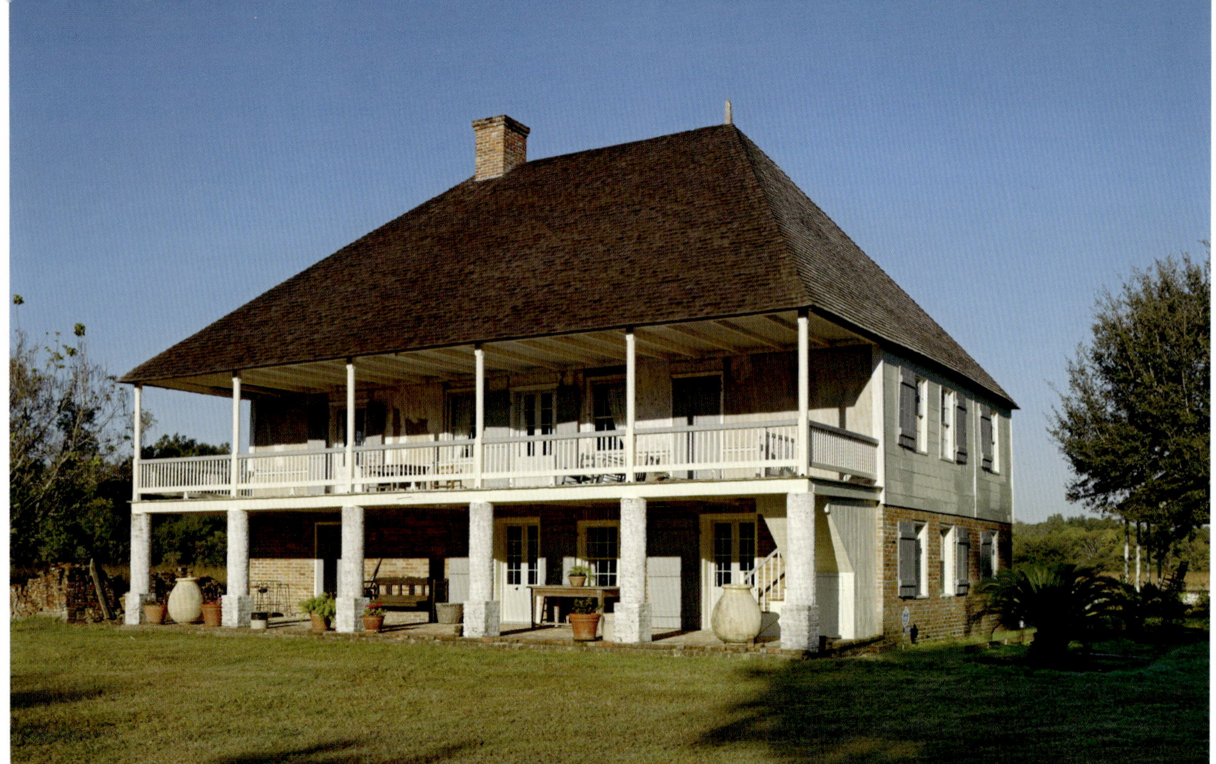

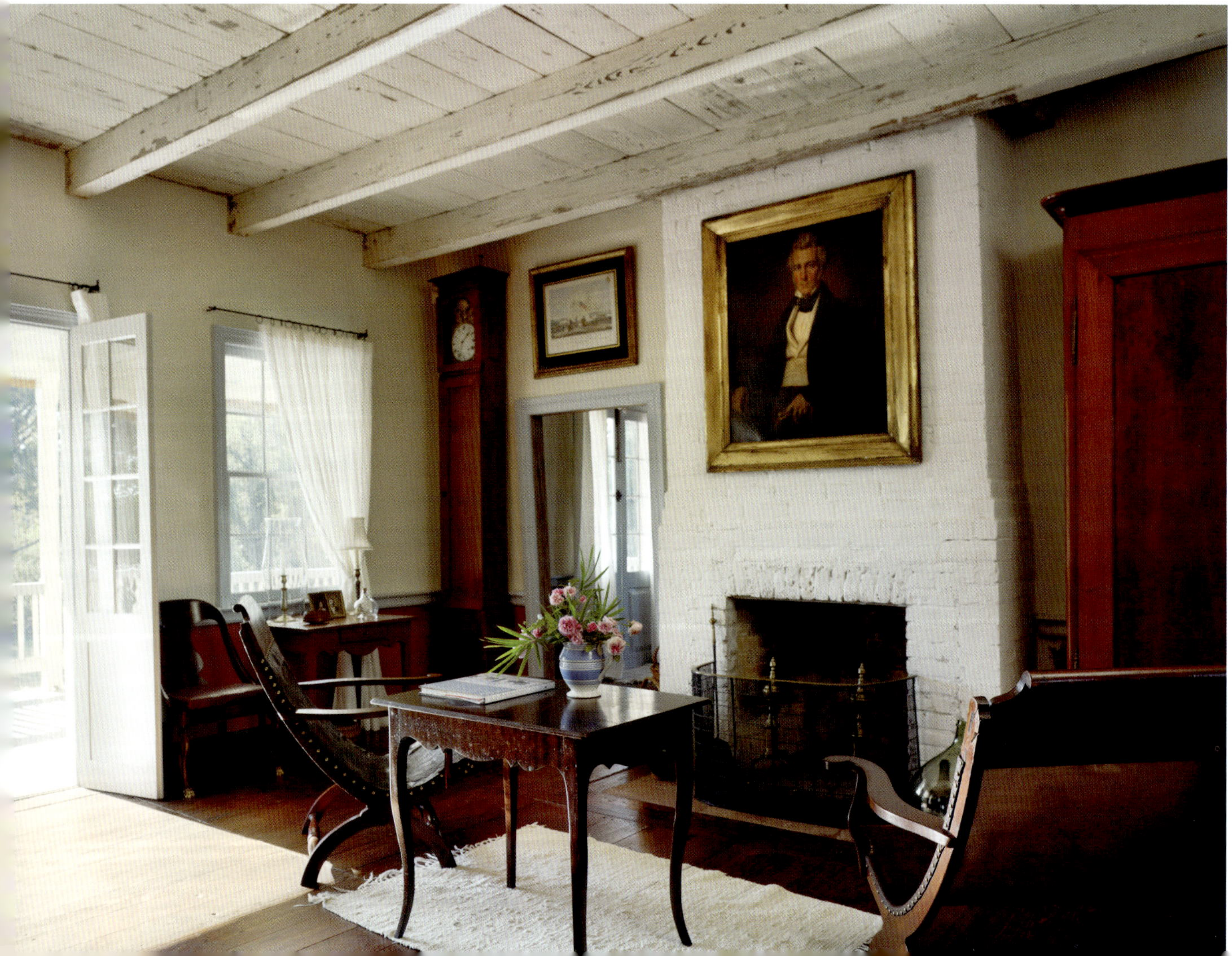

The Jaques Dupré House sat empty, abandoned in a field near Nuba in St. Landry Parish, when Sis Hollensworth first saw it in the 1970s. In 1994 she had it carefully disassembled and moved to her property at Chenal. There she painstakingly rebuilt the house, paying close attention to every detail of the historic structure. Six years later she moved into the house to live.

The owner of the house for whom it is named was the eighth governor of Louisiana, in 1830–31. Jaques Dupré (1773–1846) married Theotoste Roy of Pointe Coupee in 1792.

Hollensworth believes the house may have been built as a single-story residence on cypress blocks in the late eighteenth century. Dupré may have moved the house and added the brick foundation to elevate the primary living space about 1815.

An heirloom pitcher in the airy *salle* of the Jaques Dupré House holds a bouquet of antique roses picked from the garden.

A bowl of satsumas takes center stage on the dining table of the Jaques Dupré House. Satsuma is one of Pointe Coupee's favorite citrus fruits. Cold-hardy to about 15° F., satsuma trees seldom require extra protection from local freezes, and the fruit can stay ripe on the tree for more than a month quite successfully. Satsumas were brought to Louisiana in the early 1880s. Louisiana sweet oranges, navels, and kumquats are also found frequently in local gardens.

A steep double-pitch roof, dovetailed corners, and roman numerals carved into the building parts suggest that the barn behind the Jaques Dupré House may have been built before 1800. Hollensworth moved it to Pointe Coupee in 1996.

Lady Banks roses bloom profusely behind *baïonnettes espagnoles* (Spanish bayonets) at the entrance gates to the Jaques Dupré House. The yuccas called Spanish bayonets date to Spanish colonial days, when they were used for their ability to dissuade unwelcome visitors. (Any gardener who has had to transplant one knows why.)

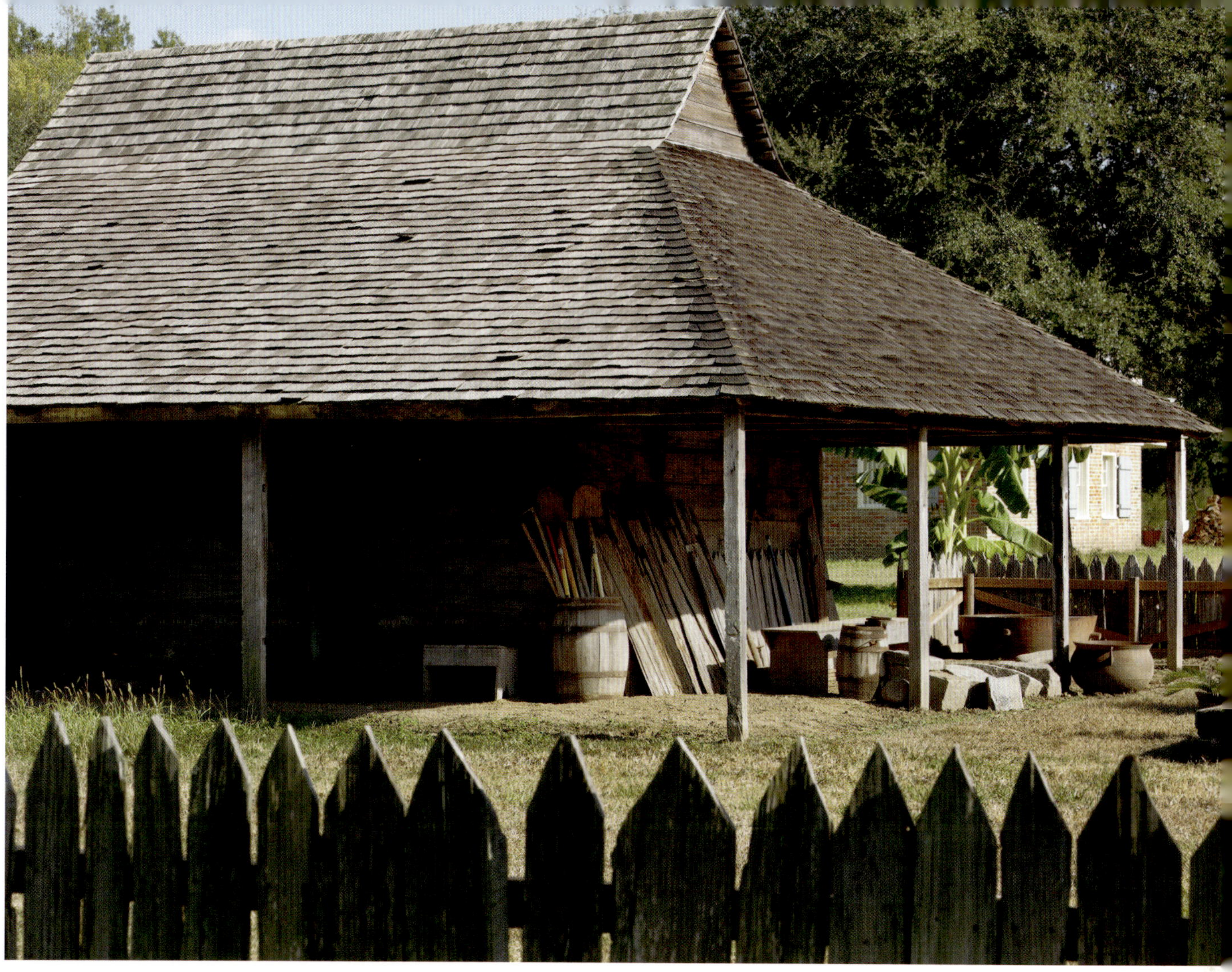

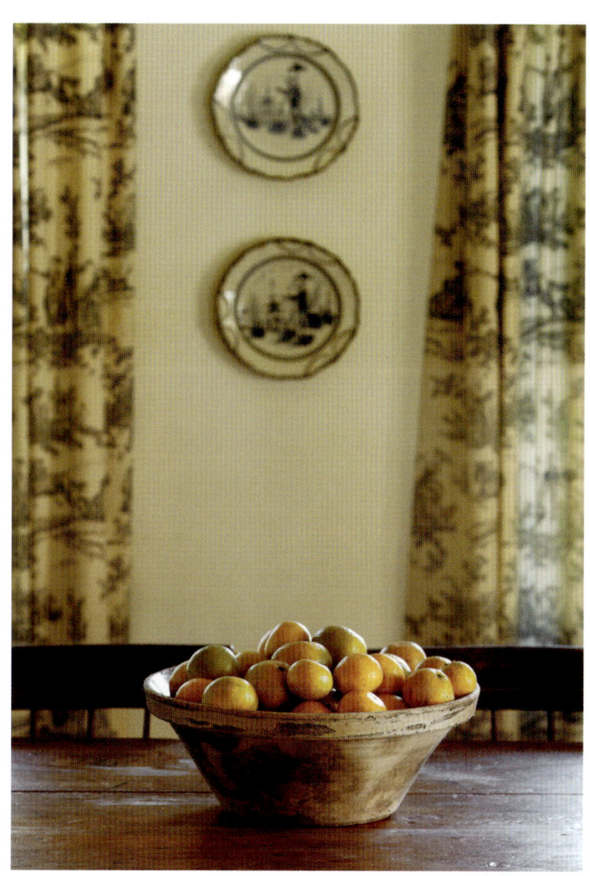

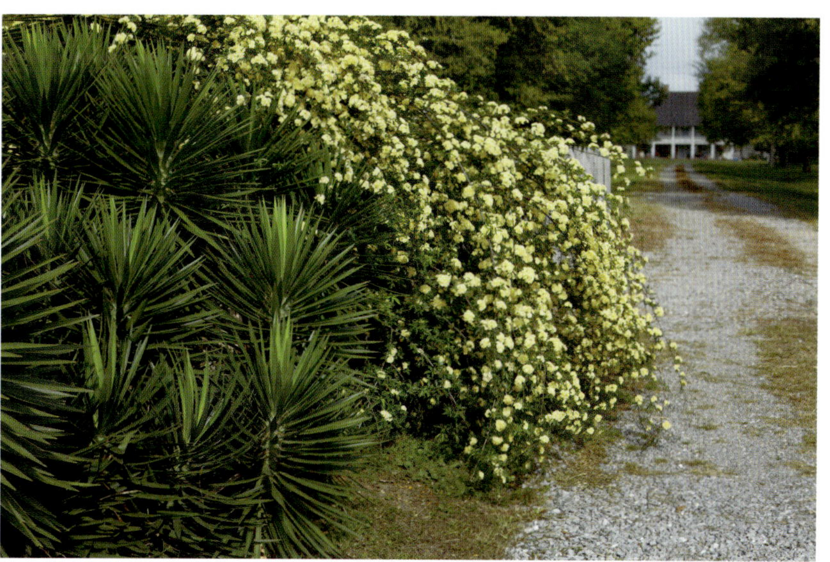

Chez Coteau (Hill House) is an early Creole house that sits on the old Coteau Road (called Cline Drive today) on the bank of the Chenal, very close to the Mississippi River. Possibly built by 1830, it was owned around 1850 by Martin Tounoir, a free man of color. Next to the cottage, current owner, landscape architect, and garden historian Suzanne Turner created a fruit orchard and kitchen garden based on nineteenth-century measured drawings from the New Orleans area. *Parterre* (ornamental garden) beds hold fig and peach trees, vegetables, and herbs. Today the property also houses the headquarters of Purdin Koi Farm.

Fig trees grow and produce fruit especially well in the rich soil of Pointe Coupee. The fruit does not travel well, so figs are generally grown for home use and put up as preserves. Most trees in the parish are old varieties such as Brown Turkey or Celeste.

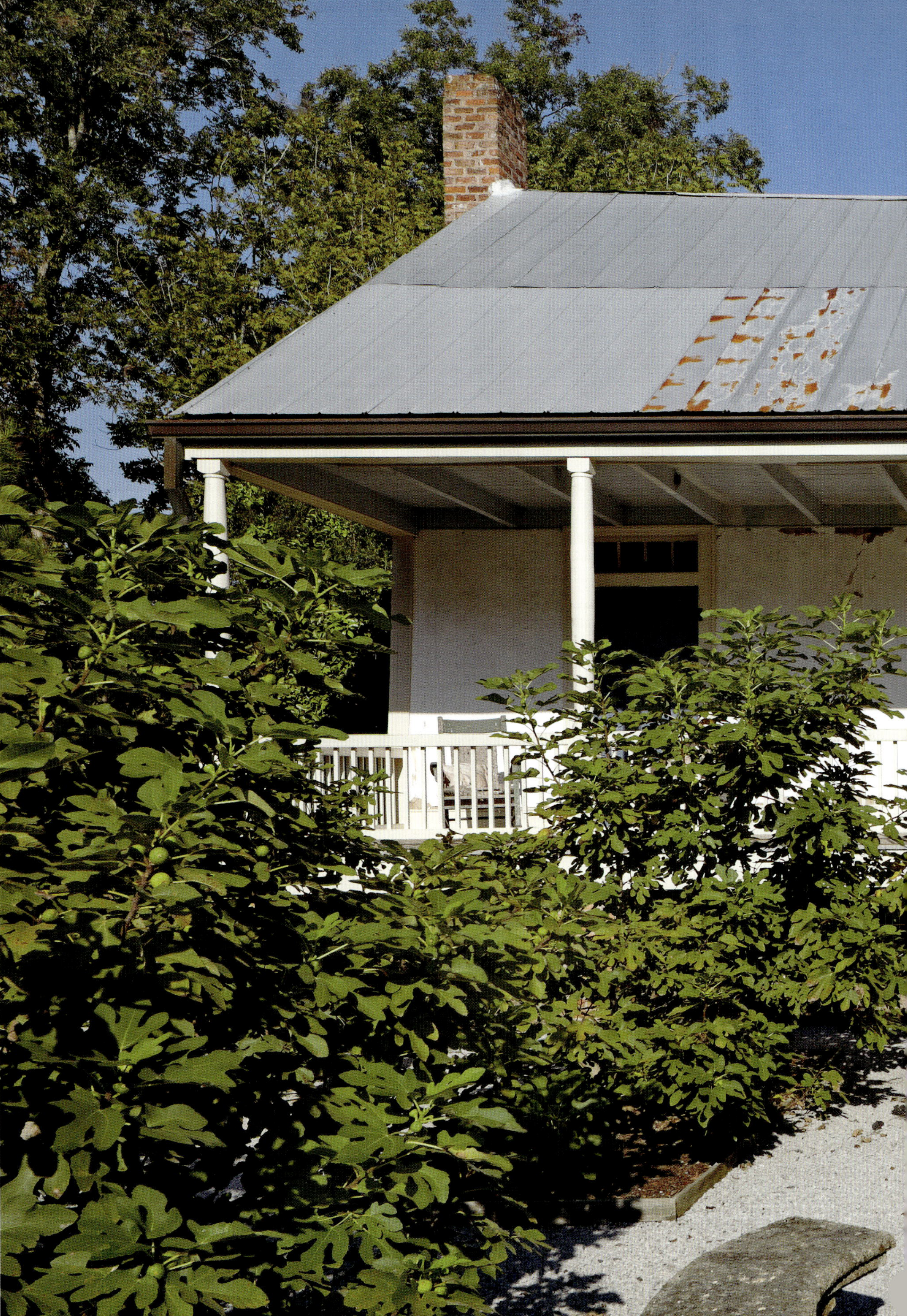

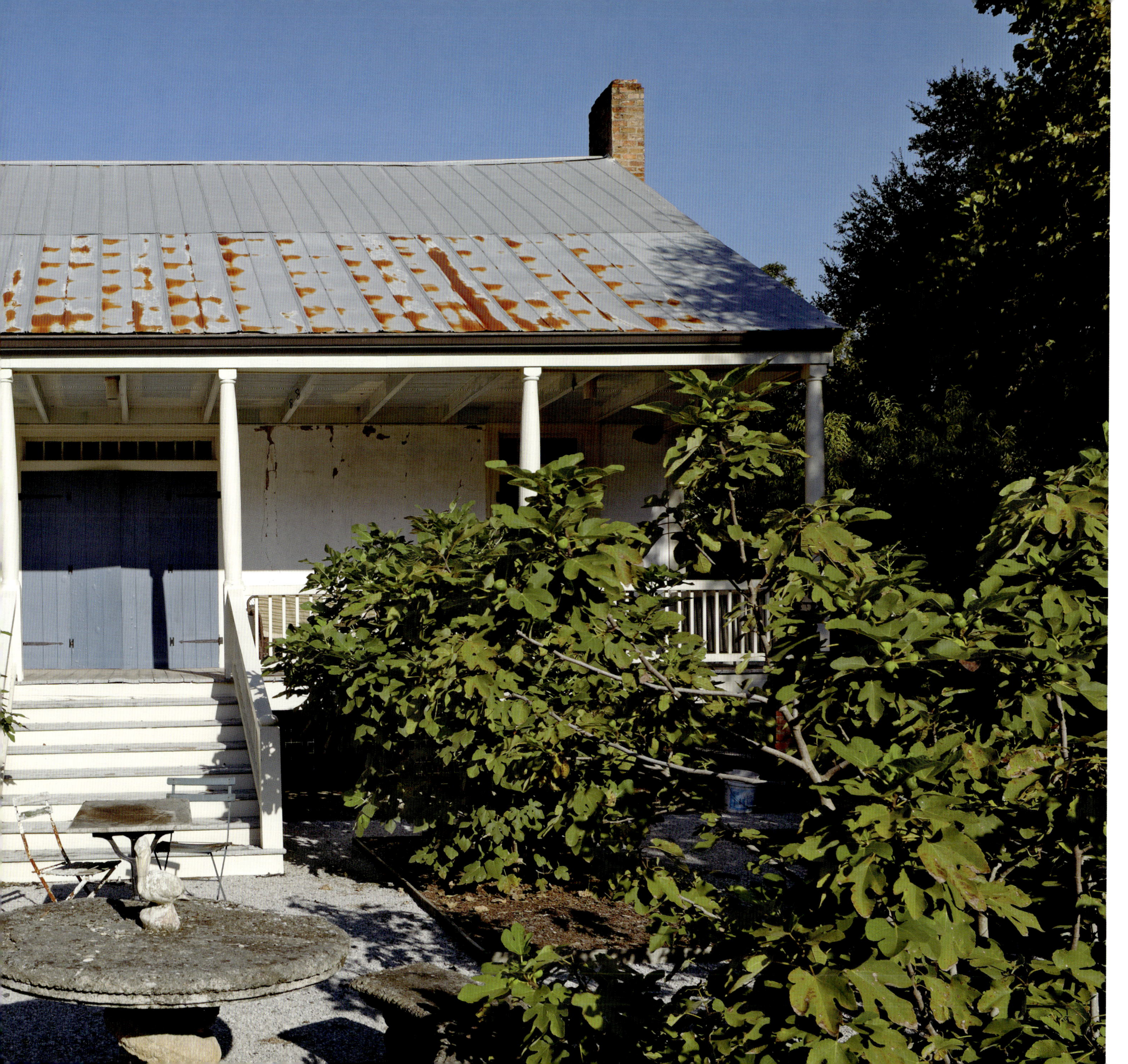

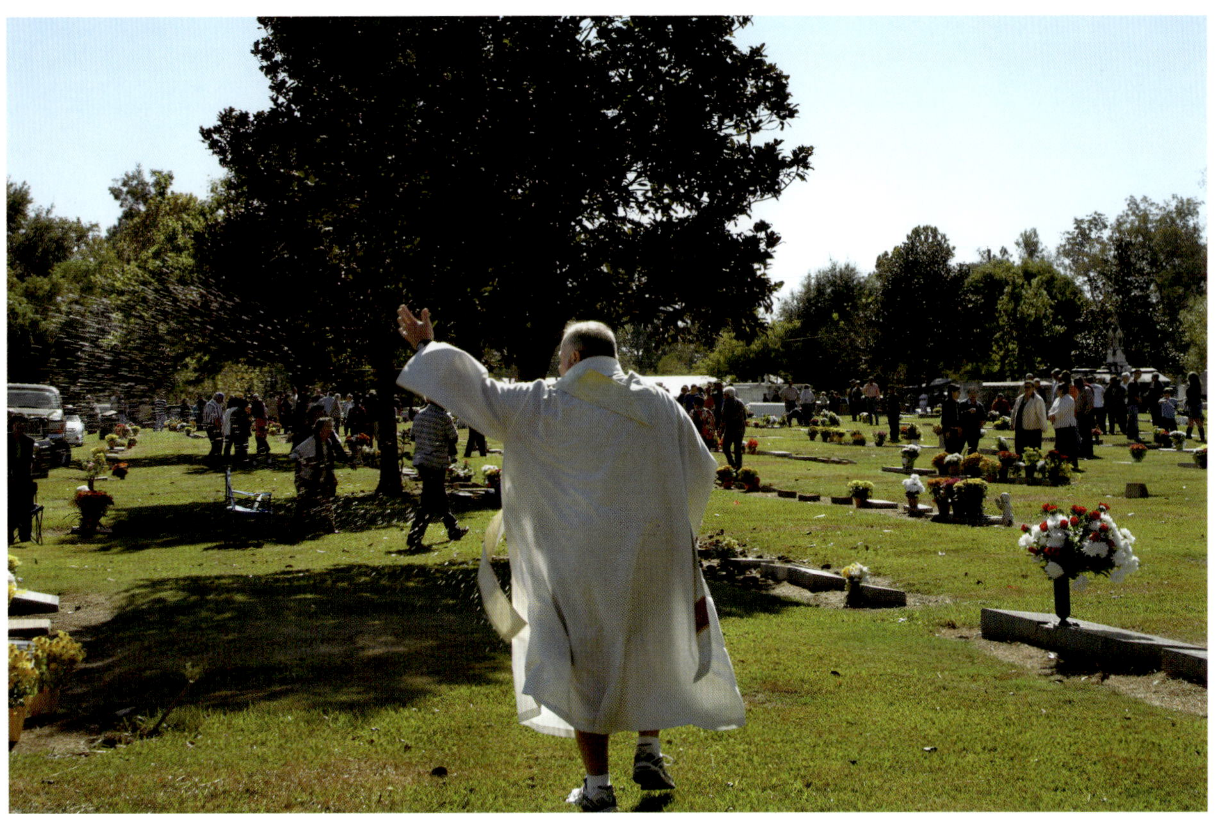

CHENAL CEMETERY

Father Greg Daigle sprinkles holy water, blessing the graves in the old Immaculate Conception Cemetery at Chenal, one of the oldest cemeteries and the largest in the parish. All Saints' Day, November 1, is an important feast day in Pointe Coupee. For weeks in advance, graves are swept clean, scrubbed, weeded, painted, then decorated with fresh flowers. Family members of all ages come to the cemeteries, keeping close touch with each other and with those gone before.

THE CHENAL

Duckweed densely covers the surface of the old Chenal at the southeast end of False River, which empties into Bayou Cirier, flowing eventually into Choctaw Swamp. *Cirier* is French for "wax myrtle," an evergreen shrub or small tree that grows along the banks of the bayou.

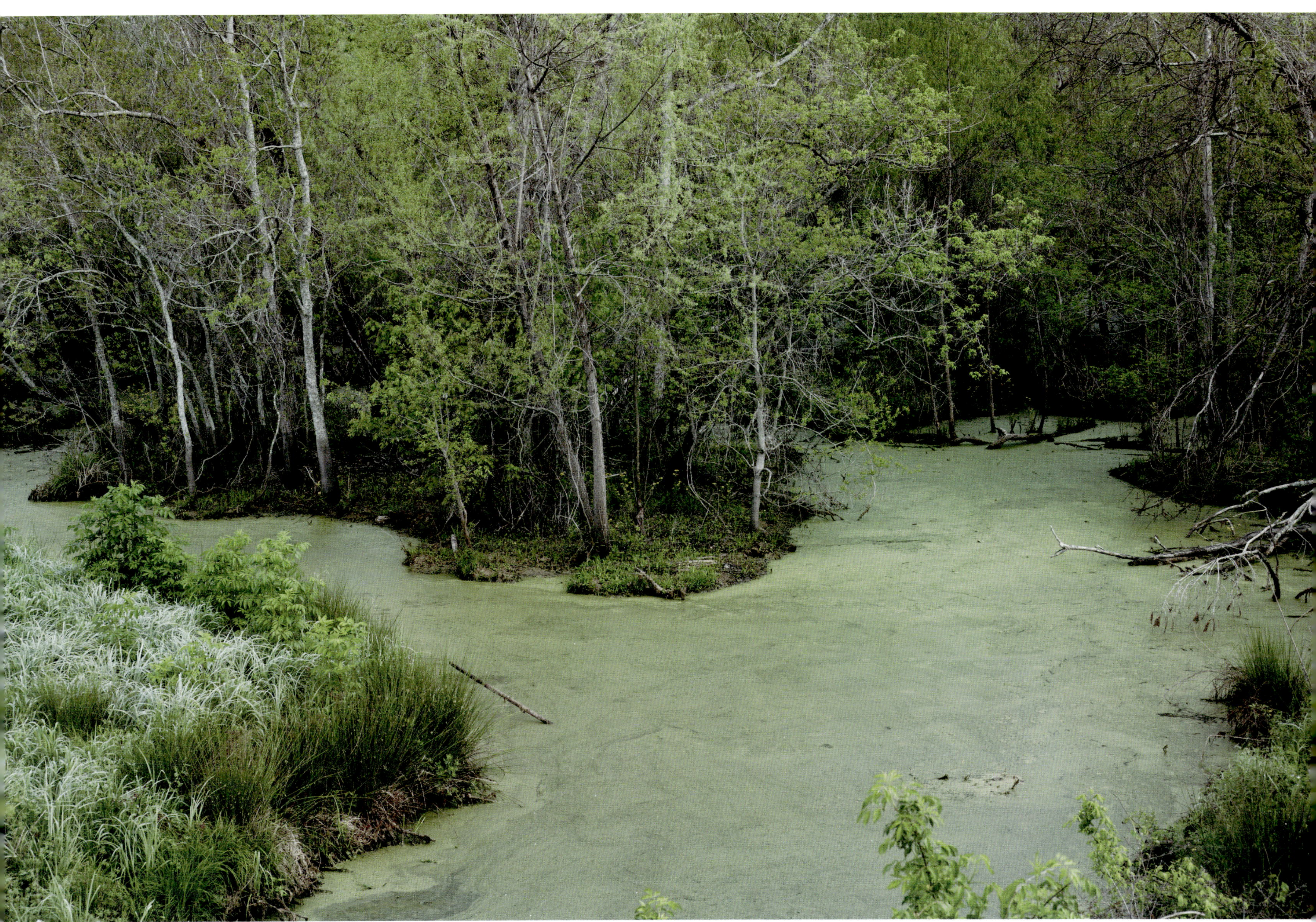

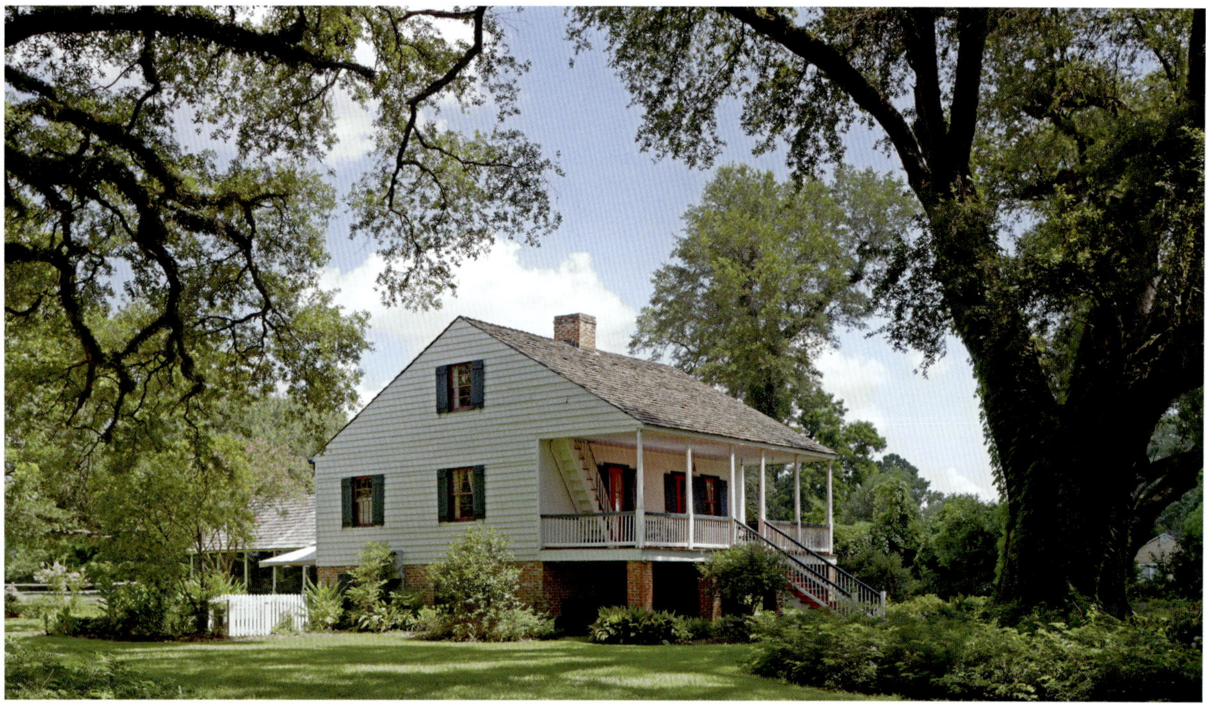

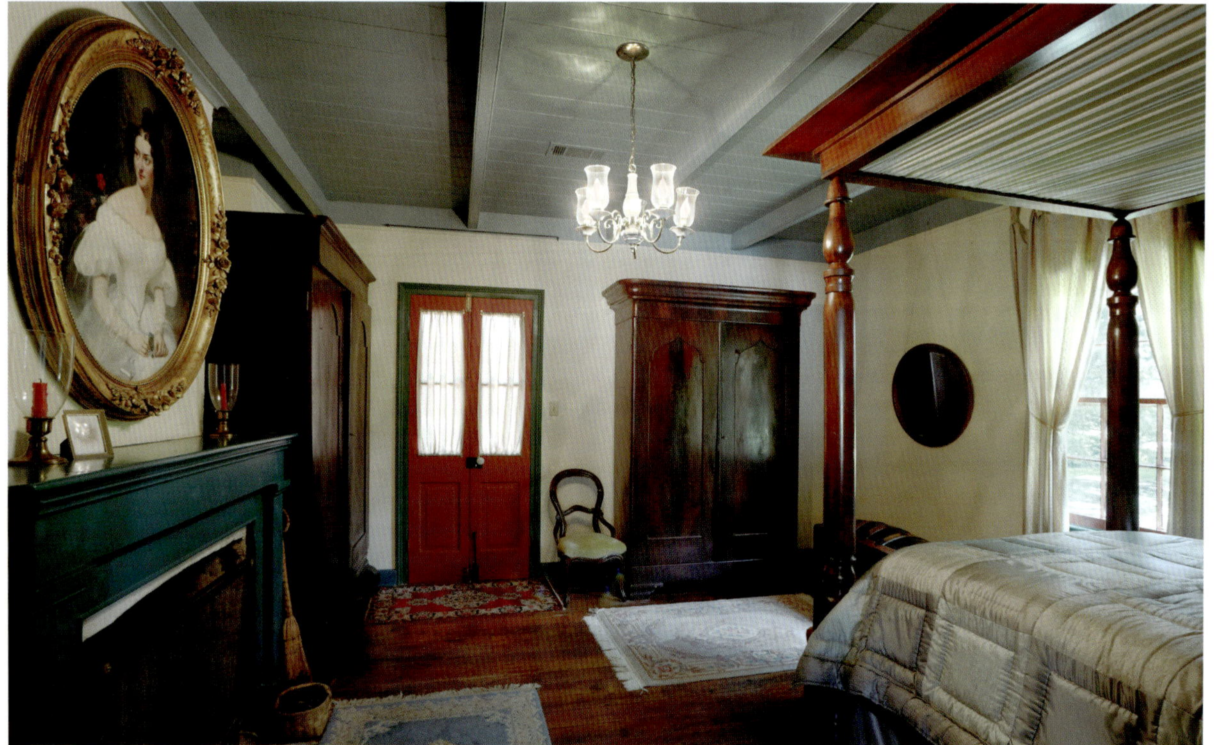

Built around 1838 by Saint Ville LeBeau, this Creole home was one of a number of such houses lining the banks of the Chenal. Only a few survive, this one thanks to the vision and hard work of Stuart and Betty Wooddy, who discovered and purchased the house in 1971. Antiquarian Robert Smith of Breaux Bridge was one of several friends and professionals who helped guide the restoration of the house. The LeBeau House was the first of a number of house restorations undertaken by the Wooddys. This one is still their home.

An oil portrait of Eugenie Marie Becue Brierre hangs in her great-great-grandson's master bedroom in the LeBeau House. The bold colors of the doors, mantel, trim, and ceiling reflect the Louisiana Creole aesthetic and love of life.

Horses graze peacefully in the field behind the LeBeau House. The French long lot system of land division is easily seen in this picture. The tract is long and narrow, with access to the water of the Chenal in front of the house and to fuel and lumber in the woods at the back of the lot. The house was probably built of cypress cut from this same stand of trees. A typical lot of one arpent wide by 40 arpents deep is about 192 feet across by 1½ miles deep, amounting to about 34 acres of land.

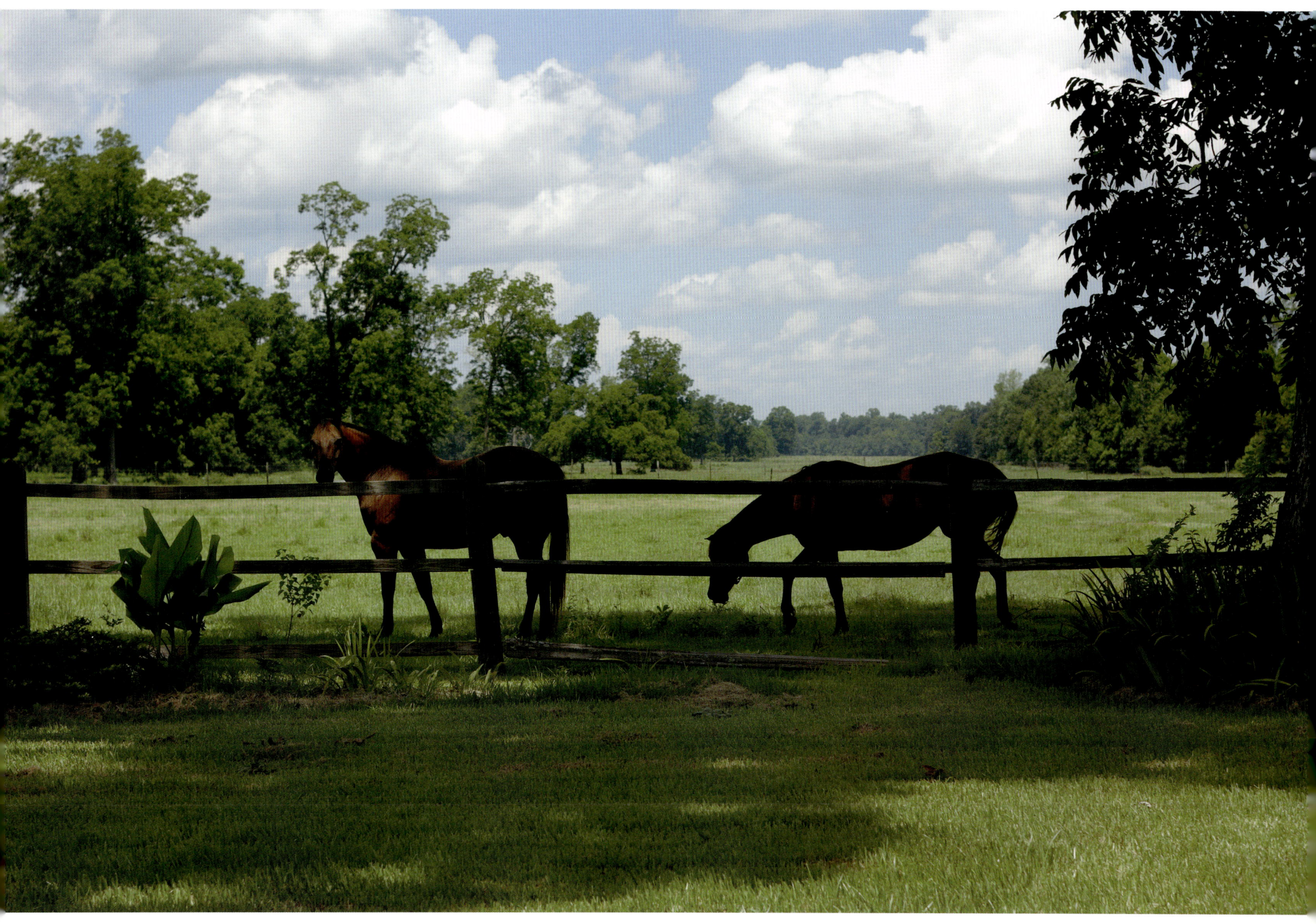

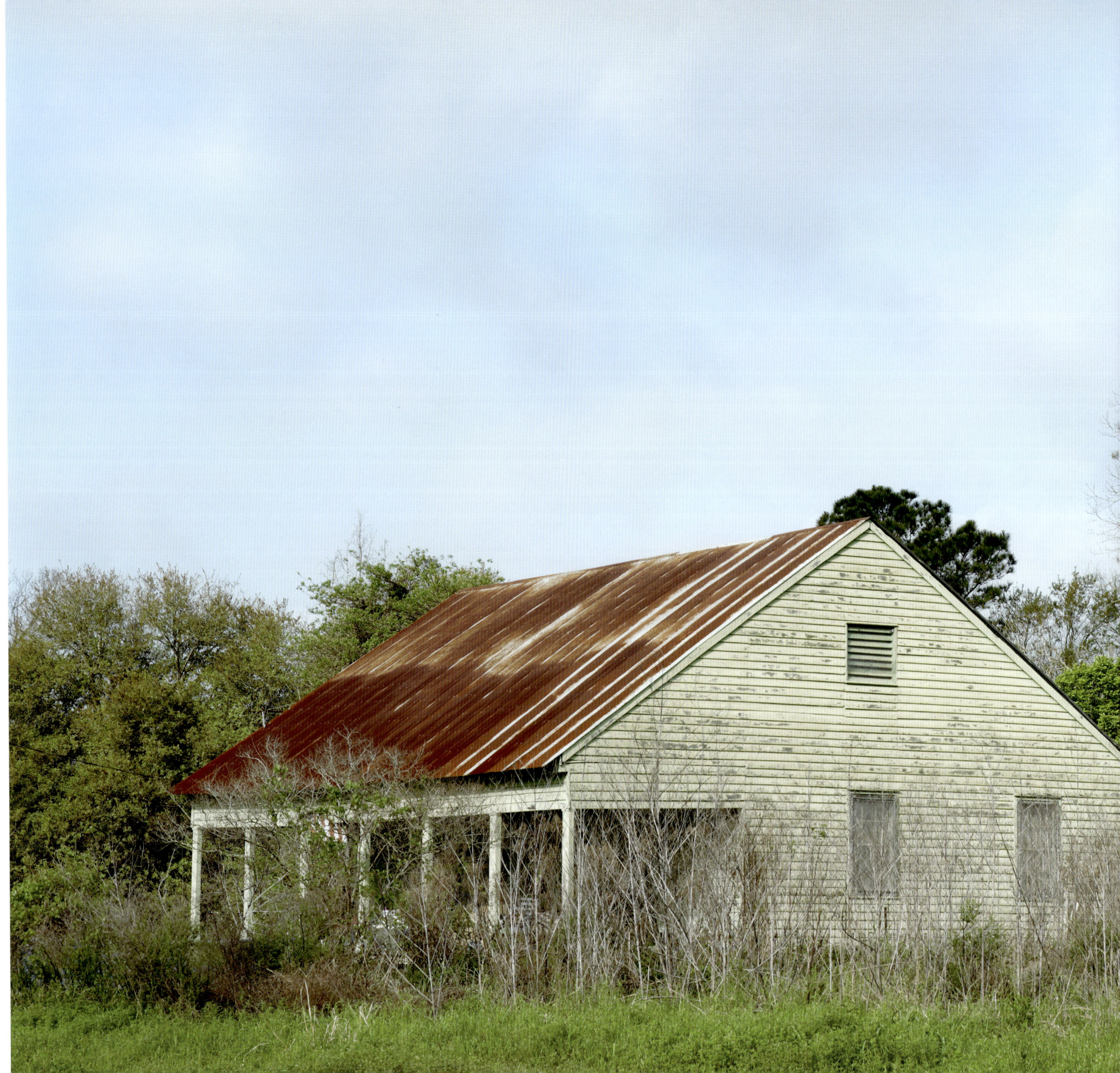

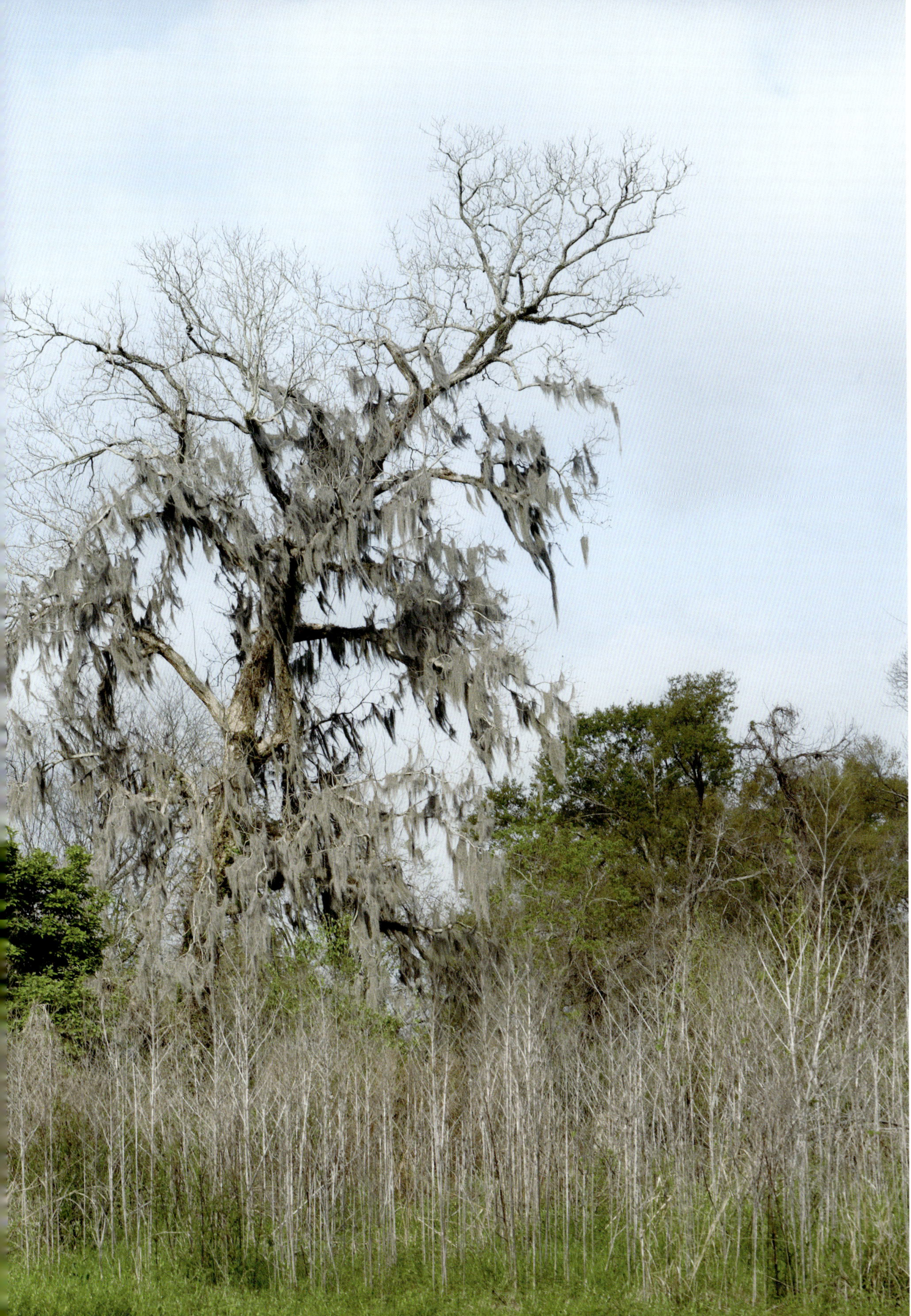

VALMONT BERGERON HOUSE
National Register of Historic Places

Built around 1840, the Valmont Bergeron House still has bullet holes recalling a violent time during the Civil War when jayhawkers—criminal deserters from both Federal and Confederate armies—attempted to break into the house. According to legend, the crime was foiled when a young lady overheard the jayhawkers planning a night raid on the house and family. Speaking in English, the men assumed the Creole girl would not understand, but having learned English at school in Kentucky, the girl told Valmont Bergeron of the plot. He armed himself and his family, and they were ready when the unwelcome visitors arrived.

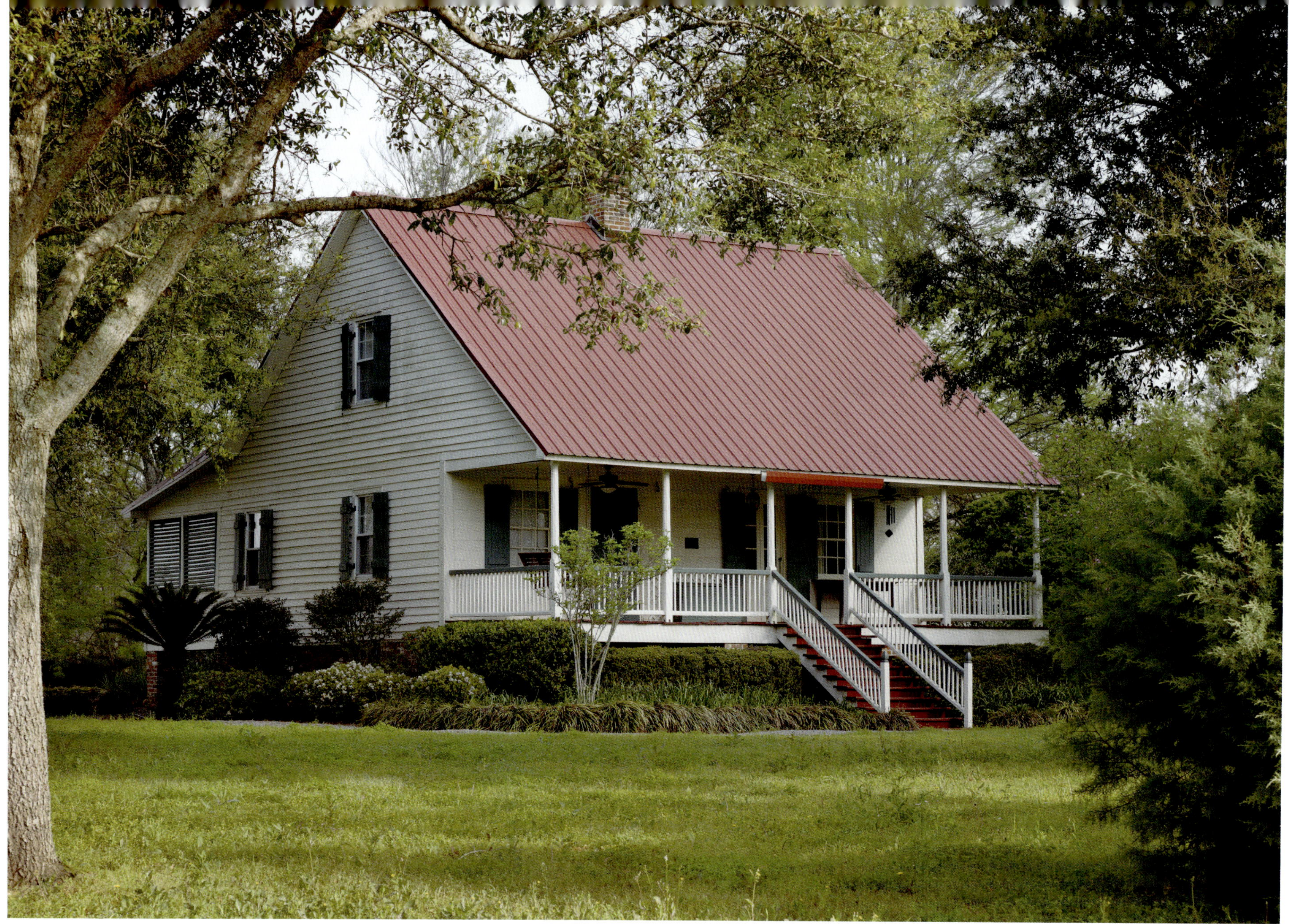

National Register of Historic Places

Around 1840, Jean Baptiste Bergeron built this traditional raised Creole cottage near his brother Valmont.

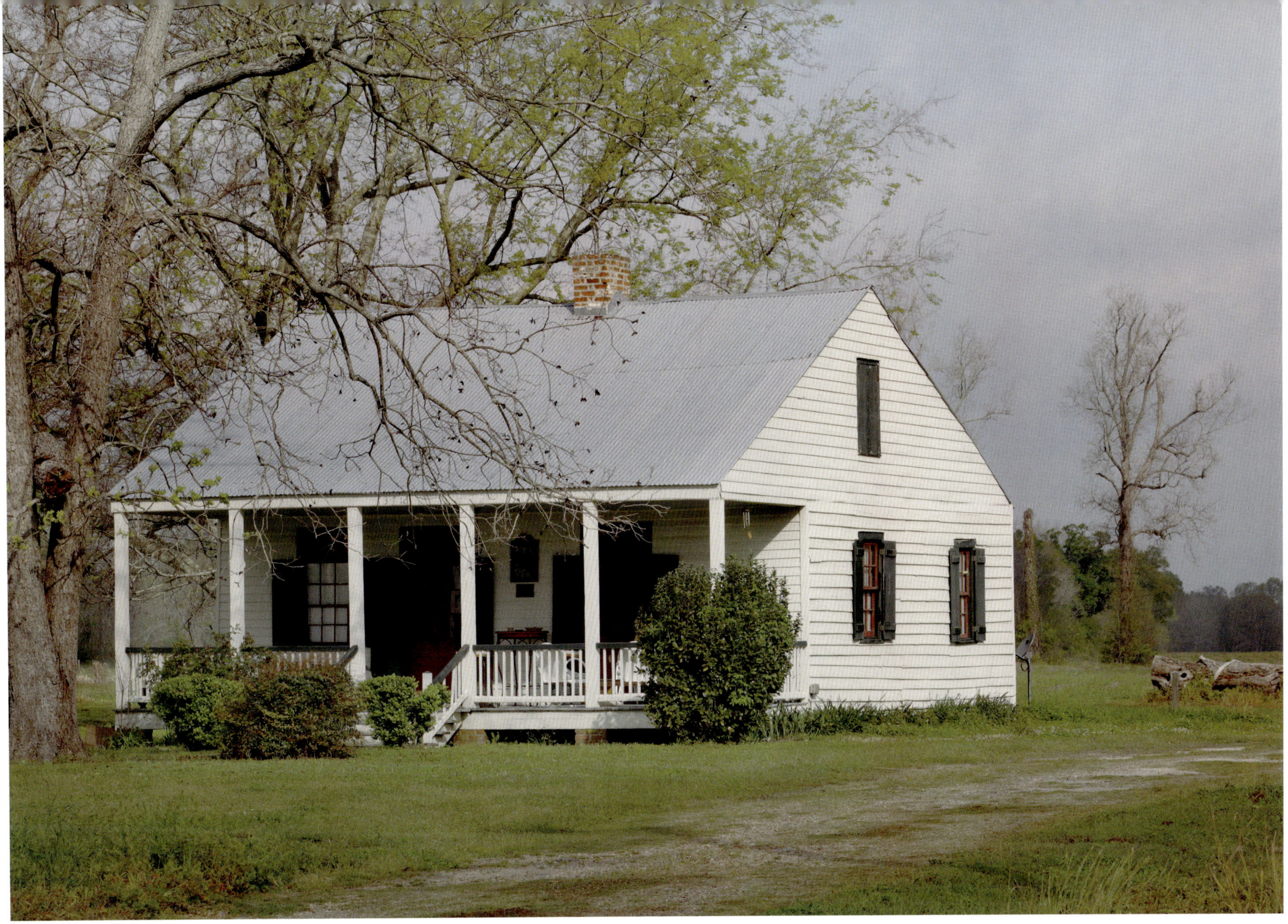

Built for Troisville LeBeau around 1840, this simple cottage was home to George Saizan and his family for many years. Red and green have always been popular trim and floor colors for Creole houses.

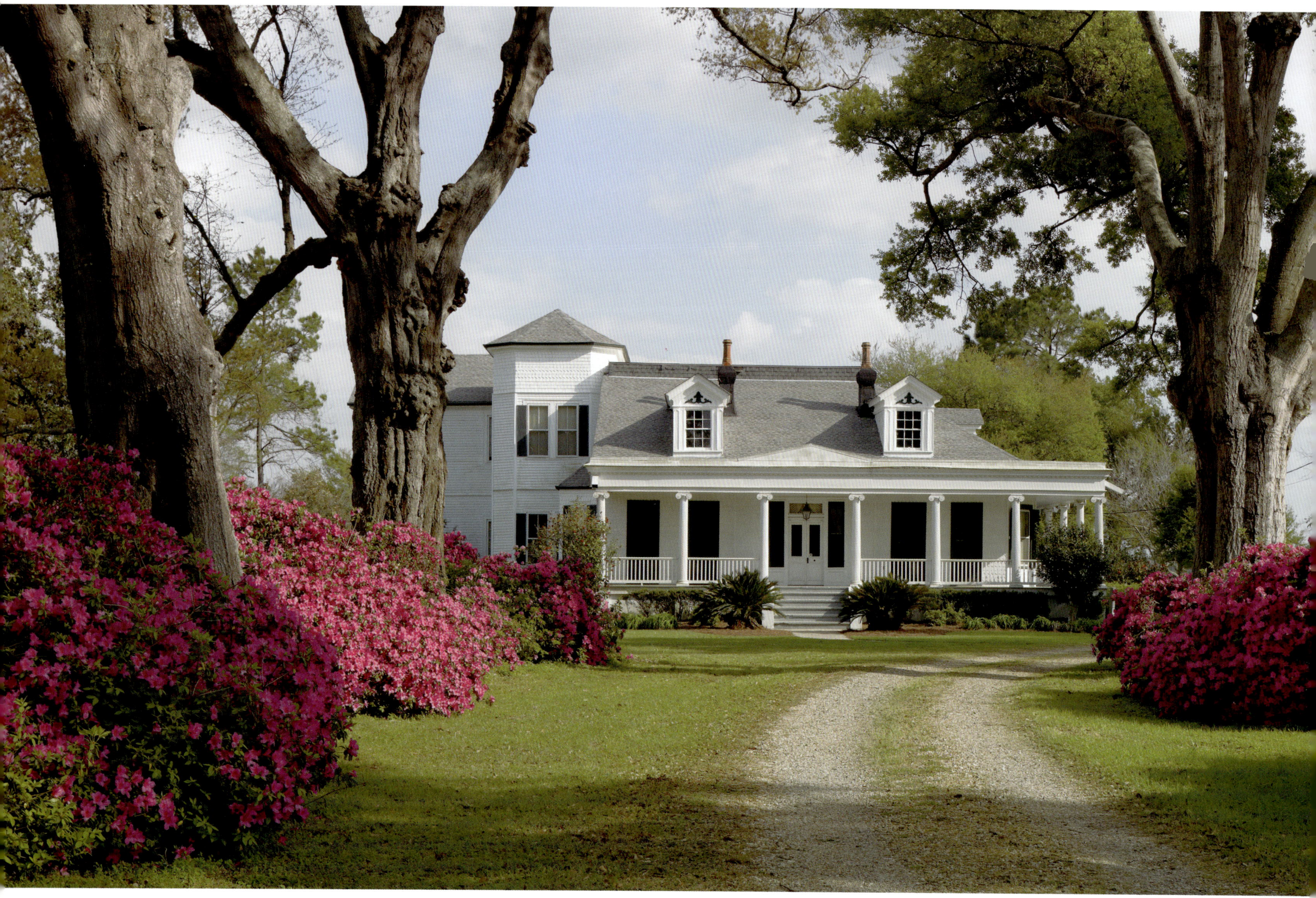

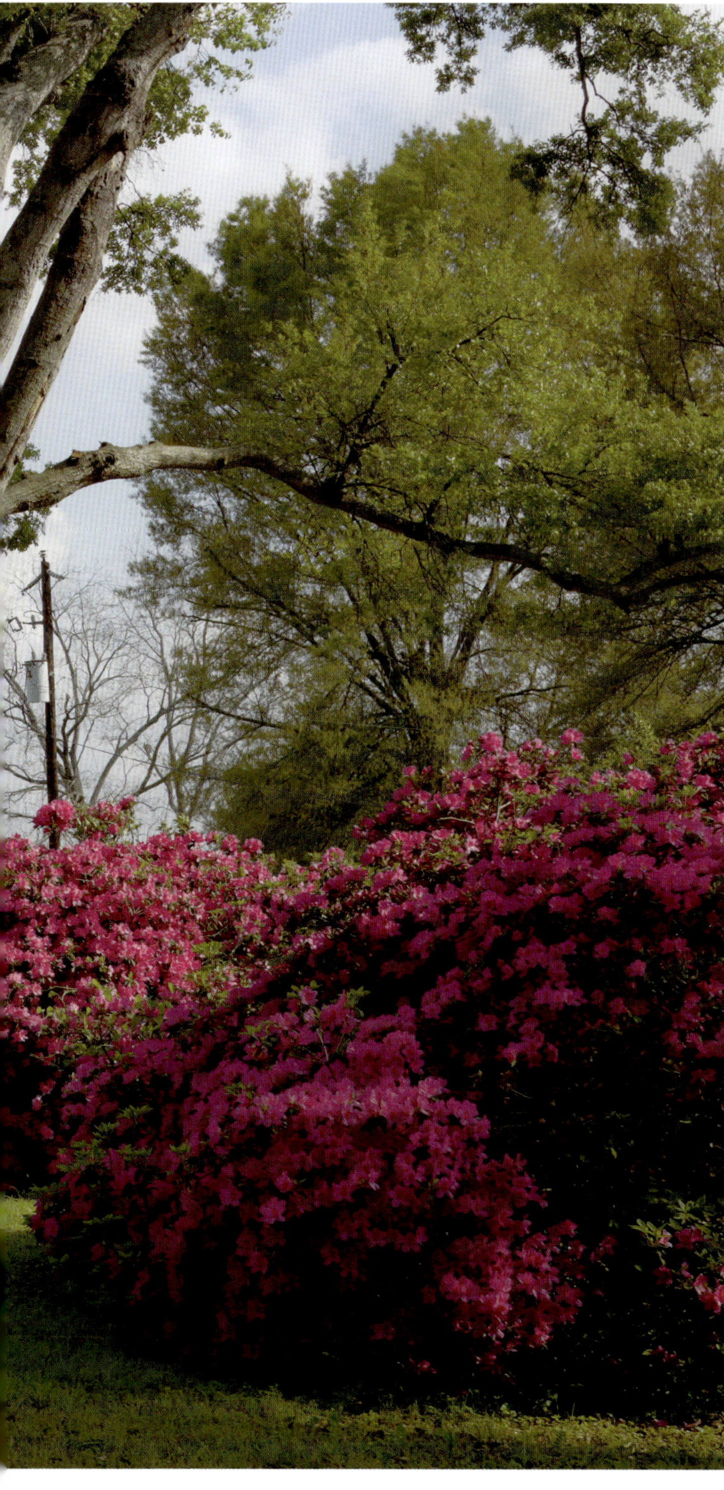

Azaleas bloom along the drive to Glynnwood. Indica azaleas were called Chinese honeysuckle when they were first planted in southern gardens in the 1850s.

The bronze plaque at the gate to Glynnwood is unusual in that it claims three dates for the house: 1836—1875—1890. The house today is an assemblage of three separate dwellings moved together and made into one building by the formidable Martin Glynn. Born in Ireland in 1829, Glynn moved to New Orleans in 1847 during the Irish potato famine. He got into the wholesale grocery business, and as he made his fortune, he bought farmland in the parishes of Iberville, West Baton Rouge, and Pointe Coupee. After the Civil War, Glynn moved with his family to the plantation that would become Glynnwood in a place that would eventually take his name: Glynn, Louisiana. Over the years a large family of eleven children prompted Glynn to increase the size of his house to include ten bedrooms.

Martin Glynn was president of the Pointe Coupee Police Jury for twenty years and state senator for eight. He died in 1921, and his descendants still live in the house today.

An old telephone hangs on the wall in Glynnwood. Martin Glynn was one of the first people in Pointe Coupee to install telephone service, in 1906. False River Telephone Line proudly announced on July 1, 1908, that the company was "Twenty-two Months Young to-day, 120 Subscribers, fifty miles of poles, over 100 Miles of Wire and Growing Every Day."

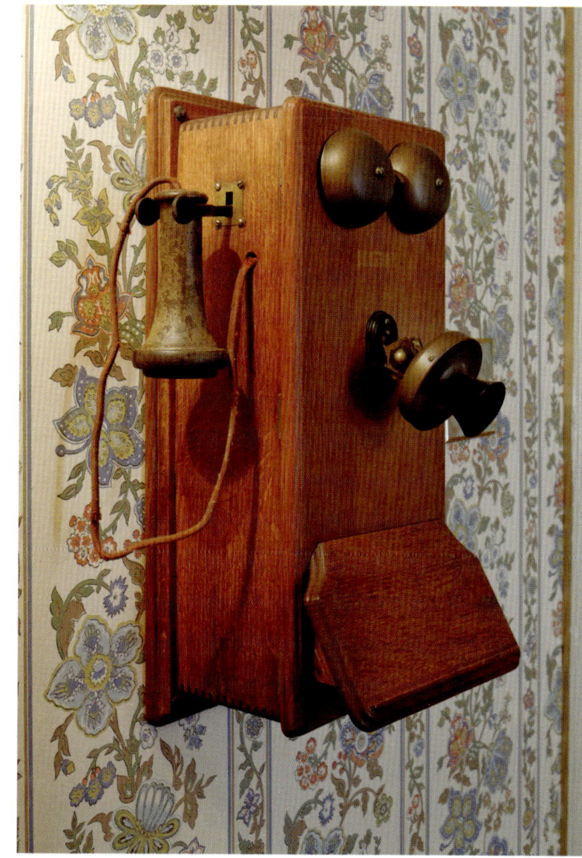

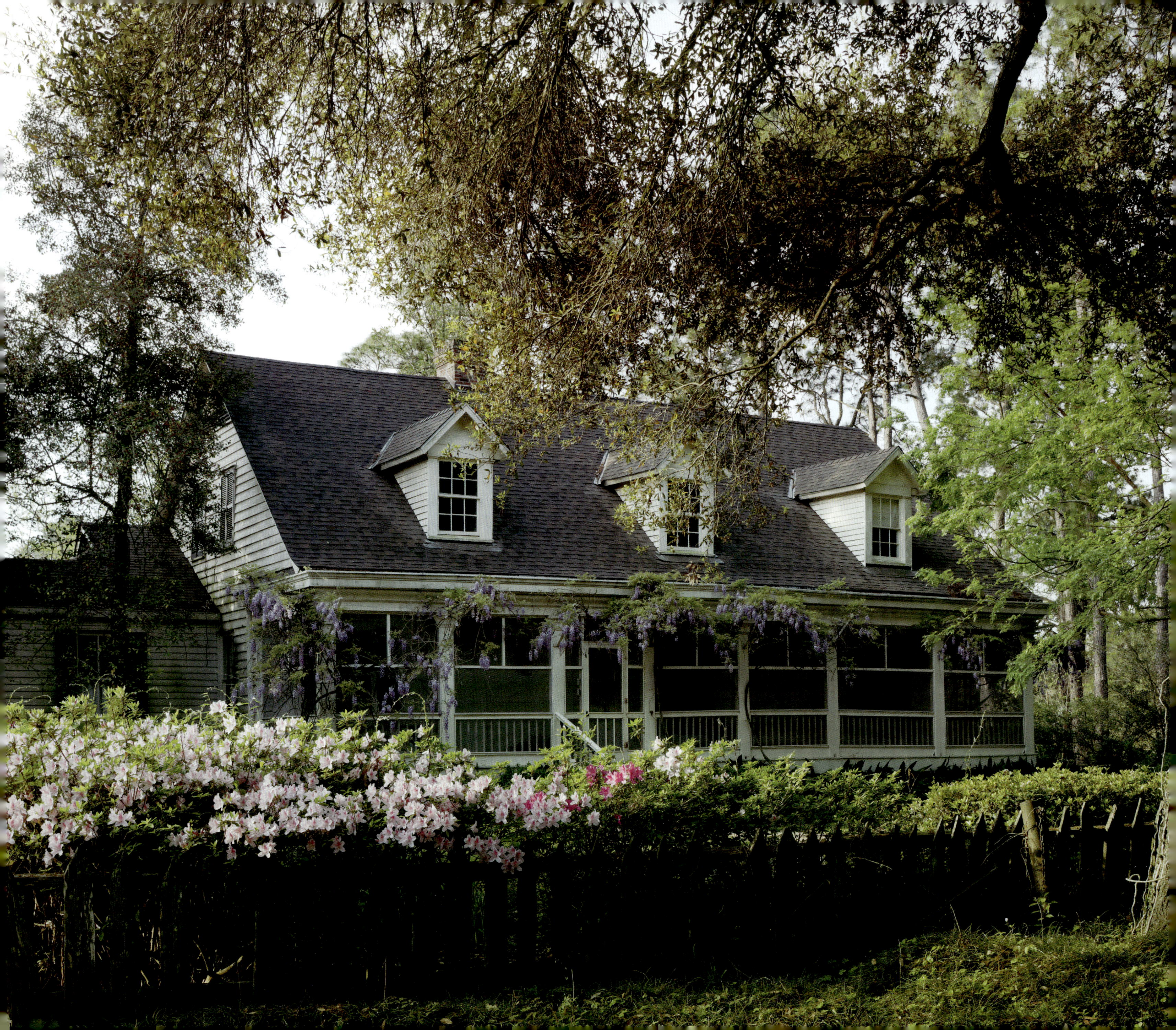

Blooming wisteria graces the screened porch of the Alma plantation home in Lakeland. The lovely old house has had many additions and renovations, but is said still to contain two rooms of the first house, built as early as 1789.

Early owners included Julien Poydras. Later David Barrow of St. Francisville, the wealthiest planter of West Feliciana and owner and builder of Afton Villa, purchased Alma. Barrow sold a one-third share of the property to his partner George Pitcher (1815–1885) in 1859. Over the years Pitcher bought out the Barrow shares, and went on to make a success of growing cane and producing sugar at Alma. Unlike many plantation owners who lost their livelihoods after the Civil War, Pitcher and his family cultivated a loyal workforce, developed productive farming techniques, and mastered efficient methods of granulating sugar. George Pitcher's great-grandson, David Stewart, owns and manages Alma today.

Bayou Poydras, originally known as Grand Bayou, flows through the cane fields of Alma Plantation and beside the family home.

The color, texture, and fragrance of Alma's raw sugar add to the elegance of afternoon coffee in a setting prepared by Georgia Morel. In Pointe Coupee the first cup of coffee, taken in bed, was traditionally a *café noir* (black coffee) to "awaken the soul." Later in the day, cream or milk was added, making the drink *café au lait* (coffee with milk).

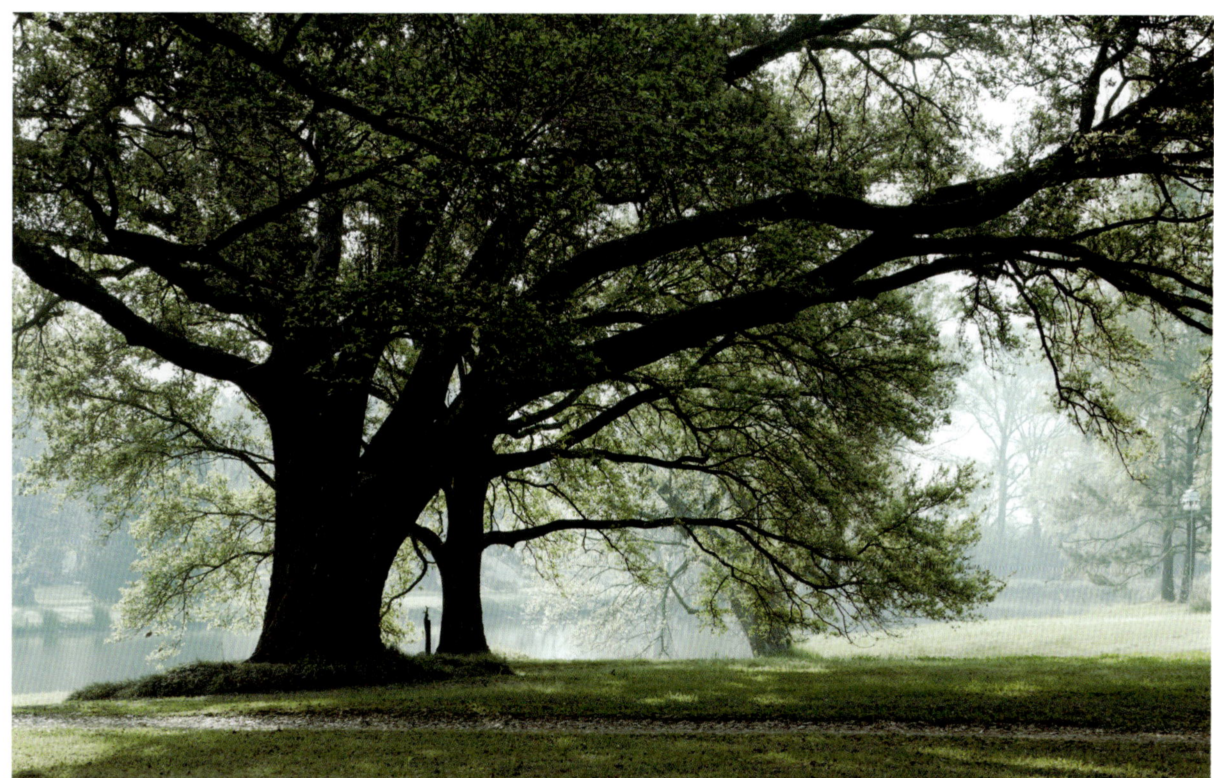

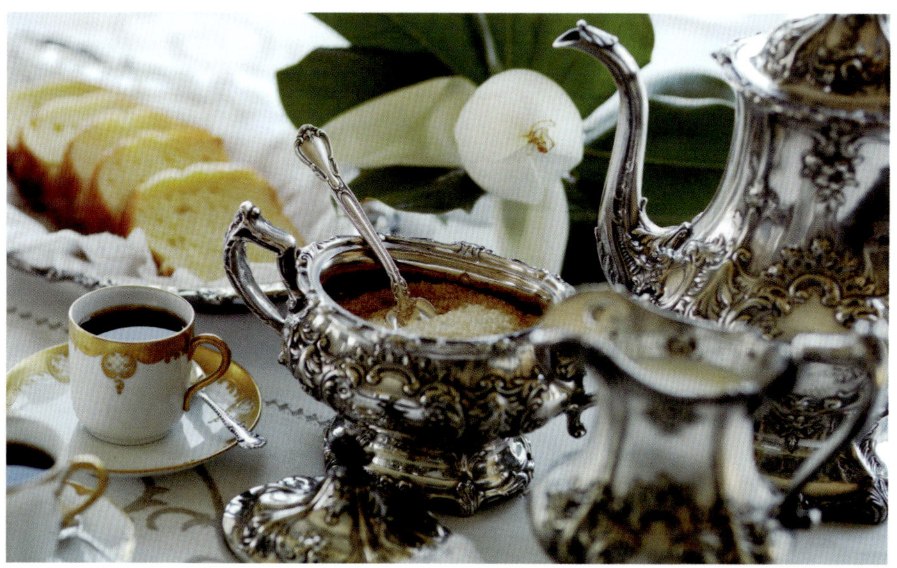

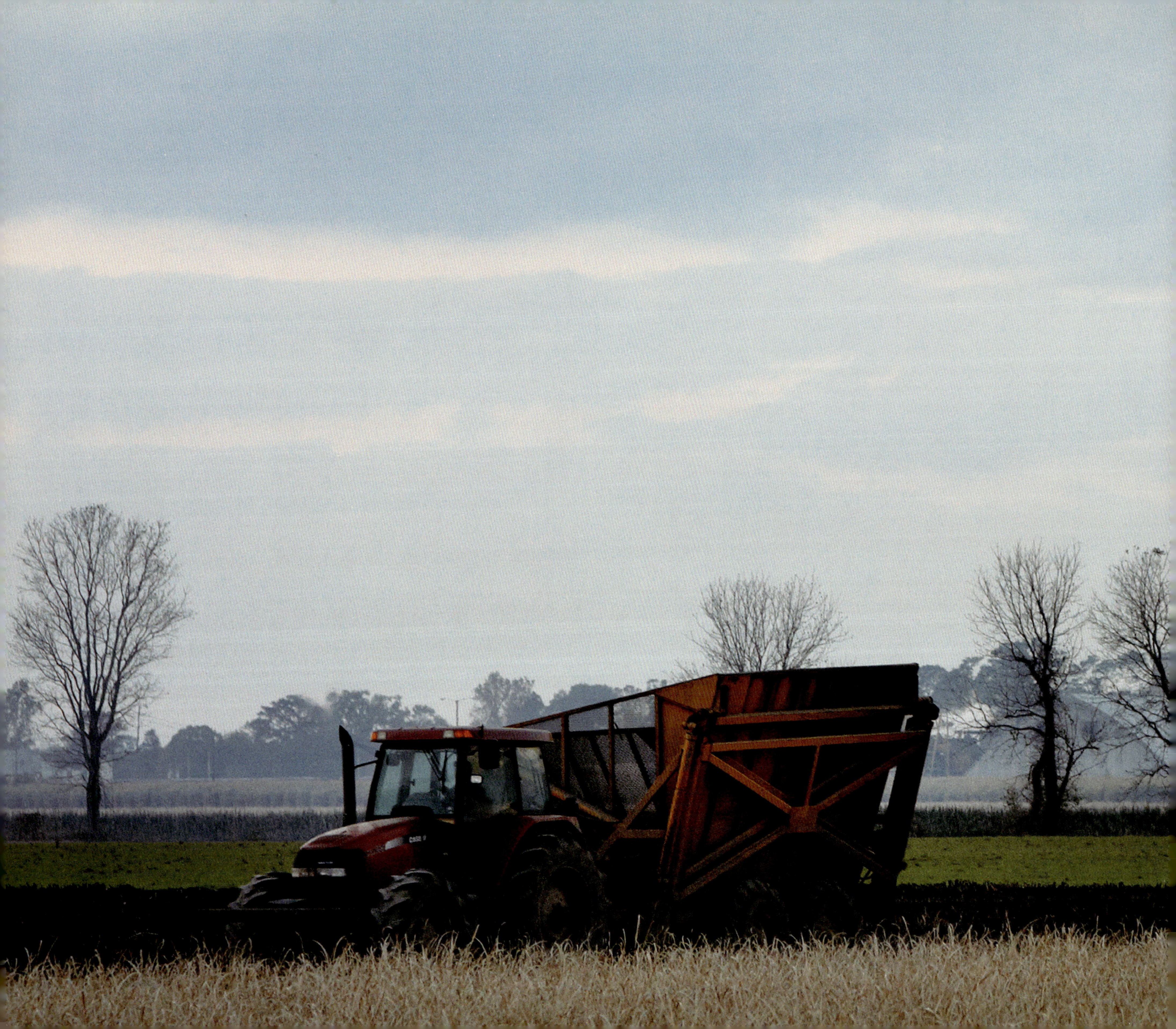

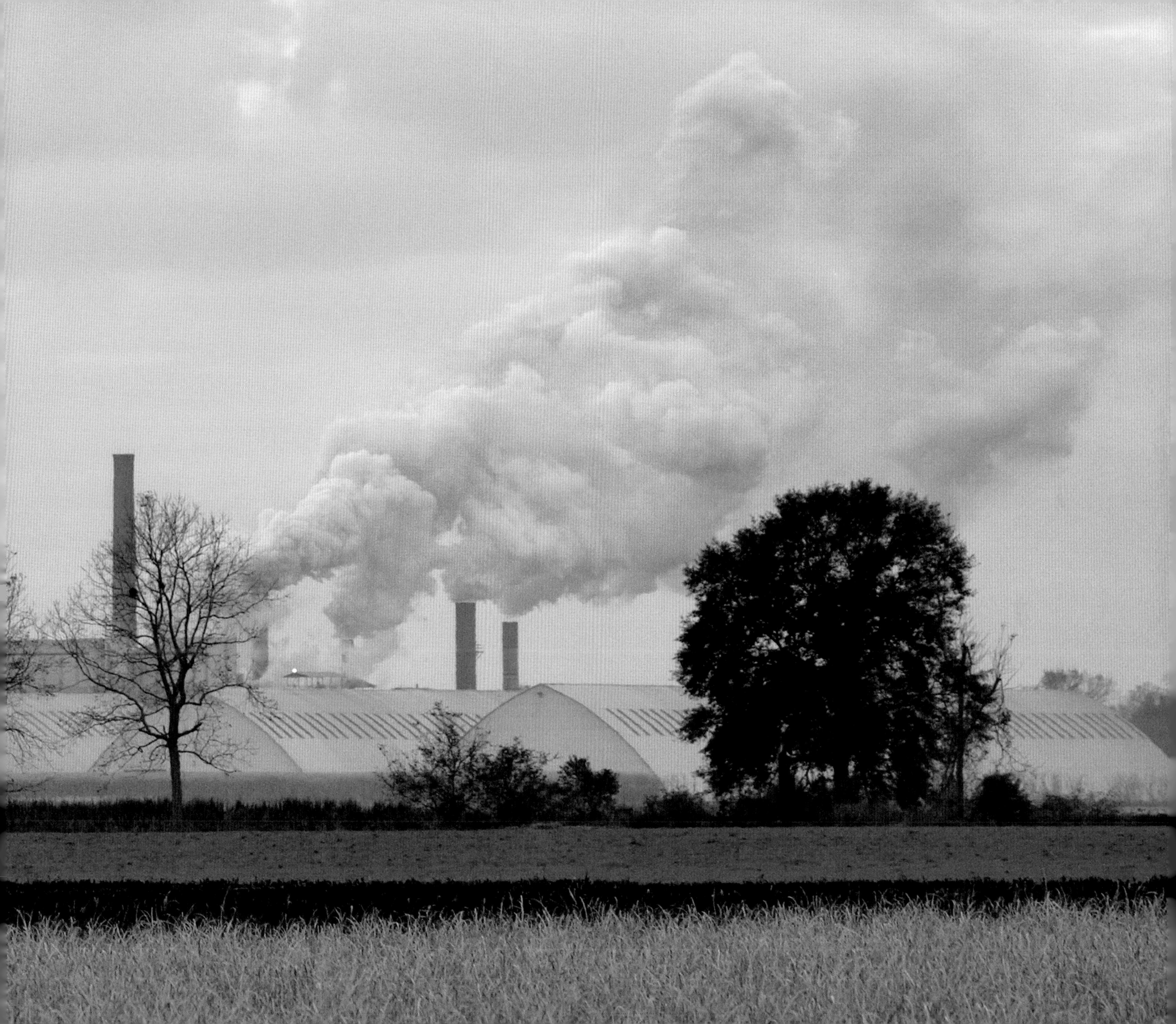

Sugarcane is grown and harvested in the fields of Alma Plantation as it has been for more than 150 years. Alma is the last complete sugar plantation in Louisiana: It still has a plantation home in which the owners live, plantation bell, overseer's house, fields in which the sugarcane is grown, a mill in which the cane is processed to become raw sugar, sugar warehouses to store raw sugar until it can be delivered to the refinery, housing devoted to the labor force of the fields and mill, a plantation store for the community, mule barn, other barns and storage buildings, and a plantation office from which the considerable business of Alma is managed.

Alma's sugar mill today, one of eleven still operating in Louisiana, is almost entirely automated. It processes cane to sugar through a carefully engineered system developed over the 200-year period since Jean Etienne de Boré, first mayor of New Orleans, demonstrated a reliable method for making granulated sugar at his Louisiana plantation.

Cane cut in the field and delivered by truck to the mill is washed, then crushed. The sugarcane juice is extracted, separated from fiber and debris (bagasse), purified, boiled to thicken through evaporation, and finally crystallized, spun, and dried.

Sparks dance around the doors of the boilers that burn bagasse, the fiber separated from the sugarcane juice, to generate both electricity and steam used in the crystallization process. Alma produces more than 70 percent of the energy it uses to create sugar—all from the discarded fiber of the sugarcane itself.

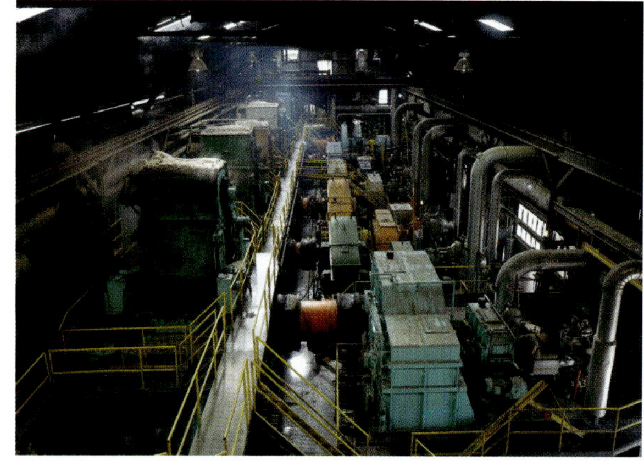

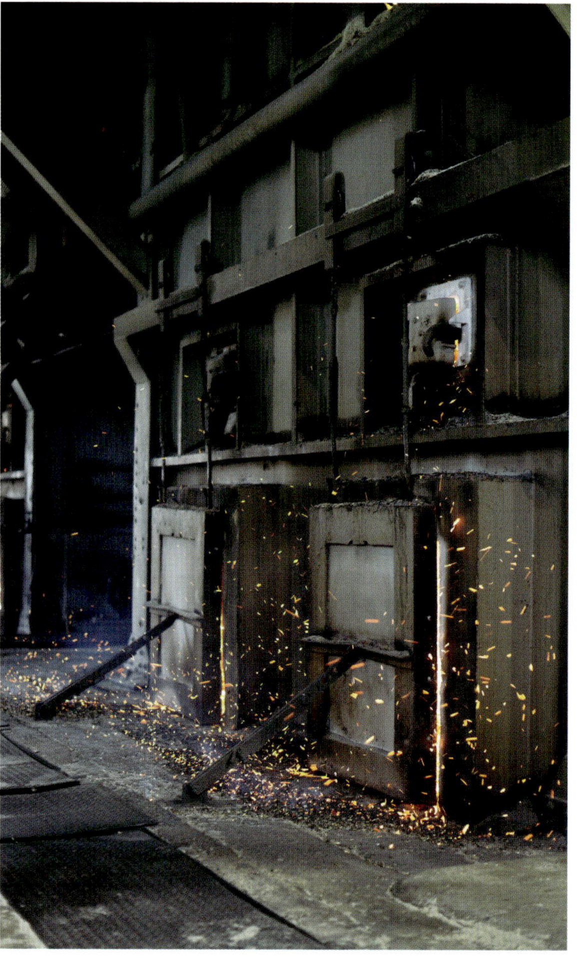

An enormous sugar warehouse holds the raw sugar until it is ready to be loaded and shipped to Colonial Sugar Refinery in Gramercy. The smell is rich and sweet. In the photo below, the truck to the right is dumping sugar brought directly from the mill. The backhoe to the left is pushing sugar up into the pile. The machine at the center is shooting sugar to the top of the pile to maximize storage space in the warehouse.

Alma's plantation store is one of the last of its kind in Louisiana. Still providing staples and hot lunches for Alma employees, the store also sells Alma's own raw sugar to many area residents, who prize the rich brown crystals in coffee and for baking.

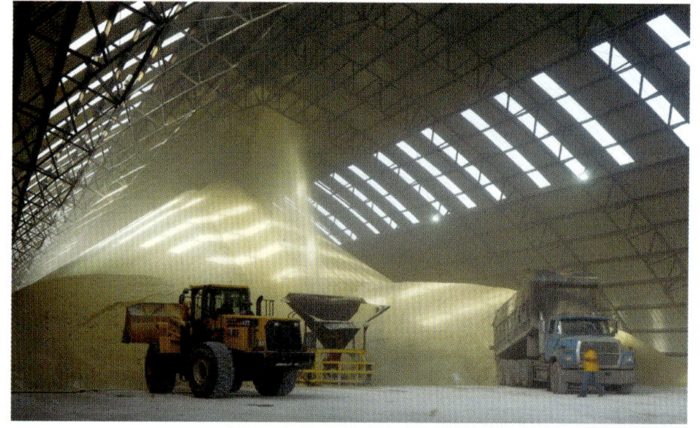

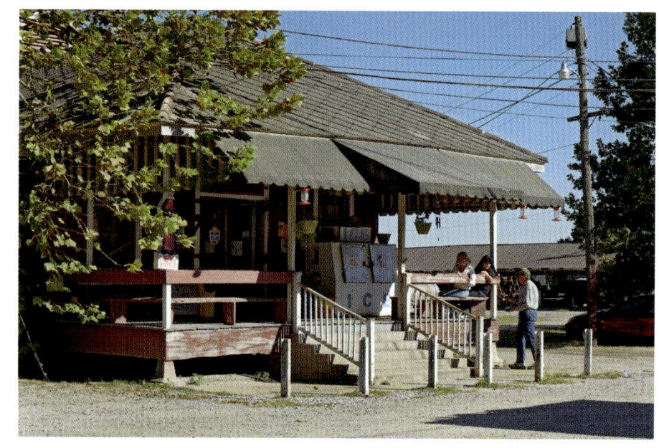

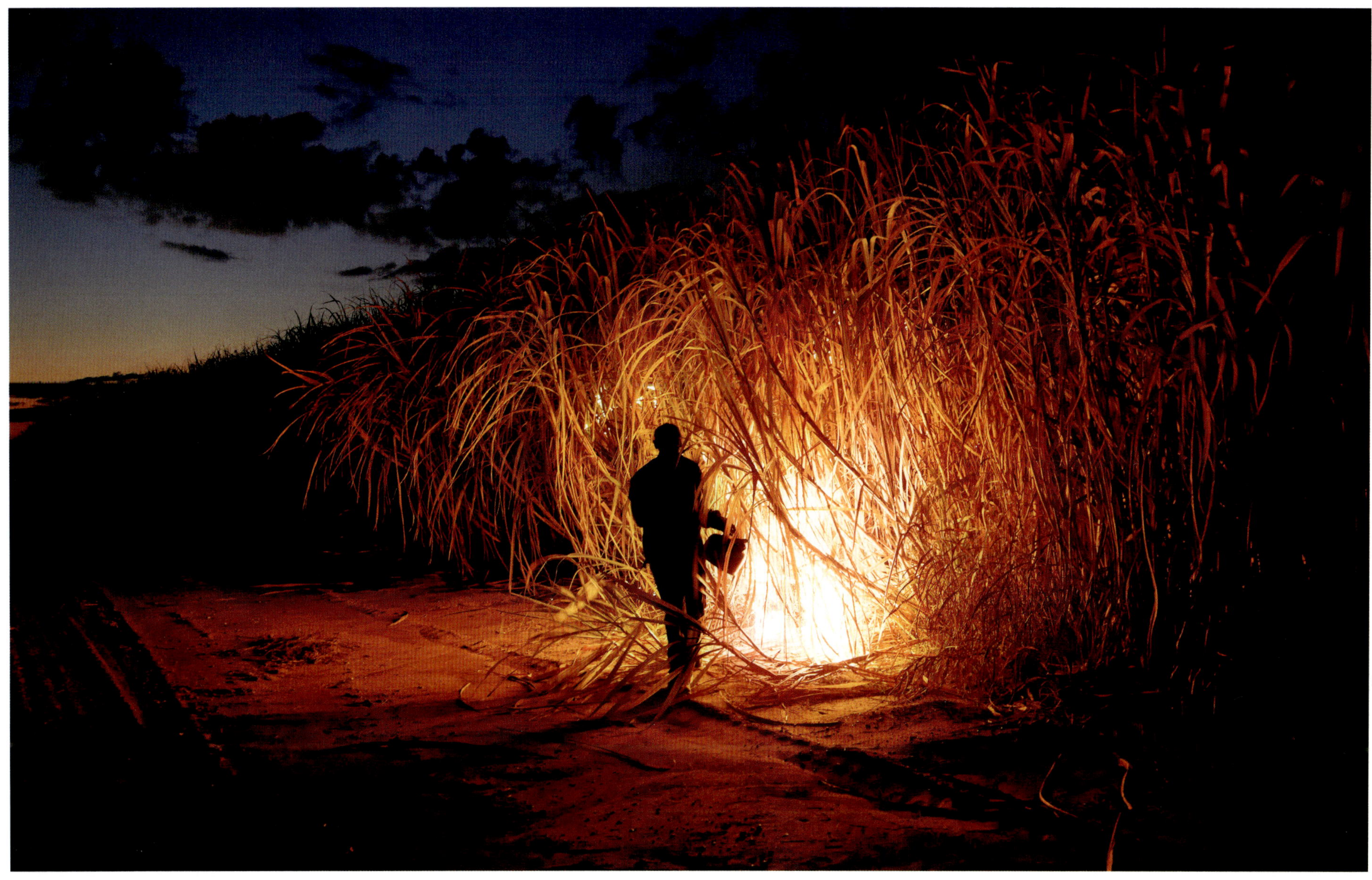

Mitch Pinsonat sets fire to one of Alma's cane fields at dusk. The fire quickly burns away the dry outer leaves but doesn't harm the sweet sugarcane juice inside. This process makes it easier to harvest the cane.

The sight of burning cane fields and the sweet smell of the smoke are timeless reminders of the continuity of agricultural life in Louisiana over almost three hundred years.

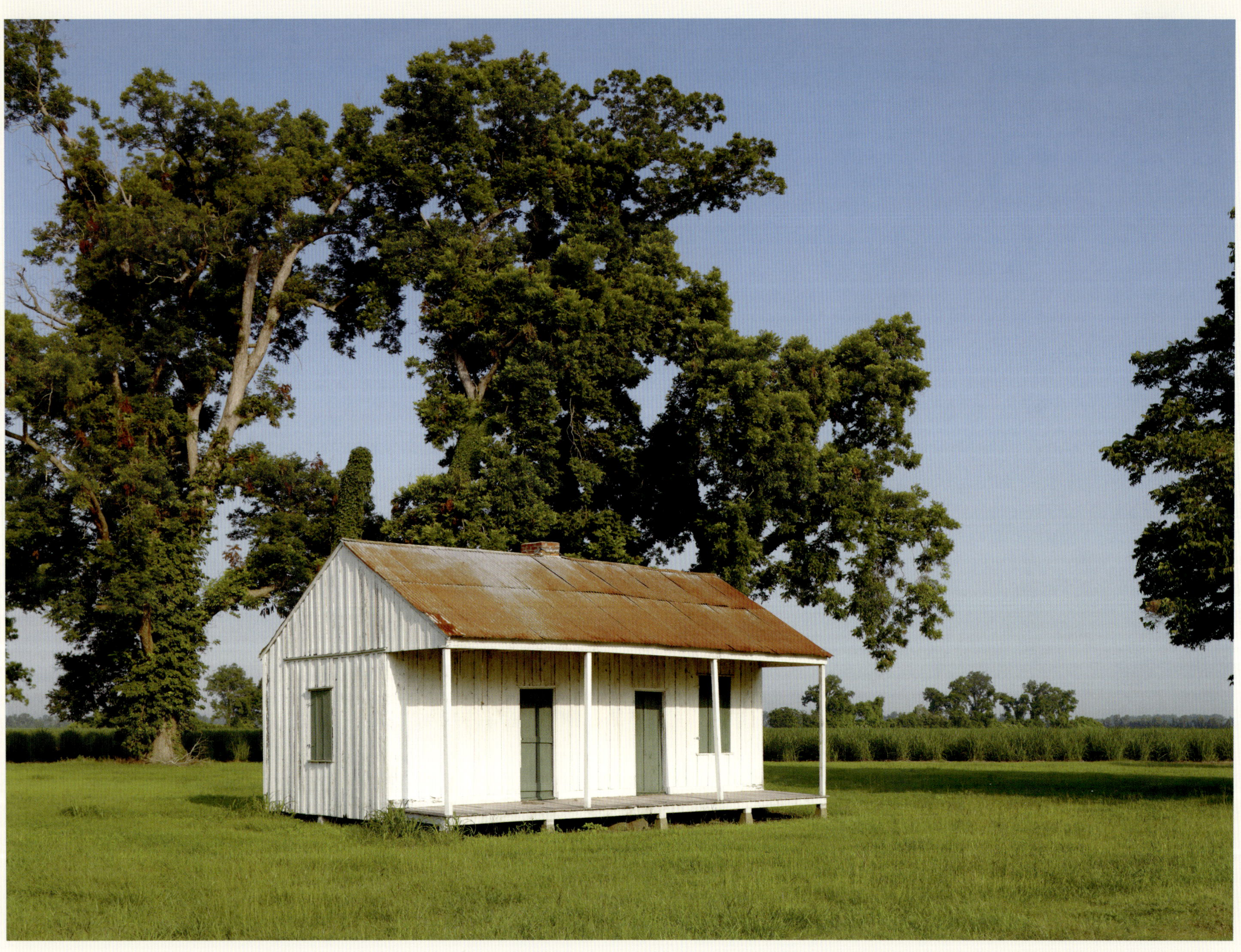

CHAPTER 3

False River Road, False River, and the Island

MISS JANE PITTMAN OAK

A very old live oak in Lakeland near Bayou Cirier, dating from a hundred years or more before the Civil War, inspired the young author Ernest J. Gaines as he wrote one of his early short stories, "Just like a Tree." It was published by the *Sewanee Review* in 1963 and compiled in Gaines's *Bloodline: Five Stories* in 1968. Gaines says that tree, and the character it inspired in the early short story, led directly to the title character of his most famous novel eight years later. Today the tree is known as the Miss Jane Pittman Oak.

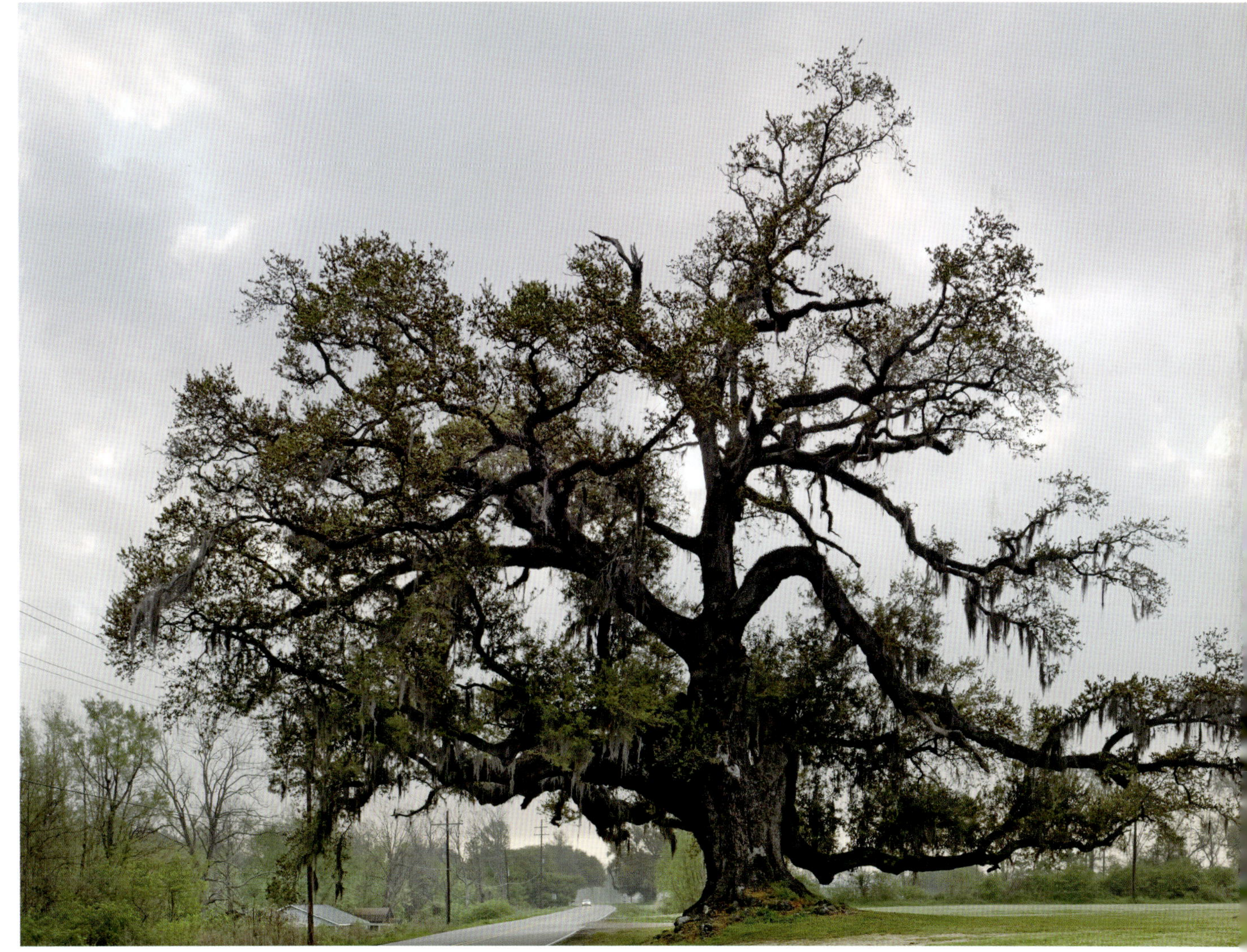

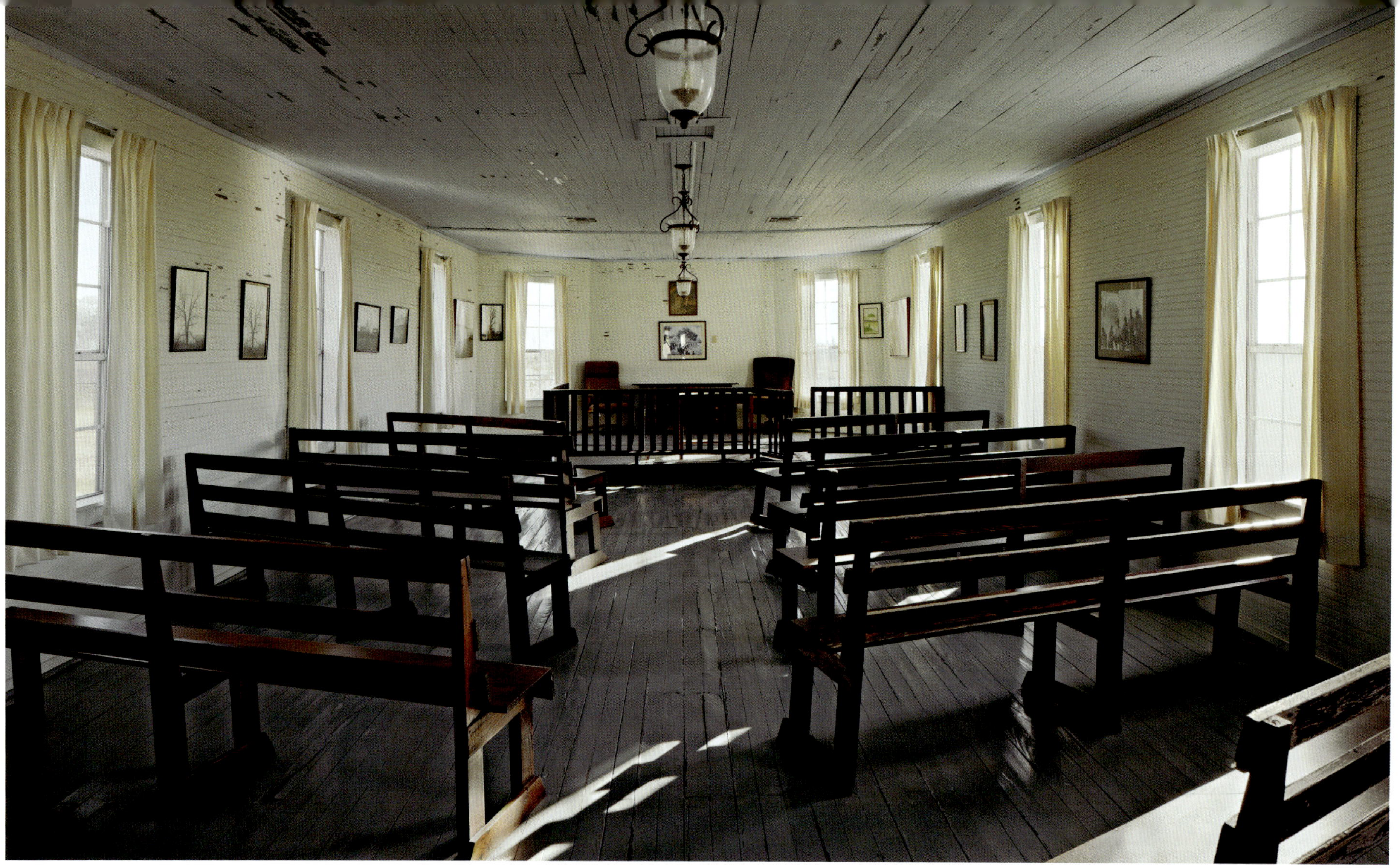

Ernest Gaines went to church and school in the Mount Zion Baptist Church, built at River Lake in the early twentieth century. When it was no longer used as a church or school, Mr. and Mrs. Gaines saved the old building by moving it to their own land, a portion of River Lake Plantation they purchased and on which they built their home.

Graves are scrubbed, scraped, and repainted yearly on the Saturday before All Saints' Day at Mount Zion Cemetery in the cane fields of River Lake Plantation. Mr. and Mrs. Gaines joined with other local people to clean up and preserve the cemetery. The annual cleanup day has turned into a community event with a morning of hard work made pleasant by sharing with friends and leading to a big social Louisiana lunch.

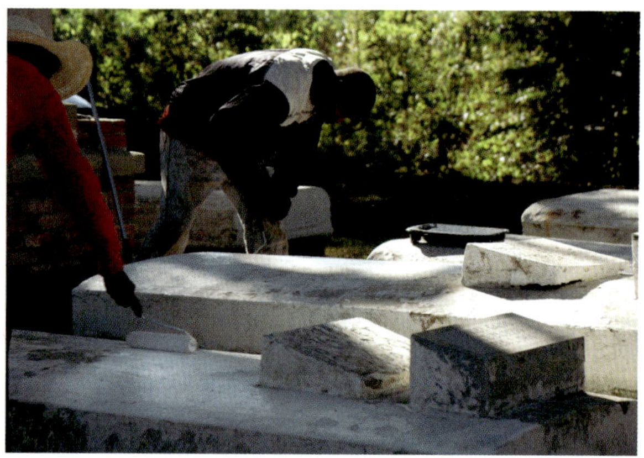

PHOTOGRAPH © 2012 BY JONATHAN TRAVIESA

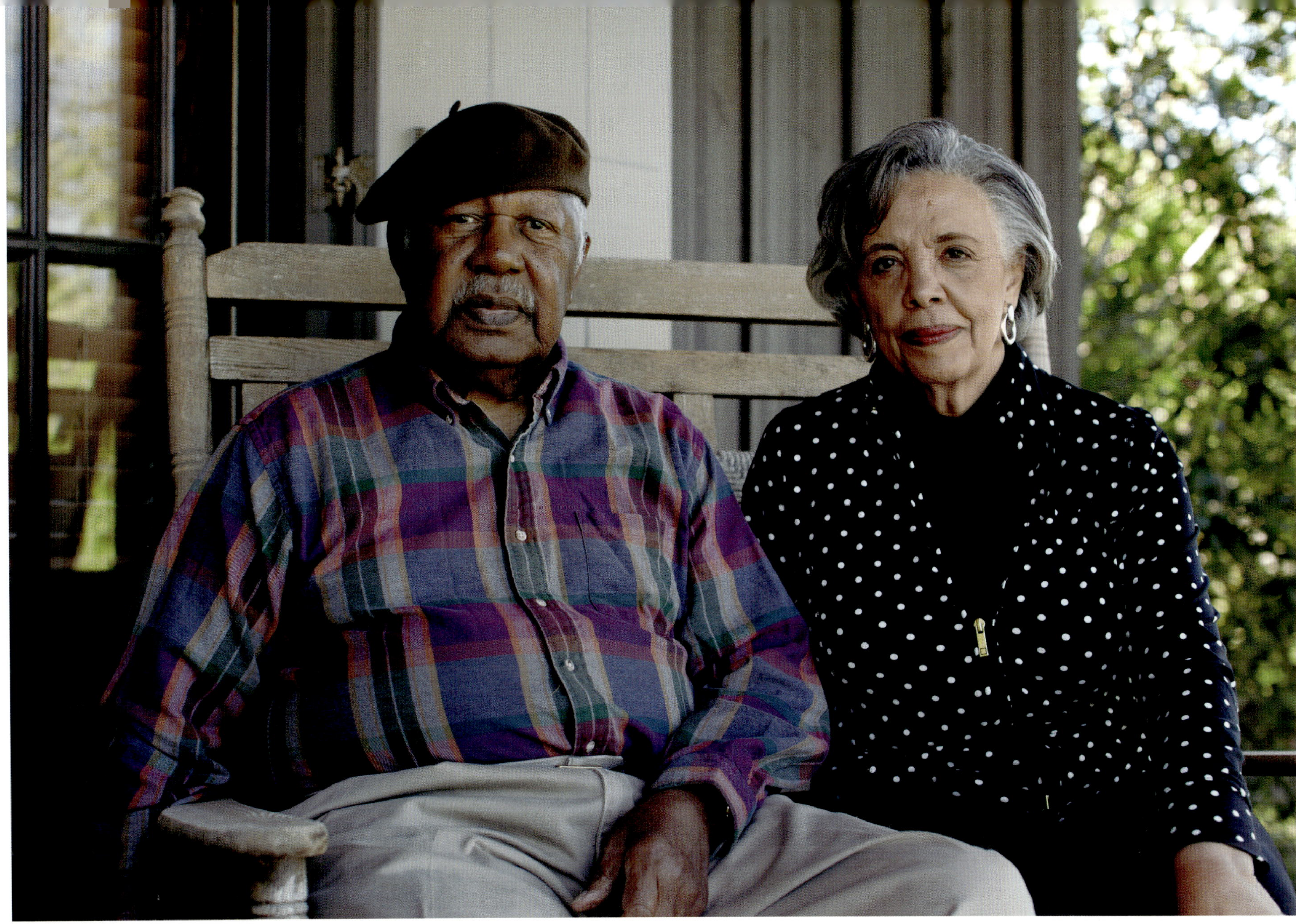

Author Ernest Gaines and his wife Dianne sit on the front porch of their home in Oscar. Gaines is one of the fifth generation of his family born and reared on River Lake Plantation. He is the author of *A Lesson before Dying,* winner of the National Book Critics Circle Award in 1993; *The Autobiography of Miss Jane Pittman;* seven other books; and numerous short stories and essays. In 2010 the University of Louisiana at Lafayette opened the Ernest J. Gaines Center for scholarship on the esteemed author's work and to honor his contribution as ULL writer-in-residence emeritus. Gaines taught at ULL for twenty-four years.

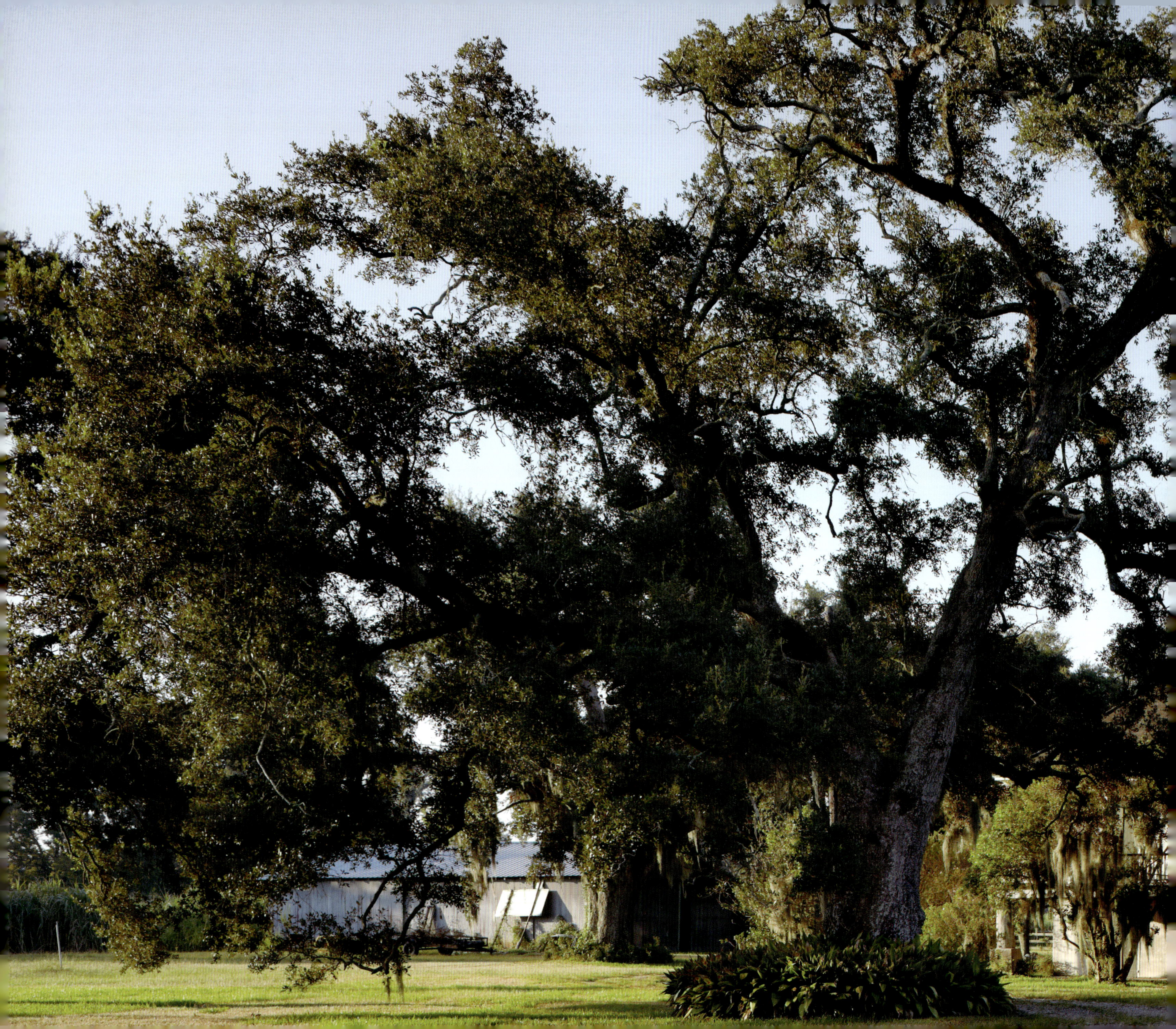

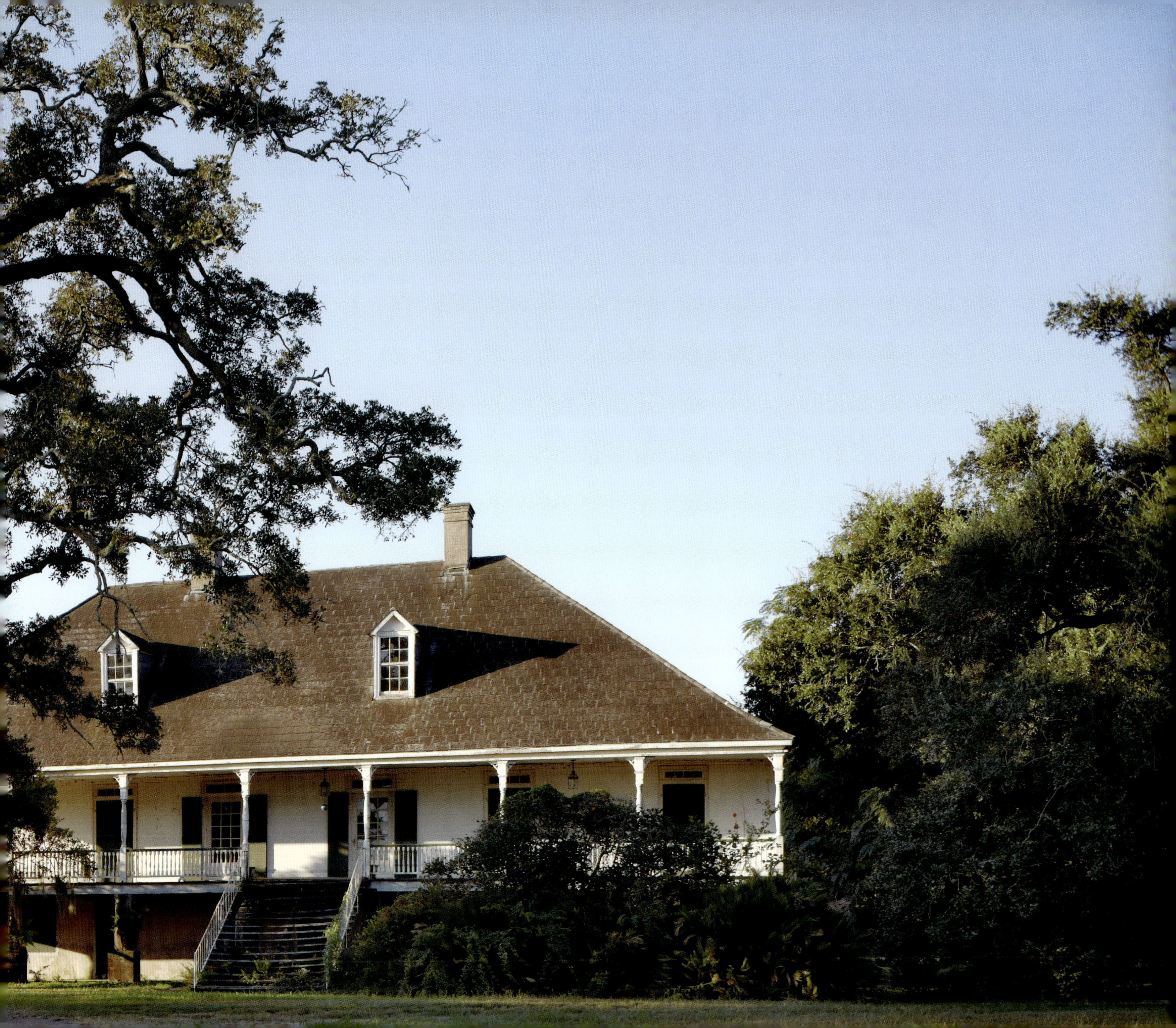

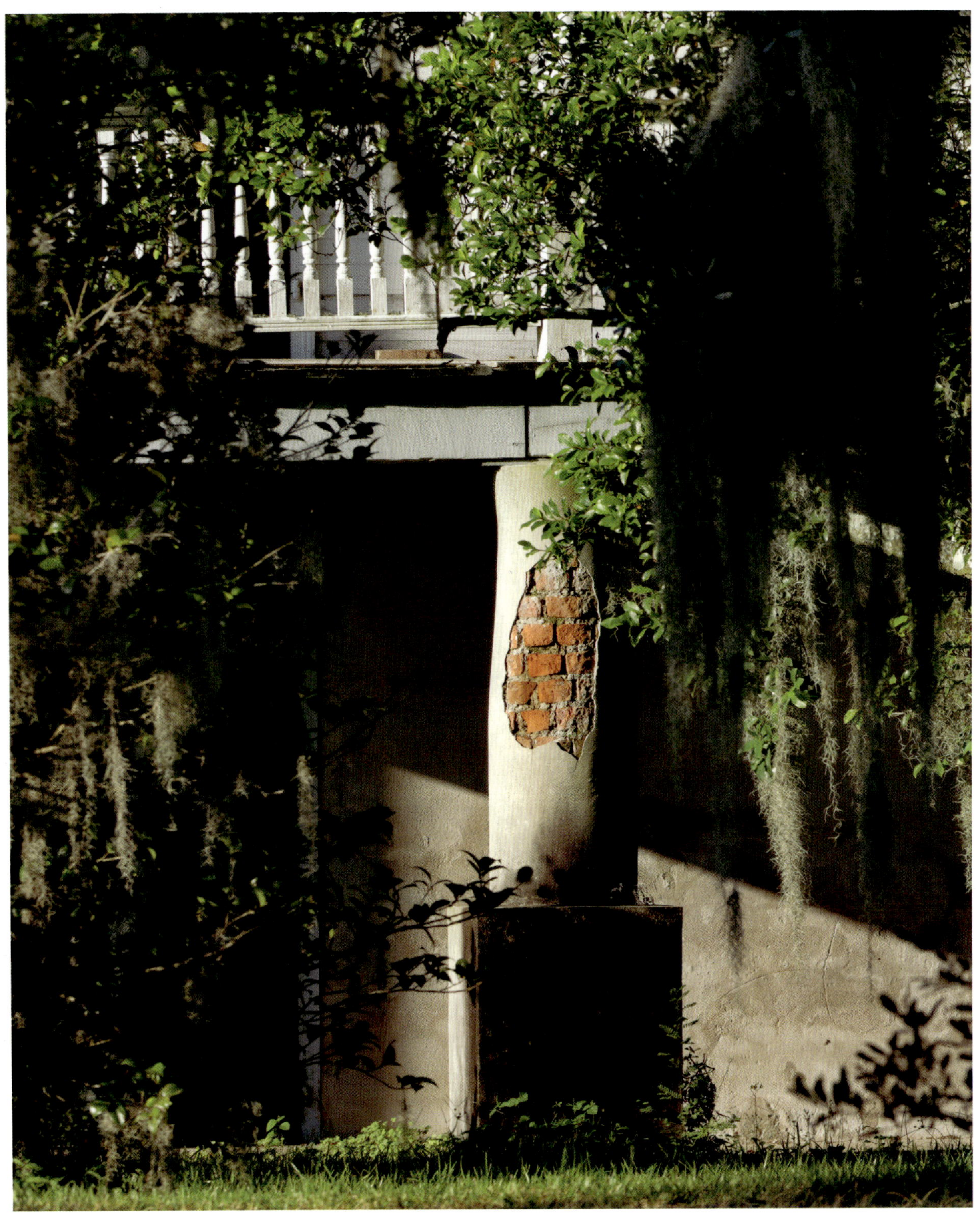

River Lake is probably one of the earliest large plantations established on False River, and one of the oldest surviving homes in Louisiana. Isaac Gaillard received the original Spanish land grant in 1790. Antoine Decuir purchased the property from him, and may have had the house built for his bride, Louise Beauvais. (Civil records include real estate transfers, but virtually no dates associated with the building of houses, so dating any early house in Pointe Coupee is usually based on style and conjecture.)

The house's name, of course, refers to False River—the lake that was once a river.

Barbe espagnole (Spanish moss), an air plant in the pineapple family and closely related to greenhouse bromeliads, grows lushly in the live oaks and camellias at River Lake. Spanish moss is one of the plants most identified with Louisiana in the popular imagination, and several folk tales tell of how this ghostly plant came to reside in Louisiana's trees. The plant is absolutely harmless to the trees in which it grows. Very sensitive to air pollution, it has failed to thrive in modern times in some places where automobile exhaust or other air pollution is prevalent.

Spanish moss was used to stuff mattresses until the mid-twentieth century, and thriving moss gins were located for many years in New Roads and Livonia.

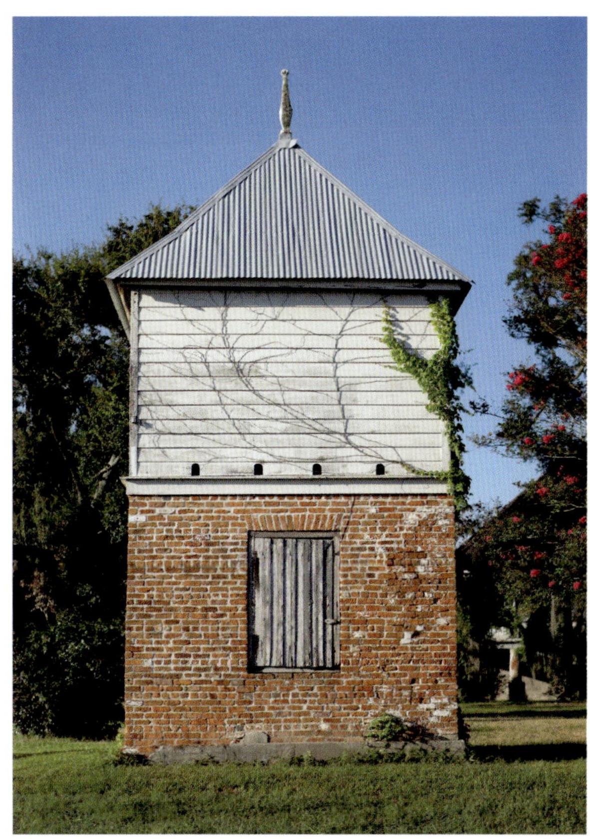

A true landmark of Pointe Coupee, an antebellum *pigeonnier* (pigeon house or dovecote) stands near False River Road. Two stood sentry before the great house River Lake until the late twentieth century. One was finally dismantled, but the other was restored and has been maintained. It is one of only six remaining in the parish, monuments to two centuries of change and transformation.

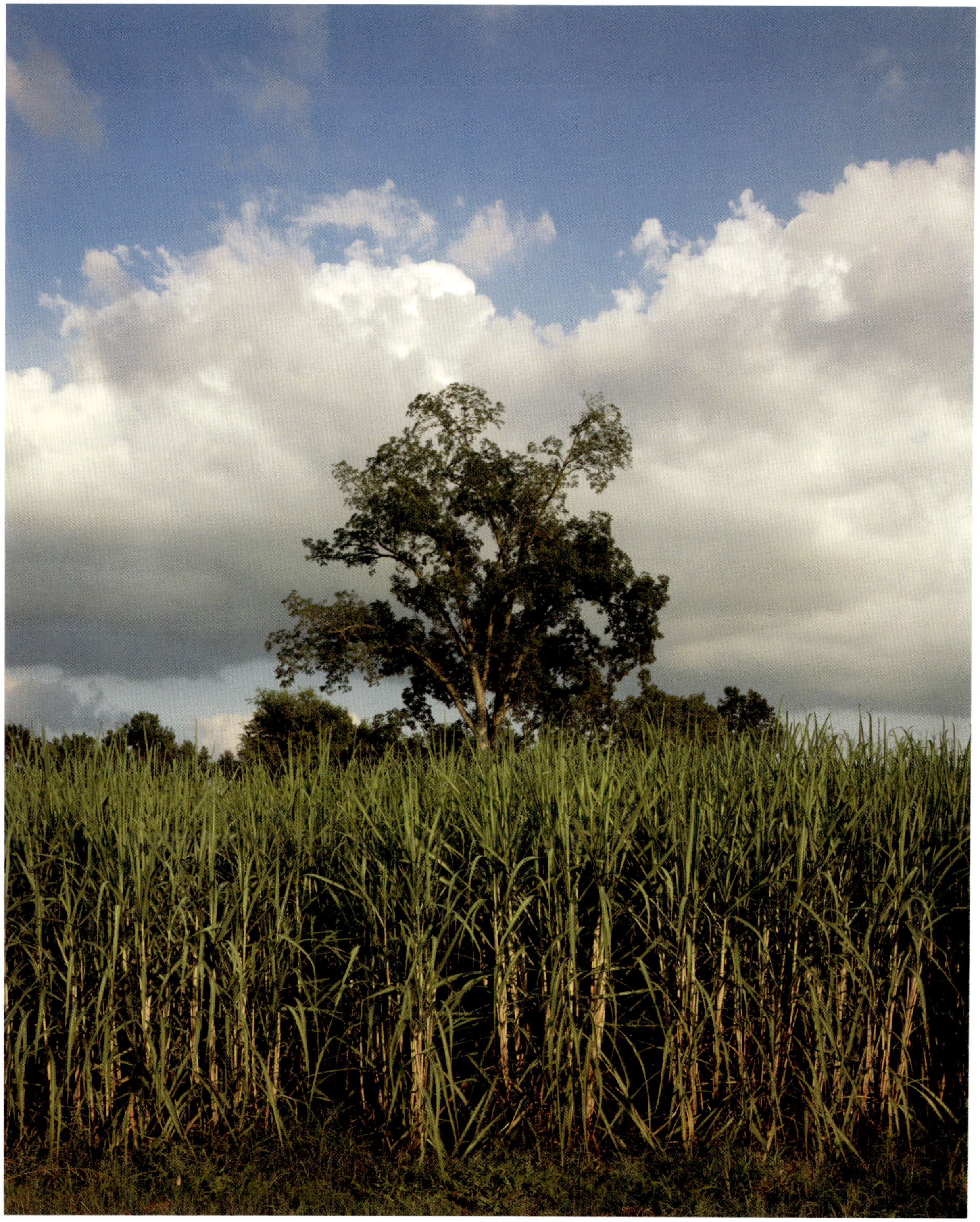

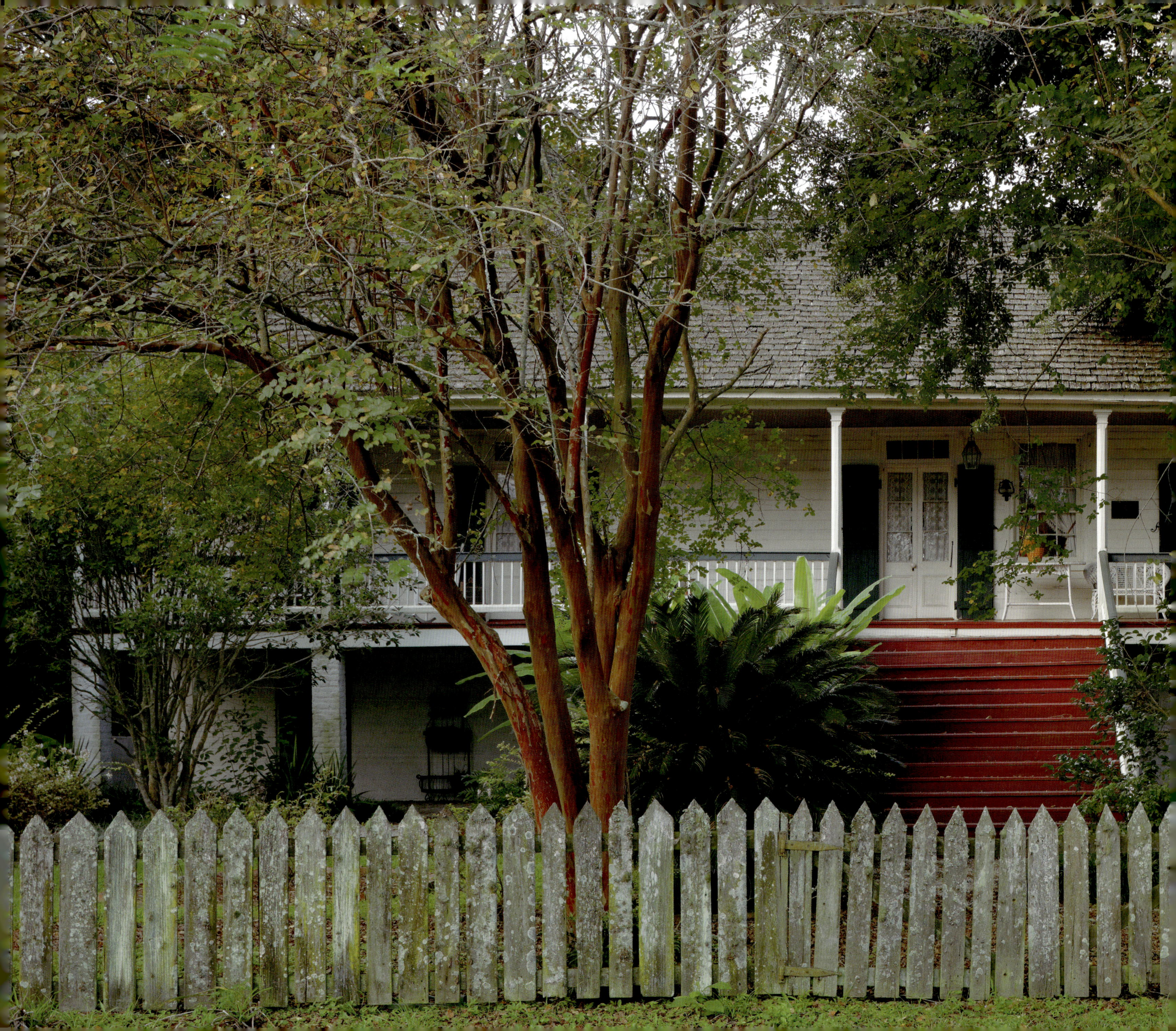

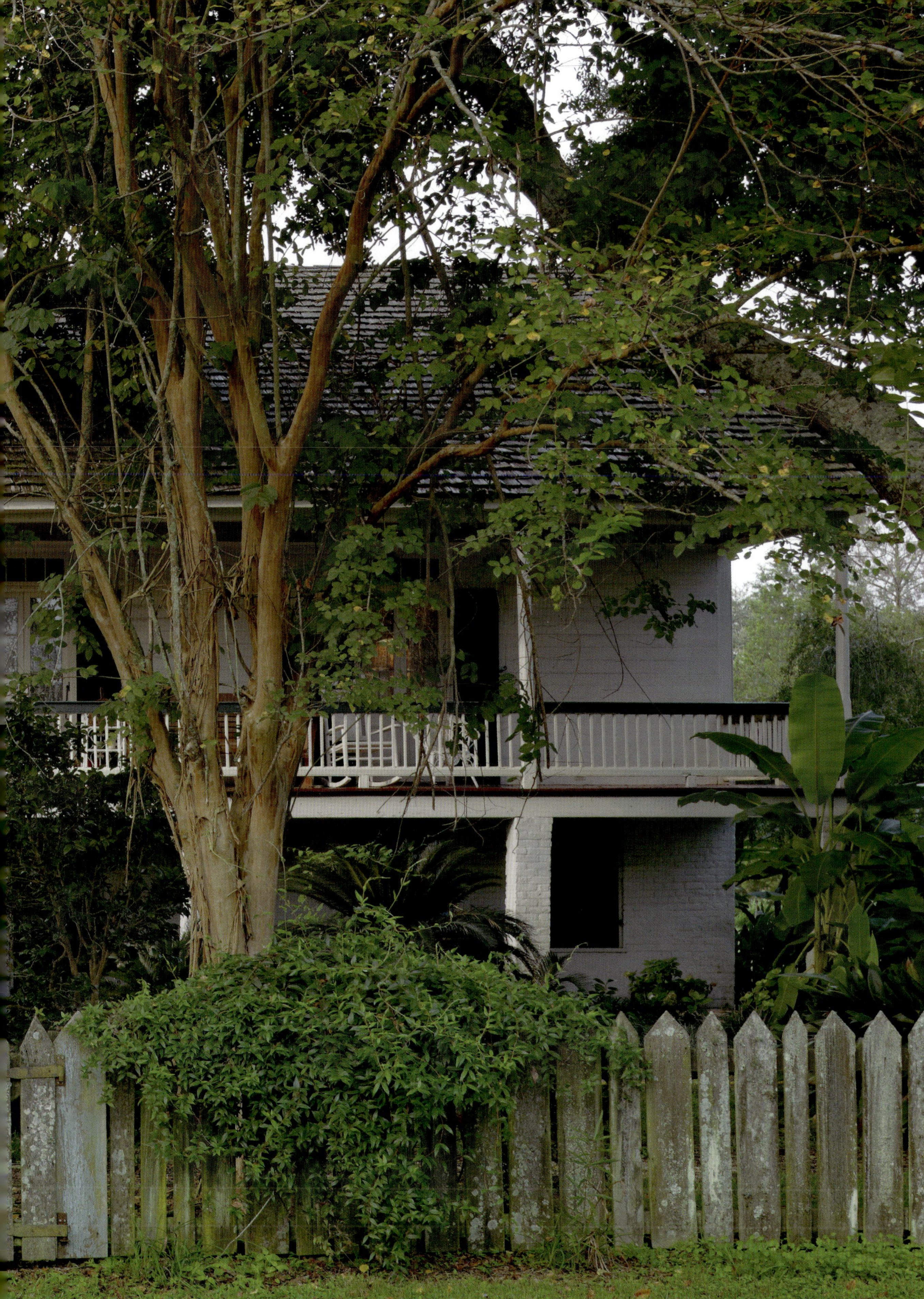

National Register of Historic Places
Historic American Buildings Survey

North Bend is an early Creole raised plantation home owned by Julien Poydras from 1800 to 1824. New, it was four rooms wide on both floors, with broad galleries (porches) front and back. About 1850 it was made larger with one more room added to each floor on the western end. Typical of French houses, there were no interior halls or stairs. Circulation was from room to room or on the outdoor galleries.

The old cypress *pieux* fence is often seen enclosing Pointe Coupee gardens. True to the period of the house, this one encloses a parterre garden accented by crape myrtle, camellia, sago palm, and banana. In the nineteenth century the cypress fence would have kept animals out of the homegrown vegetables, herbs, and flowers.

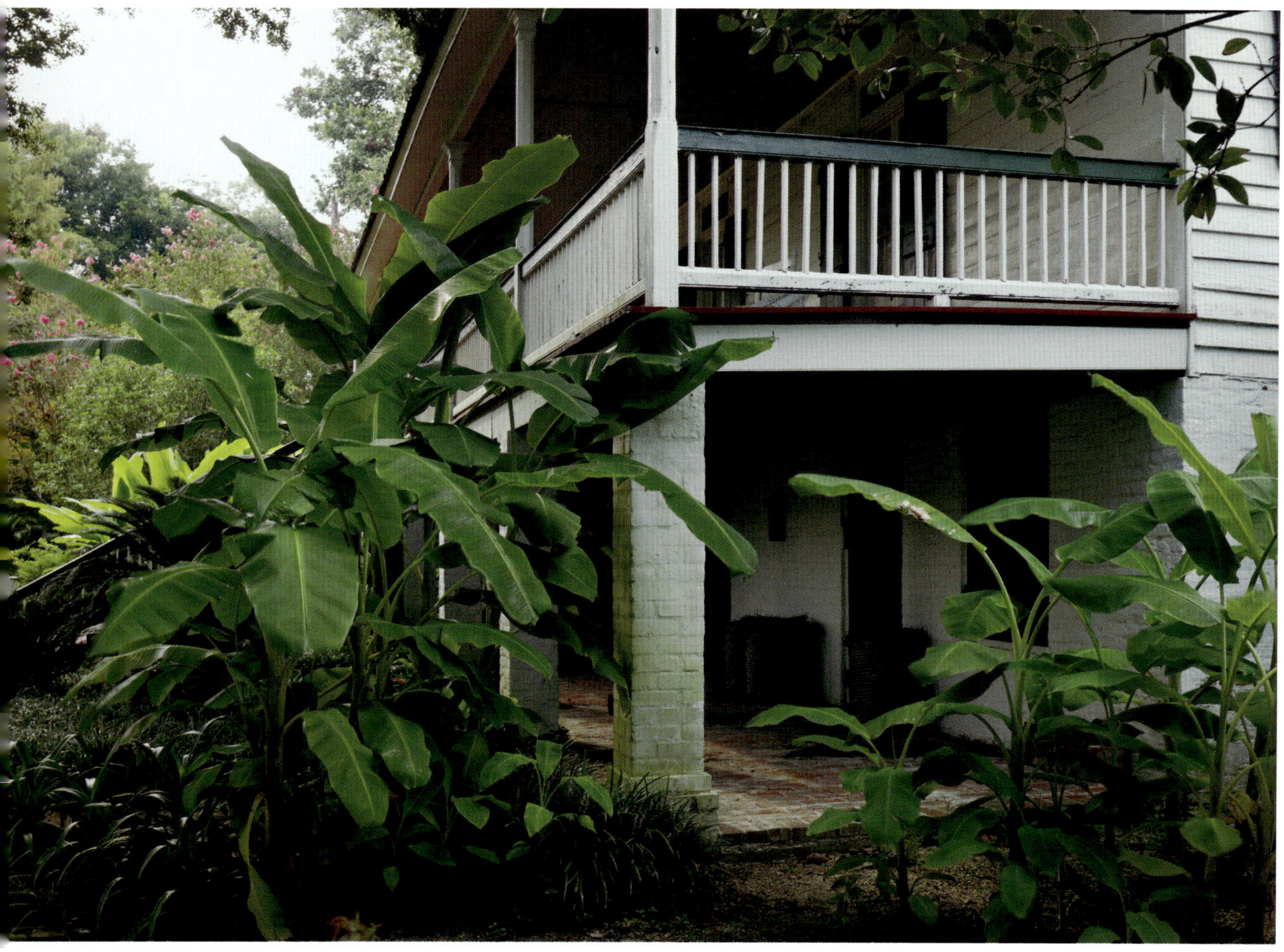

Bales of pine straw, a favorite garden mulch, stand at the ready under the gallery of North Bend. The first floor is built of brick and the upstairs of wood, which is typical of early French houses in Pointe Coupee. When the Mississippi River got high enough to overtop the levees and flood the Chenal and False River, the brick basement was relatively water-resistant. Residents could move upstairs until the waters subsided.

Banana trees are favorites of Louisiana gardeners. In seasons of long, mild autumns, they may even manage to produce fruit.

North Bend's homey modern kitchen is in the enclosed upstairs back gallery. When the house was new, the kitchen was out back in its own building to keep the home safe from the danger of frequent kitchen fires.

A Creole gold ceiling glows above an antique bed inherited by Mrs. Alfred Pickett from her Provosty ancestors at Evergreen Plantation, down the Mississippi River in Edgard. The atypical fireplace on an outside wall indicates that this room was not original, but added later in the history of the house.

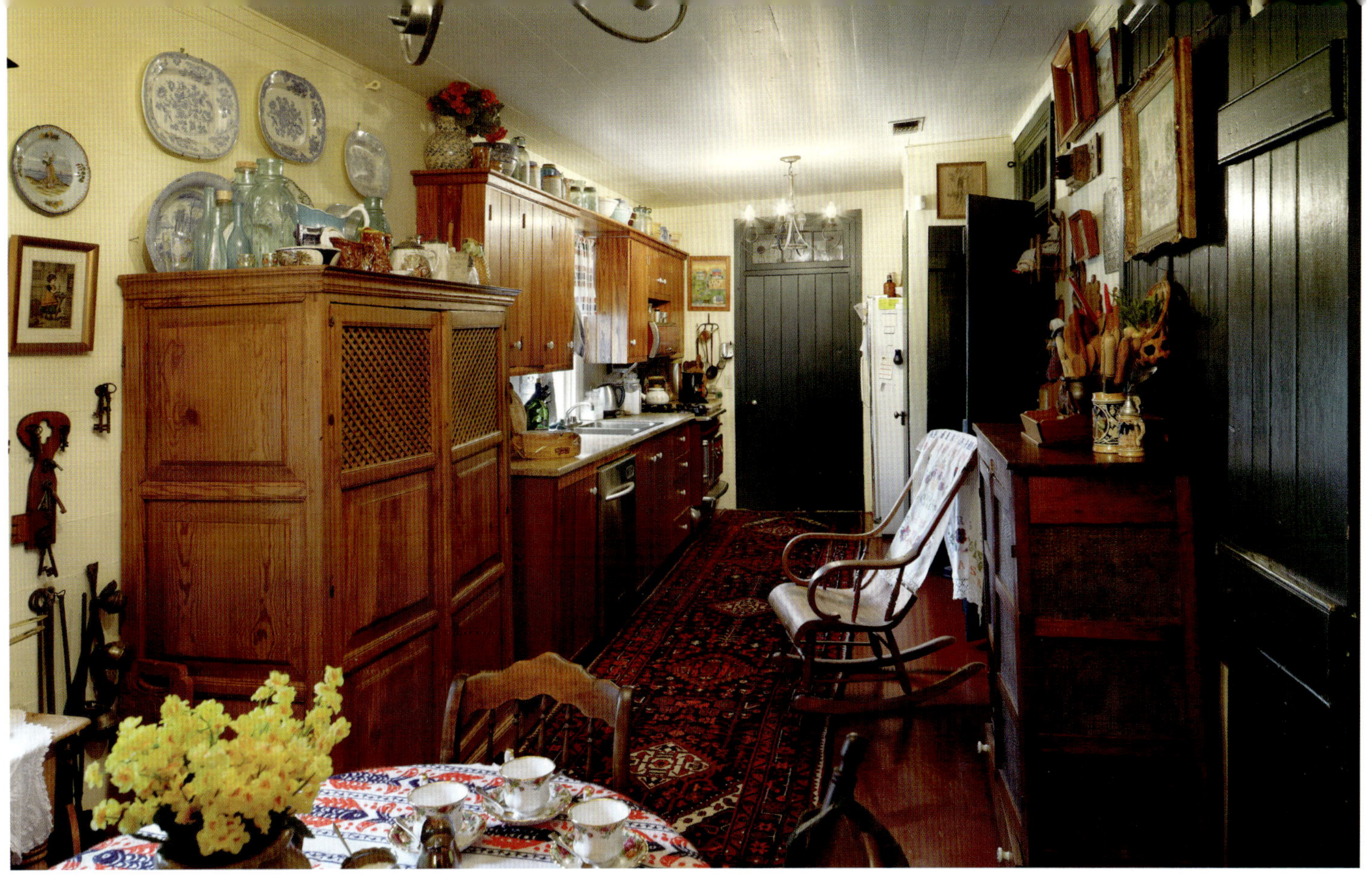

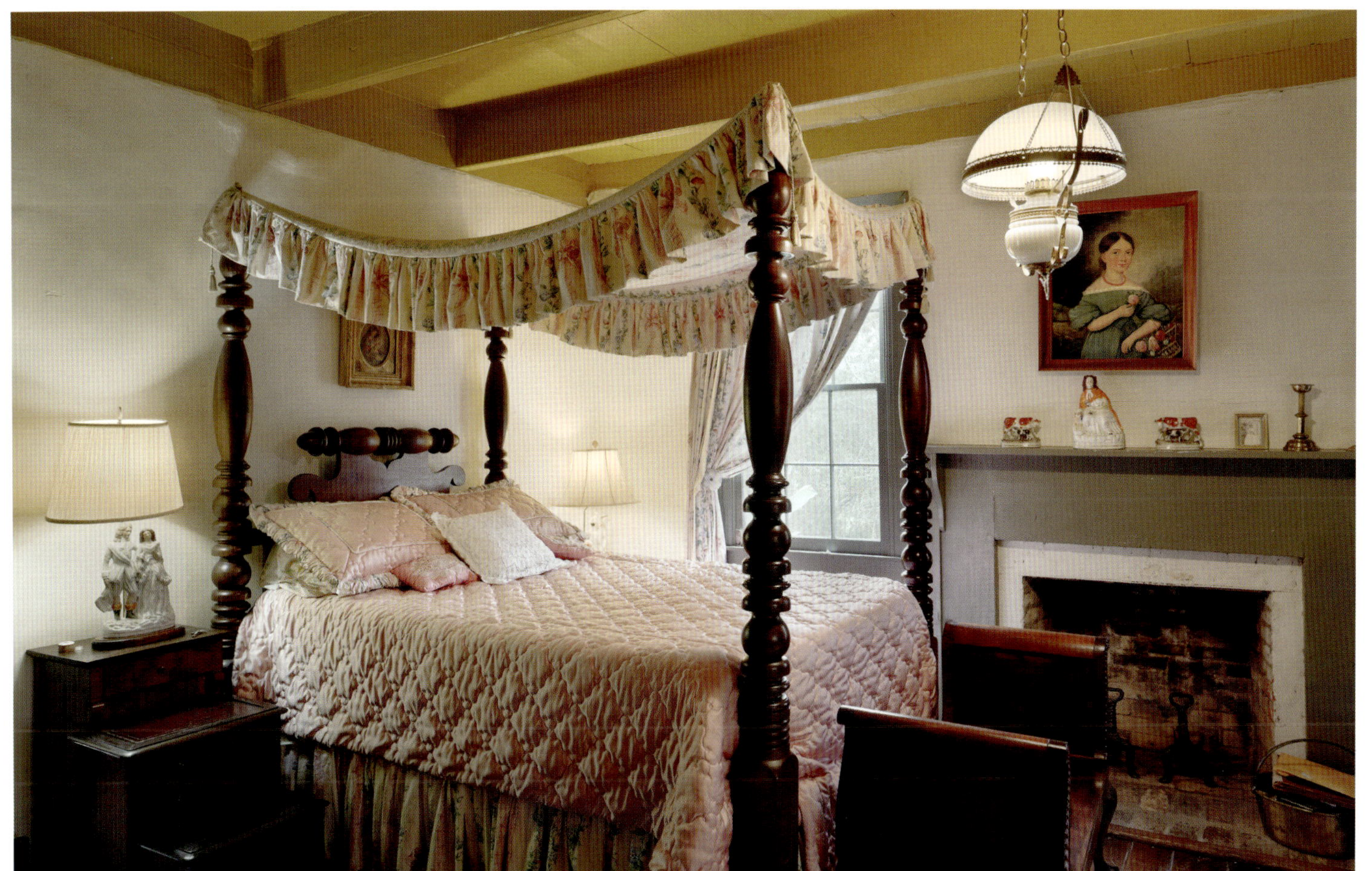

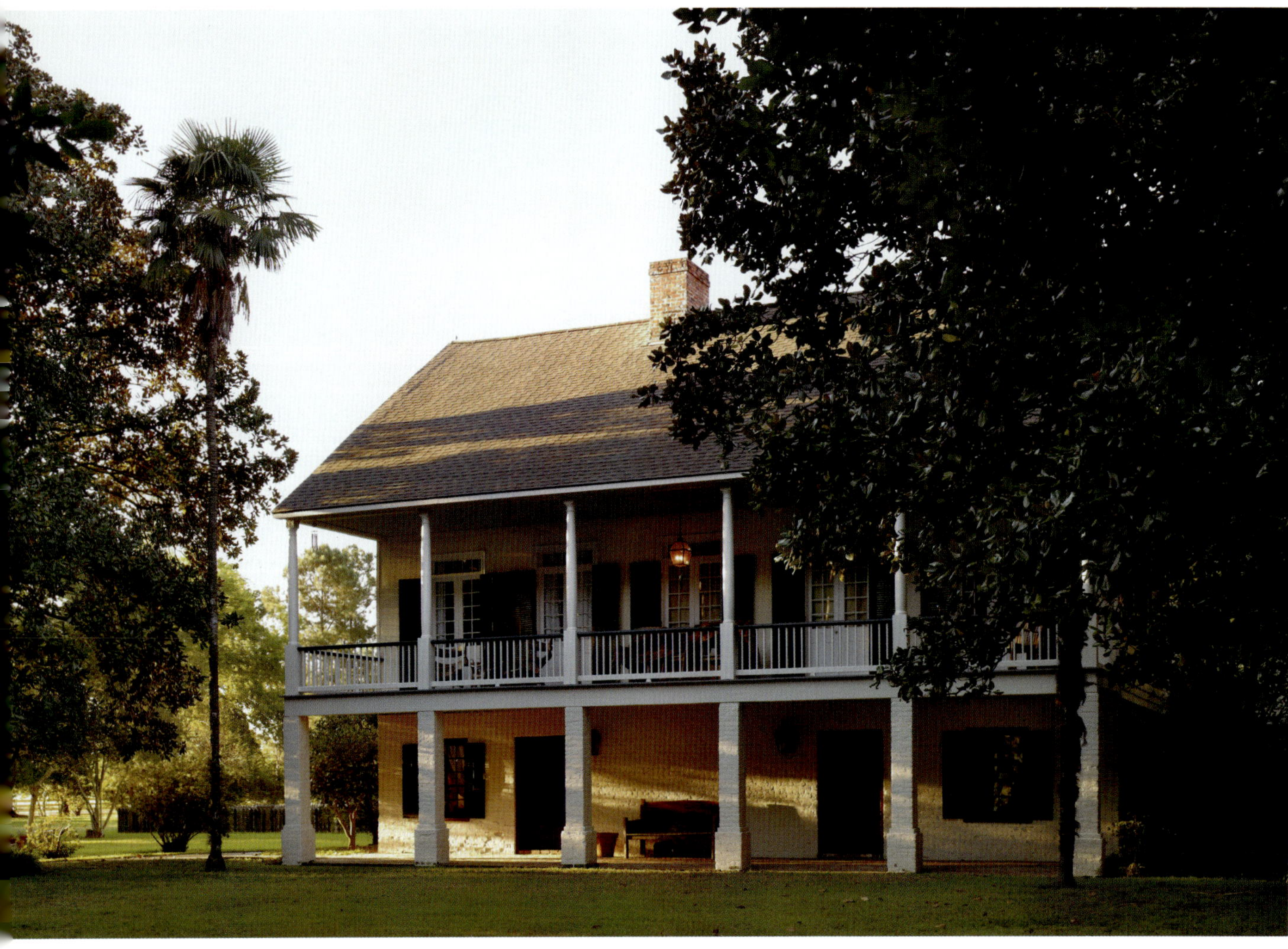

Missing from this classic Creole plantation house is its outdoor staircase, removed from the front galleries and replaced by an indoor stair in the twentieth century. Otherwise, Pleasant View retains its pristine Old Louisiana architecture: brick basement and columns downstairs holding up a frame-built second story with beautifully turned colonettes and French doors below glazed transoms. The house has no central hall, eschewing the popular Classical Revival style that gained prominence elsewhere along the Mississippi River in antebellum Louisiana. This house was already under construction in 1842 when Louis Amazan Hubert, a native of Saint-Domingue (Haiti), purchased the plantation.

A wooden cistern standing on a strong brick base gathers rainwater from the roof of Pleasant View. The antique cistern was brought to Pointe Coupee from Manresa, formerly Jefferson College in Convent, Louisiana, chartered in 1831 and today a Jesuit retreat center.

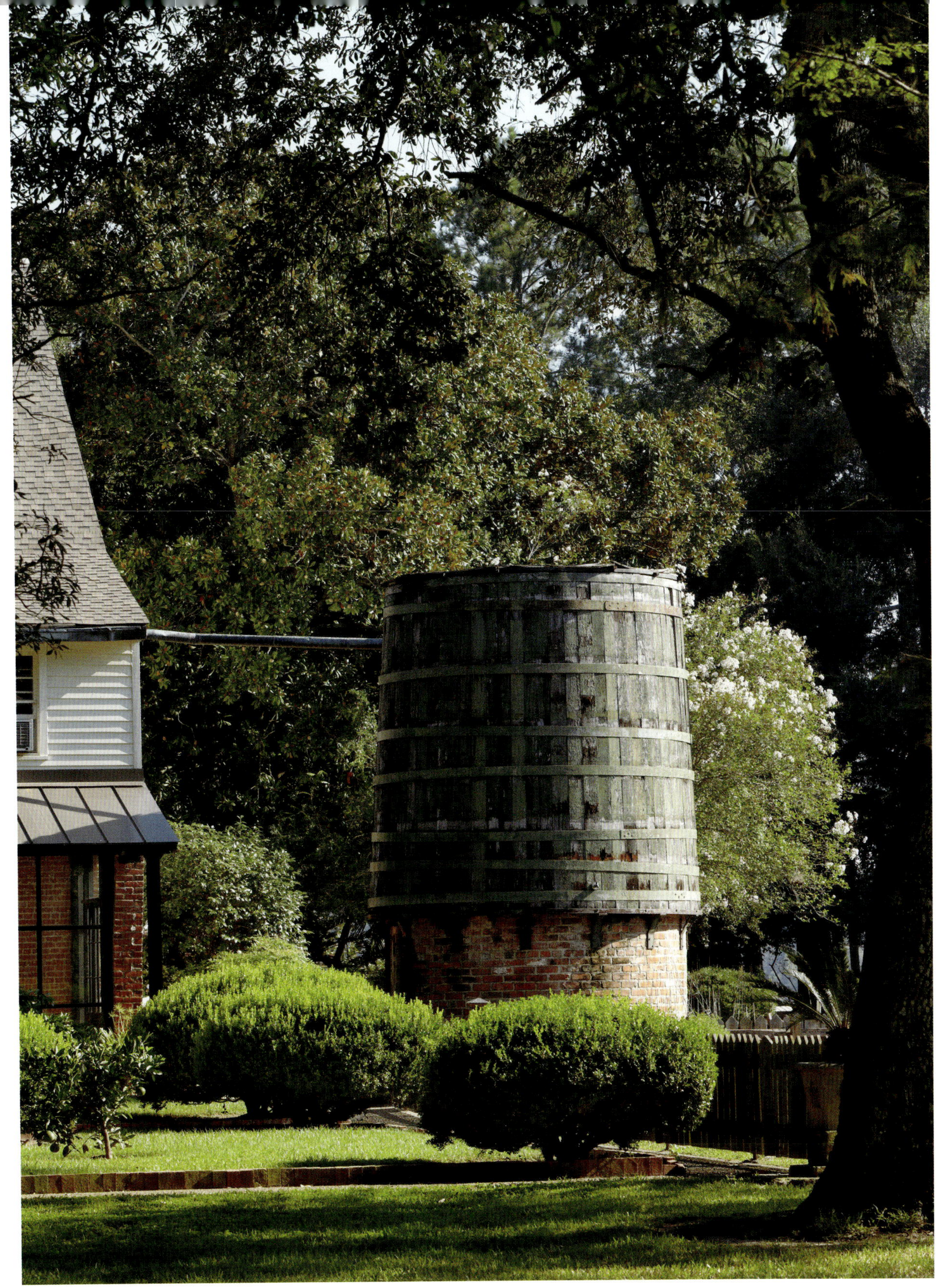

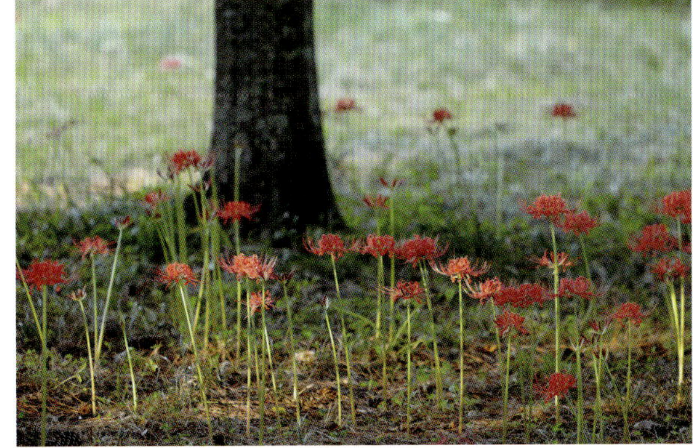

Red spider lilies bloom plentifully in the lawns and fields around Pleasant View in early fall. Southerners call the flowers "naked ladies" because they make their leaves in the spring, die away in the summer, then pop up overnight with fanciful red flowers on bare stems after the first rains of late September. The plants survive with no care, so one can tell where gardens used to be by the prevalence of "naked ladies" in fields and ditches throughout Pointe Coupee in the fall. The bulbs were first brought from Japan to the United States in 1854.

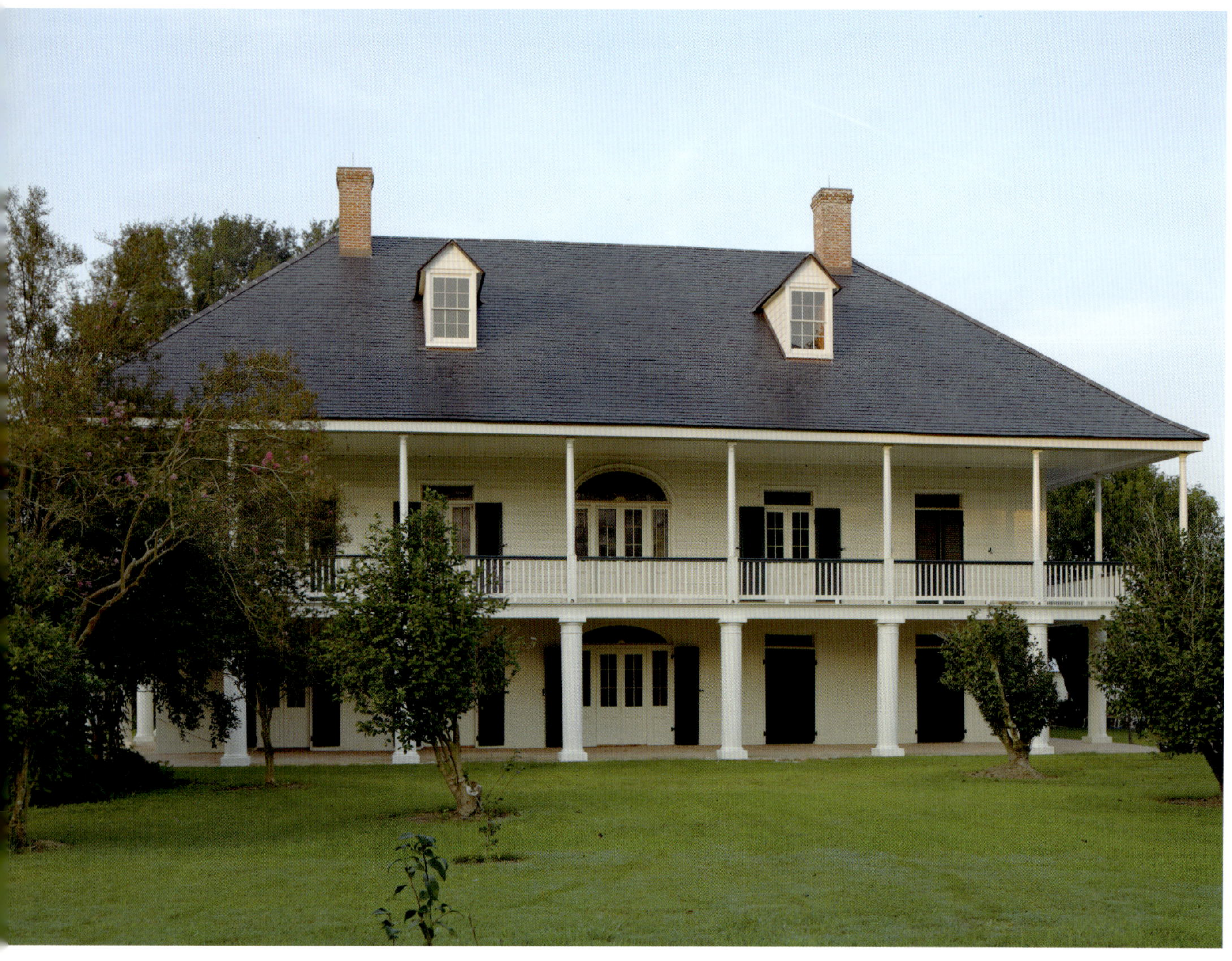

Austerlitz was built around 1832 by Antoine Decuir, a free man of color. His father had purchased the land from Indians on False River in 1783. It is a grand home with a wide central hall and French doors with transoms on both floors. Very unusual for Pointe Coupee Parish!

In 1886 the house was purchased by Joseph A. Rougon, which began a line of ownership surviving to the present. Joseph's son, Colonel Henry Rougon, created camellia gardens in front of the house facing False River in 1939. These beautiful old shrubs still bloom profusely through Pointe Coupee's mild winters.

The current owners, Beth and Joe Rougon and their children, are the fourth and fifth generations of the family to live at Austerlitz.

The house was named for Napoleon's 1805 victory at Austerlitz. If you follow False River Road all the way to the Mississippi River, you will reach a village called Waterloo, the name of the place where Napoleon met his final defeat in 1815.

The light and air and sophisticated color scheme of the ground-level center hall bely its original utilitarian function. Walls are plastered brick, built to withstand the fairly frequent flooding of False River through the nineteenth century. The inverted-bell glass lantern appears to be lit with candlelight, as it might have been 180 years ago. Only the simple plank doors remind one that this is the less formal floor of the house.

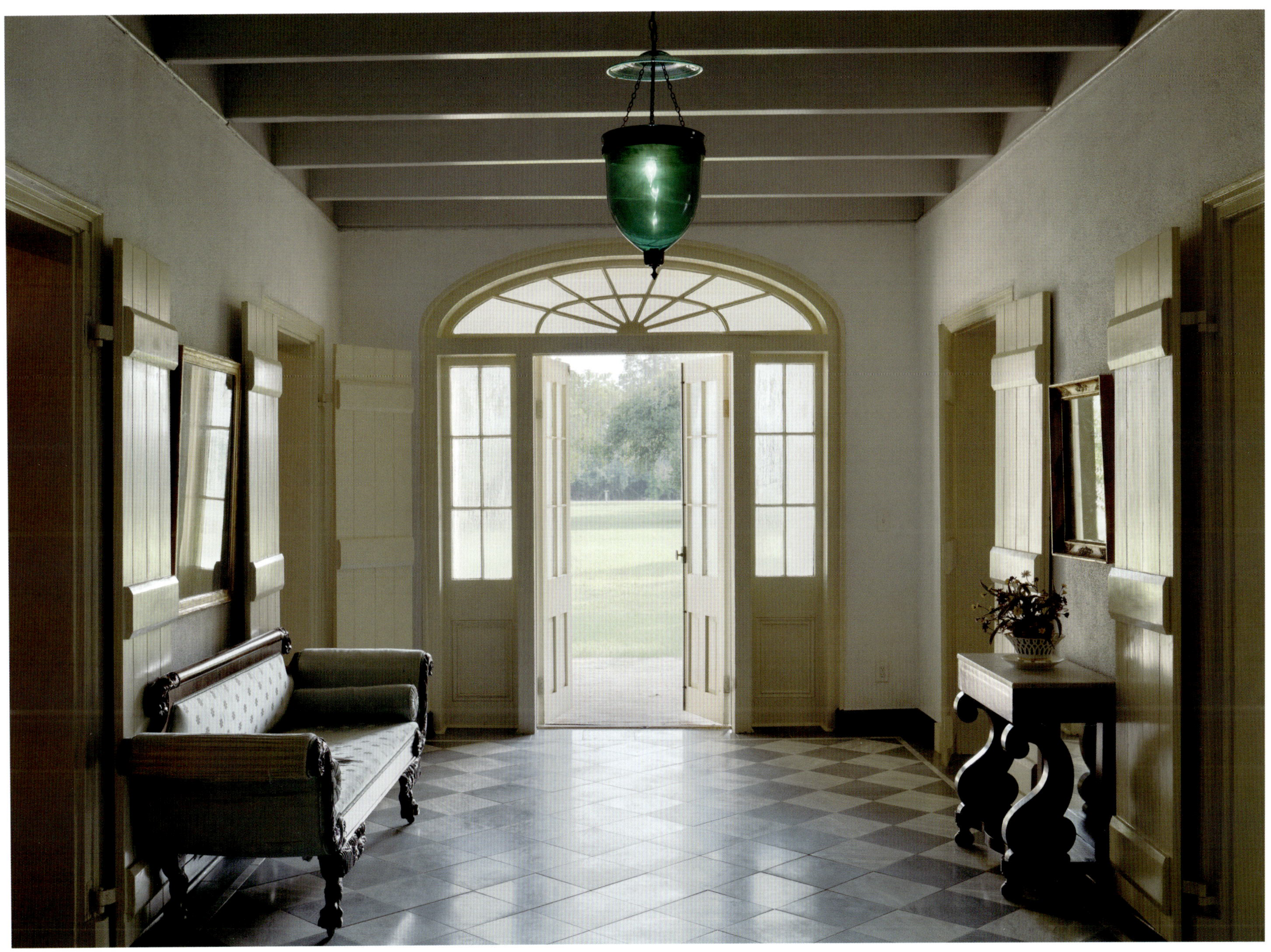

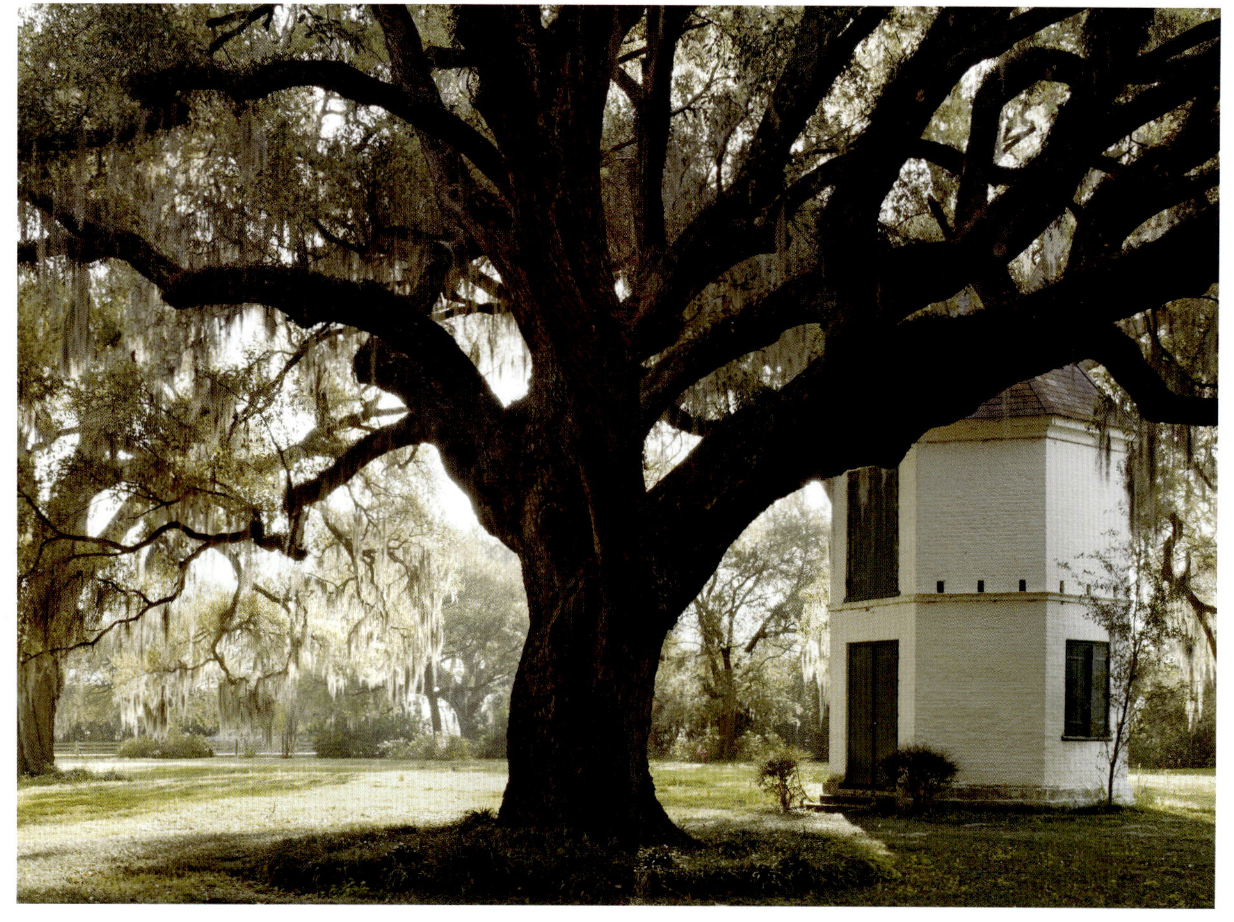

National Historic Landmark
National Register of Historic Places
Historic American Buildings Survey

Parlange's curving drive enters the property in the center of a broad lawn, providing a beautiful view of the *allée* (formal avenue) of cedar and live oak. Two-story brick *pigeonniers* stand in perfect symmetry on either side of Parlange, creating an enchanting view from False River Road. A *pigeonnier* was built to raise squab, or domesticated pigeon, which was a popular food of the French. Serving squab was seen as an indication of wealth. These are the only octagonal *pigeonniers* in Louisiana.

A bronze satyr cavorts on a sugar kettle in a garden designed in part by the Parlanges' friend, landscape designer Steele Burden. Water lily and parrot's feather ornament the surface of the water.

Parlange is one of the finest plantation homes in the South. Surrounded by live oaks and cedar trees draped in Spanish moss, it seems not to have changed much in two hundred years, and conveys a timeless sense of place. In fact, the same family has lived in the house and worked the land for most of the plantation's history. The palpable magic of Parlange is part and parcel of the charm and vivacity of the Parlanges themselves.

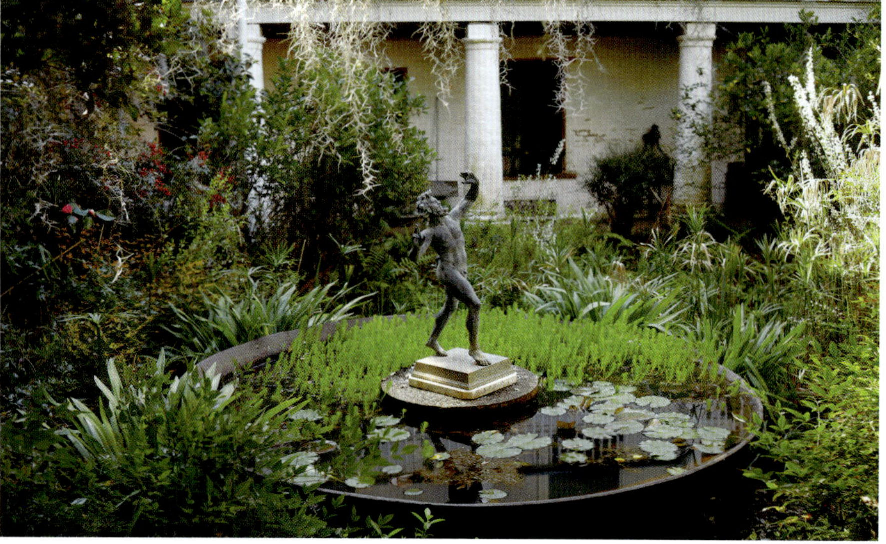

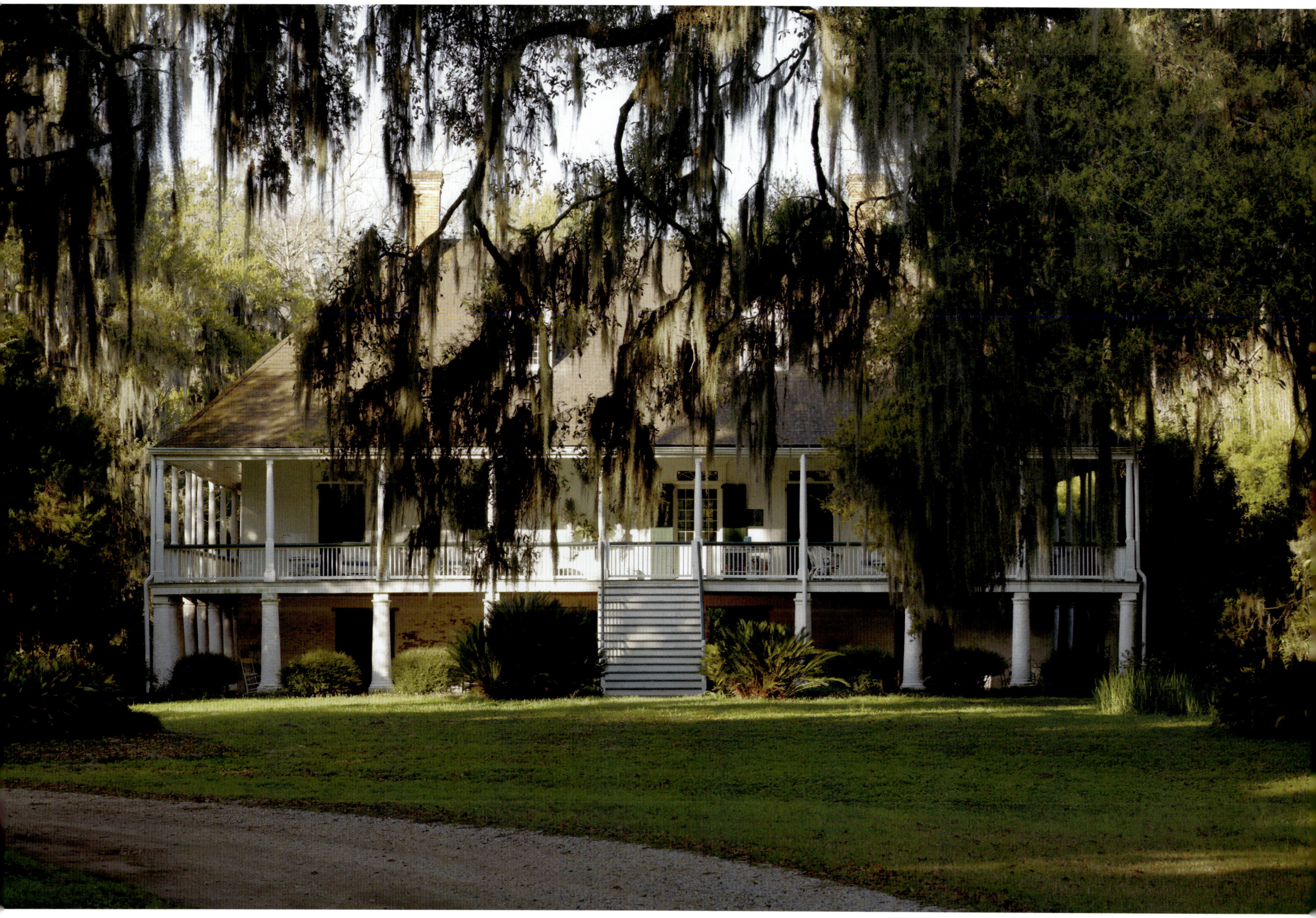

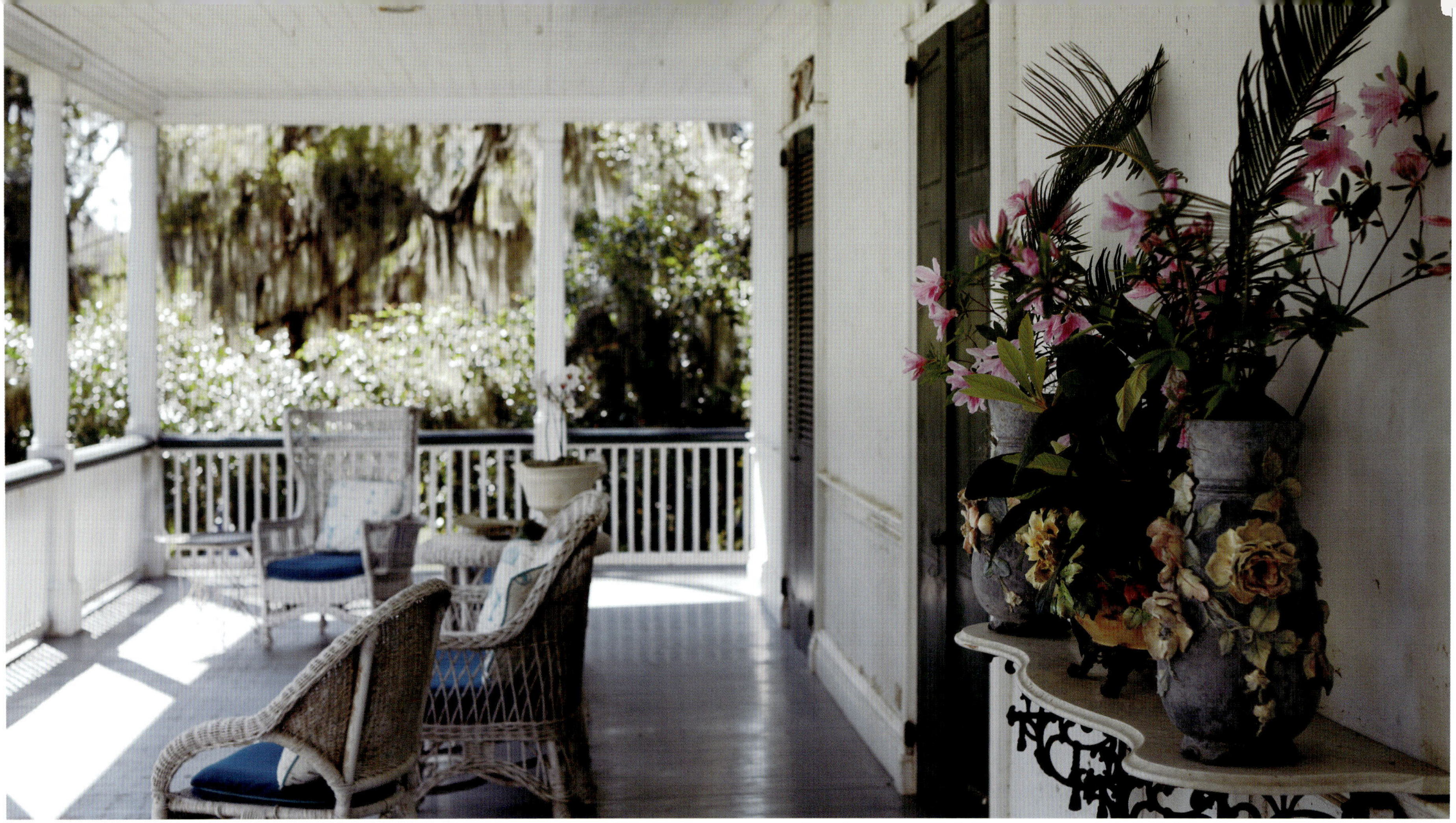

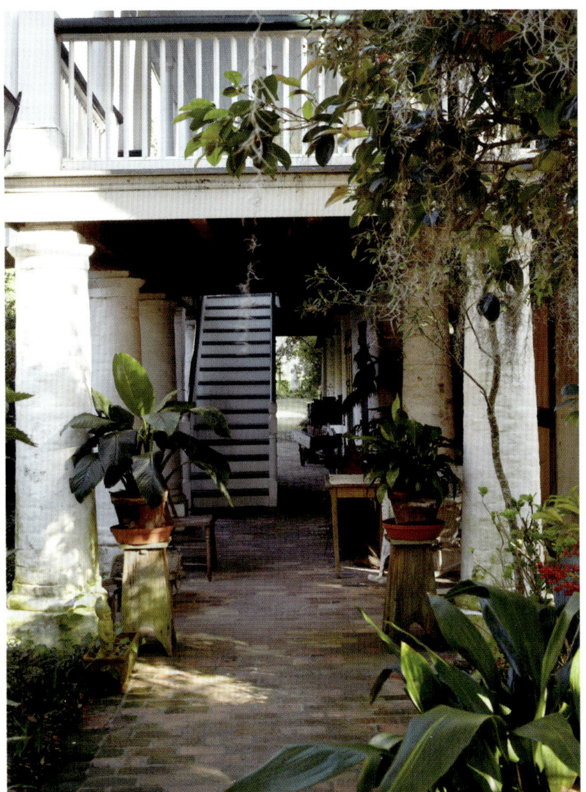

Azalea blooms, sago fronds, and loquat foliage brighten the gallery of Parlange looking out to False River. Upstairs and downstairs, porches encircle the house on all four sides.

As in almost all early French Louisiana houses, the stairs from first to second floor are outdoors on the gallery. The first-floor brick basement is painted with lime wash, a slurry of slaked lime and water traditionally used to protect both brick and wood.

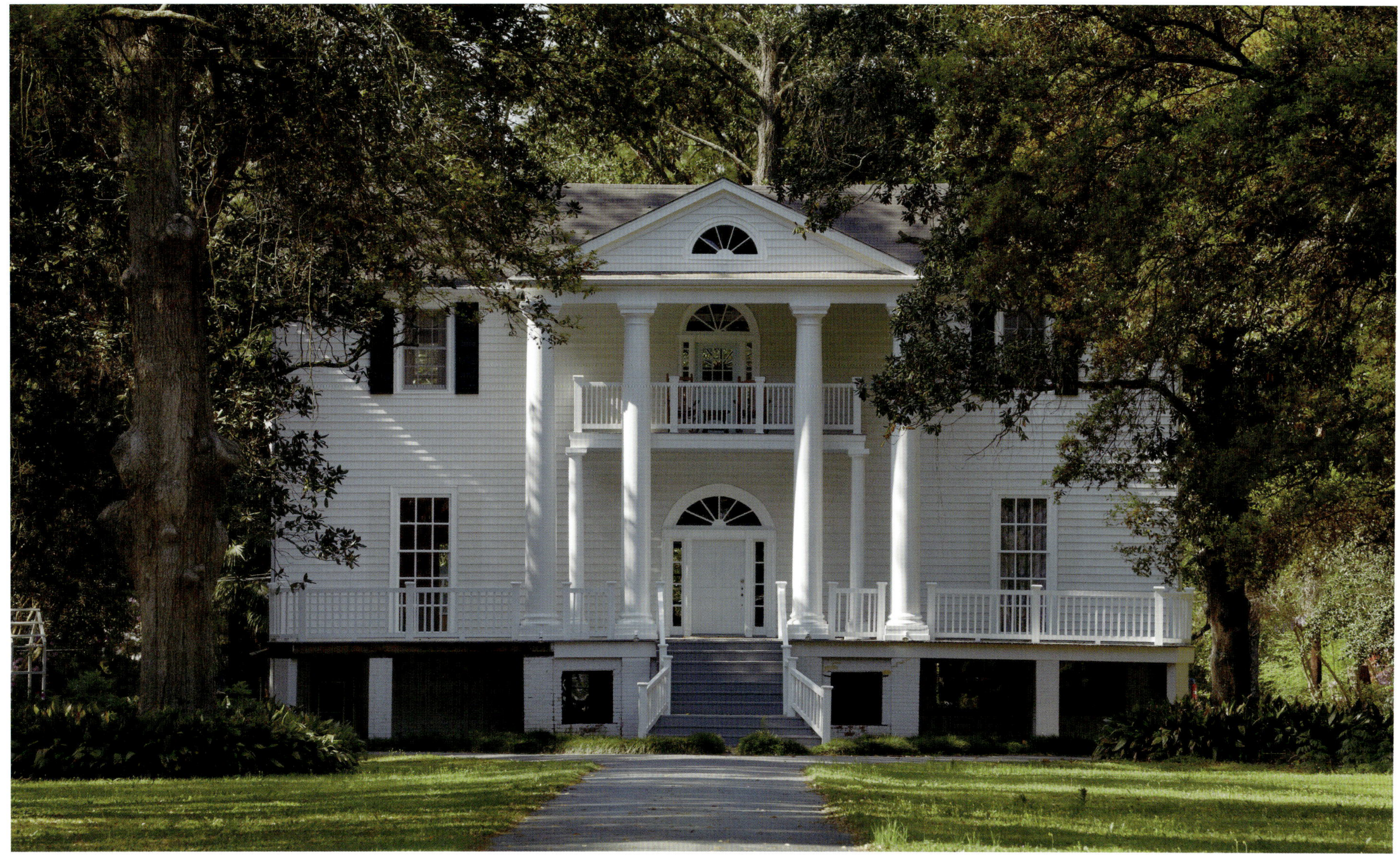

A large Colonial Revival house built in the 1930s stands at the end of a long pecan-and-oak-lined drive off False River Road. It has been known by many names: Seebold Plantation, Allendorph Mansion, and, most recently, *Mon Coeur* (My Heart).

The house was built by Dr. Herman de Bachelle Seebold from New Orleans, the author of *Old Louisiana Plantation Homes and Family Trees* (1941). The house contains antique elements from several important early New Orleans houses: mantels from the old de Marigny home in the faubourg de Marigny, glazed doors from the old de la Chaise plantation house, and other parts of lost plantation homes collected by Dr. Seebold for his fine home in Oscar.

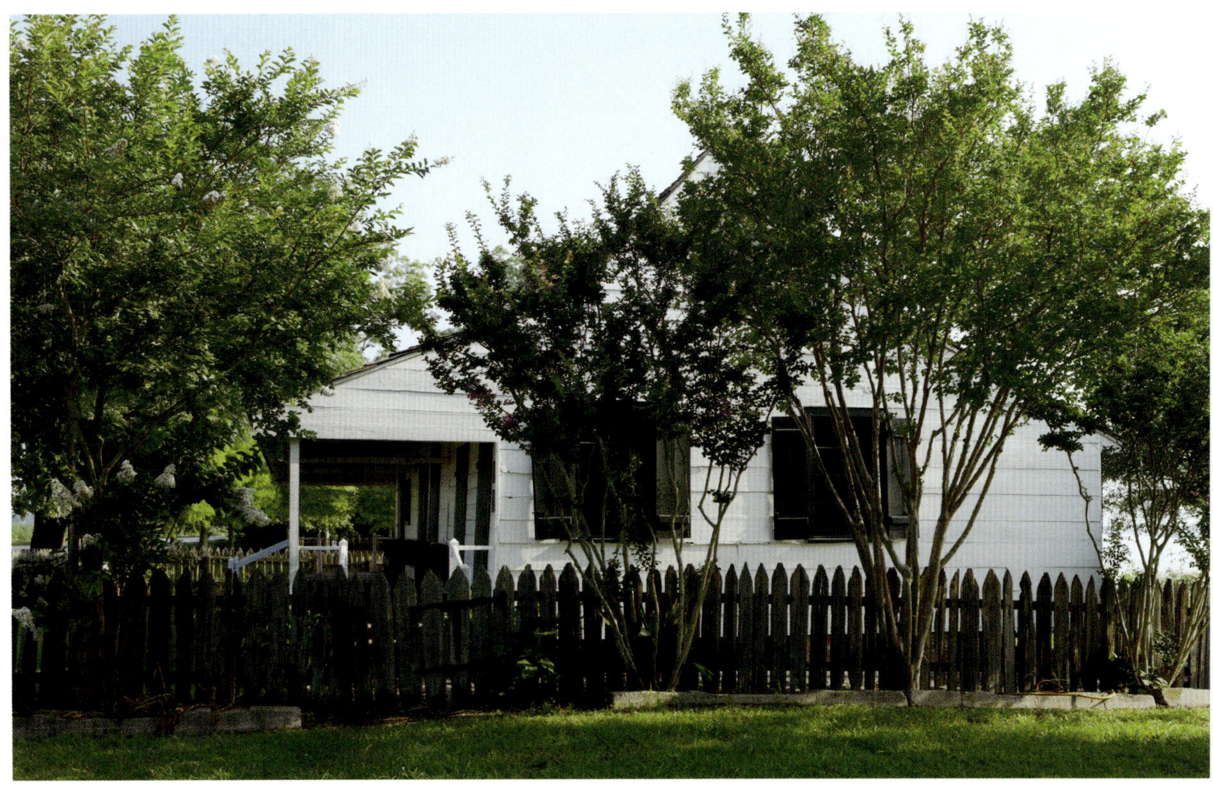

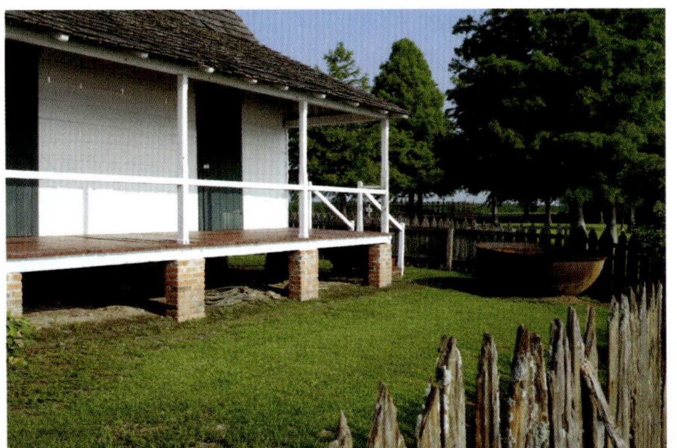

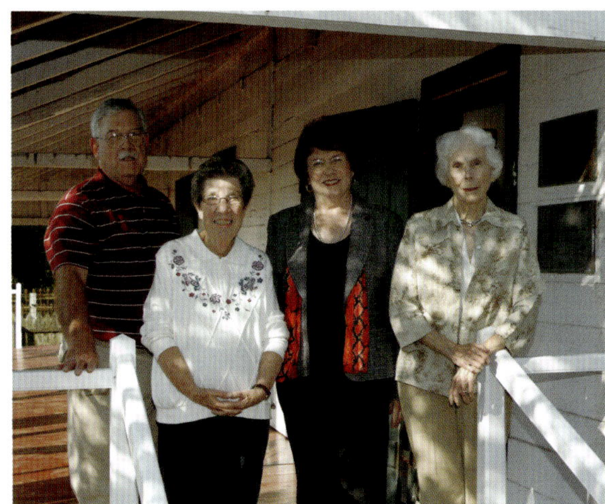

Located on the banks of False River near Parlange, this simple structure built as early as 1800 has had many uses over the past two hundred years. Some speculate it once served as a jail. In 1976, in the spirit of the United States bicentennial, Joanna Wurtele donated it to the parish in honor of her father, Allen Ramsey Wurtele. Here, museum docents greet visitors and tell the history of Pointe Coupee.

An old sugar kettle sits near the back porch of the Pointe Coupee Parish Museum. The rare construction technique of the end shown is more common in French Canada than in Louisiana: *pièce sur pièce,* horizontal planks locked with full dovetail corners.

Four citizens who take an ongoing interest in the Pointe Coupee Parish Museum stand on its front porch: Stu Braud, Winona Sicard, Charlotte Gandy, and Toppy Haag. Miss Winona is a docent; her friends sit on the museum committee for the parish police jury, Pointe Coupee's traditional form of parish government.

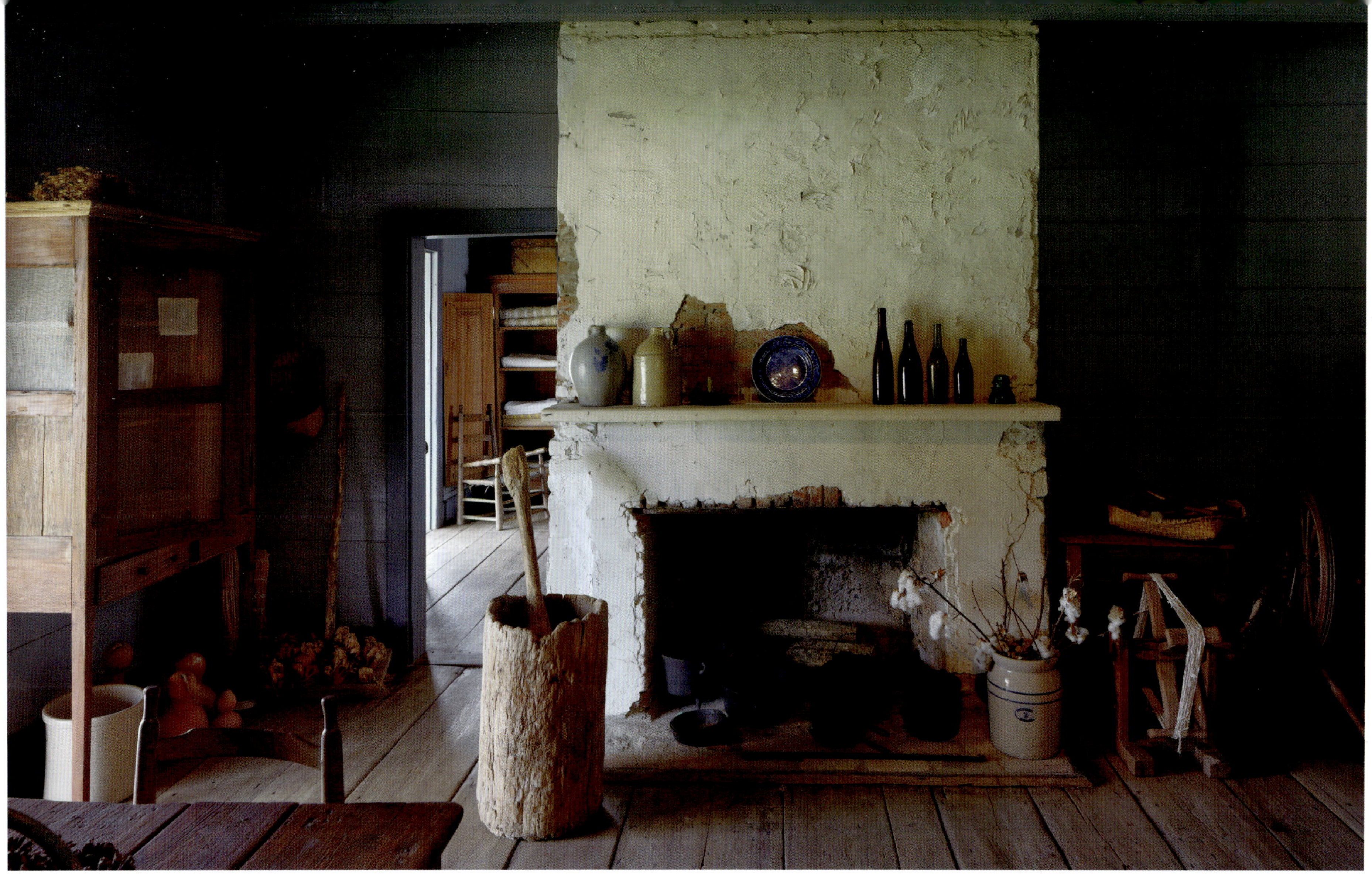

The central fireplace was the only source of heat for this small house during cold winters in the eighteenth and nineteenth centuries. The fabric-covered panels of the *garde-manger* (pie safe) to the left kept insects off fresh-baked foods. The mop close by is made with corn shucks. The *pile et pilon* was used for grinding wheat or corn to make flour or meal. To the right, a spinning wheel sits near the weasel holding a length of cotton yarn.

The blue plate on the mantel is English trans-ferware. Even in French Pointe Coupee, people ate from dishes made in England, for "Brittania ruled the waves" of manufacture and trade throughout the 1800s.

An Acadian coverlet dresses an old cypress bed in the museum. The quilt on the trunk to the left is pieced together with undyed cloth of brown and white cotton, and blue dyed with indigo. At the time this building was constructed, indigo was an important crop grown in the parish.

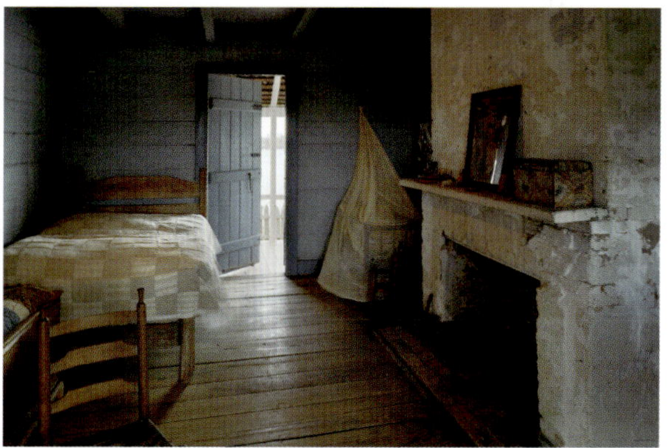

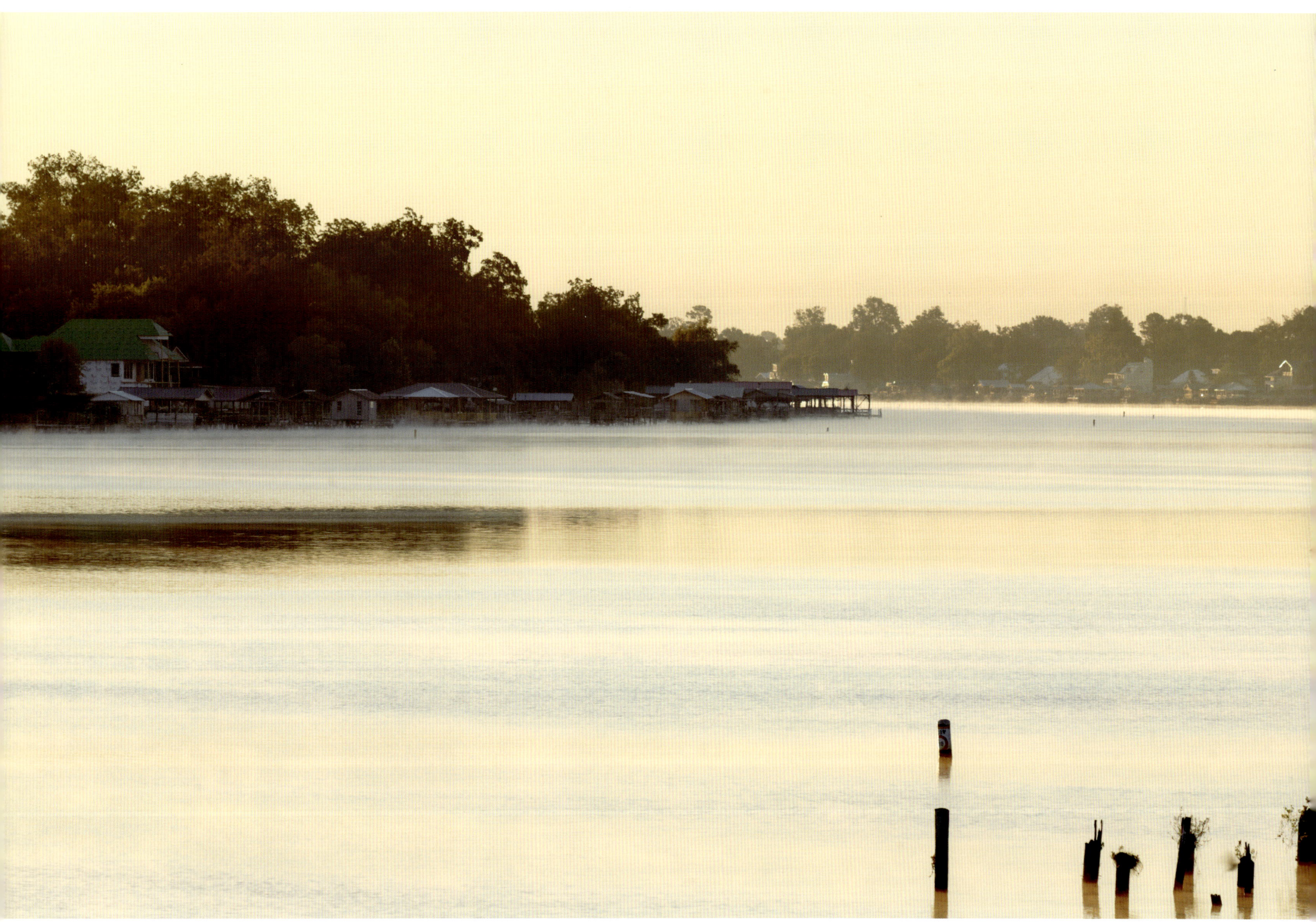

Mist rises from the surface of False River early on a spring morning. False River is a lake about sixteen miles long in roughly the shape of a horseshoe. Before 1700 it was a 22-mile-long meander bend of the Mississippi River. Once the river changed its course, it began to flow past the old channel, and the river became a lake. Within a few years the channel at either end of the lake began to fill with silt and debris. Areas of the *chenal* (channel) were kept open for water access. For a long time plantations on False River used the lake and the chenals to transport their produce to the Mississippi. This process required portage, carrying the product across dry ground from the edge of the lake to the river.

Today the lake is primarily recreational. Boats with or without water skiers share the lake with fishermen, kayakers, and folks enjoying the view from the dock. About 20 feet deep generally, False River reaches depths of 65 feet in the middle. Near the ends, "the flats" are shallow enough to walk across. Fishermen catch bass, bream, and catfish as a rule. Public fishing docks are located in downtown New Roads near the public boat launch, just below City Hall. Feeding the ducks is popular sport there, too.

Camps and docks line the banks of False River. Small cottages sit next to mobile homes and McMansions in the democratic tradition of American homeownership. Every house has its piece of the waterfront and its view across what used to be the Mississippi River.

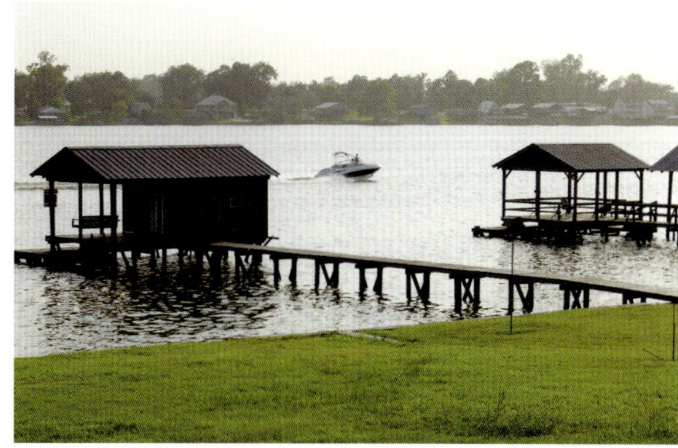

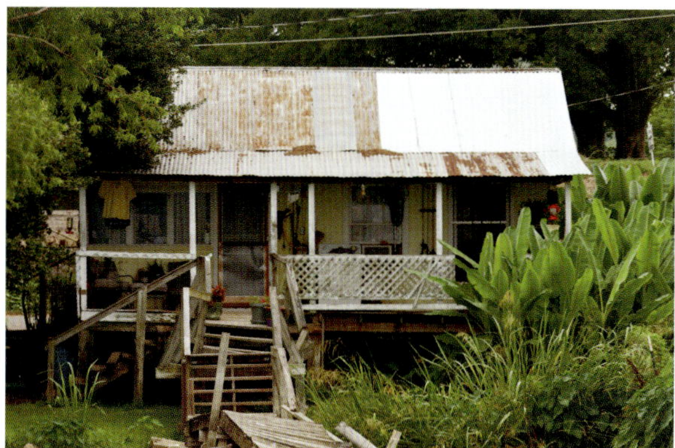

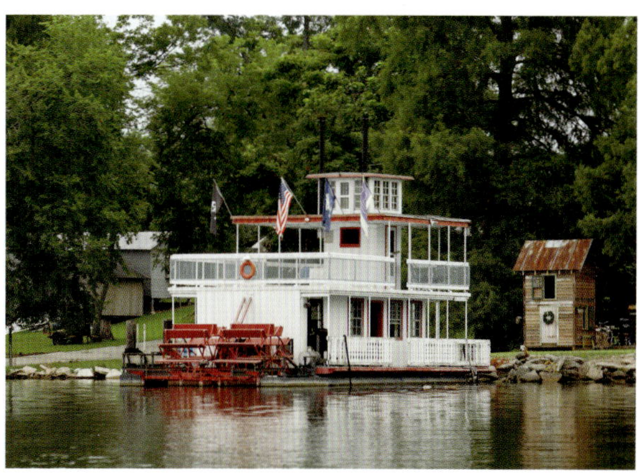

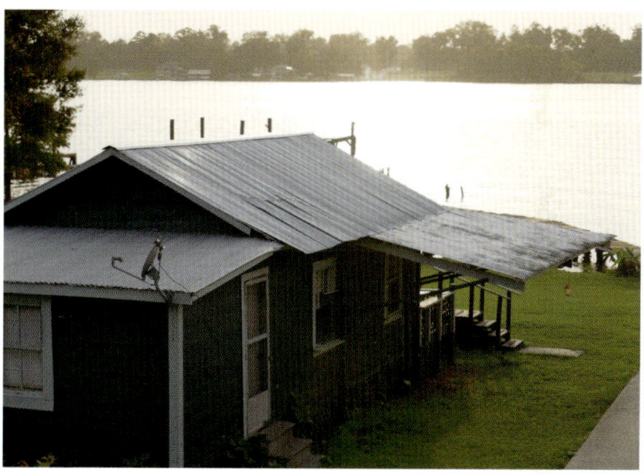

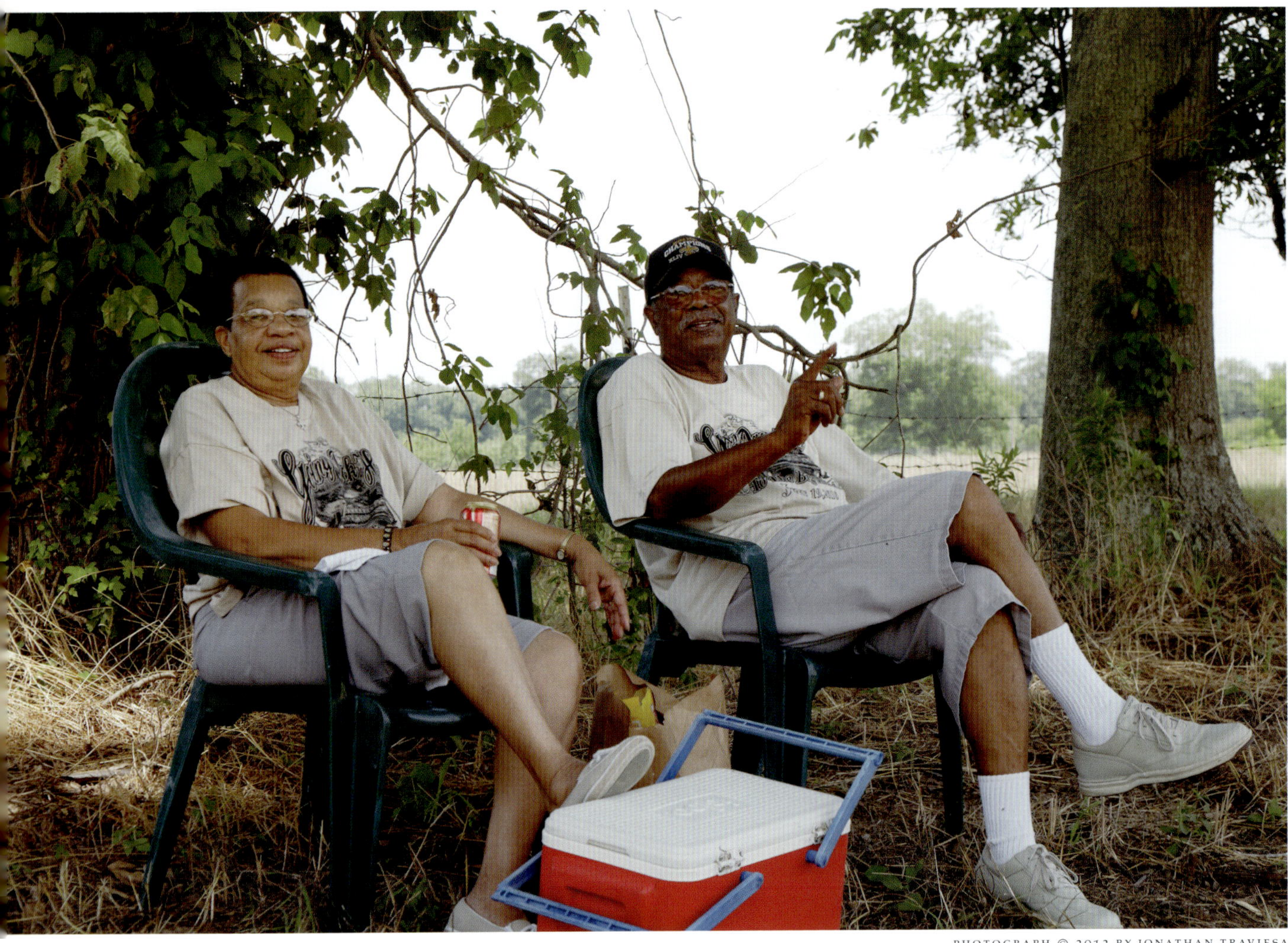

PHOTOGRAPH © 2012 BY JONATHAN TRAVIESA

Annamora and Jesse Joseph enjoy a pleasant day catching up with friends at the Island Family Reunion, a reunion of not one family but all the people who grew up on "the Island." They like to get together. It's part of the culture.

Today the Island is connected by land to the mainland at both ends of False River, but when the oxbow was first cut off, the Island had water all the way around it.

Islanders enjoy a day of fun: Alton Warr and friends; Heisman and Chenette Cador, Gloria He-bert Cador; Charles Joseph; Chad Barrios, James "Big Brown" Joseph, and Lane Ewing.

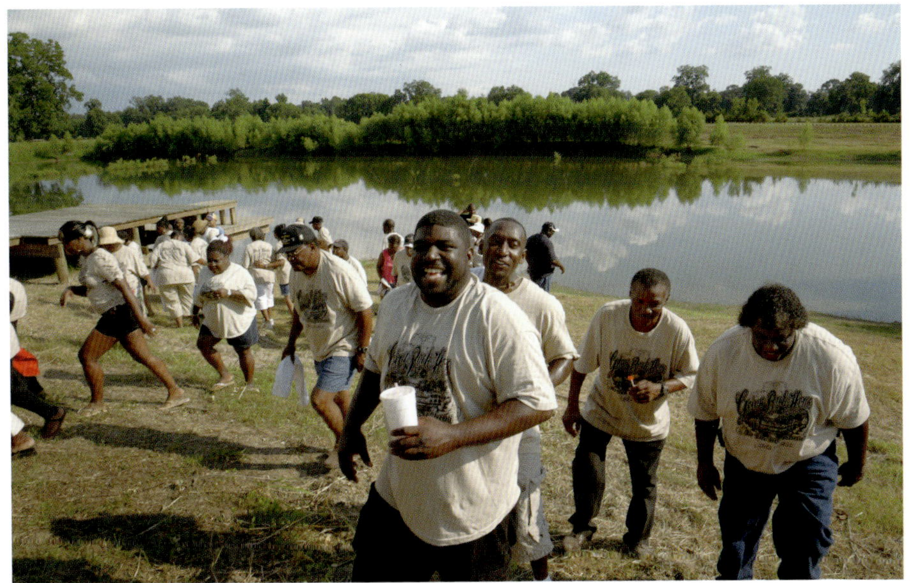

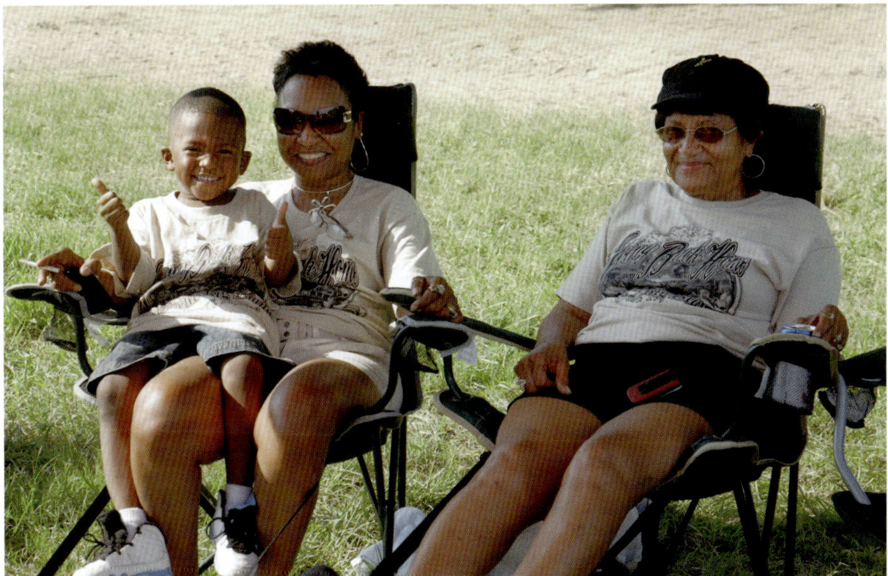

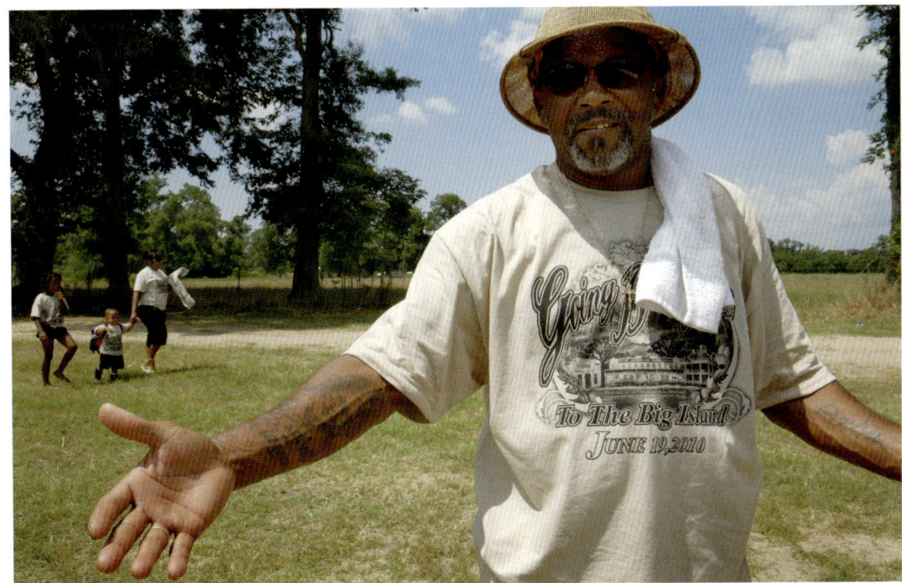

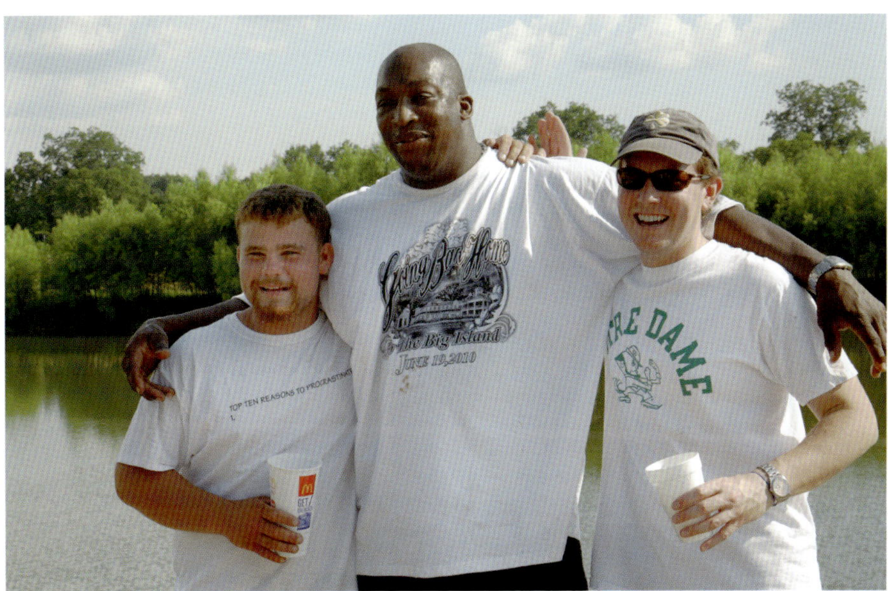

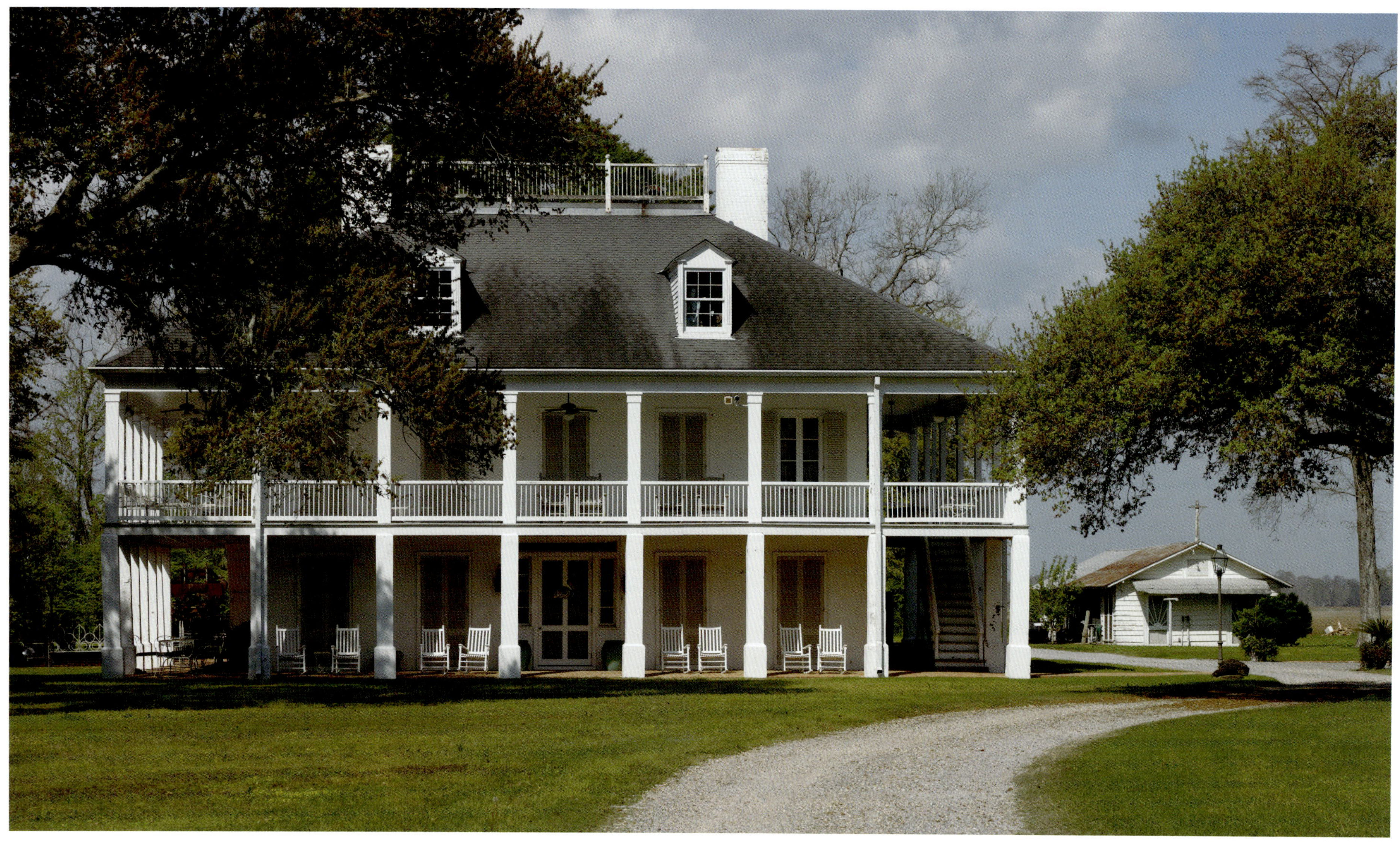

Ramsey was built in 1944 by Allen Ramsey Wurtele, a planter, inventor, and author. The house sits on the site of Wurtele's previous house, the 1860 New Olivo House, which was struck by lightning and burned to the ground in 1944. Wurtele owned the property from 1927, and is remembered as the inventor of the mechanical sugarcane harvester. His daughter, Joanna Wurtele, lives in the house today.

In 1958 Hollywood found Pointe Coupee. Director Martin Ritt brought a brilliant cast, including Paul Newman and Joanne Woodward, to Ramsey to film scenes for a movie based on stories by William Faulkner. *The Long, Hot Summer* was the resulting film.

The vapor trail of a jet airplane seems far away in time and space from the misty fields of Ramsey.

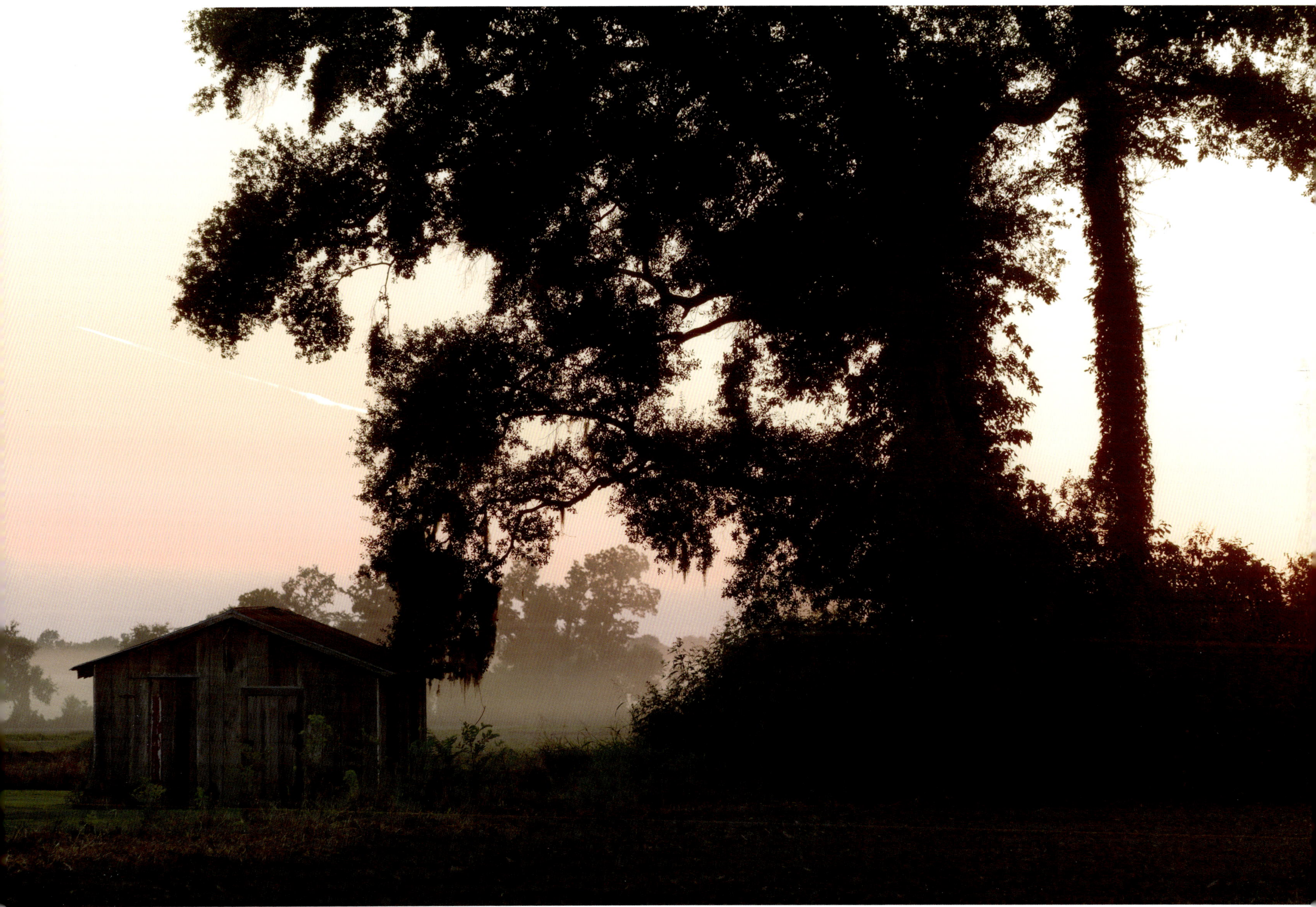

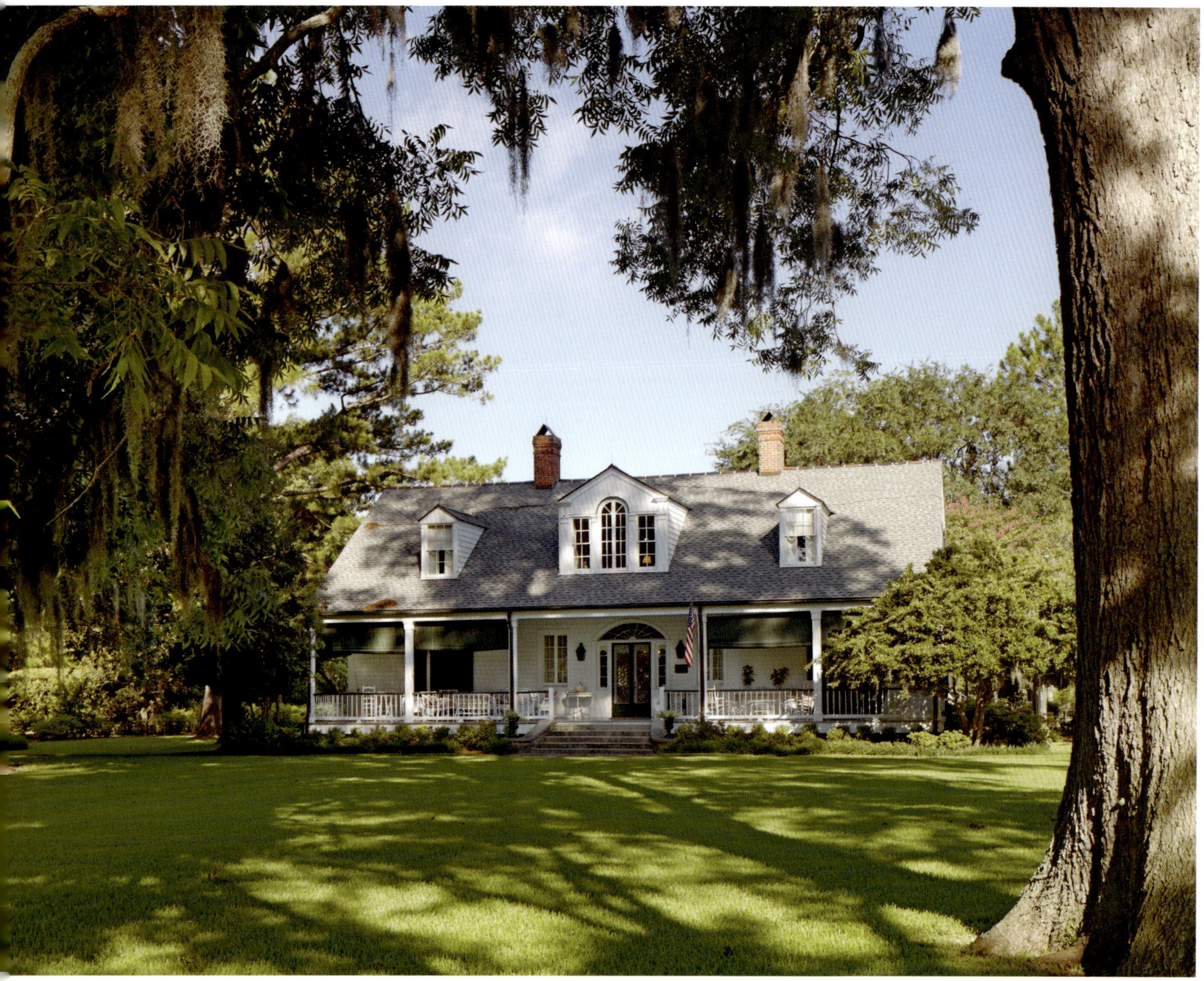

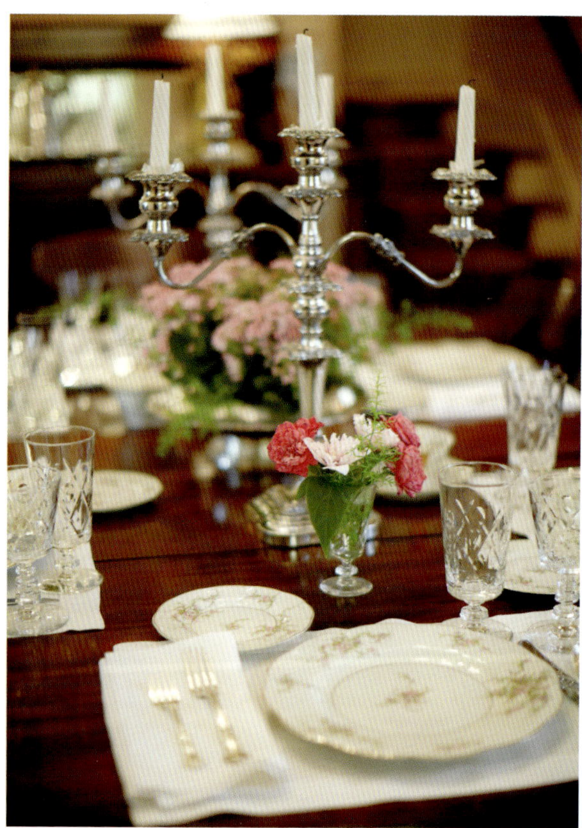

Bonnie Glen was built about 1830 by Antoine Gosserand. In 1935 his great-grandson, Louis Henry Gosserand, renovated the house in the Colonial Revival style, adding the fanlight over leaded-glass doors and three handsome dormers. Bonnie Glen has remained in the same family since the land was purchased in 1805.

Jeanne Curet James, sixth generation to Bonnie Glen, set the 1865 table with her grandmother's china and crystal and flowers cut from her garden.

In Louisiana, the dining table has long held an important place in the hearts of the people. Visit-

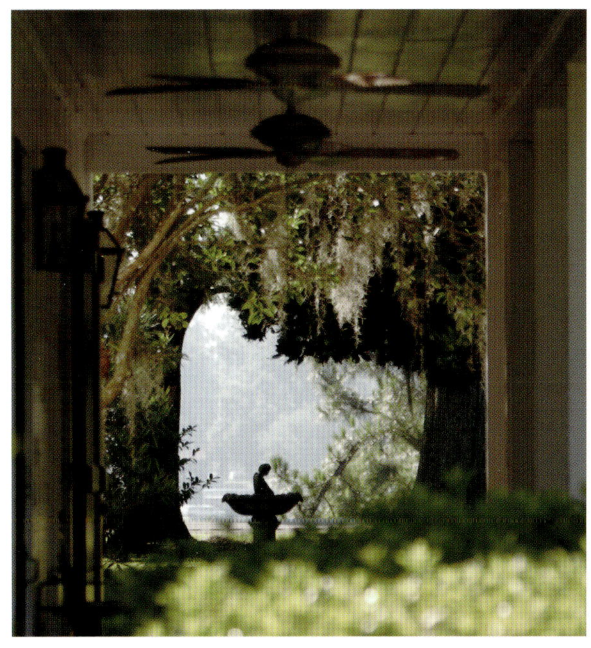

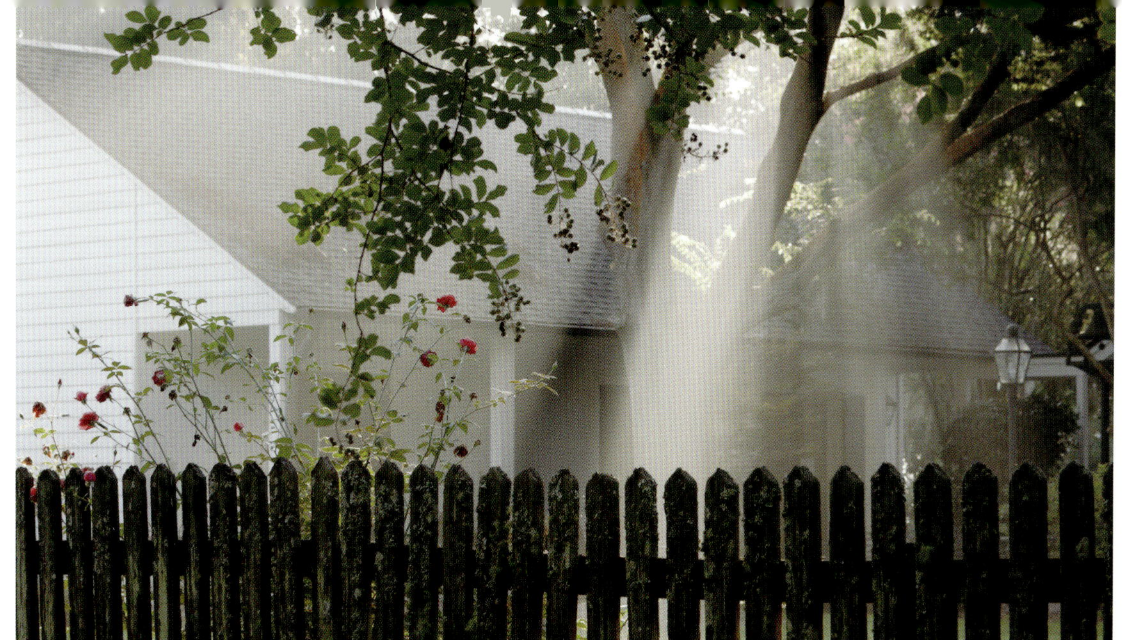

ing from his native France in 1803, C. C. Robin, author of *Voyage to Louisiana, 1803–1805*, wrote that Pointe Coupee meals were served with a European opulence he found astonishing in light of the pioneer nature of the community.

Bonnie Glen looks out over False River.

Morning sun filters through crape myrtle at Bonnie Glen.

A slave cabin behind Bonnie Glen has been preserved, and is one of the last standing in the parish.

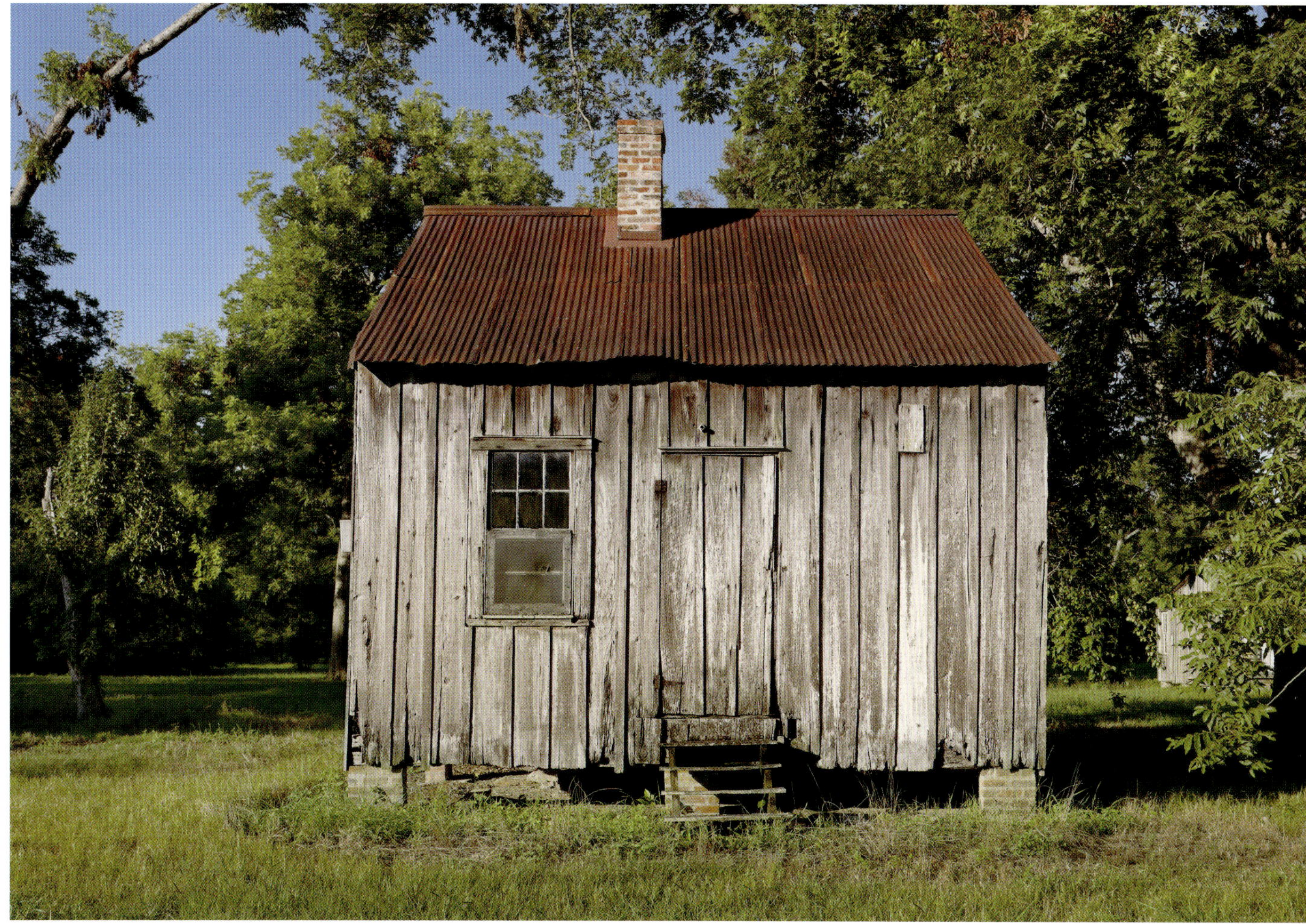

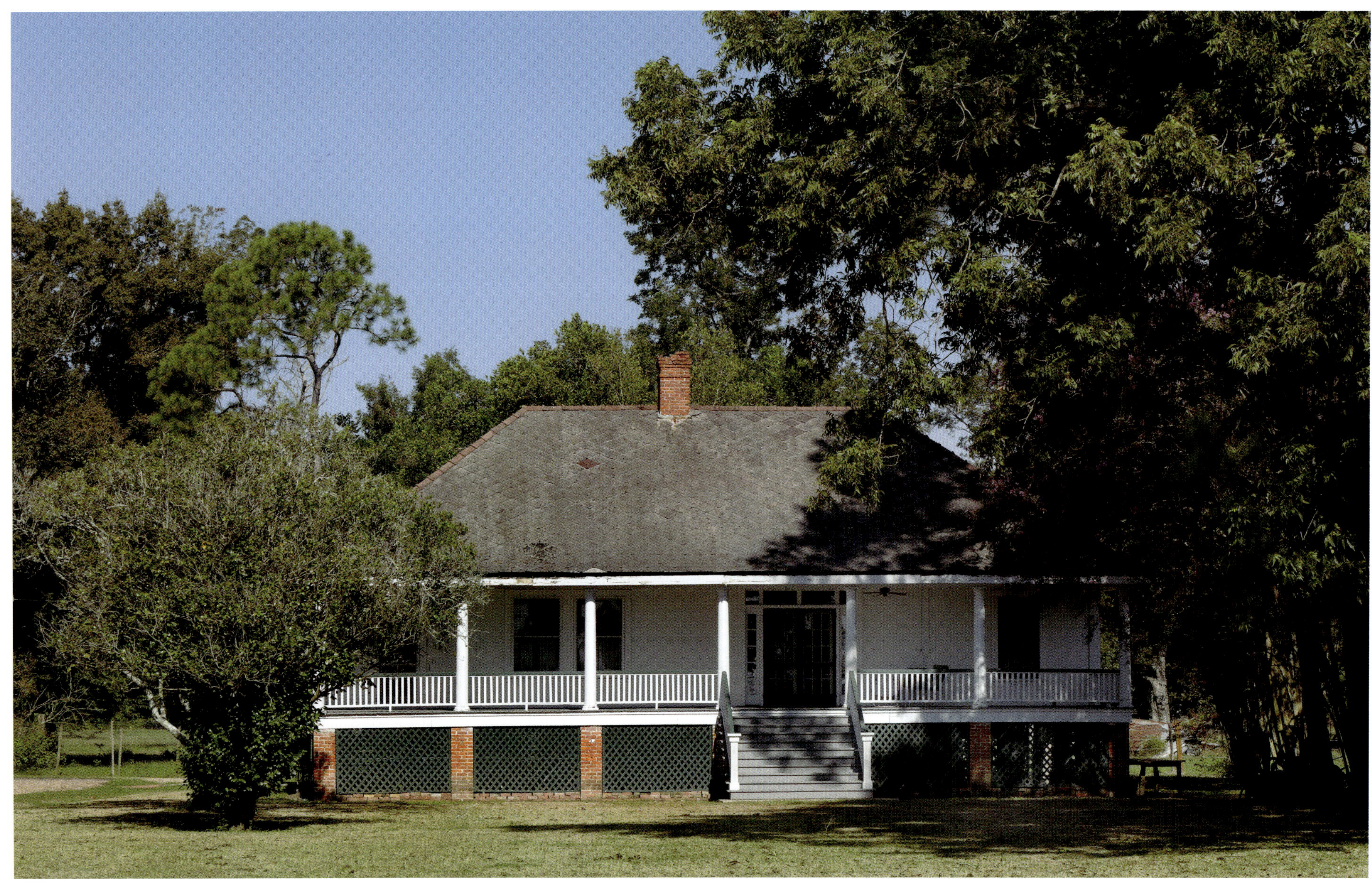

Striking in its handsome simplicity, the Hurst House was built in 1854 by Villeneuve Bergeron, one of fourteen children of Valerien and Marie St. Cyr Bergeron. With its big hip roof, full front gallery, and asymmetrically placed windows and doors, the house is a lovely late example of a Creole raised cottage. Behind the brick piers that hold up the gallery are hidden large cypress logs stacked on their sides to support the floor of the house.

The old barn that sits in the field next to the Hurst House is also an antebellum building dating to 1854.

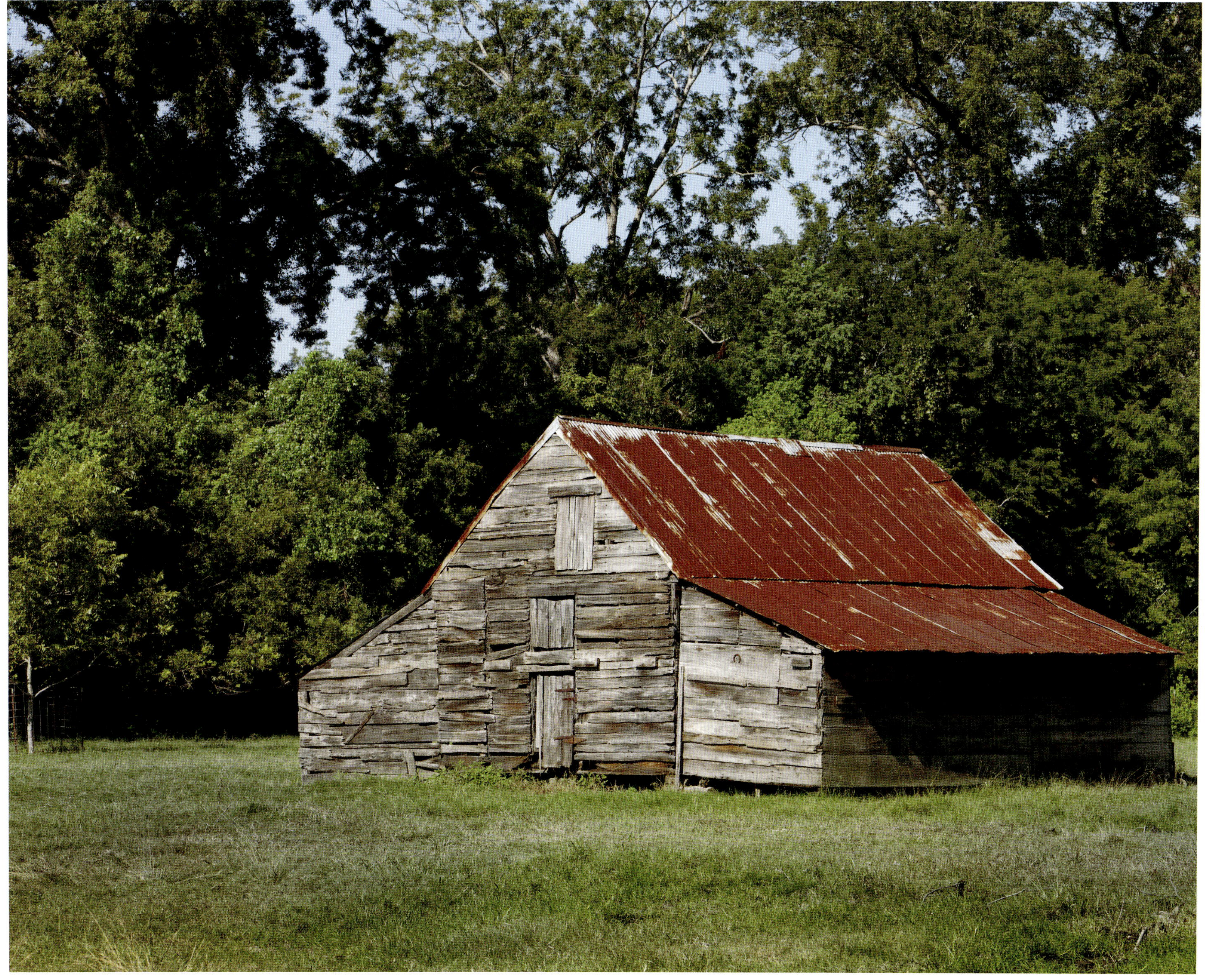

The most massive live oak in the parish, and one of the largest in the South, has been known by three names over three centuries: the Poydras Oak, the Maryland Oak, and the Randall Oak. It was first known as the Poydras Oak in honor of Poydras College. At his death in 1824, Julien Poydras left an endowment in his will to open an academy of higher learning in Pointe Coupee. Poydras College opened in 1833. By 1836 its main building was complete, located on False River just behind the enormous oak.

A young instructor from Maryland, James Ryder Randall, came to teach English and the classics at Poydras College in 1861, the year the American Civil War began. The battle of Fort Sumter began on April 12. One week later, the Baltimore Riot erupted. In a violent confrontation with Union soldiers from Massachusetts on Pratt Street in Baltimore, twelve civilians and four soldiers were killed. Some historians call it the first bloodshed of the Civil War.

When Randall learned of the death of a friend in the riot, he was moved to write the poem "Maryland, My Maryland." He composed it overnight in his room at Poydras College. Set to the tune of the German "O Tannenbaum," it became a popular Confederate anthem sung throughout the war. Long after the Civil War, in 1939, the song was adopted as Maryland's state song, and is still so today.

In the twentieth century a monument was erected by the Book Club of Pointe Coupee to commemorate James Ryder Randall and his poem written at Poydras College. By then there was little left of the old school. The main building had burned in 1881, but the grand oak lived on. In 1938 Louis Henry Gosserand, who lived at Bonnie Glen, gave the keynote address at the commemoration ceremony, accompanied by his young nephews Bernard and Louis Curet.

In 2011, at the 150th anniversary of the creation of "Maryland, My Maryland," the original monument was remounted and repositioned under the branches of the Randall Oak. The same Book Club that erected the original monument rededicated it in a ceremony attended by several hundred people—including Louis Curet and others who had been there in 1938: Toppy Smith Haag, Pauline Bondy Hernandez, Pat Olinde Laurent, and Charles Serio.

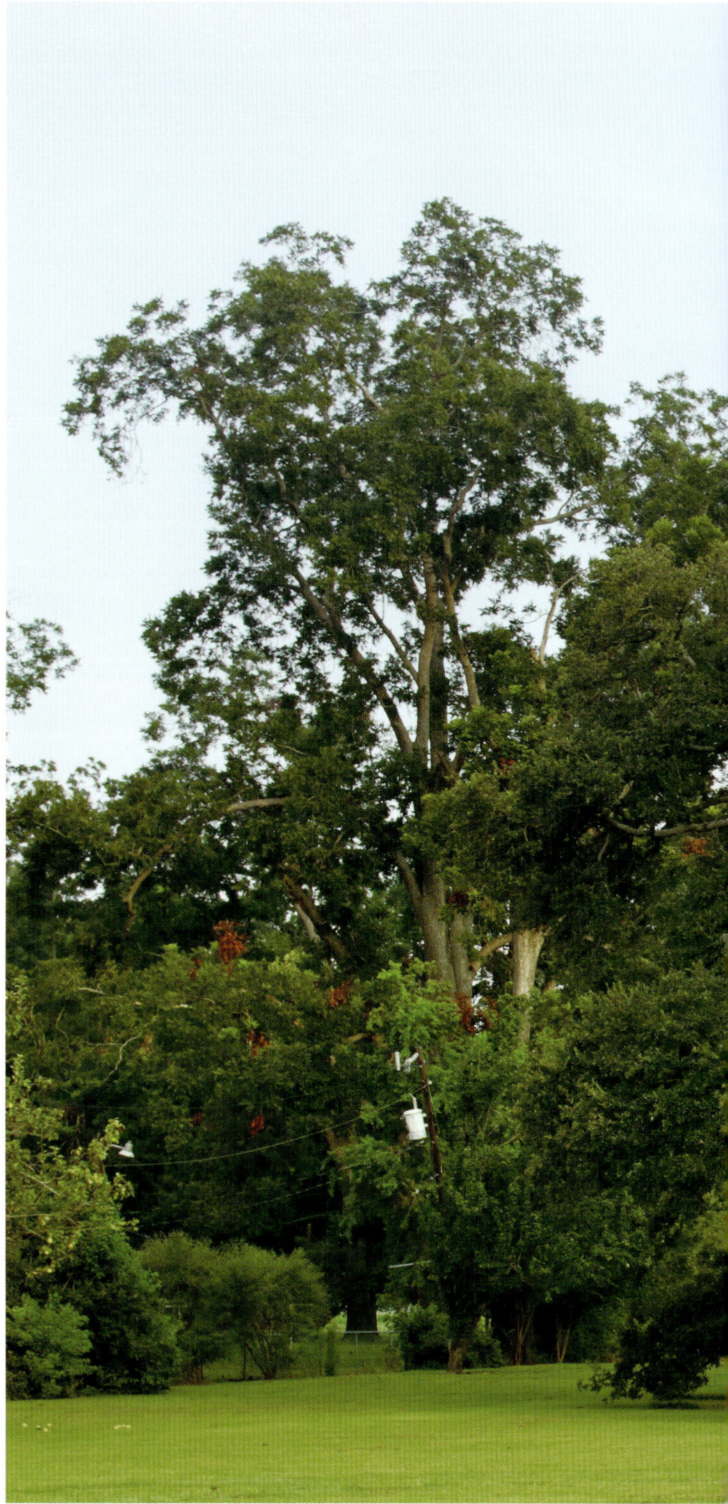

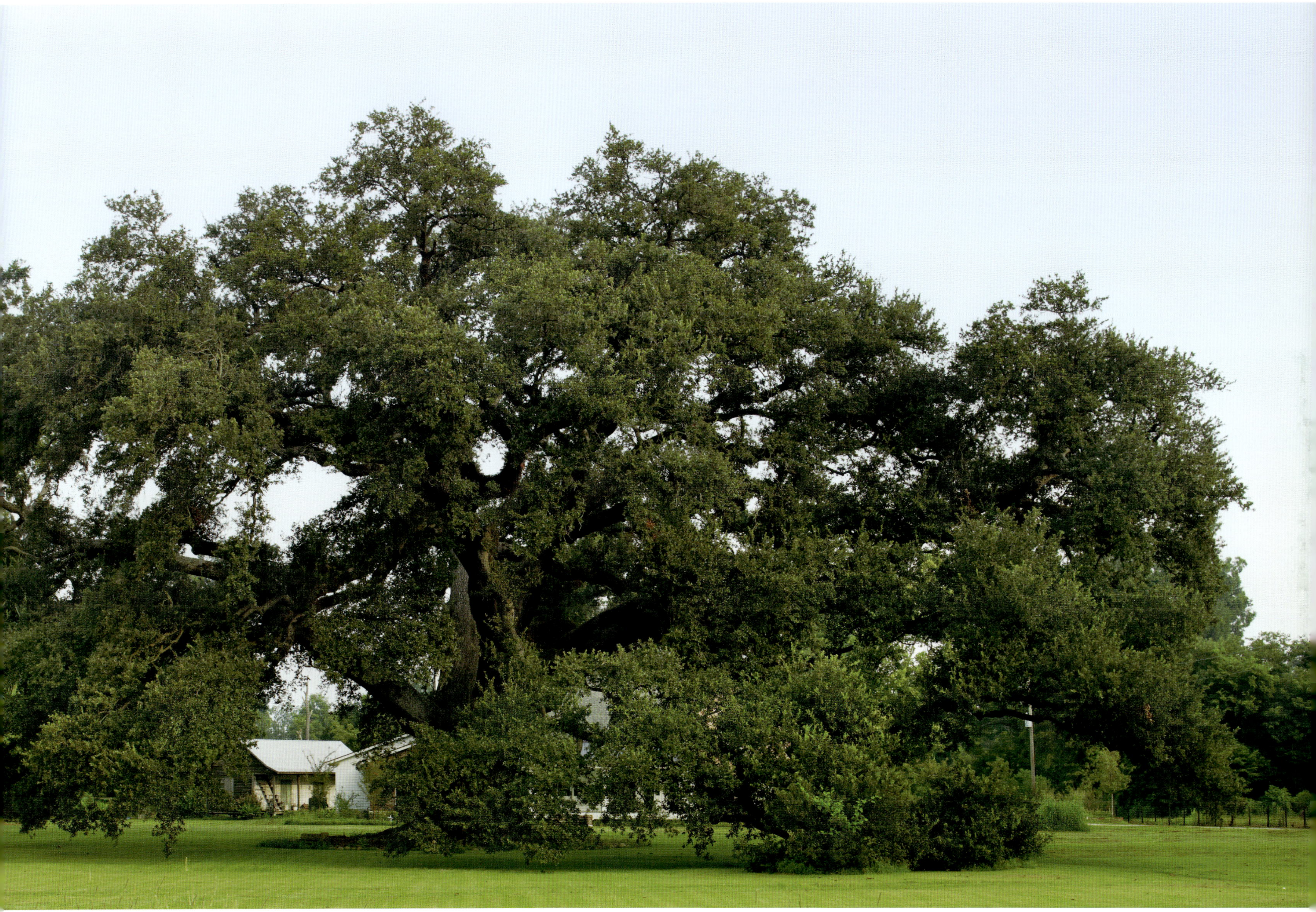

Jynell Glaser visits with a customer at the Glaser's produce stand on False River Road. She and her husband Charles, known as "Brother," make it easy for folks in Pointe Coupee to "eat local." They grow more than thirty kinds of fruits and vegetables on their 25-acre truck farm. The Glasers were some of the first farmers to take their produce to the Red Stick Farmers Market in Baton Rouge, helping to create a very successful and well-known weekend event.

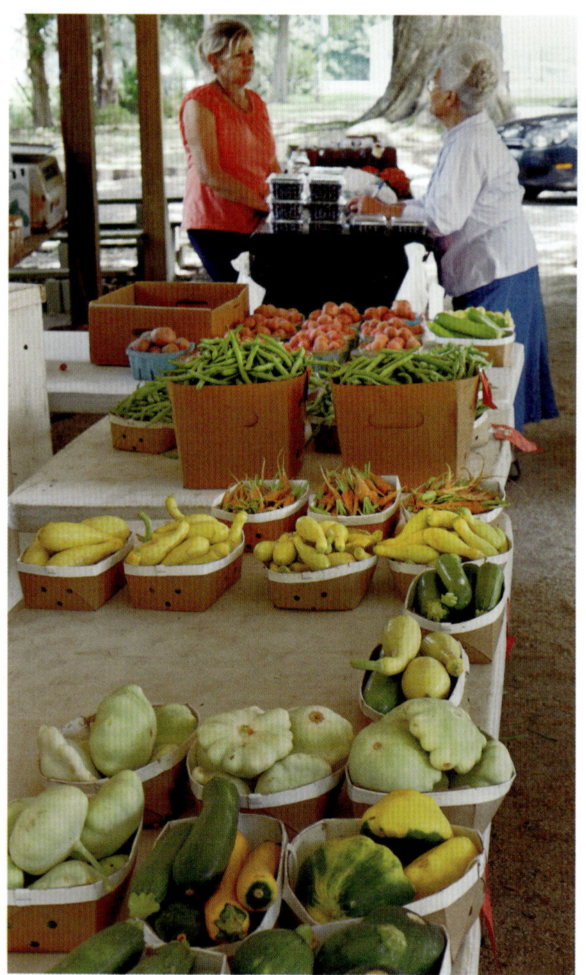

Employees of Bergeron Pecans sort and pack shelled pecans for shipping all over the world. Founded by Horace Joseph Bergeron, the plant has been family owned and operated since 1910. The modern facility was built in 1941. The third generation of Bergerons now working in the business are proud of the fact that they have never advertised. The success of Bergeron Pecans has been built over the past hundred years entirely by word of mouth.

The pecan is a North American tree that grows in abundance along Louisiana's Red River, especially in Creole country between Natchitoches and Pointe Coupee. Old trees can be as tall as 120 feet, and many still produce nuts. Modern orchards are planted with grafted varieties, usually selected for growth habit, size, and flavor. The annual yield of pecans in Pointe Coupee—some years as high as nine million pounds—is often the largest in the state.

Fresh pecans from orchards all over the parish fill bins outside the shelling plant during fall harvest season.

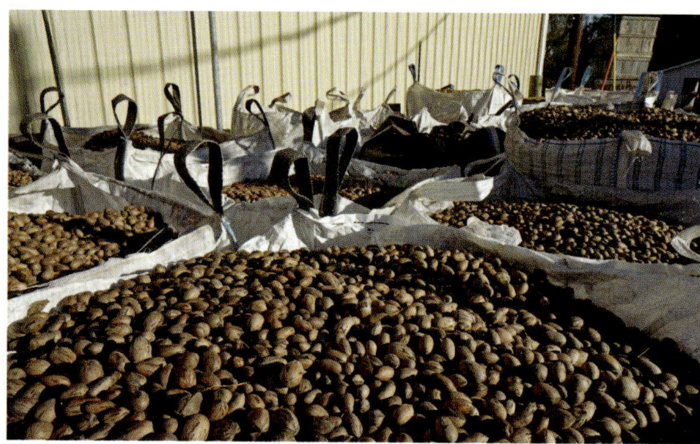

PHOTOGRAPH © 2012 BY JONATHAN TRAVIESA

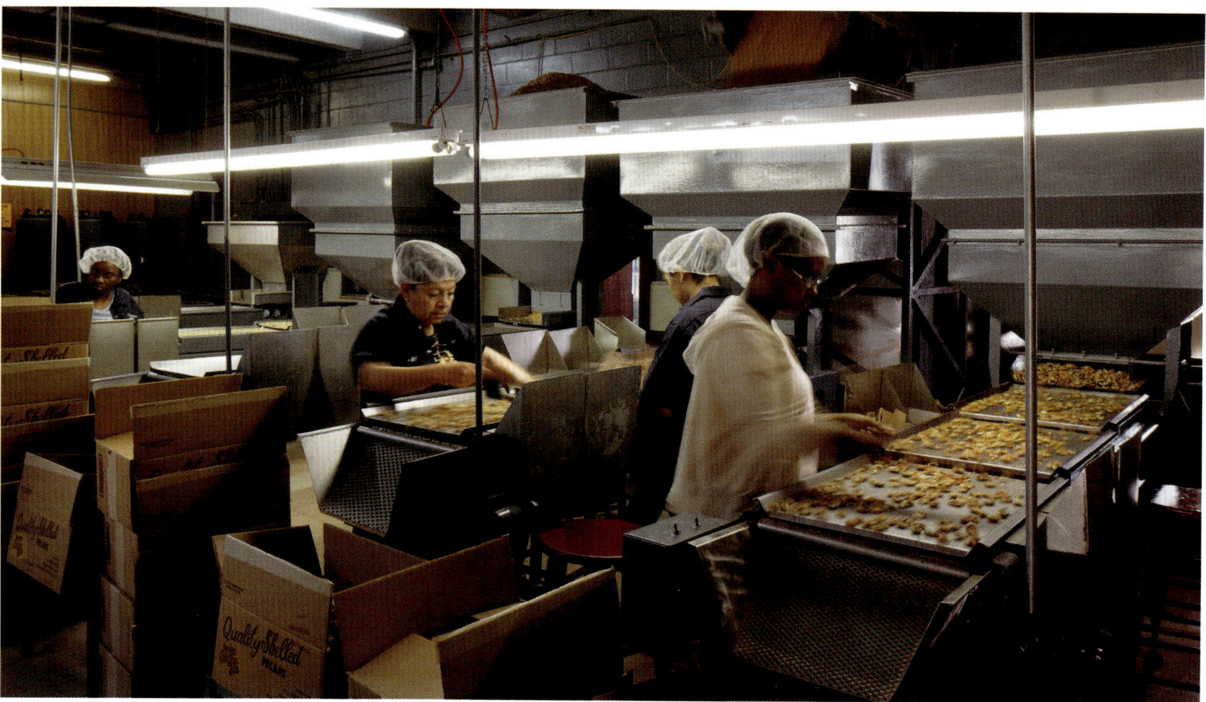

PHOTOGRAPH © 2012 BY JONATHAN TRAVIESA

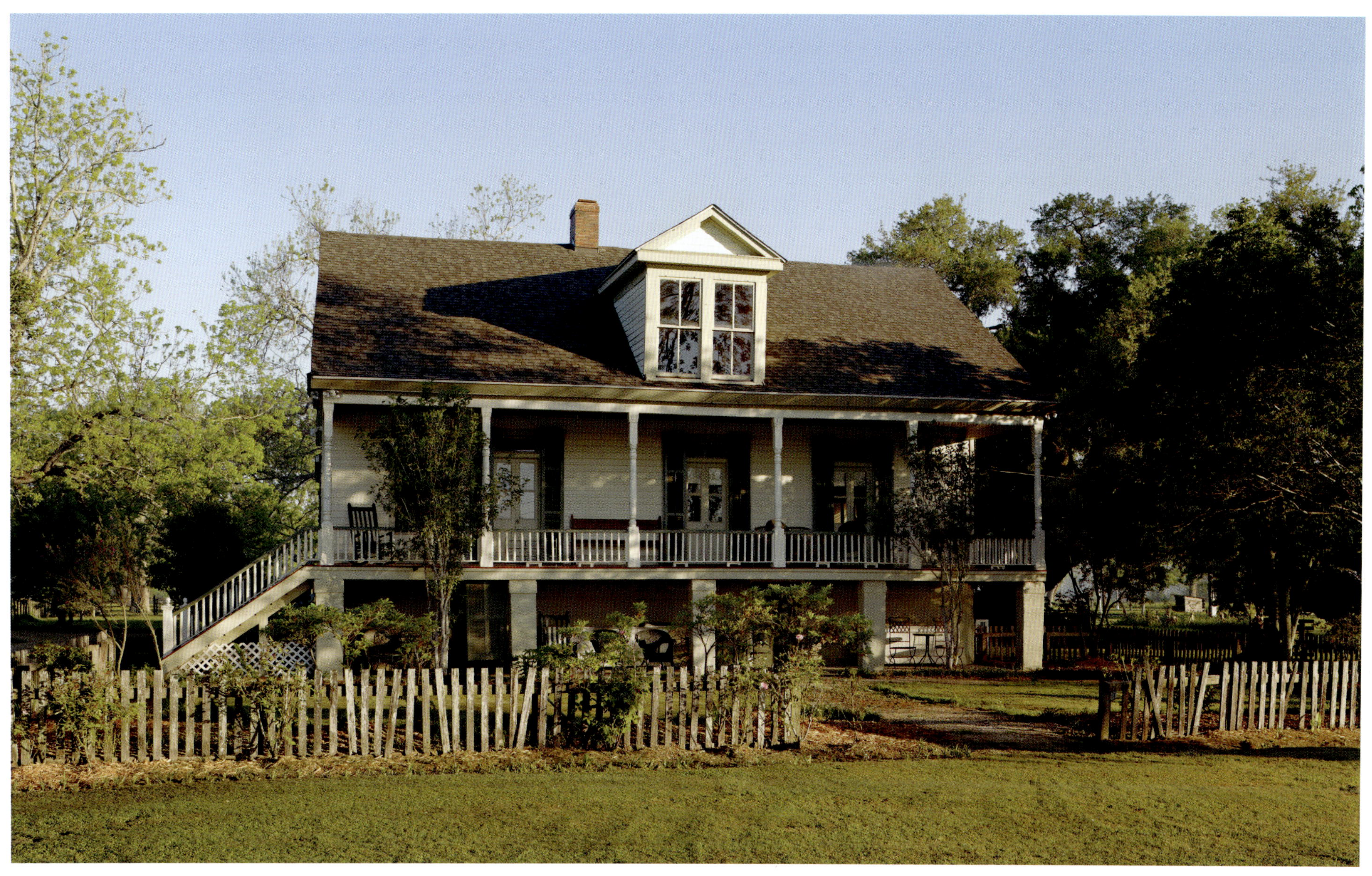

Mon Rêve, "My Dream" in French, was built about 1850 for Valerien and Marie St. Cyr Bergeron. The Bergerons were the parents of fourteen children. Many of the couple's descendants still live in the parish. Today, Mon Rêve is operated as a bed-and-breakfast.

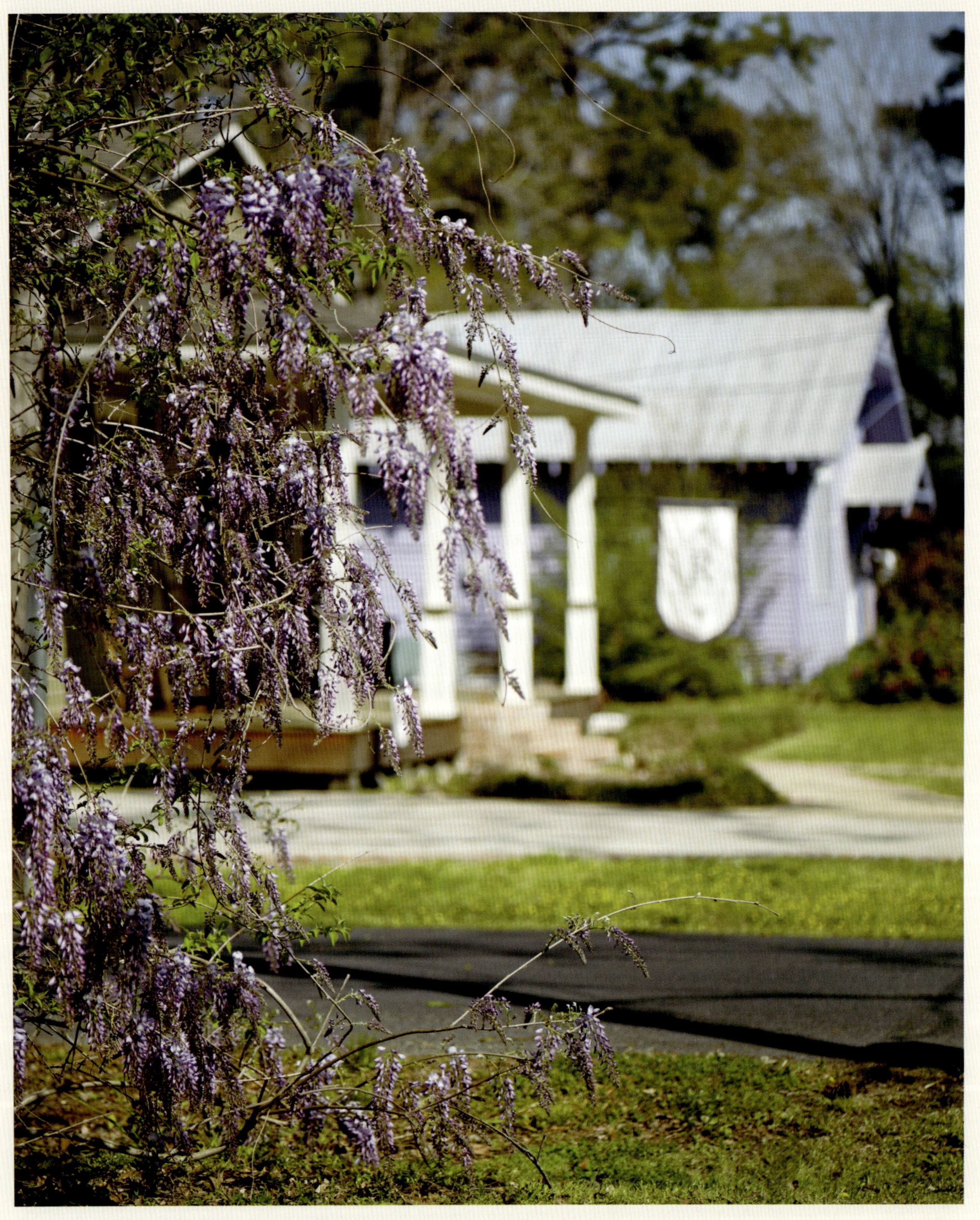

CHAPTER 4

The New Road and New Roads

Main Street runs along the natural bank of False River through the town of New Roads, the parish seat, with a population of around five thousand residents.

The courthouse is at bottom left of this picture. The old plantation home in the center is the LeJeune House.

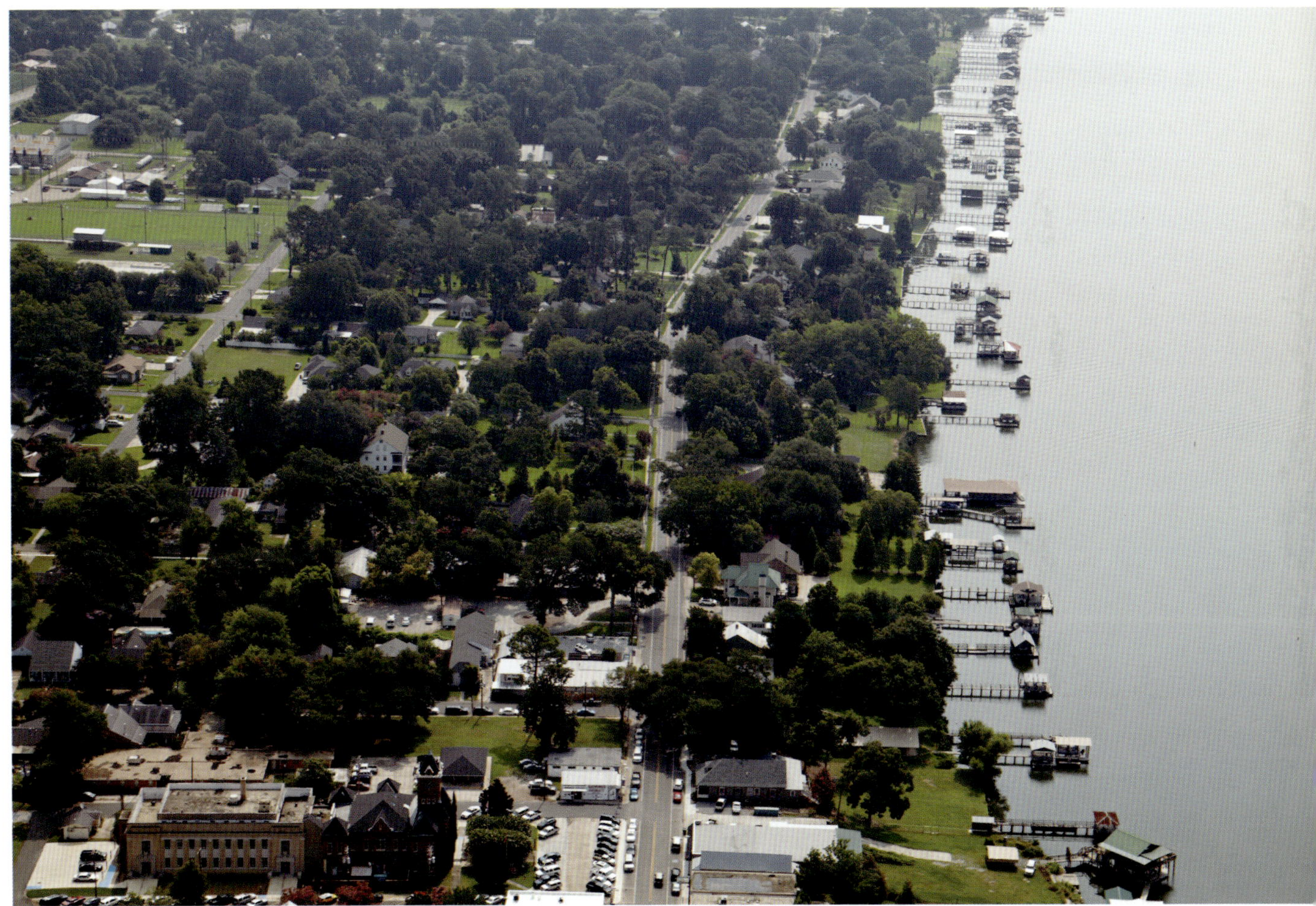

The Wagley House was built in 1901, about a century after the Albin Major House. Similar in grandeur and style to turn-of-the-century houses in the Garden District of New Orleans, this home was built for New Roads native Louise Pourciau and her husband, New Orleans merchant Antonio Marqueze. Living primarily in the big city, they saw it as a weekend retreat on False River.

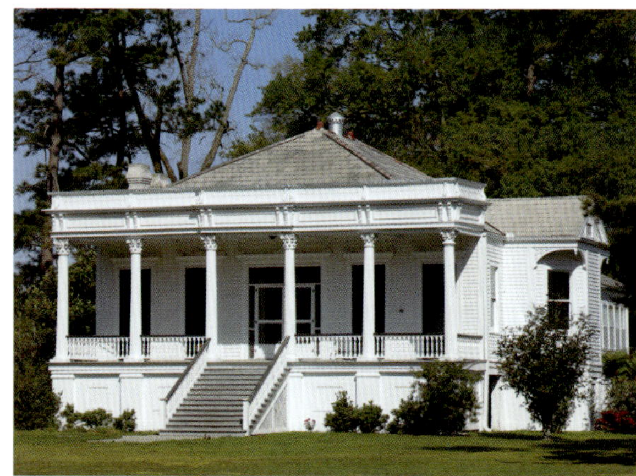

JULIEN POYDRAS
MUSEUM AND ARTS CENTER
National Register of Historic Places
Louisiana Trust for Historic Preservation Award

Mary Langlois of the Poydras Home of New Orleans speaks at a Poydras Day ceremony in front of the Julien Poydras Museum and Arts Center. The monument in the foreground marks the grave of Julien Poydras (1746–1824), whose remains were moved to this site in front of the Poydras High School in 1891. Every year as *La Toussaint* (All Saints' Day) approaches, the grave is decorated and a program is prepared to honor the memory of Poydras, one of Pointe Coupee's most renowned citizens.

The old high school, built in 1924, is a fine brick Neoclassical civic building. In a process that took more than ten years, a group of local citizens worked to purchase and restore the building after it closed as a school in 1991. In 2011 the Pointe Coupee Historical Society won a state preservation award "for preserving and restoring historic Poydras High School from demolition, and through adaptive reuse, returning it to the community as an asset for present and future generations."

Today the building provides a stage for historical programs, concerts, art shows, and other productions made possible by groups such as the Arts Council of Pointe Coupee, the Centre for the Arts, and the Pointe Coupee Historical Society. The Pointe Coupee Historical Society owns, operates, and maintains the center.

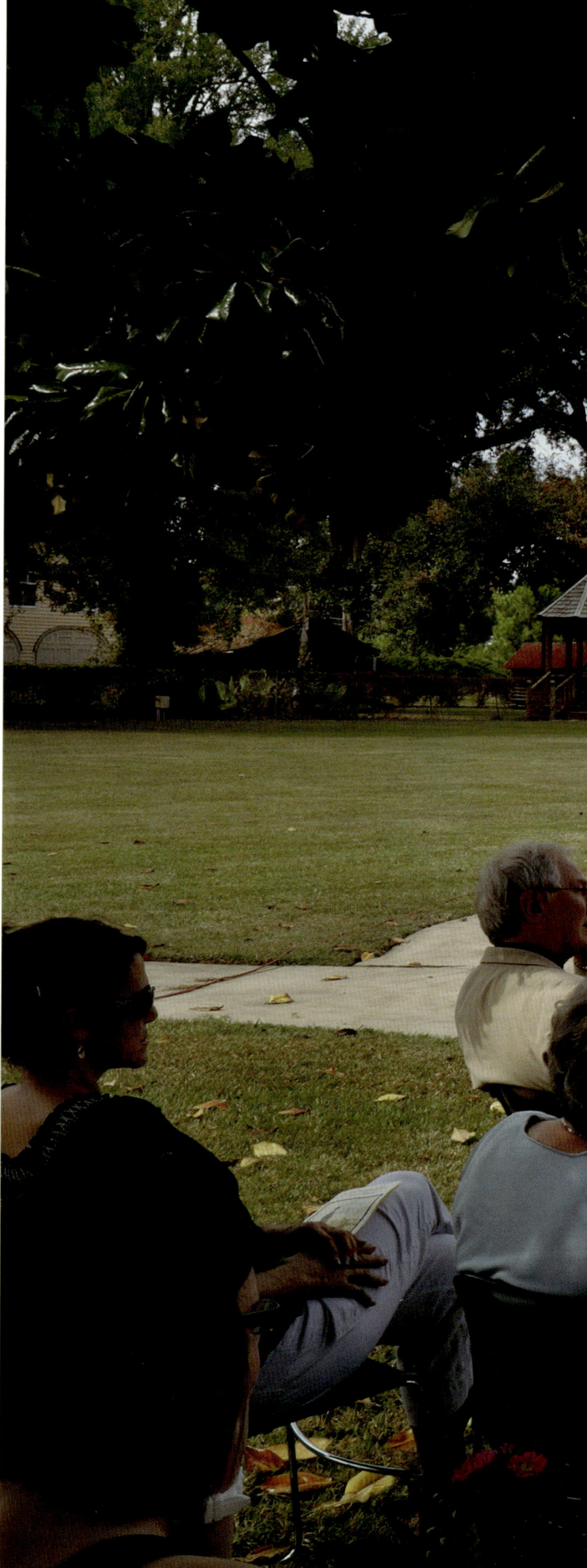

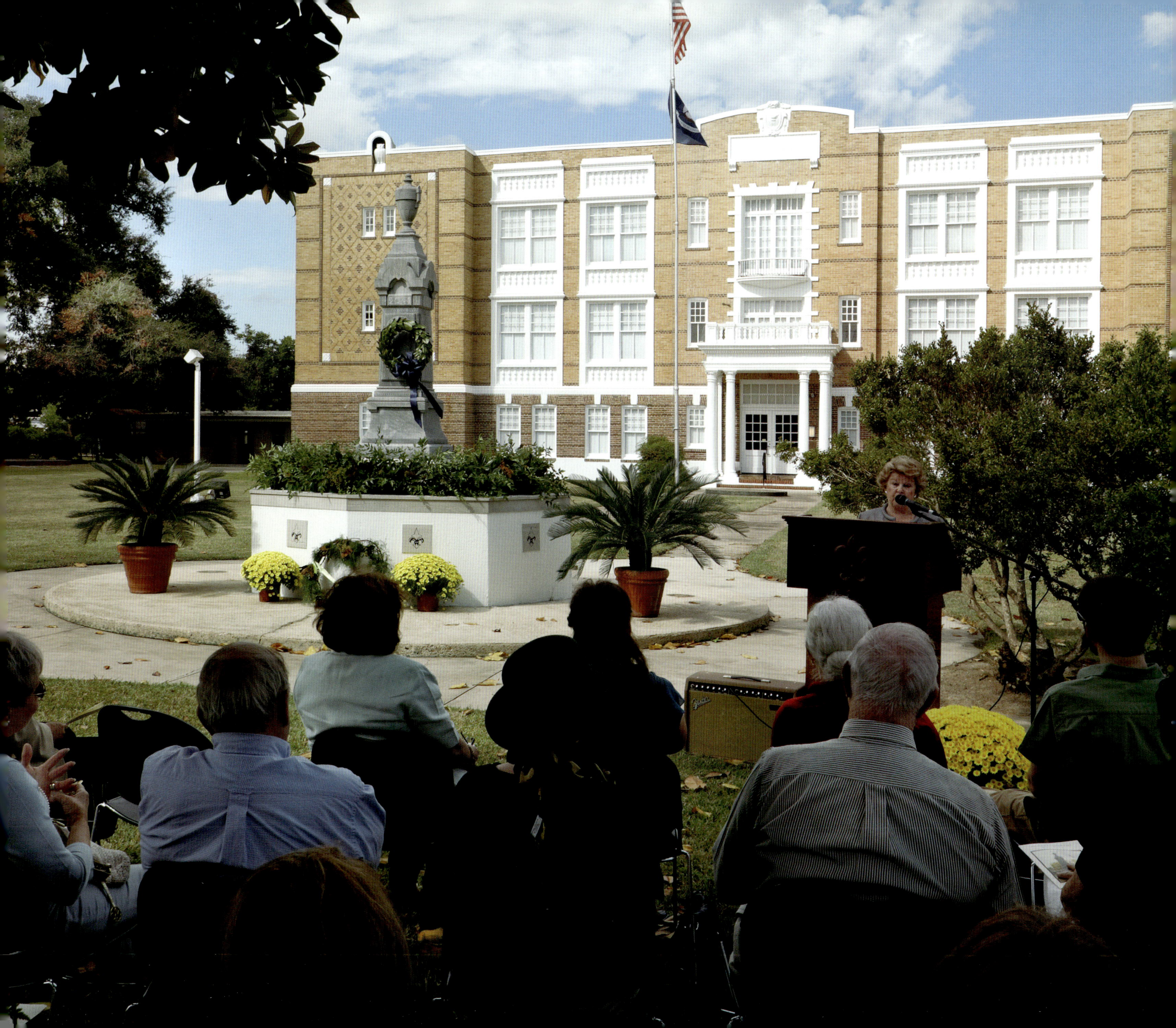

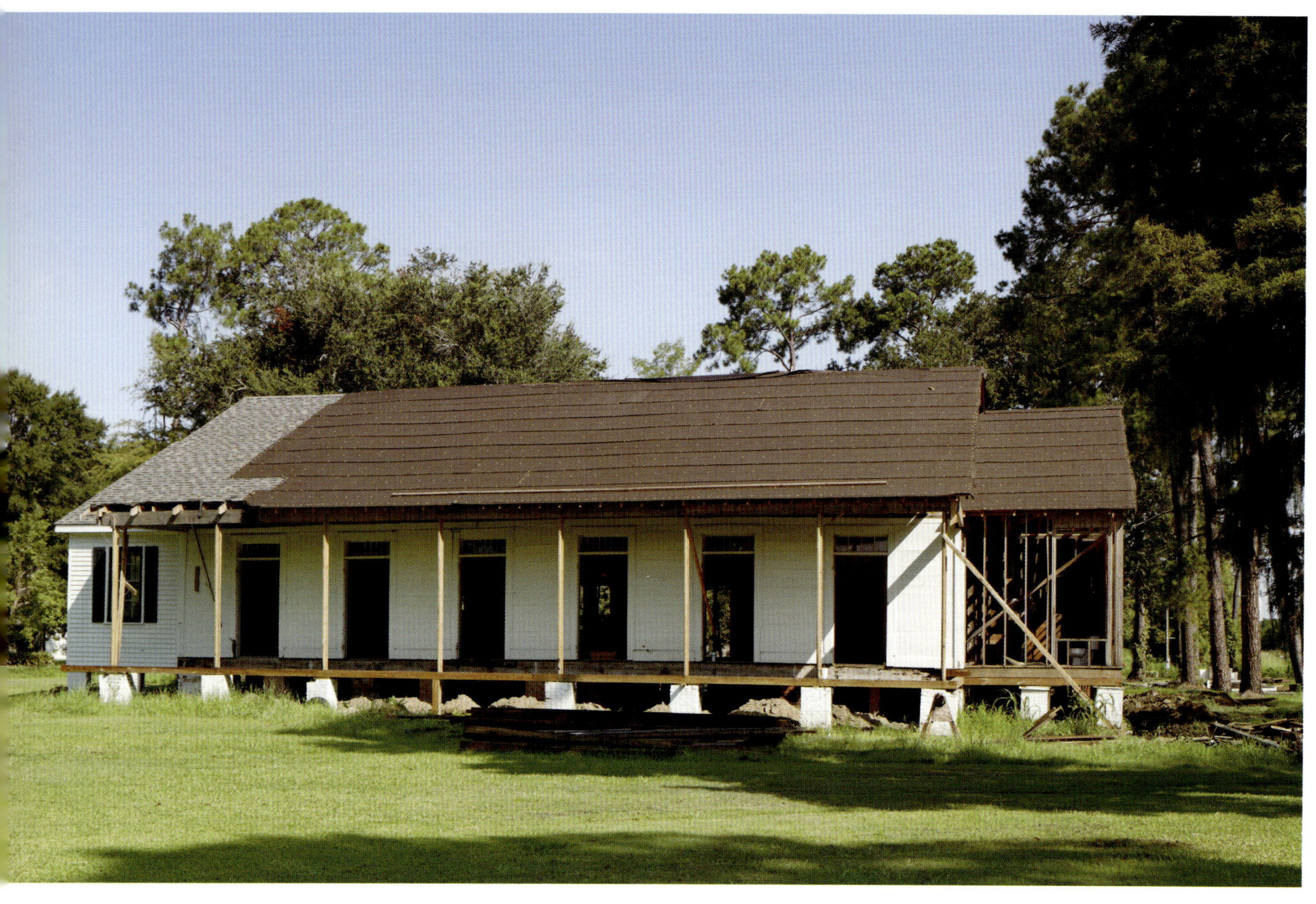

ALBIN MAJOR HOUSE
National Register of Historic Places

The Albin Major House was probably built in the first decade of the nineteenth century, and is one of the oldest houses still standing in New Roads. In 2008 Hurricane Gustav blew down a huge tree that crushed the entire roof of the house. The owner is in the process of rebuilding the historic home.

Storms have destroyed a multitude of buildings in Pointe Coupee over the centuries. Saving old houses for future generations is largely the result of hard work by individual owners to protect their homes along the way, and to stabilize and rebuild after damage occurs.

St. Mary of False River was founded as a mission church of St. Francis of Pointe Coupee, the original church on the Mississippi River established in 1738. The wood-frame church that opened its doors in 1823 stood where St. Mary's stone grotto is today. The old church was taken down once the brick church was finished.

The present church was largely built in 1904–1907 according to plans of New Orleans architect Theodore Brune. The brick was made by J. P. Gosserand's New Roads Brickyard.

The handsome tower was completed in 1929, installed with a fine bell moved from the old church. "Marie Seraphine" is the name of the 1876 bell that still tolls on Sunday mornings and for the Angelus three times every day. It was shipped to Pointe Coupee from its foundry in Troy, New York, on the steamer *Robert E. Lee*.

Tiles depicting the Stations of the Cross were created by Sister Anne Constance Livaudais for a small prayer garden behind St. Mary. Steele Burden, the creator of Windrush Gardens in Baton Rouge, helped develop the gardens at St. Mary with Father Frank Uter in the late 1970s.

Aspidistra, the cast iron plant, crowds around a small bust of the Christ set in a garden birdbath.

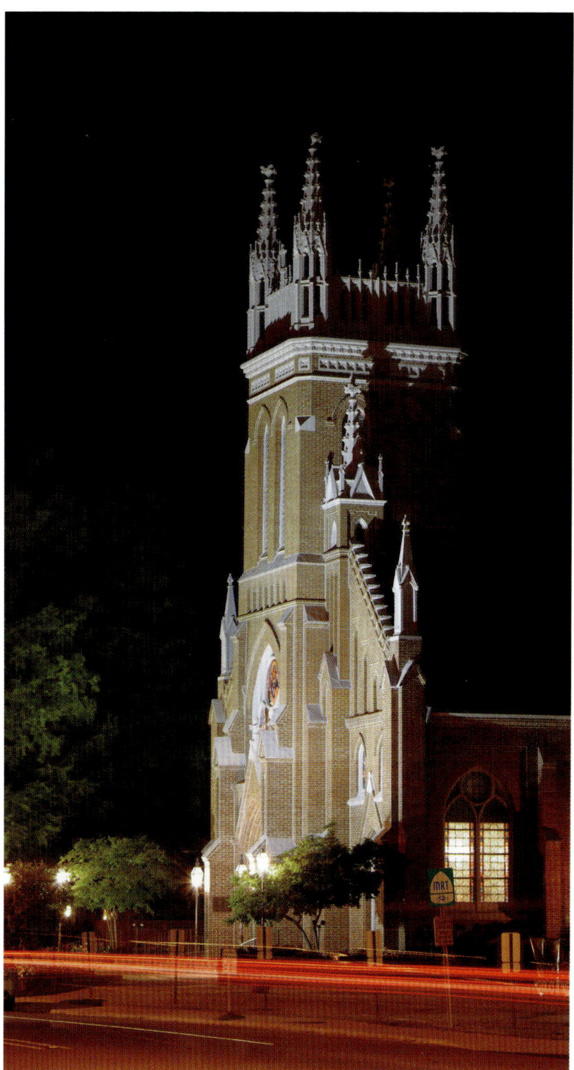

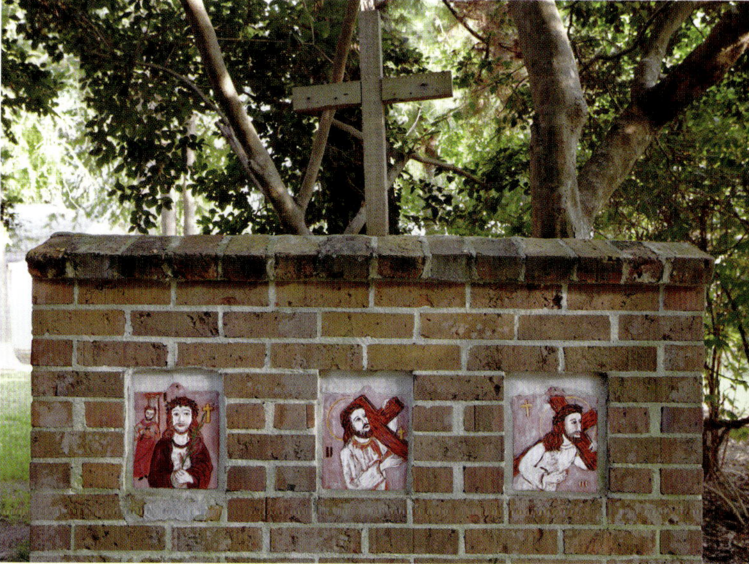

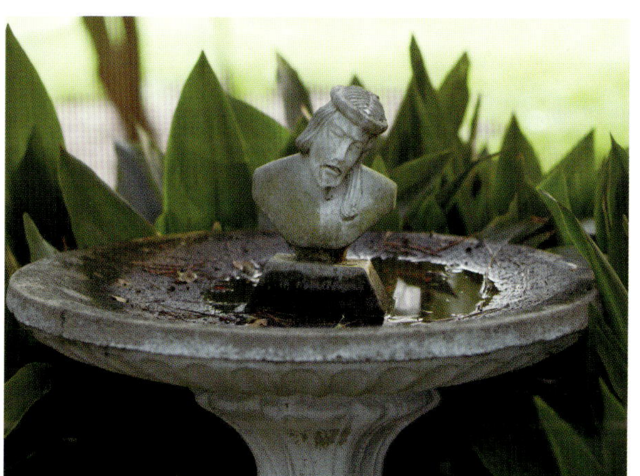

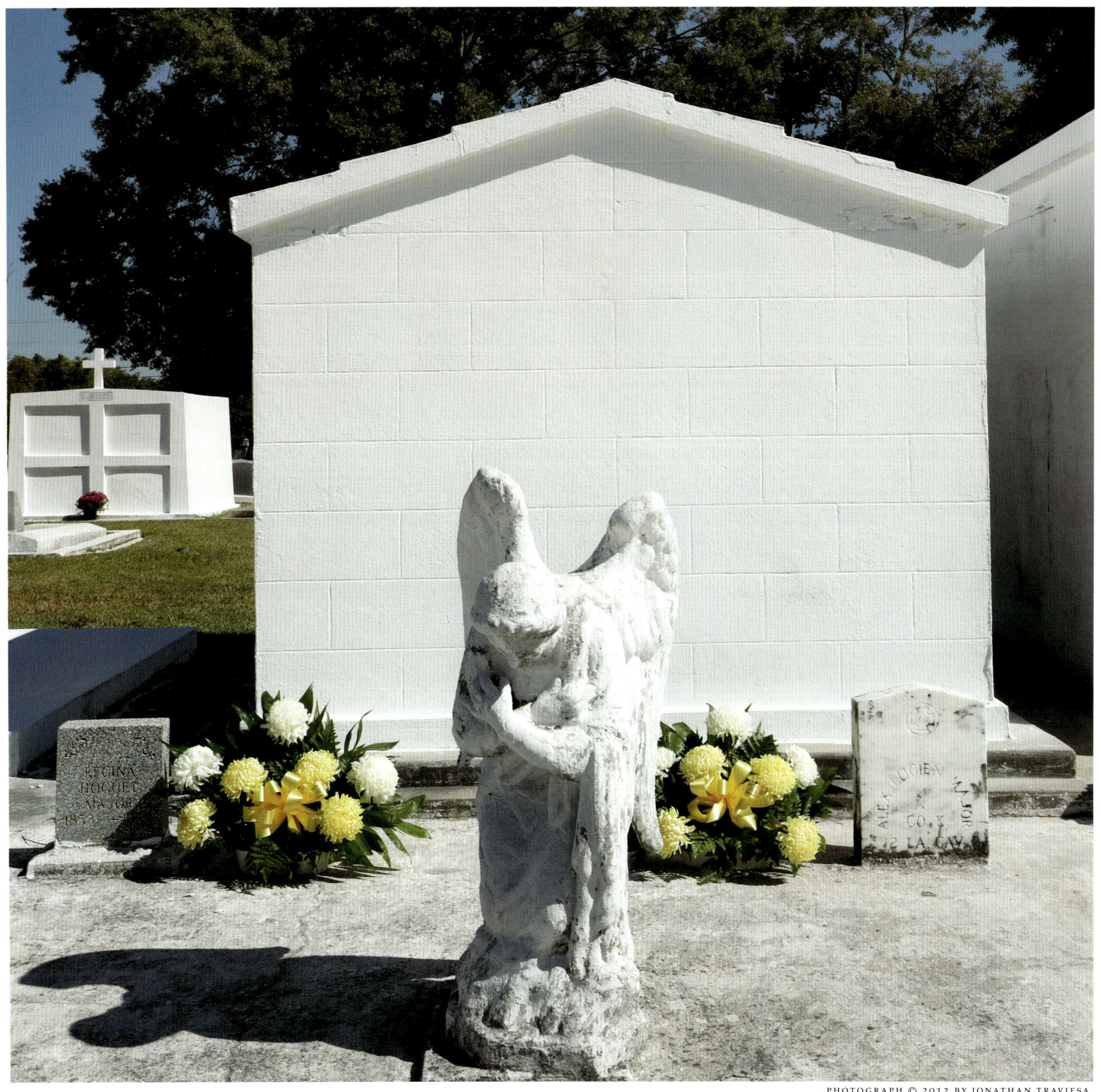

PHOTOGRAPH © 2012 BY JONATHAN TRAVIESA

Flower arrangements are placed in front of freshly painted tombs in a display of respect for the dead on All Saints' Day, November 1. Chrysanthemums are the traditional flowers used. In earlier days *crête de coq* (cockscomb) was popular, and it is still grown in old-fashioned gardens on the Island.

Pointe Coupee and New Orleans share the tradition of burying their dead in above-ground tombs, a cultural practice that originated in France and Spain. As a rule, Catholic settlers in Louisiana buried their dead above ground, Protestants and Jews below ground.

St. Mary Cemetery is located on the Chemin Neuf, the "new road" that gave the town its name, on donated land that was originally part of the François Samson Plantation. Opened in 1865, it contains some of the markers and remains from Old St. Francis cemetery, which was abandoned during 1888–1892 when the Mississippi River encroached.

Marble tablets are carved with the names of Provosty family dead, many whose remains were relocated from the earlier graveyard near St. Francis Church. The mausoleum that holds these remains is about a foot away from its neighbor, so the names can only be read at an angle looking between the tombs.

The Passionate Walk has been conducted on Good Friday yearly since 2005. Several hundred people walk, carrying a wooden cross, from Immaculate Conception Church in Lakeland to St. Mary in New Roads. The walk is about twelve miles along False River.

The group passes the Beauregard Olinde House, built in 1897 by a New Roads merchant. Olinde's descendants still live in the house.

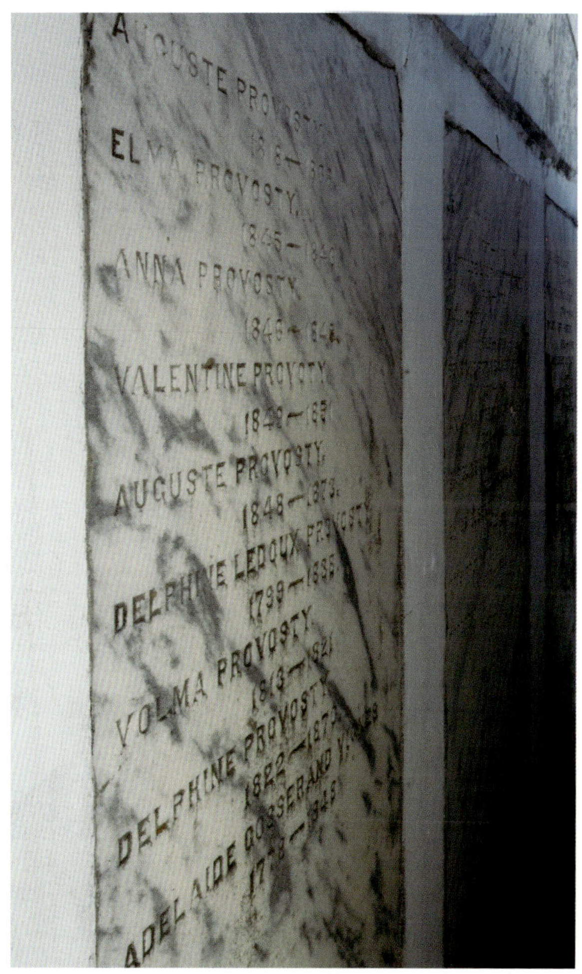

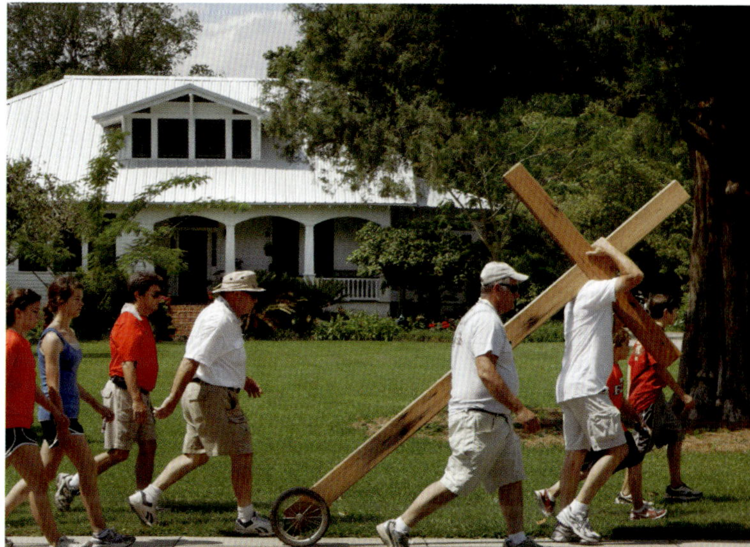

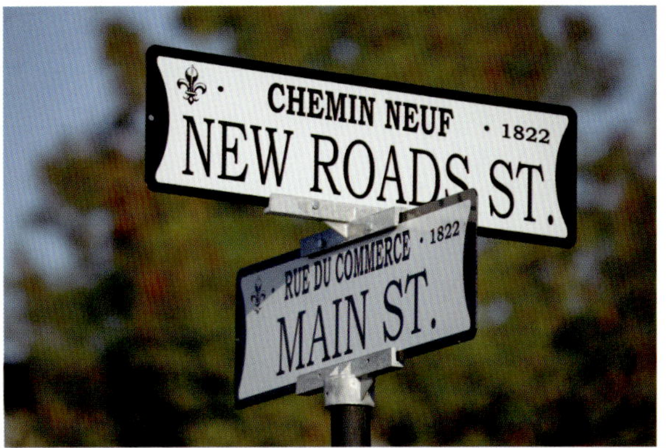

Modern street signs read in English and French. *Chemin Neuf,* the "new road" for which the town was named, was created by the Spanish colonial government about 1776 as a shortcut from False River to the Mississippi. The road has moved over the years from St. Mary to New Roads Street, but the path is essentially the same as it was in 1776.

In 1822, the free woman of color Catherine Depau, nicknamed *la fille Gougis* (Gougis's daughter), created a small town by drawing up a six-block, 20-lot subdivision of her own False River plantation. These six blocks are still the heart of downtown New Roads.

The post office was first known as "False River" (1858) and "St. Mary's" (1878), and sometime before it became "New Roads" (1879) it was the singular "New Road." The name has been misspelled as "New Rhodes" more than once, but has stayed true to its meaning in a town that still calls its 1776 Spanish road new.

The clock in front of City Hall faces north, south, east, and west, and announces not only the time but the date of the original division of downtown New Roads, 1822. The four-face Howard Post Clock was made for the city by the Electric Time Company of Medfield, Massachusetts, and installed in 2005. The clock was donated by H. T. "Bubber" Olinde Jr.

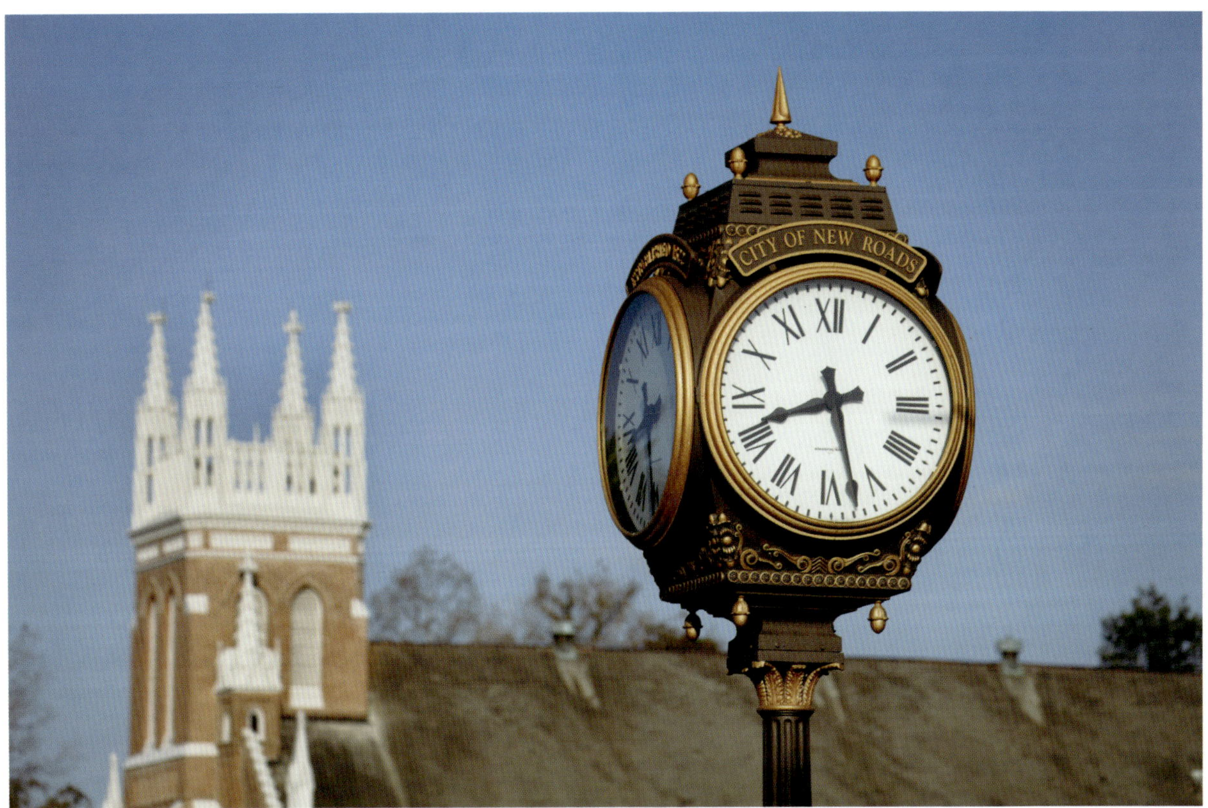

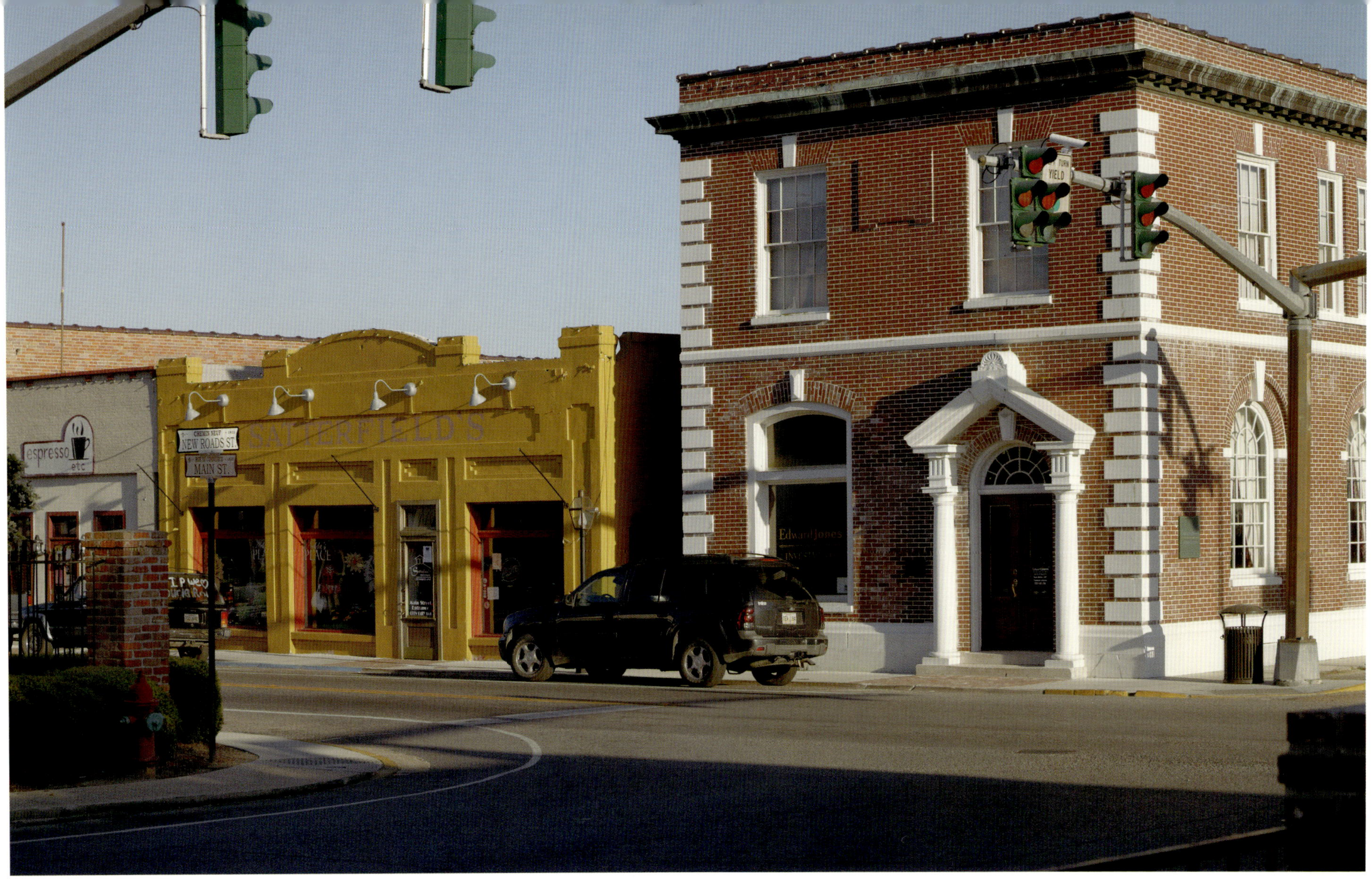

SATTERFIELD MOTOR COMPANY
FIRST NATIONAL BANK OF NEW ROADS
National Register of Historic Places

Two historic twentieth-century buildings stand side by side in New Roads. The Creole gold building is the Satterfield Motor Company, an early automobile showroom built in 1917. Today the building houses several shops and the entrance to a popular restaurant on False River called Satterfield's. The two-story brick building is the old First National Bank of New Roads, built in 1909 and handsomely restored by Brent Labatut almost a century later. Today it houses a financial investment company.

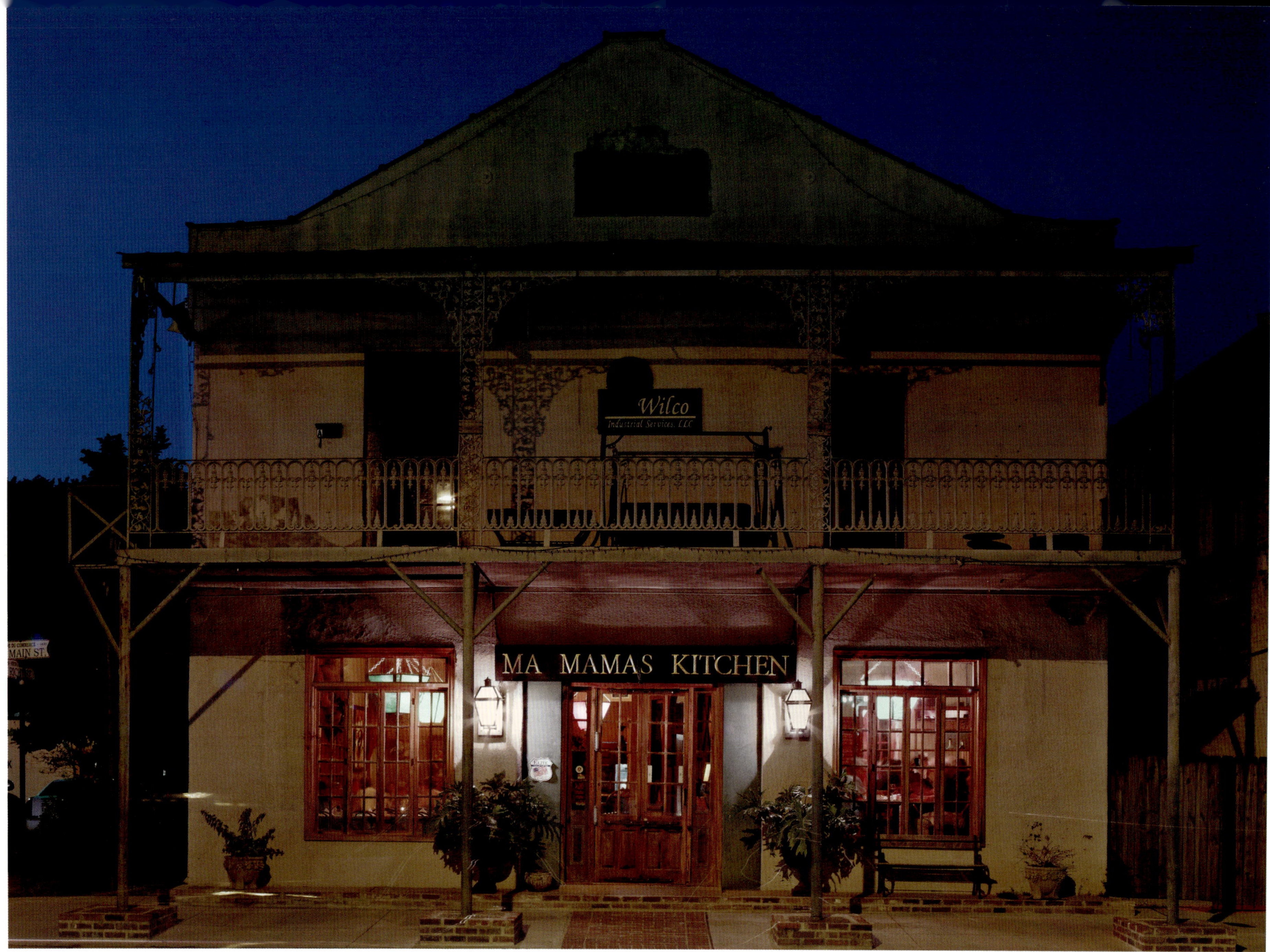

The Graugnard-Richy Building dates to the 1850s, and is the oldest surviving commercial structure in the parish. Presently home to one of the most acclaimed restaurants in Pointe Coupee, the old stucco building has nineteenth-century ironwork similar to that found in the New Orleans French Quarter. This is the last standing of eleven downtown buildings with second-floor balconies.

Christmas lights illuminate the Romanesque Revival façade of the parish courthouse, built in 1902 on the site of an earlier courthouse in downtown New Roads. Original records maintained by the clerk of court date back to 1770.

A life-size statue of John Archer LeJeune stands in front of the Pointe Coupee Parish Courthouse. The bronze monument was created by Louisiana sculptor Patrick Dane Miller and donated to the parish by Patrick F. Taylor in 2000. John Archer LeJeune (1867–1942) was born at Old Hickory Plantation in Batchelor near what is today the Morganza Spillway. Known as "the greatest of all leathernecks," LeJeune served in the Marine Corps almost forty years, and as commandant from 1920 to 1929. Camp LeJeune, North Carolina, was named in his honor.

In 1976, America's bicentennial year, the Daughters of the American Revolution presented an honor roll to be installed permanently in the parish courthouse. It lists the names of Pointe Coupee men who are known to have fought against the British in America's War for Independence. Other honor rolls grace the halls of the courthouse as well.

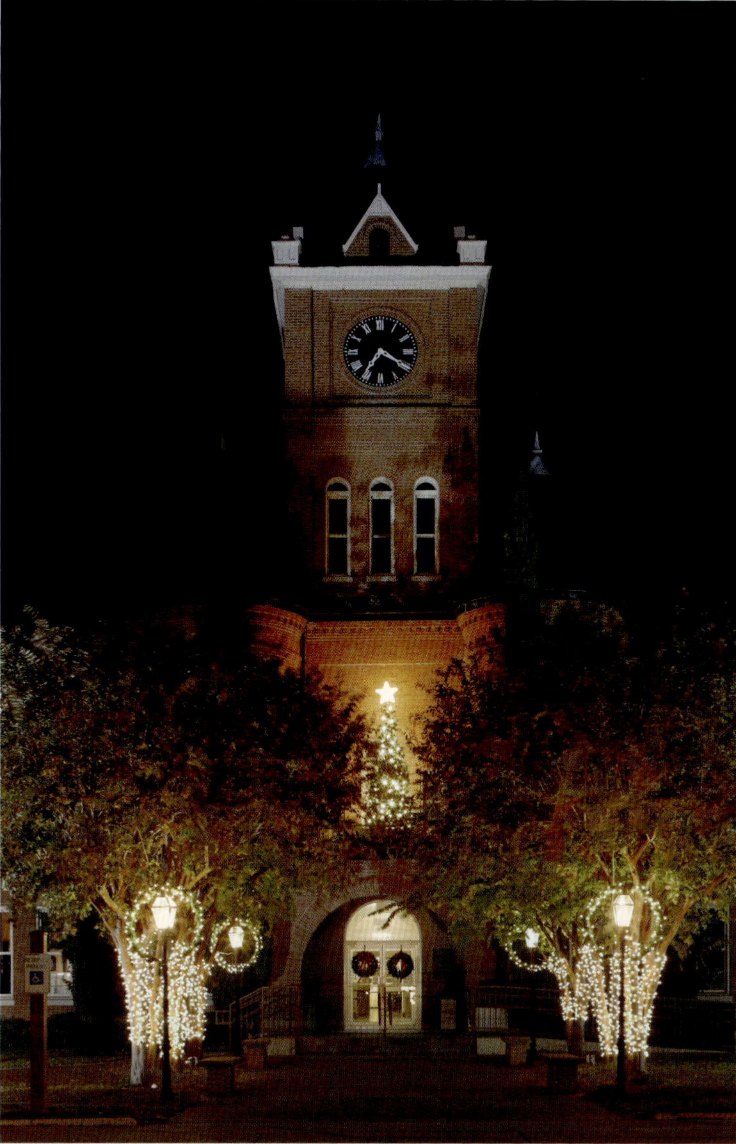

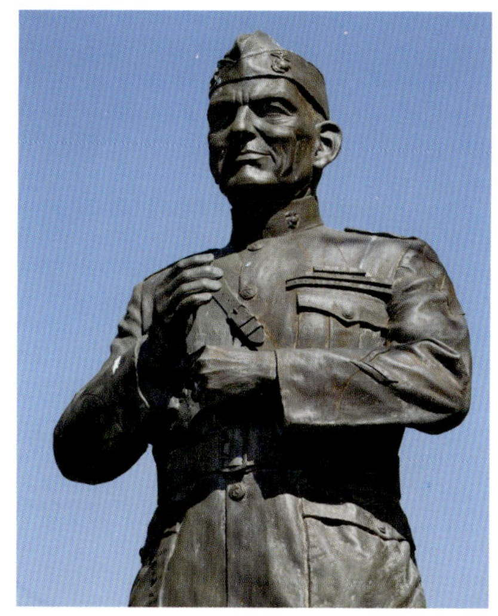

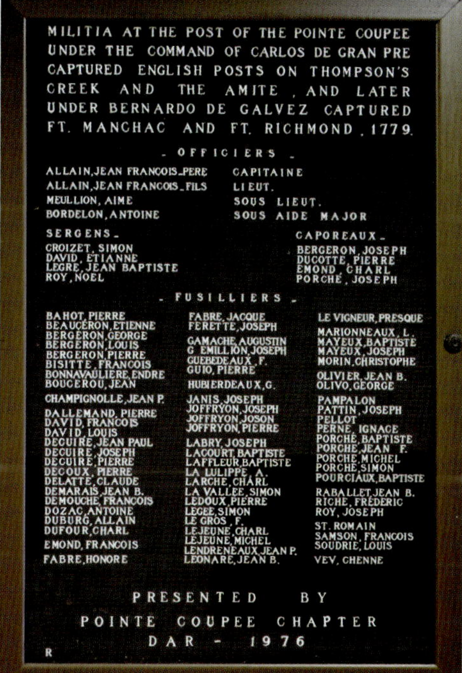

MILITIA AT THE POST OF THE POINTE COUPEE UNDER THE COMMAND OF CARLOS DE GRAN PRE CAPTURED ENGLISH POSTS ON THOMPSON'S CREEK AND THE AMITE , AND LATER UNDER BERNARDO DE GALVEZ CAPTURED FT. MANCHAC AND FT. RICHMOND , 1779.

. OFFICIERS .

ALLAIN, JEAN FRANÇOIS _ PERE	CAPITAINE
ALLAIN, JEAN FRANCOIS _ FILS	LIEUT.
MEULLION, AIME	SOUS LIEUT.
BORDELON, ANTOINE	SOUS AIDE MAJOR

SERGENS _

CROIZET, SIMON
DAVID, ETIANNE
LEGRE, JEAN BAPTISTE
ROY, NOEL

CAPOREAUX _

BERGERON, JOSEPH
DUCOTTE, PIERRE
EMOND , CHARL
PORCHE , JOSEPH

. FUSILLIERS .

BAHOT, PIERRE
BEAUCERON, ETIENNE
BERGERON, GEORGE
BERGERON, LOUIS
BERGERON, PIERRE
BISITTE, FRANCOIS
BONNAVAULIERE, ENDRE
BOUCEROU, JEAN

CHAMPIGNOLLE, JEAN P.

DALLEMAND, PIERRE
DAVID, FRANCOIS
DAVID, LOUIS
DECUIRE, JEAN PAUL
DECUIRE, JOSEPH
DECUIRE, PIERRE
DECOUX, PIERRE
DELATTE, CLAUDE
DEMARAIS, JEAN B.
DEMOUCHE, FRANCOIS
DOZAC, ANTOINE
DUBURG, ALLAIN
DUFOUR, CHARL

EMOND, FRANCOIS

FABRE, HONORE

FABRE, JACQUE
FERETTE, JOSEPH

GAMACHE, AUGUSTIN
G EMILLION, JOSEPH
GUEBEDEAUX, F.
GUIO, PIERRE

HUBIERDEAUX, G.

JANIS, JOSEPH
JOFFRYON, JOSEPH
JOFFRYON, JOSON
JOFFRYON, PIERRE

LABRY, JOSEPH
LACOURT, BAPTISTE
LAFFLEUR, BAPTISTE
LA LULIPPE, A.
LARCHE, CHARL
LA VALLEE, SIMON
LEDOUX, PIERRE
LEGEE, SIMON
LE GROS, F.
LEJEUNE, CHARL
LEJEUNE, MICHEL
LENDRENEAUX, JEAN P.
LEONARE, JEAN B.

LE VIGNEUR, PRESQUE

MARIONNEAUX, L.
MAYEUX, BAPTISTE
MAYEUX, JOSEPH
MORIN, CHRISTOPHE

OLIVIER, JEAN B.
OLIVO, GEORGE

PAMPALON
PATTIN, JOSEPH
PELLOT
PERNE, IGNACE
PORCHE, BAPTISTE
PORCHE, JEAN F.
PORCHE, MICHEL
PORCHE, SIMON
POURCIAUX, BAPTISTE

RABALLET, JEAN B.
RICHE, FREDERIC
ROY, JOSEPH

ST. ROMAIN
SAMSON, FRANCOIS
SOUDRIE, LOUIS

VEV, CHENNE

PRESENTED BY POINTE COUPEE CHAPTER DAR - 1976

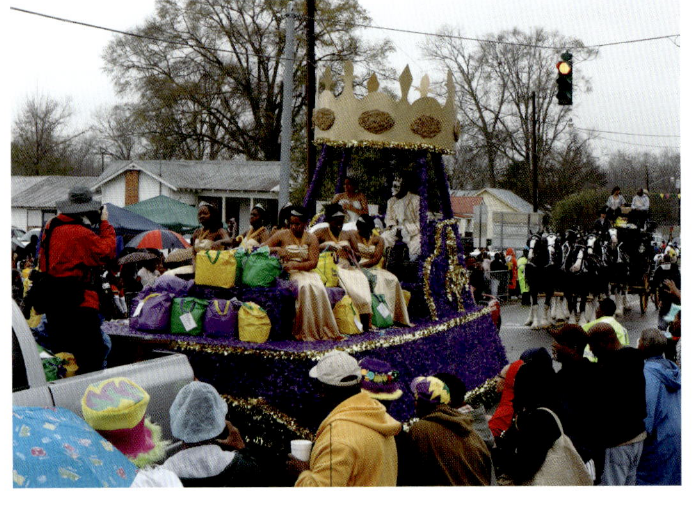

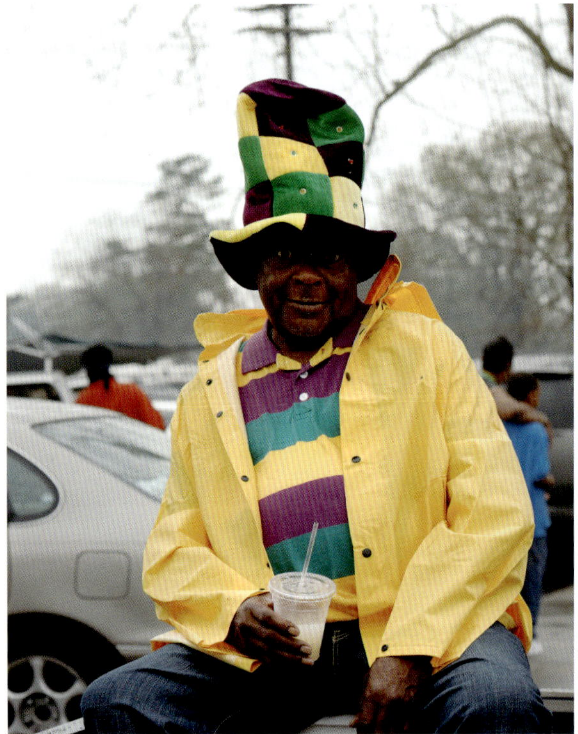

The Community Center of Pointe Coupee gets its parade rolling on Mardi Gras morning in 2011. Latrice Richard and Spencer Duhe are the reigning queen and king.

The morning parade is the older of New Roads' two Mardi Gras parades. It was started by Jimmy Boudreaux in 1922. Unlike exclusive krewes in other cities, both of New Roads' krewes are open to public participation.

A spectator takes in the sights, and happily makes a sight himself, at Mardi Gras in New Roads. As many as 100,000 people—residents and visitors—turn out for one of the largest Mardi Gras celebrations outside of New Orleans.

"Louisiana" was the theme of the Cub Scouts' prizewinning float in 2011.

King Stephen David and Queen Rebecca Maggio greet New Roads mayor Robert Myer as Tommy Guidry keeps everyone dry on a rainy Mardi Gras day, 2011. The afternoon parade is sponsored by the Lions Club and has been rolling since 1941. It is the first known Mardi Gras parade to roll as a charitable fundraiser.

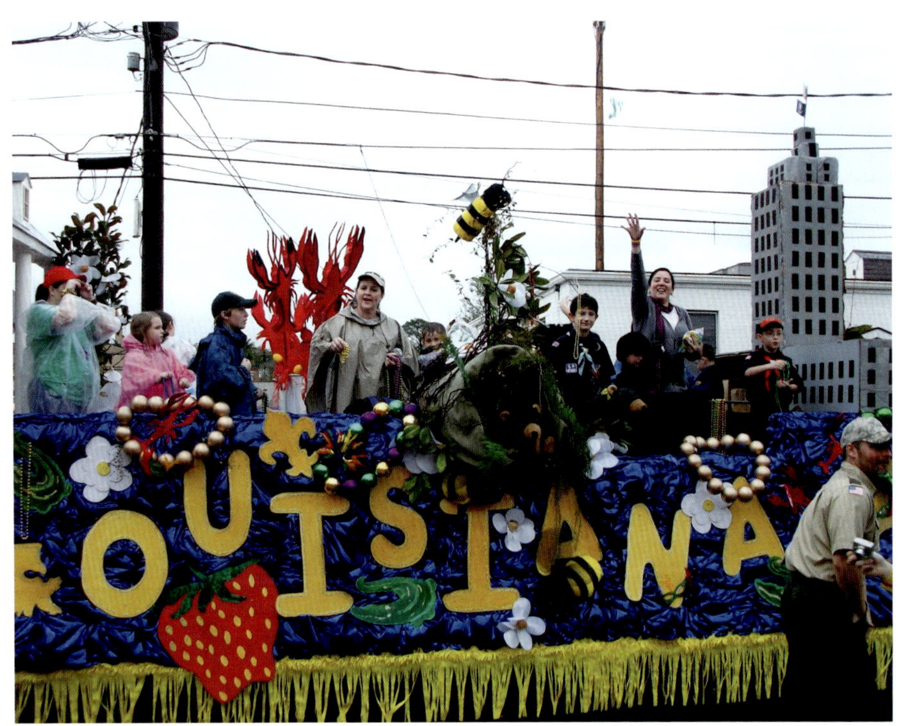

PHOTOGRAPH COURTESY GRACE HEBERT

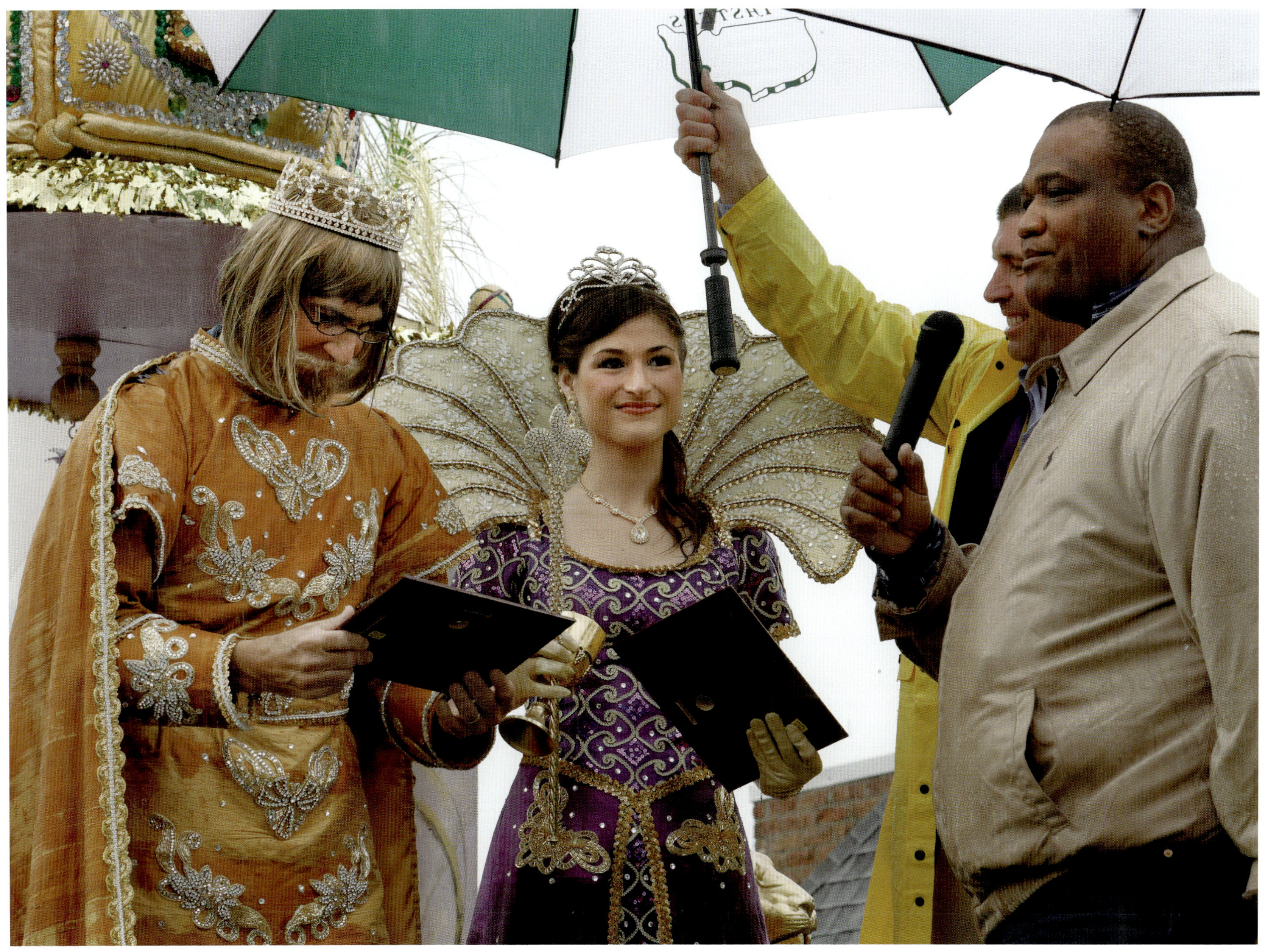

St. Augustine Catholic Church was established in 1922 by the Josephite Fathers, an order devoted to ministry among African Americans. The church was built in 1923 on New Roads Street, on land donated by St. Mary of False River. St. Augustine operated a school for black children from 1932 until school desegregation in the late 1960s.

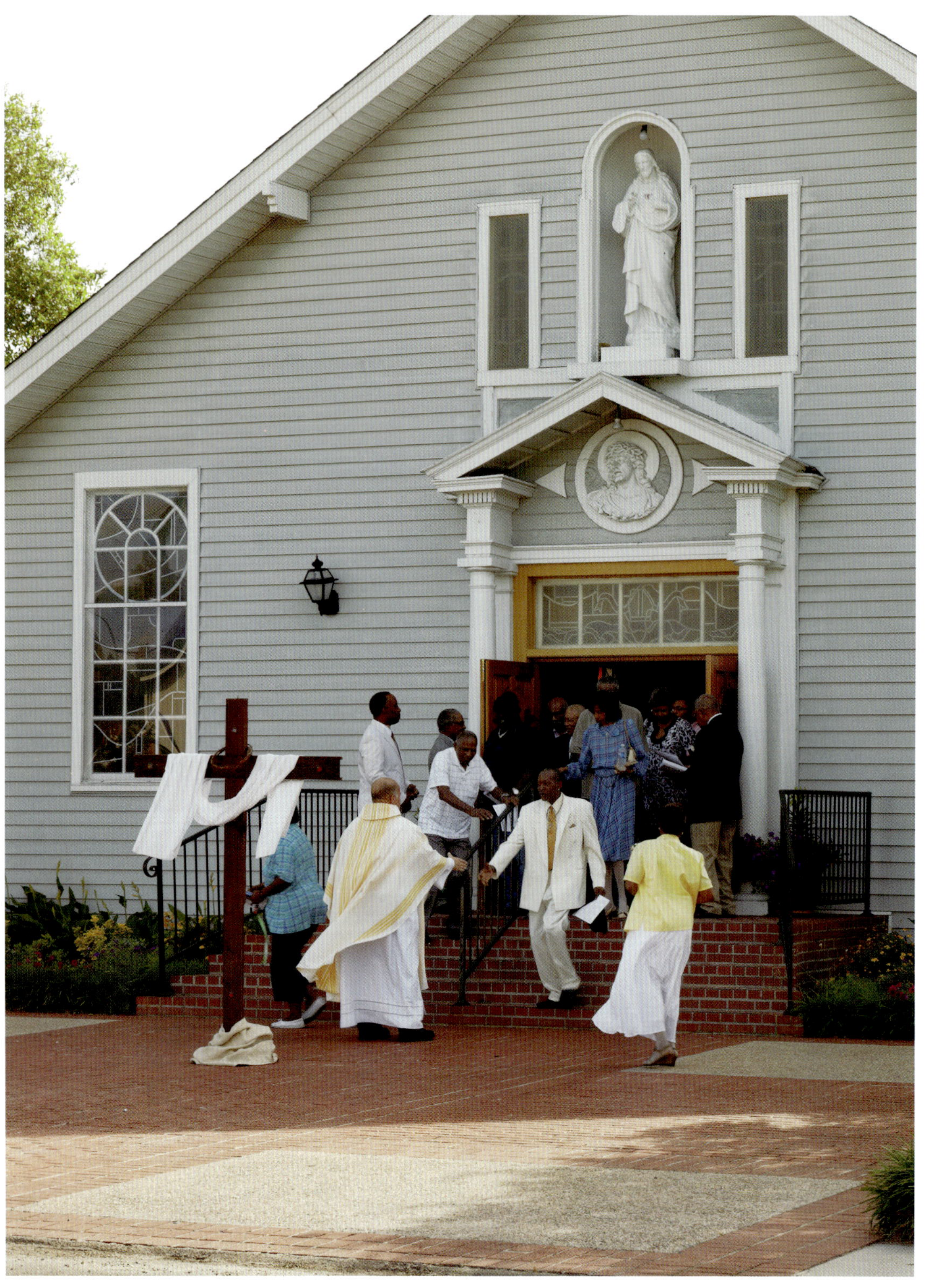

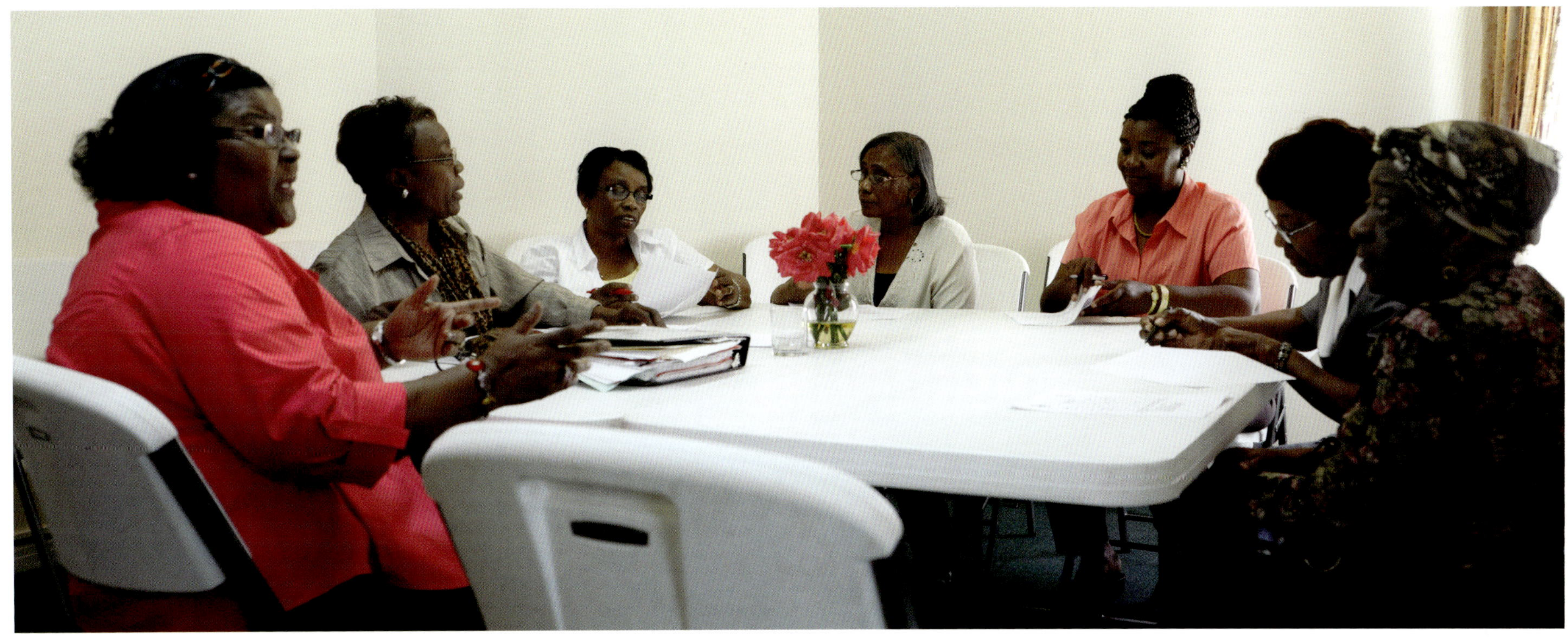

A group of ladies mostly from *L'Ile* (the Island of False River), gather weekly to speak and sing together in Creole French. (*From left to right: Gail Hurst, Mary V. Jackson, Mary Derozin, Gracie Armstrong, Constance Joseph, Mildred Duhe, and Mary Geneva Croom.*)

Les Créoles de Pointe Coupée is the only formal group of Creole speakers known to meet regularly to enjoy and preserve their unique linguistic heritage. From the early 1700s until after the Civil War, French was the primary language of Pointe Coupee. French immigrants brought their own varieties of French from Hainaut (now Belgium), France, French Canada, and the West Indies. People from Africa, Spain, Italy, Germany, Switzerland, and England altered the language in ways that have made Pointe Coupee's Creole French distinct among all the dialects spoken in Louisiana.

Today some of the residents of the rural island side of False River, as well as descendants of those who once lived there, maintain the spoken Creole language of Pointe Coupee.

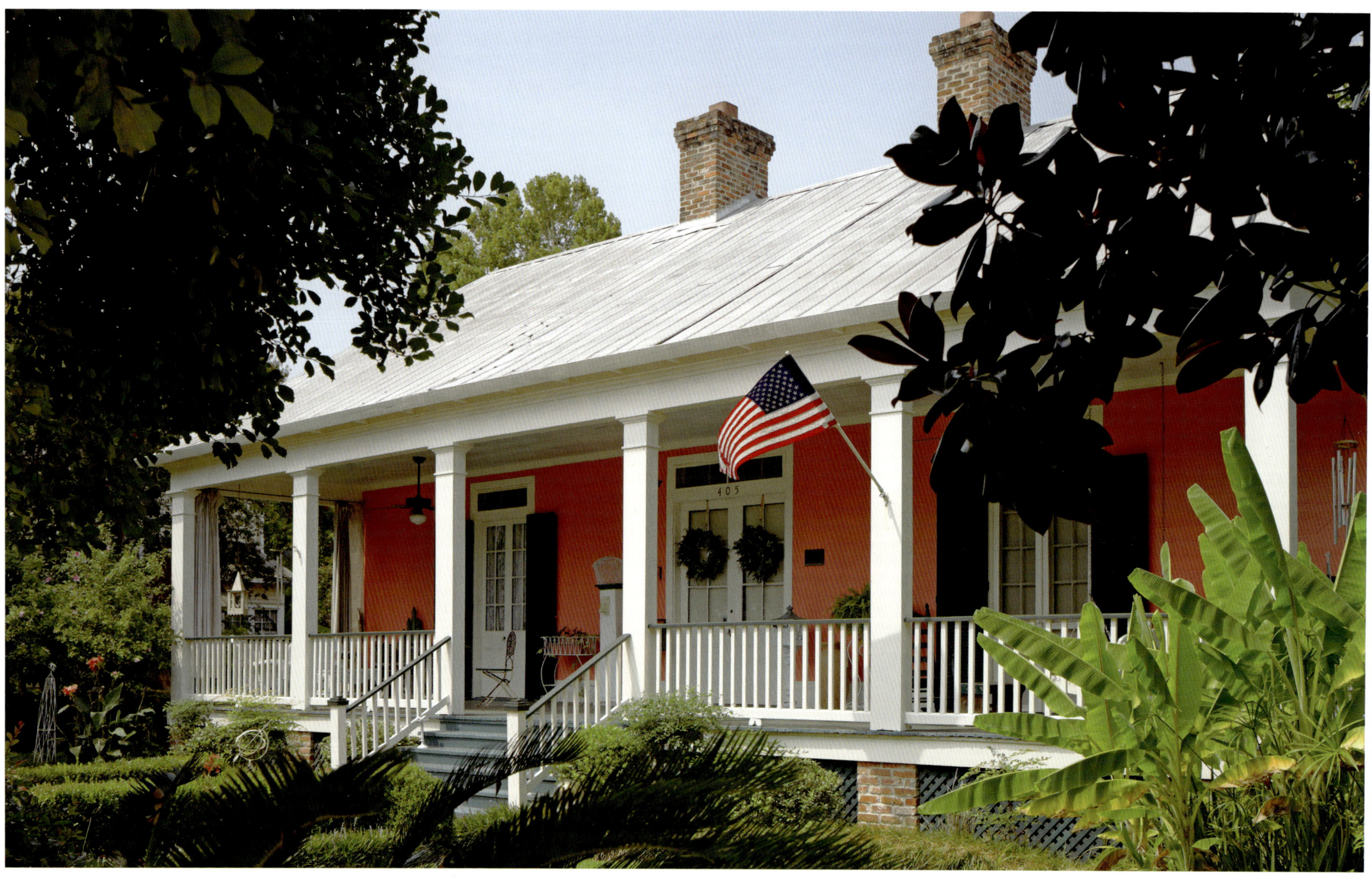

SAMSON HOUSE
National Register of Historic Places

The Samson House bed-and-breakfast is operated in a fine home built in the 1830s. It is known more fully as the Samson-Claiborne House in recognition of two notable residents: Clement Samson, a pharmacist in the later nineteenth century and a son of Terence Samson, who built Wickliffe; and Norbert Claiborne, father of Judge Ian Claiborne and at one time a sugar chemist in South America. The house was moved from its original location at the corner of Pennsylvania Street and East Main to its present spot on Richey Street. A wide center hall makes the house unusual in a town of Creole houses typically having no hallways whatsoever.

Woodworker Kerry Callegan planes a cypress board by hand in a tradition of building with local wood that goes back to the earliest settlement of Pointe Coupee. Callegan says, "It just feels good when you're working it." He and his coworker Mitchell Purpera conduct business in a shop that used to house Callegan's father's auto repair business.

Roger Jones removes a big cypress board to a pile as his son Chad runs the hydraulic saw from an enclosed room. The family has operated the Jones and Jones Sawmill in Innis since 1998. Cypress is the only wood they handle, milling boards as large as 28 inches wide by 24 feet long. Bald cypress, native to Louisiana, has been cut for lumber since the 1700s. Most old Pointe Coupee homes are built primarily of cypress.

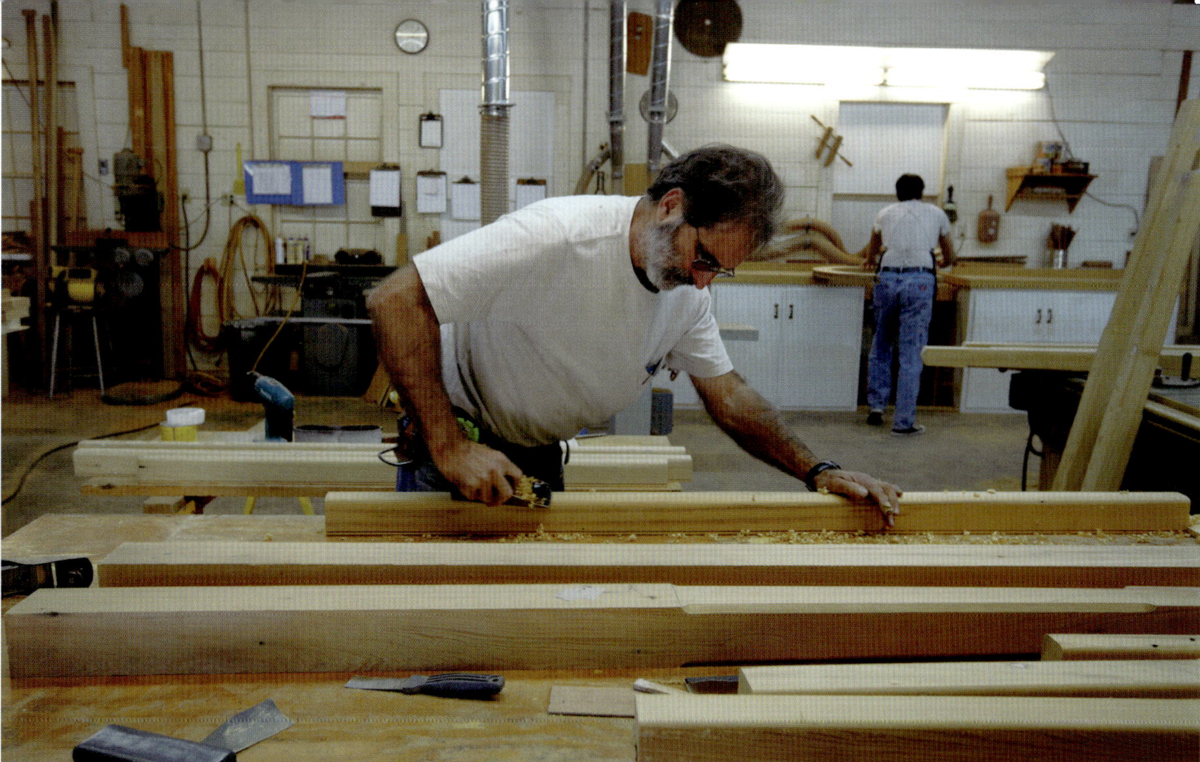

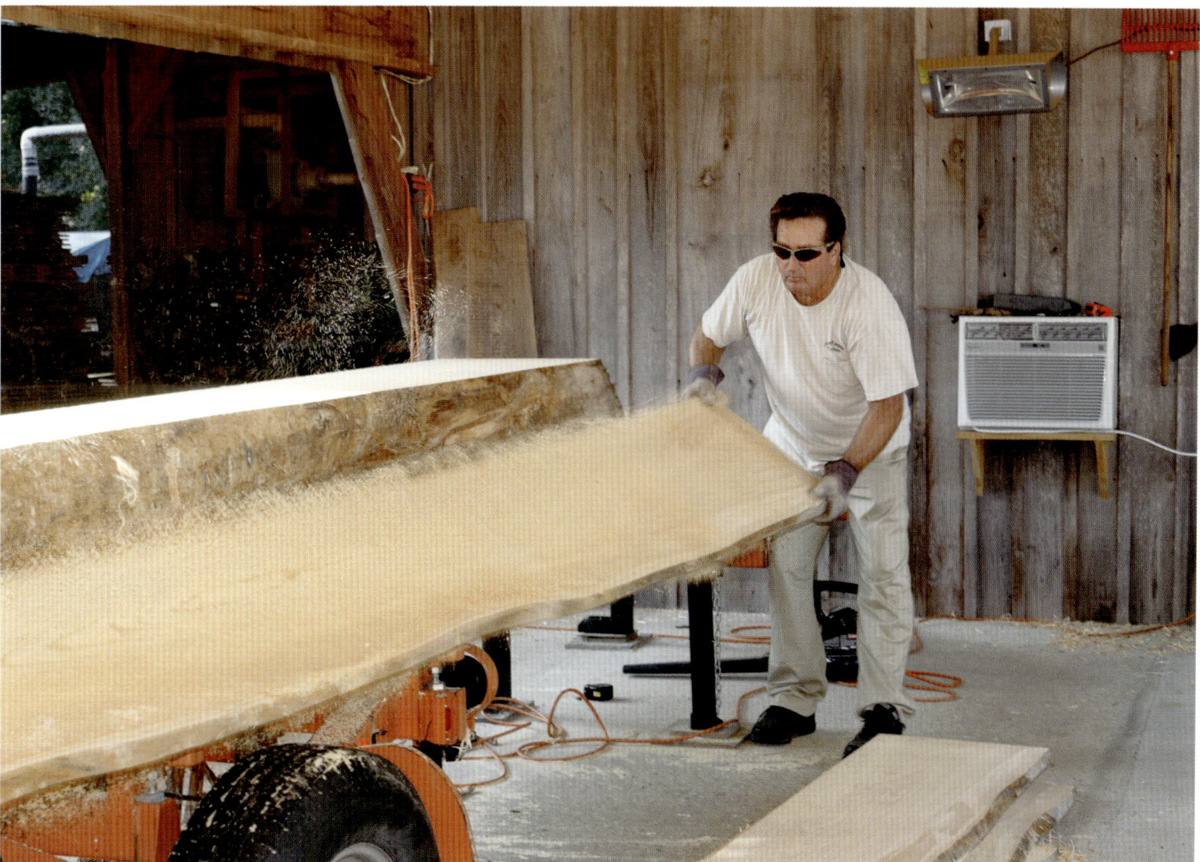

Two enormous southern magnolias dwarf the LeJeune House, set back beyond an acre of lawn stretching down to False River.

The LeJeune House was the centerpiece of a 500-acre plantation extending from the present-day St. Mary's Street to Oak Street, and from False River back to the *Chemin Neuf,* where it bends east toward the Mississippi. Especially after the Civil War, the land was sold and developed to build a sizable portion of the town of New Roads today. Appropriately, the LeJeune House was the first building in New Roads to be listed on the National Register of Historic Places.

As evident in the floor plan, the LeJeune House is a traditional Creole house, almost identical to Parlange. The basement is built of *briquette entre poteaux* (brick-between-posts), and the main living floor upstairs is constructed of wood frame filled with *bousillage.* The house appears to have been remodeled in the Greek Revival fashion, perhaps in 1834 when the plantation passed to new owners. The strong "Greek" columns of the renovation somewhat obscure the random placement of doors on the façade of the old French house, but the wrap-around fireplaces and lack of hallways suggest an early-nineteenth-century building date.

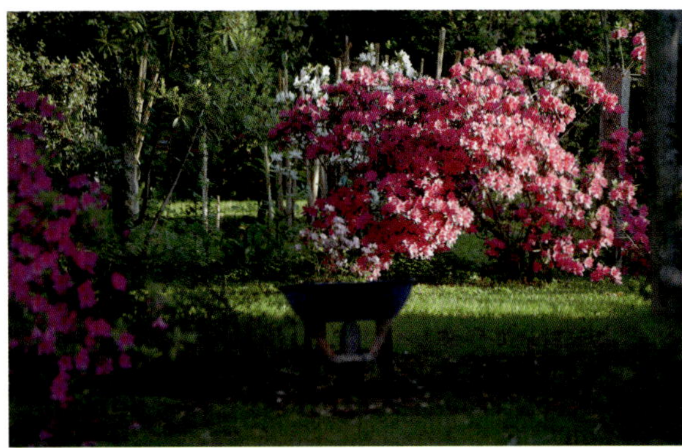

Big-flowered and eye-popping, Formosa azaleas are favorite spring shrubs in the old gardens of Louisiana.

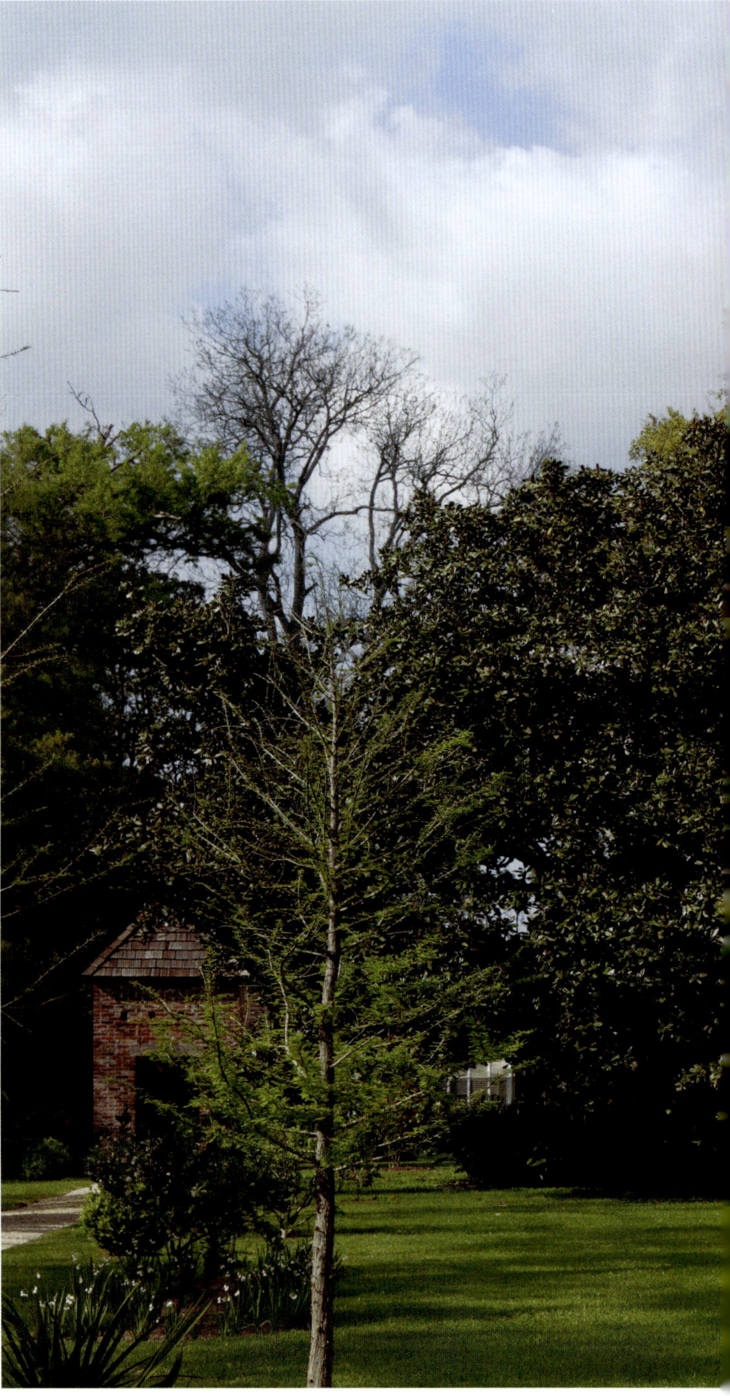

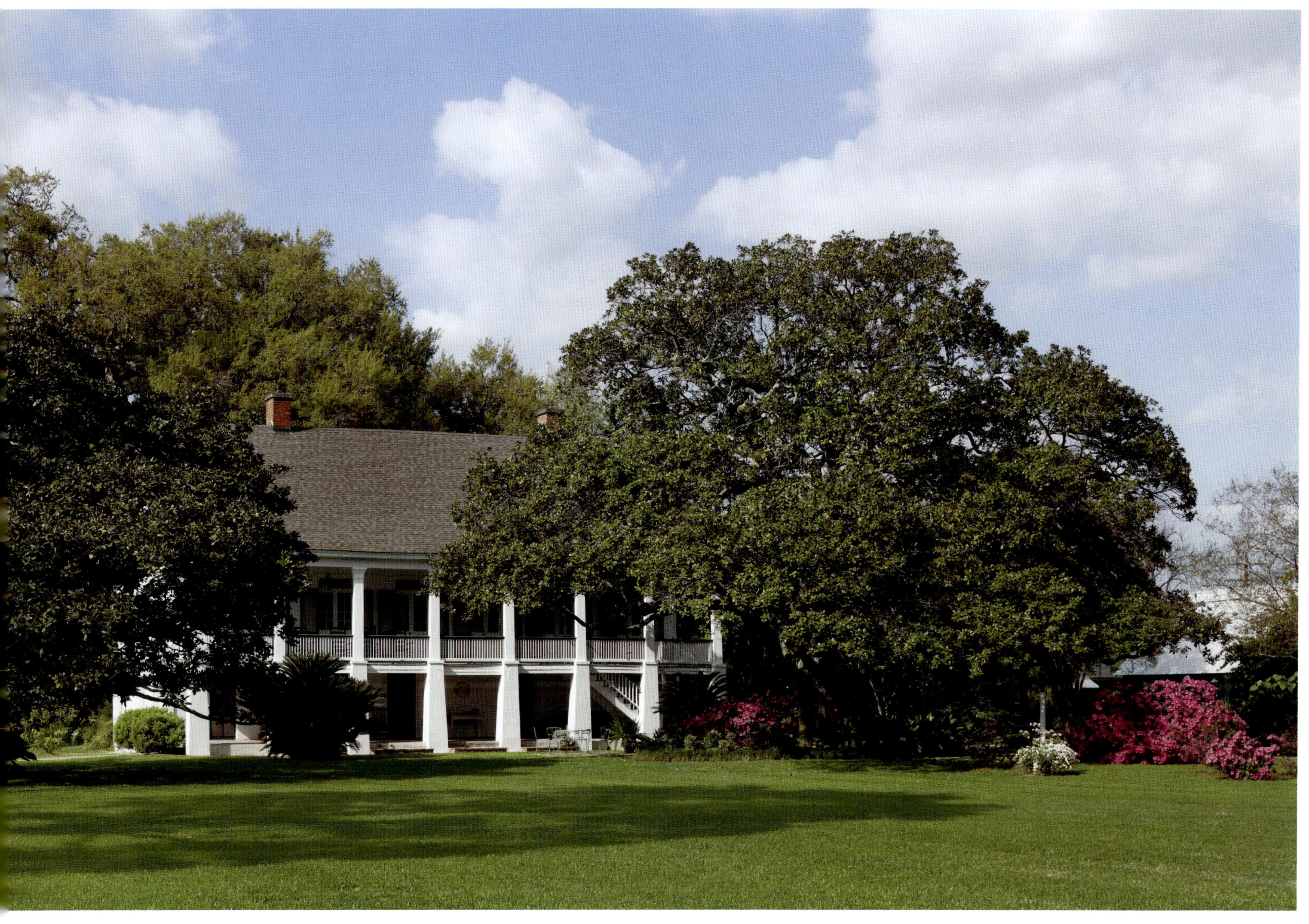

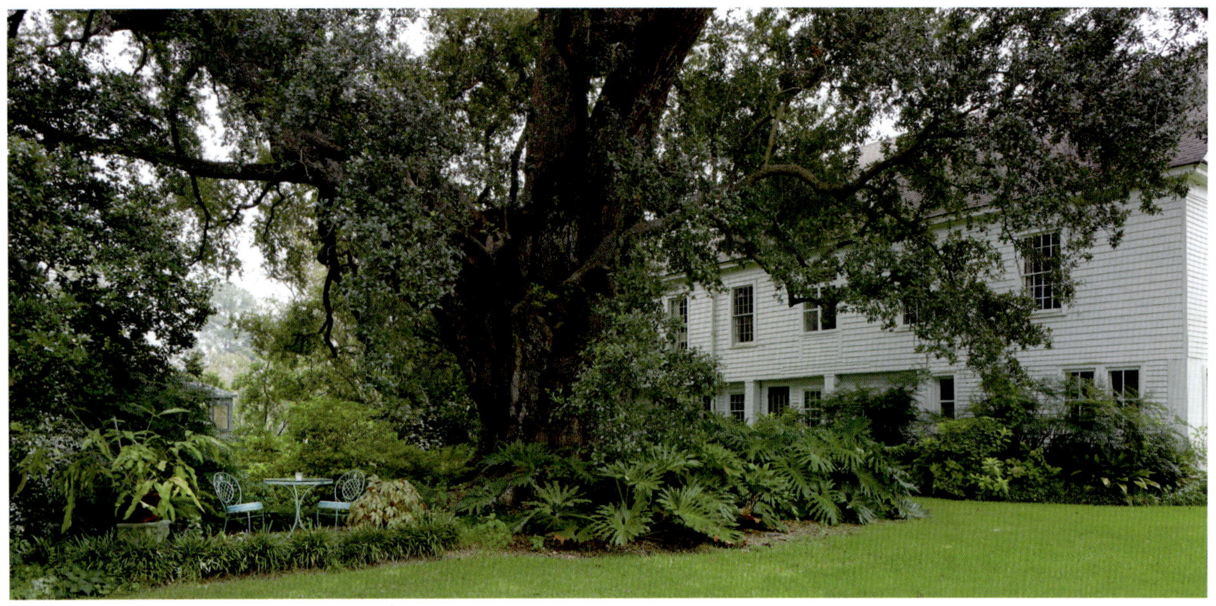

The live oak behind the LeJeune House was already a grand old tree when the house was built almost two hundred years ago. More than 28 feet in circumference, the tree is a member of the Live Oak Society and was named for the plantation's first owner, François Samson.

François Samson was born in St. Malo, France, but served at the *poste* of Pointe Coupee by 1772. In 1779 colonial governor of Spanish Louisiana Bernardo de Gálvez led a march to rout the British in West Florida. Samson fought with Gálvez in the Battle of Fort New Richmond (now Baton Rouge), one of the only battles of the American Revolution fought outside the original thirteen colonies.

SALLE

Local history says a Frenchman named François Avernant came from Bordeaux to remodel the LeJeune House, and spent two years accomplishing the work. The unusual transoms between rooms as well as above French doors, the coffered ceiling, the intricately designed paneling with pilasters and capitals—all handmade of local cypress—make the *salle* one of the most unusual rooms in Pointe Coupee. Current owners painted the room a drab white based on the earliest color their scrapings uncovered. The light blue of the ceiling panels was, however, purely a choice meant to delight.

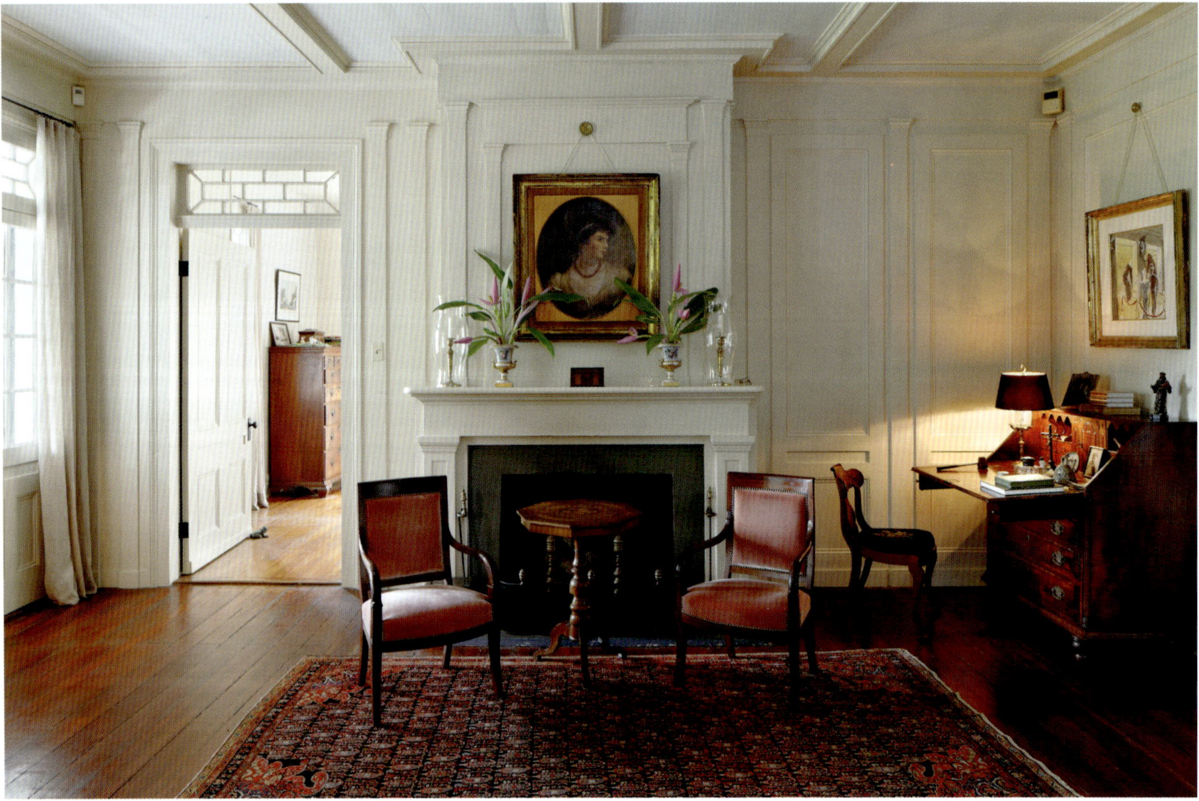

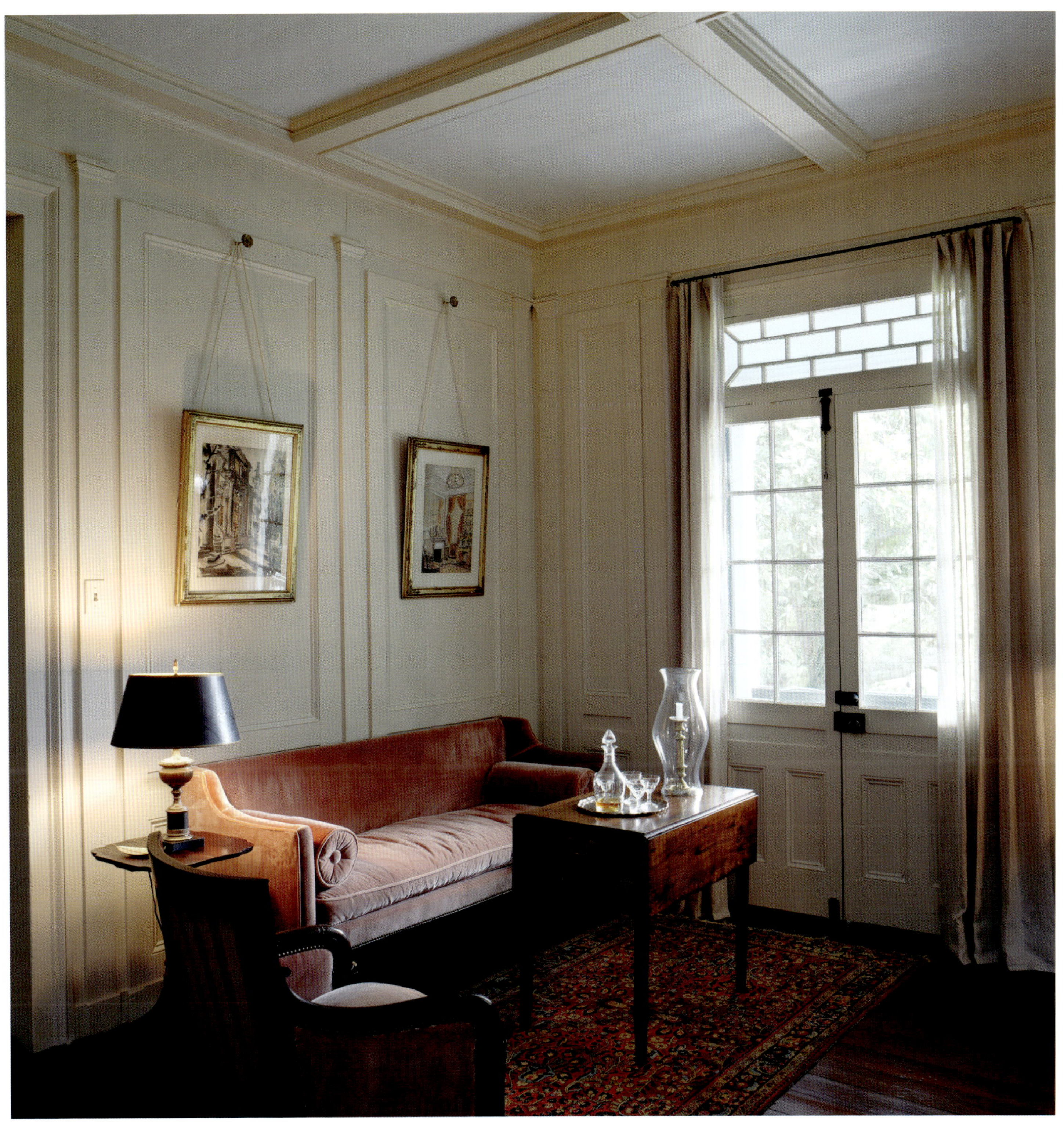

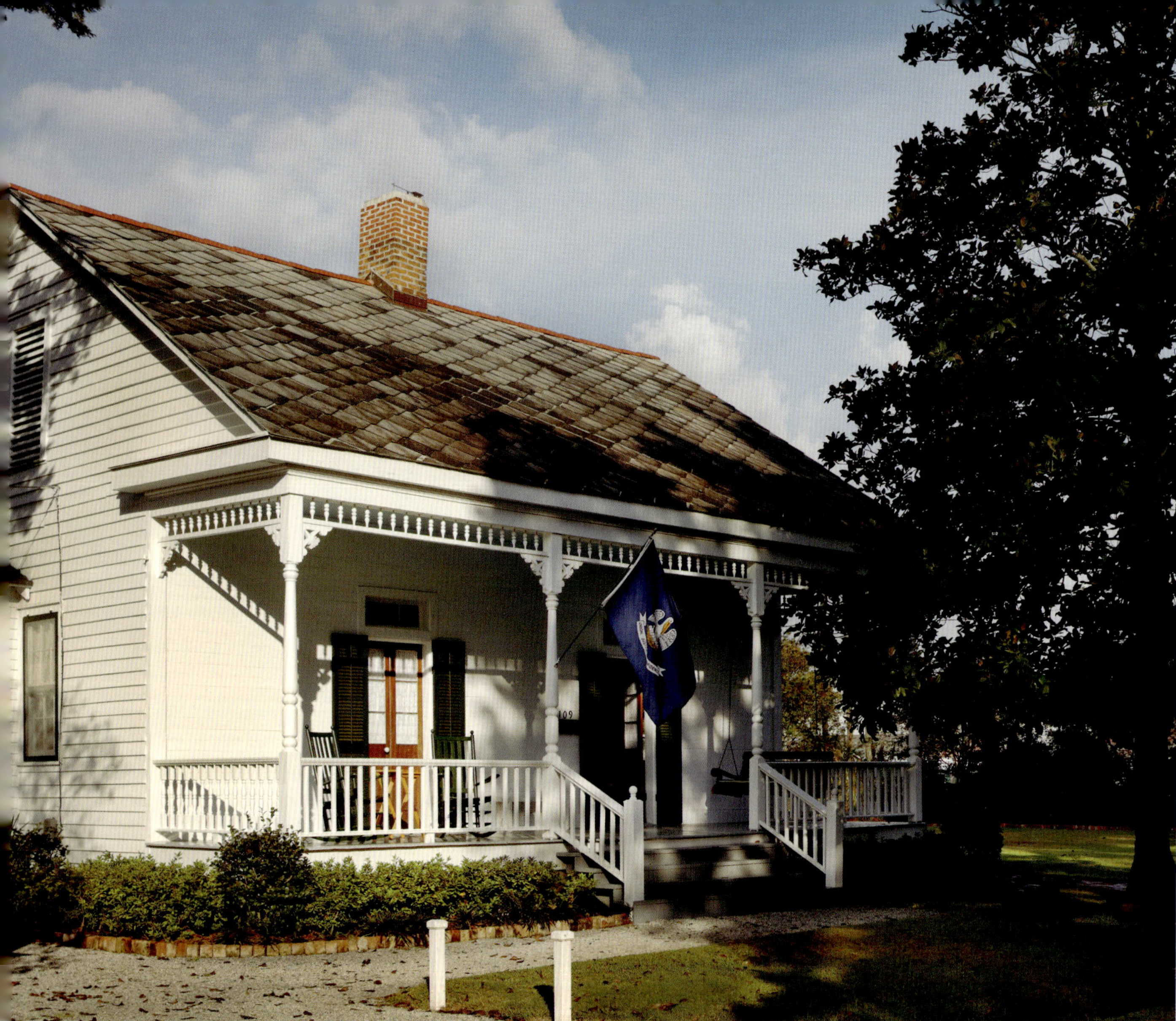

Built in the 1890s for the Anatole Sanchez family, the Pourciau House on Peach Street is a good example of a late Victorian Creole cottage ornamented in the Eastlake fashion. The house still has its broad front gallery and two front doors, indicating the traditional *salle et chambre* floor plan of the previous hundred years. But now the columns are turned on a lathe and dressed up with playful, intricately cut brackets and rows of turned spindles. The period between 1890 and 1912 was a prosperous, hopeful time in New Roads and Pointe Coupee in general, ending abruptly with the terrible flood of 1912. But many of these delightfully decorative, if simple, cottages survived, and are still used as residences throughout the parish. The Pourciau House, "a Wayfarer's Retreat," is operated as a bed-and-breakfast today.

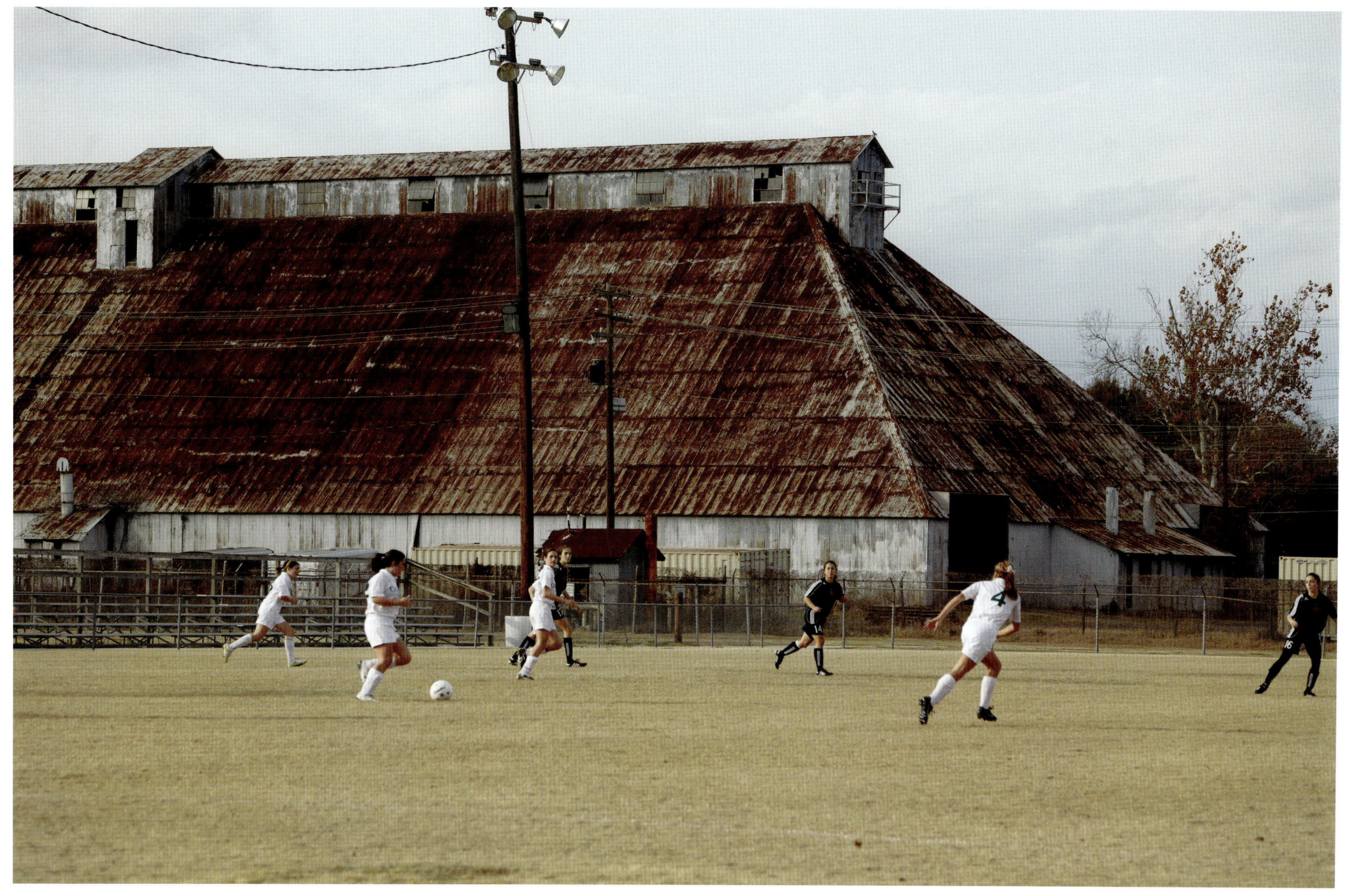

COTTONSEED OIL MILL

The Catholic of Pointe Coupee girls' soccer team plays on the ball field in front of the old cottonseed oil mill in New Roads. The mill dates back to 1900 and operated until 1979.

Alcide Bouanchaud, captain of the Pointe Coupee Artillery, assembled this home by placing two antebellum Creole cottages end to end around 1880. His descendants continued to own and occupy the home for the next century.

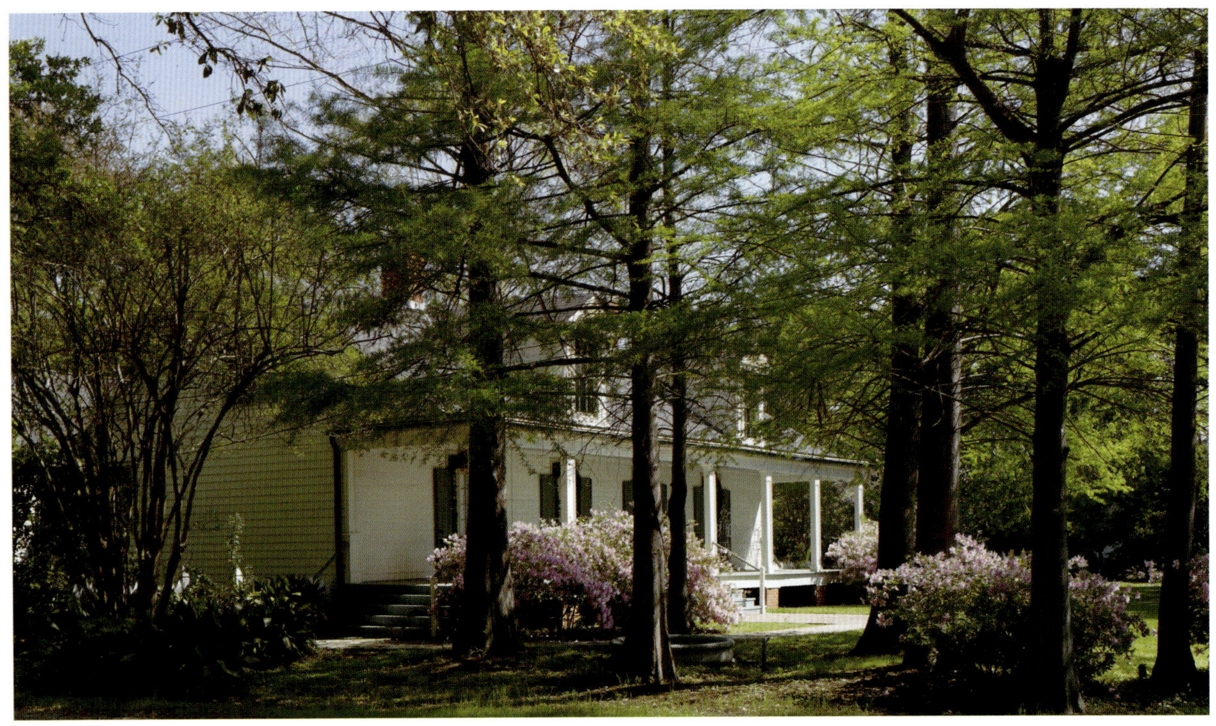

MISS SARITA'S GARDEN

Built in 1886 for Joseph LeJeune, this house was renovated a century later by James and Sarita Bouanchaud. In Miss Sarita's garden a large fan palm shades gingers, begonias, impatiens, ferns, and aspidistra, all bordered with monkey grass, a southern favorite.

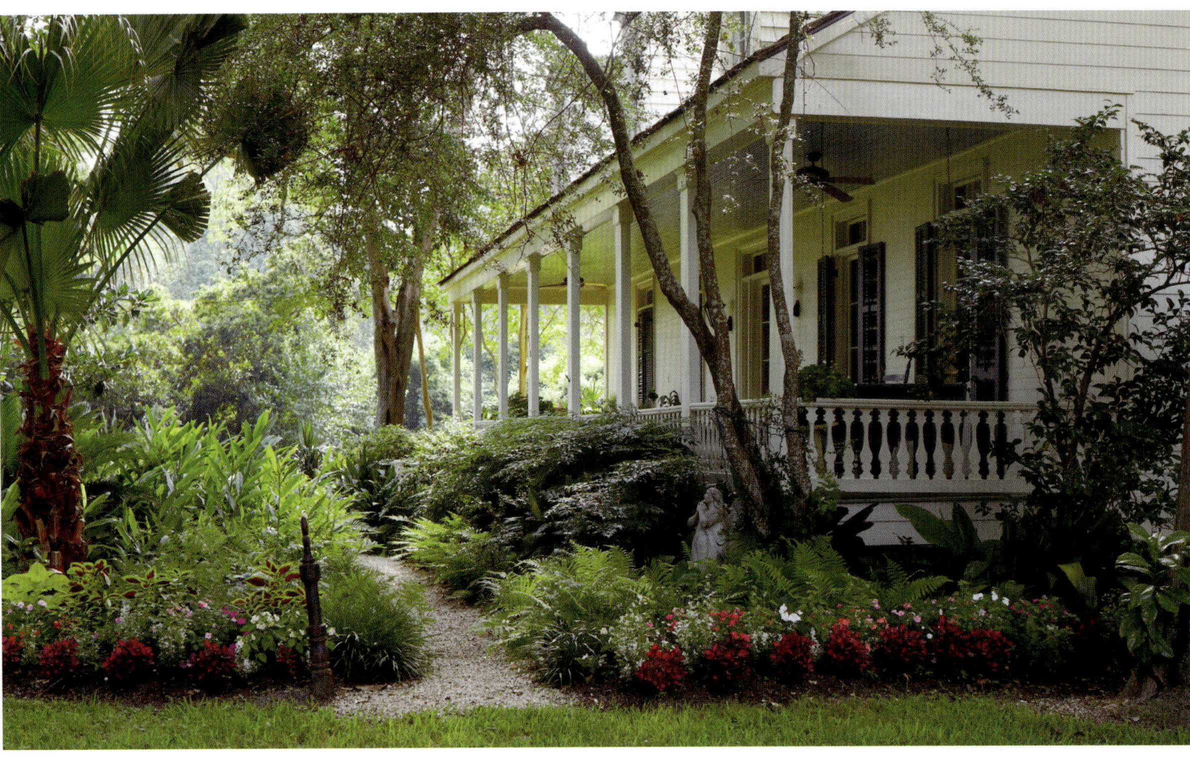

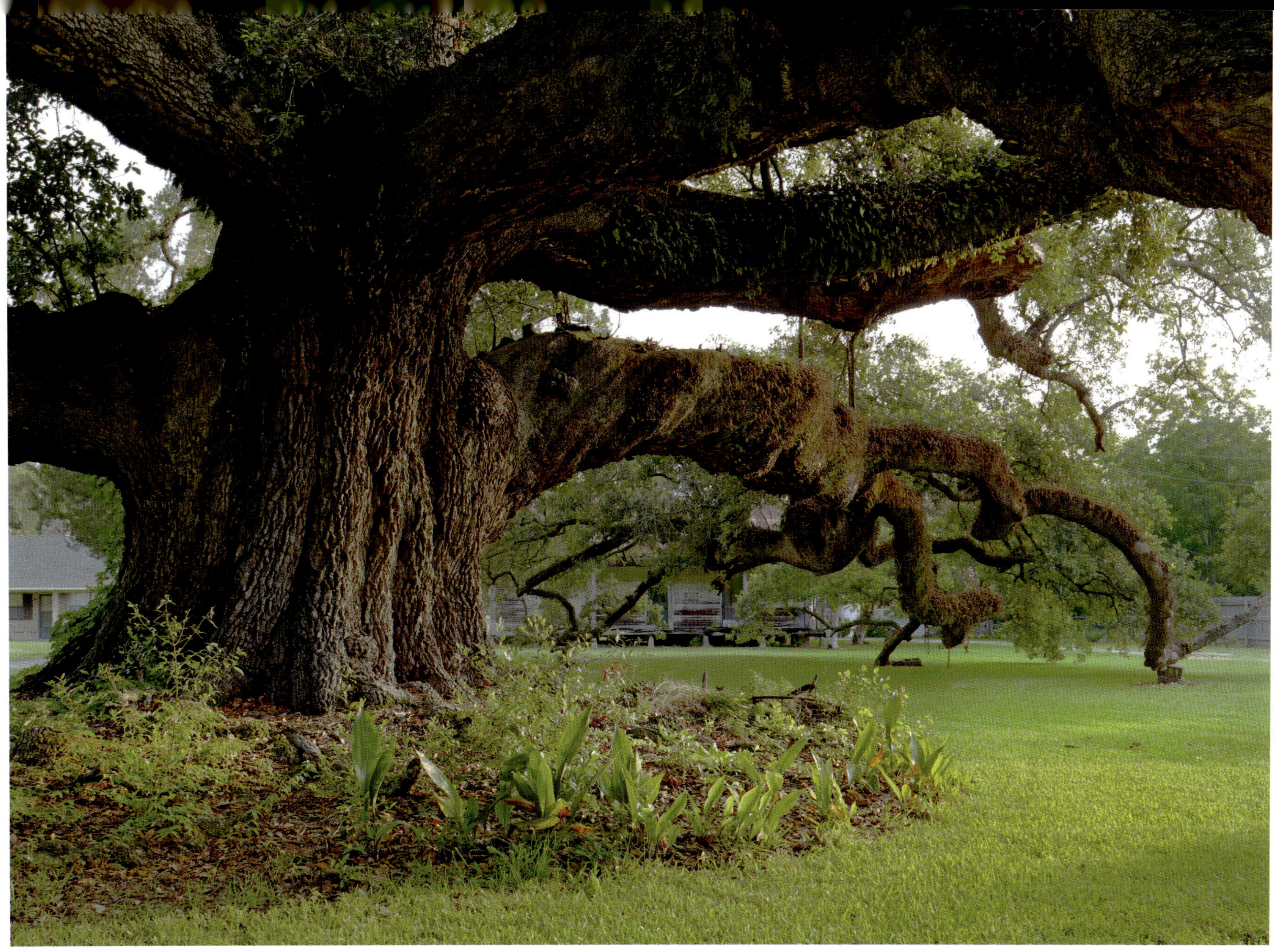

The Langlois Oak on Main Street near Morningside has limbs that touch the ground and a trunk more than 25 feet around. It is one of 62 live oaks in Pointe Coupee registered with the Live Oak Society under the auspices of the Louisiana Garden Club Federation. Edwin Lewis Stephens founded the society in 1934 with 43 trees in Louisiana, Texas, Mississippi, and Florida. Today more than 6,000 live oaks throughout the South have been registered.

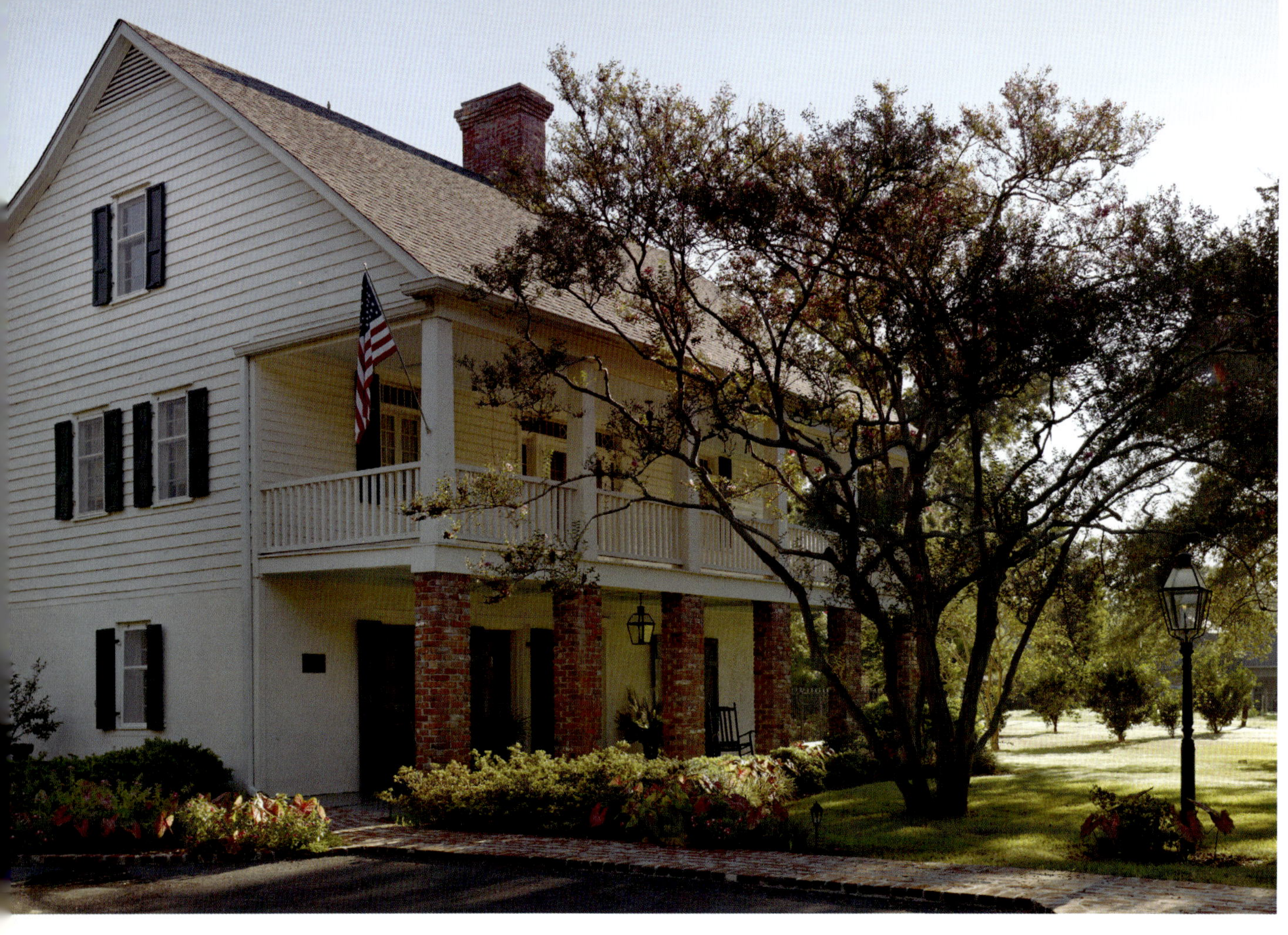

Wickliffe was named for the nearby Wickliffe Post Office, which in turn was named for Louisiana's fifteenth governor, Robert C. Wickliffe. Generally, Creole plantations and great houses were known by the surname of their owners, for example *L'Habitation Samson*, for Terence Samson, Wickliffe's first owner. The manner of naming houses such as White Hall in Upper Pointe Coupee is an Anglo-Saxon tradition.

Wickliffe is situated in a part of the parish known for two centuries as *Poulailler* (Chicken Coop), a humorous name that probably refers to the wild birds that roosted in the Upper Chenal.

The lower front gallery of Wickliffe is as comfortable and elegant in the twenty-first century as when it was built almost two hundred years ago (though the painted concrete floor is relatively new). The first floor is constructed of *briquette entre poteaux* and the second floor of wood frame, typical of early French Louisiana homes.

French doors in Wickliffe's dining room open to a view across a wide lawn to the old riverbed abandoned by the Mississippi River when it changed its course and cut off False River in the early 1700s.

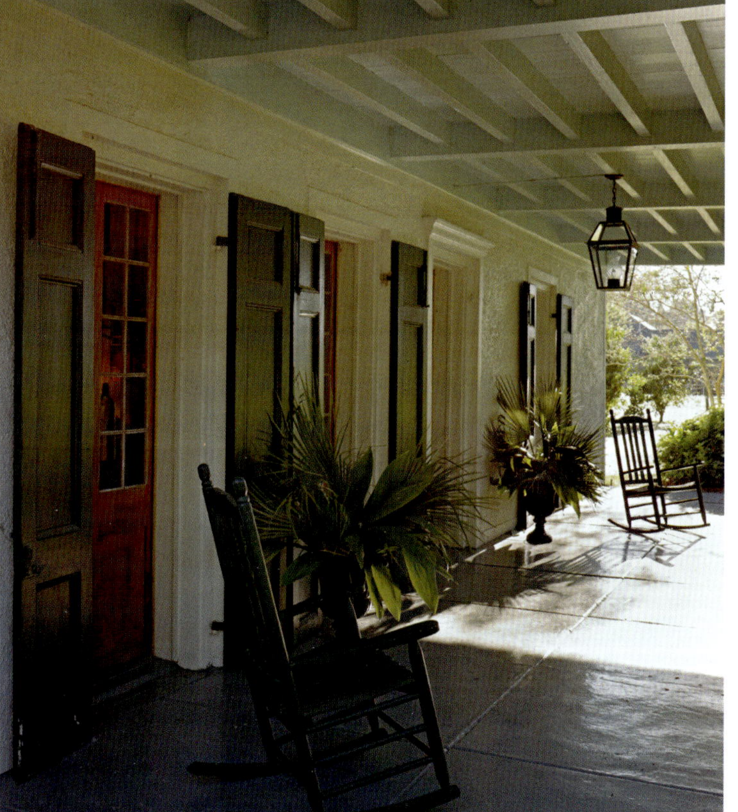

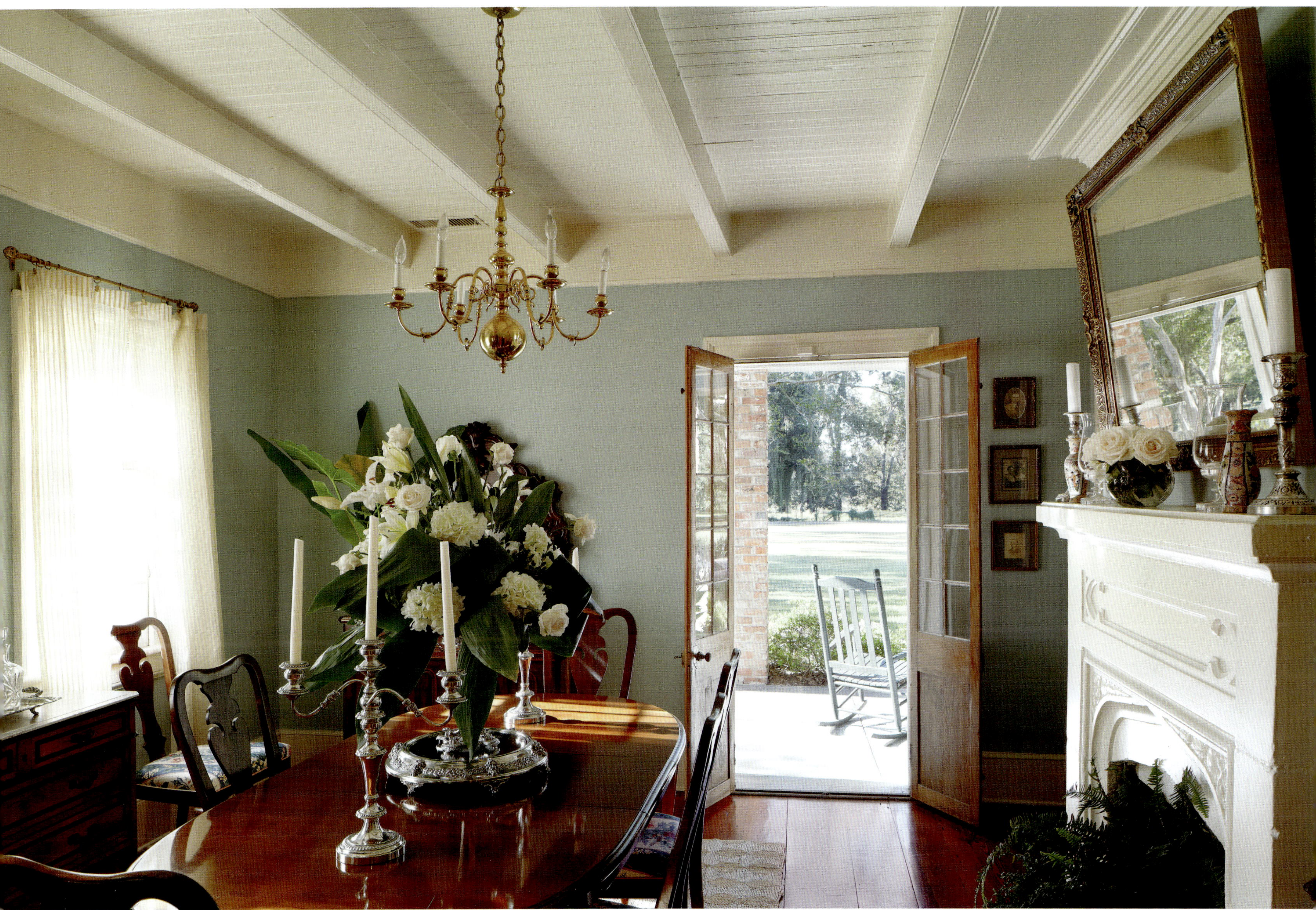

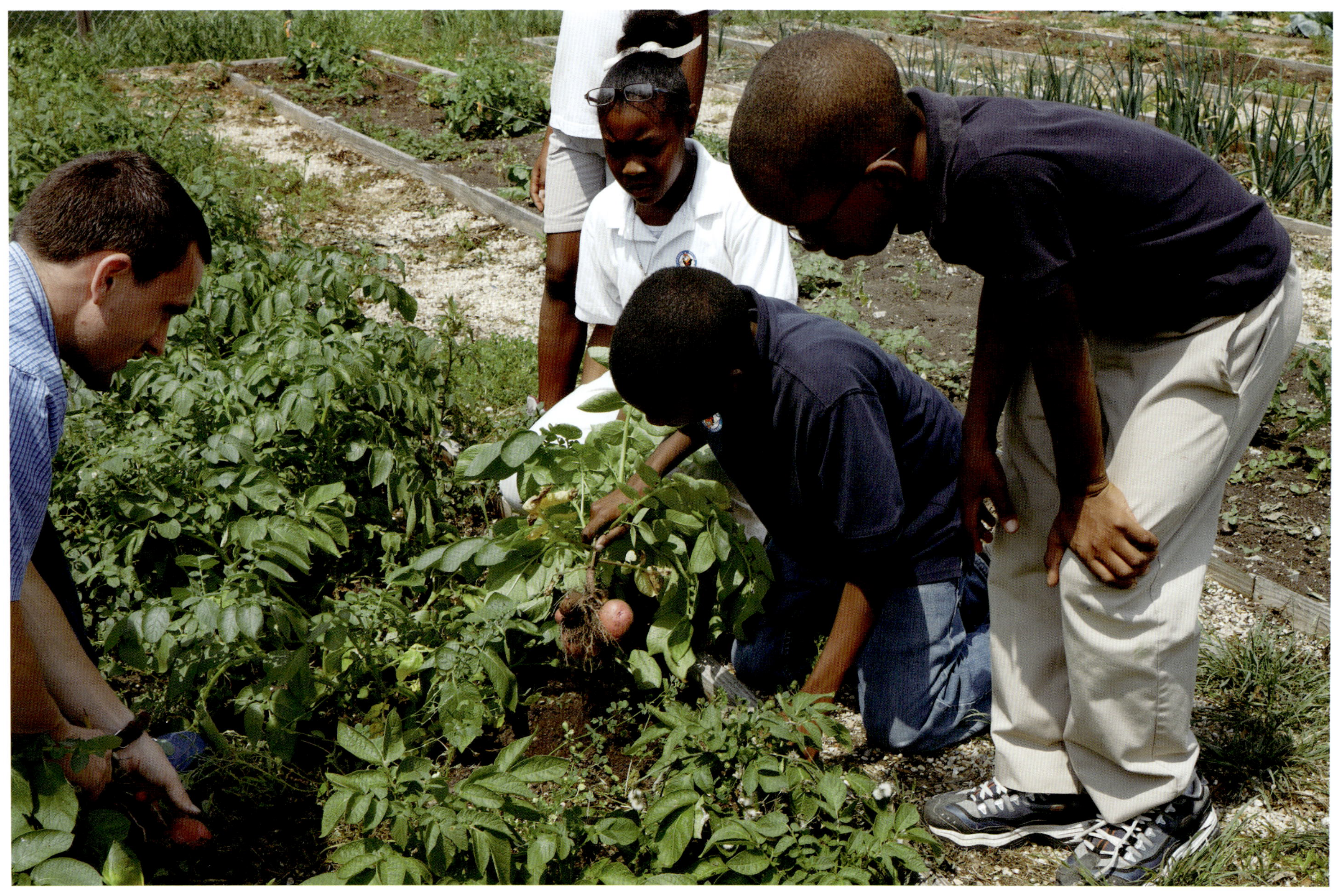

Rosenwald elementary school students show off cabbages they grew in their school garden. (*photo to right:* Micah Smothers, Tedra Brown, Jakala Jones, Chrisstana Tibbs, Brandon Davis, and Travis Franklin.) Almost every school in Pointe Coupee has created a garden with the help of County Agent Miles Brashier and many teachers who have seen the value of children growing their own food.

The first Rosenwald School in New Roads was built in 1921, funded by an ambitious program created by Chicago philanthropist Julius Rosenwald (1862–1932). Rosenwald matched local donations to build more than 5,000 schools in fifteen states from 1912 to 1932, all to support better education for African American children in the South and Midwest. In Pointe Coupee, Rosenwald schools were built in New Roads, Ventress, and Torbert.

A student presents fresh-dug potatoes on his way back to the classroom. As they grow vegetables in the school garden, children learn about the victory gardens of World War II, when many American civilians grew potatoes, carrots, and other vegetables in their home plots to add to the war effort through food production.

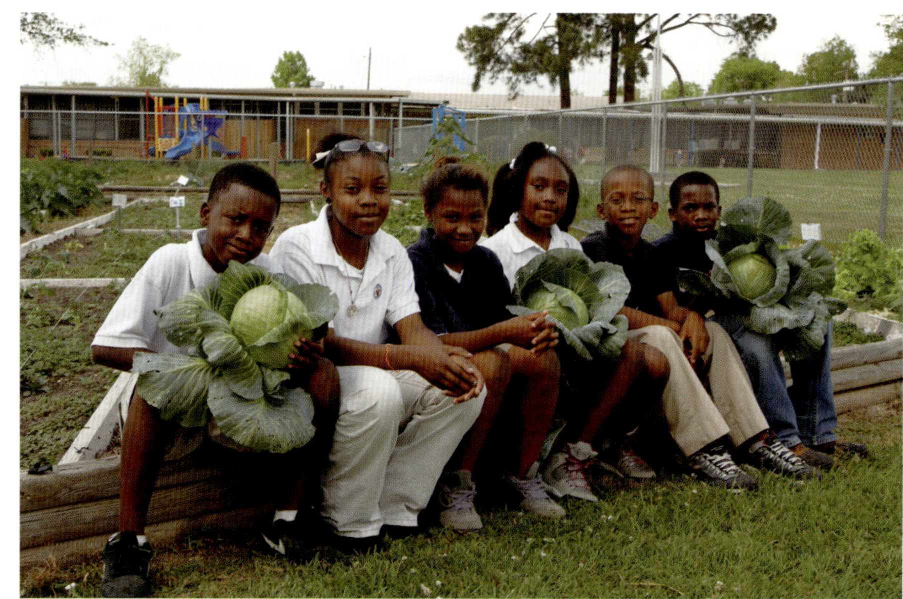

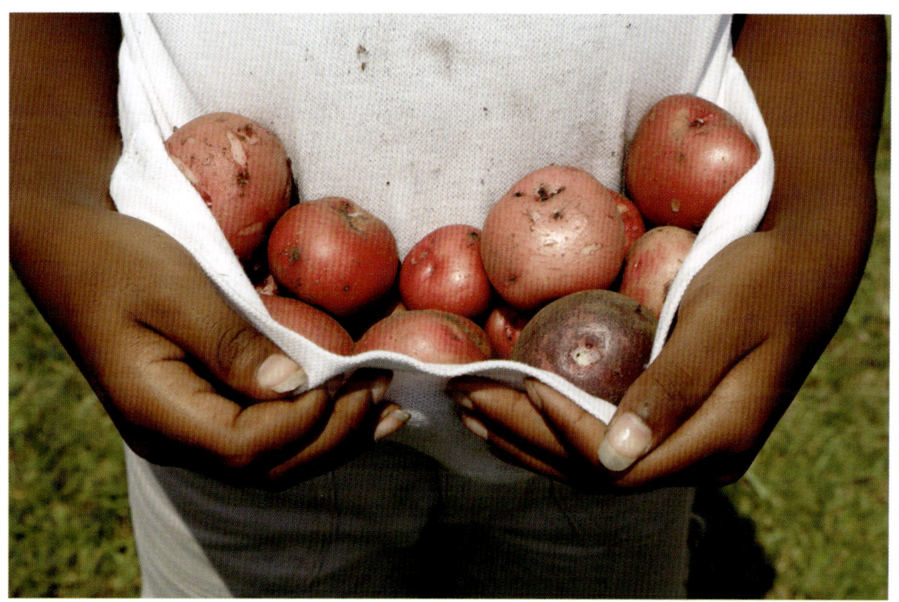

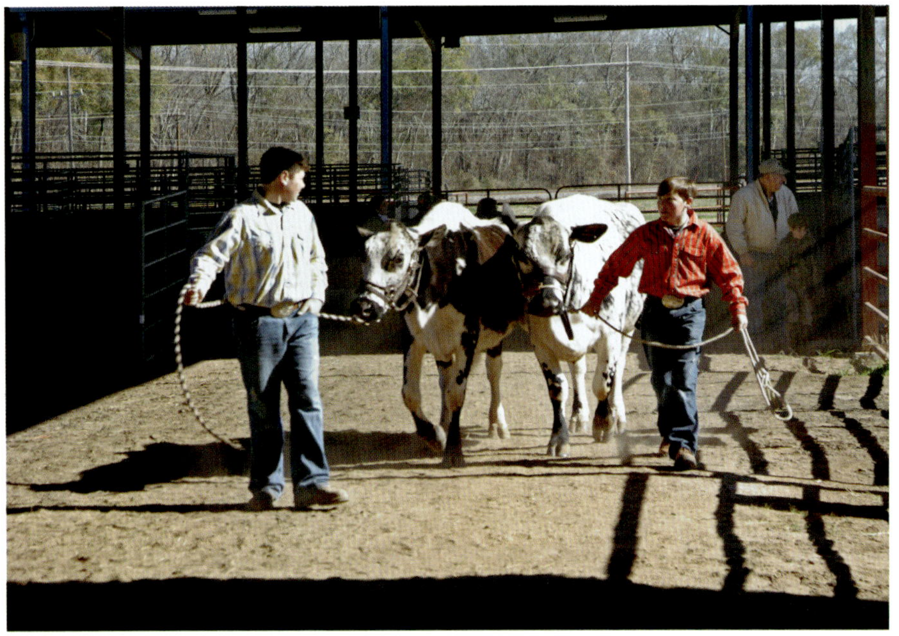

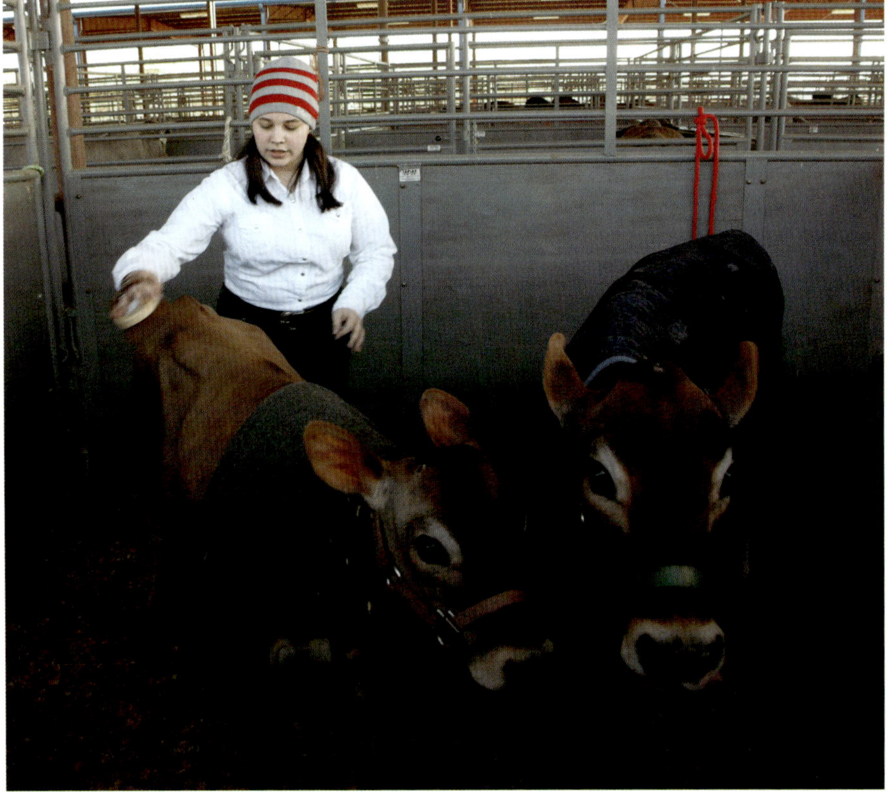

John and Trevor Jarreau of Livonia lead their dairy cows out to the Jeff Smith Memorial Arena of the Multi-Use Center in New Roads.

Rebecca Brown of Maringouin grooms her dairy calves in preparation for the cattle competition at the 4-H Livestock Show.

High school rodeo club members from across Louisiana warm up to compete in the cutting horse event at the 4-H Rodeo in New Roads.

The Louisiana 4-H program started in Avoyelles Parish, just across the Atchafalaya River from Pointe Coupee, in 1908. 4-H is the nation's largest youth development organization, open to young people nine to twenty years old. With local support from the parish school board, police jury, and the community, 4-H is run in a three-way partnership between the U.S. Department of Agriculture, the state's land grant university LSU, and Pointe Coupee's local government. The 4-H program is still incorporated into the classroom in Pointe Coupee, and every fourth-grade student in the parish is invited to join 4-H free for one year. In 2011 the parish boasted 875 members in grades 4–12, and 125 adult volunteers. The four Hs of 4-H stand for Head, Heart, Hands, and Health.

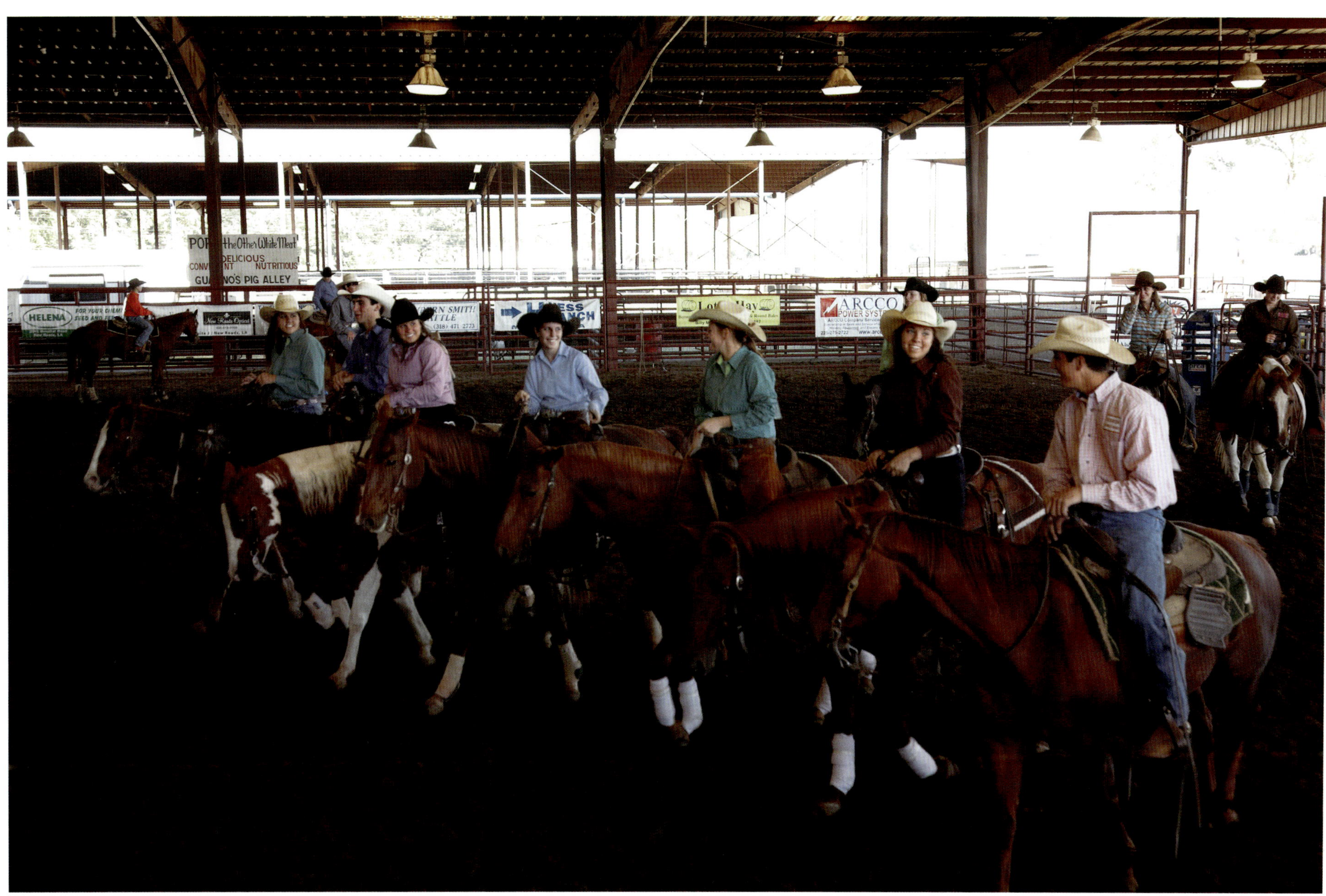

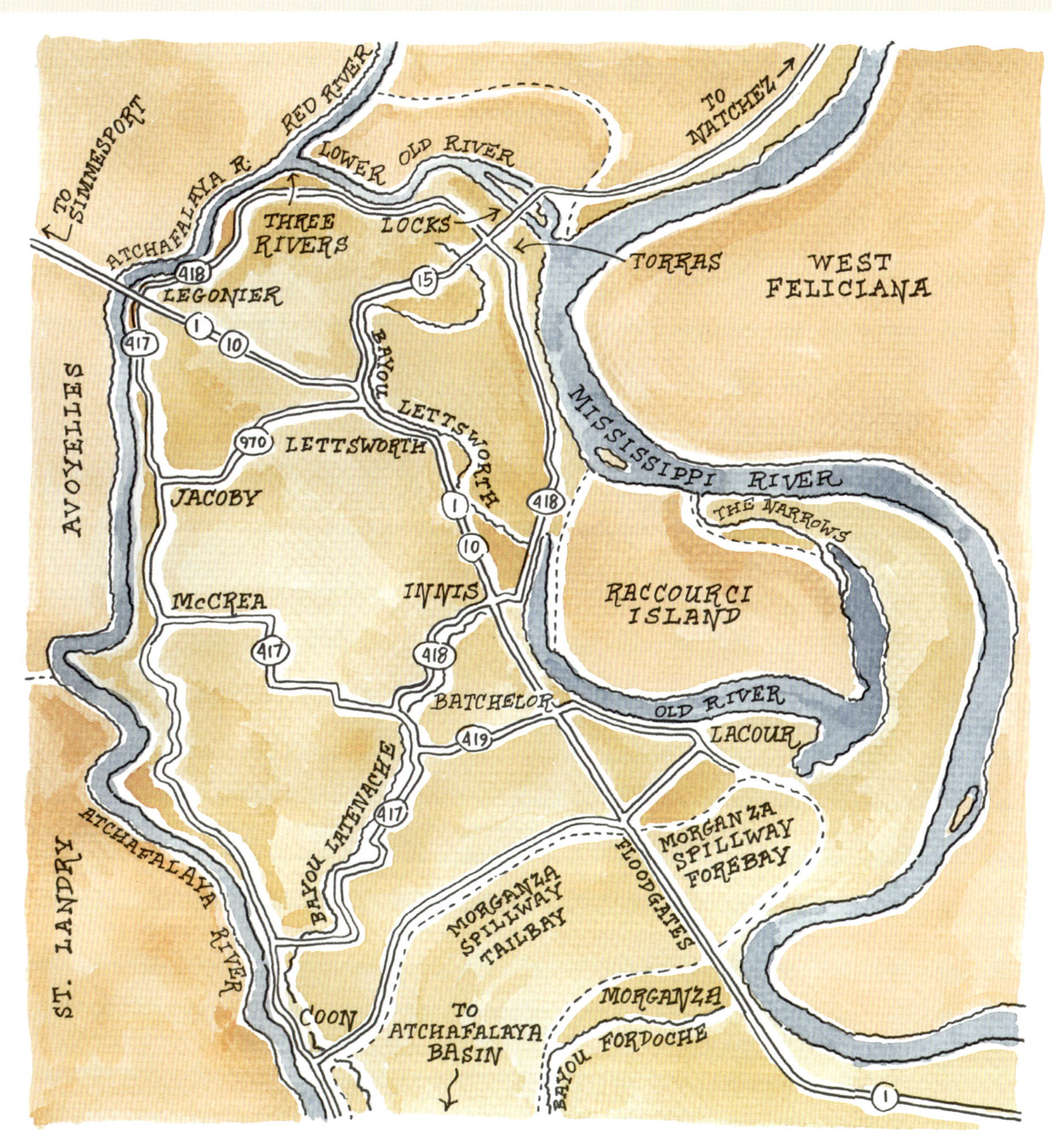
TO SIMMESPORT
ATCHAFALAYA R.
RED RIVER
LOWER OLD RIVER
TO NATCHEZ
THREE RIVERS
LOCKS
TORRAS
WEST FELICIANA
418
15
LEGONIER
417
1
10
BAYOU
LETTSWORTH
970
LETTSWORTH
418
JACOBY
1
MISSISSIPPI RIVER
THE NARROWS
10
AVOYELLES
McCREA
INNIS
RACCOURCI ISLAND
417
418
BATCHELOR
OLD RIVER
419
LACOUR
417
MORGANZA SPILLWAY FOREBAY
ST. LANDRY
ATCHAFALAYA RIVER
BAYOU LATENACHE
FLOODGATES
MORGANZA SPILLWAY TAILBAY
COON
TO ATCHAFALAYA BASIN
MORGANZA
BAYOU FORDOCHE
1

CHAPTER 5

LA-1, Morganza, and the Spillway

JOE BEAUD POTATO SHED

Joe Beaud's potato shed is a landmark on LA-1 between New Roads and Morganza. Farmer Joe Beaud (1911–2002) grew Irish potatoes for about fifty years, from the beginning of the Great Depression until the late 1970s. In the shed, he washed and graded potatoes and packed them for shipping by rail as far as Chicago.

Pointe Coupee folks still remember eating Joe Beaud potatoes, harvested in spring, drenched in butter and parsley at dinner on Easter Sunday.

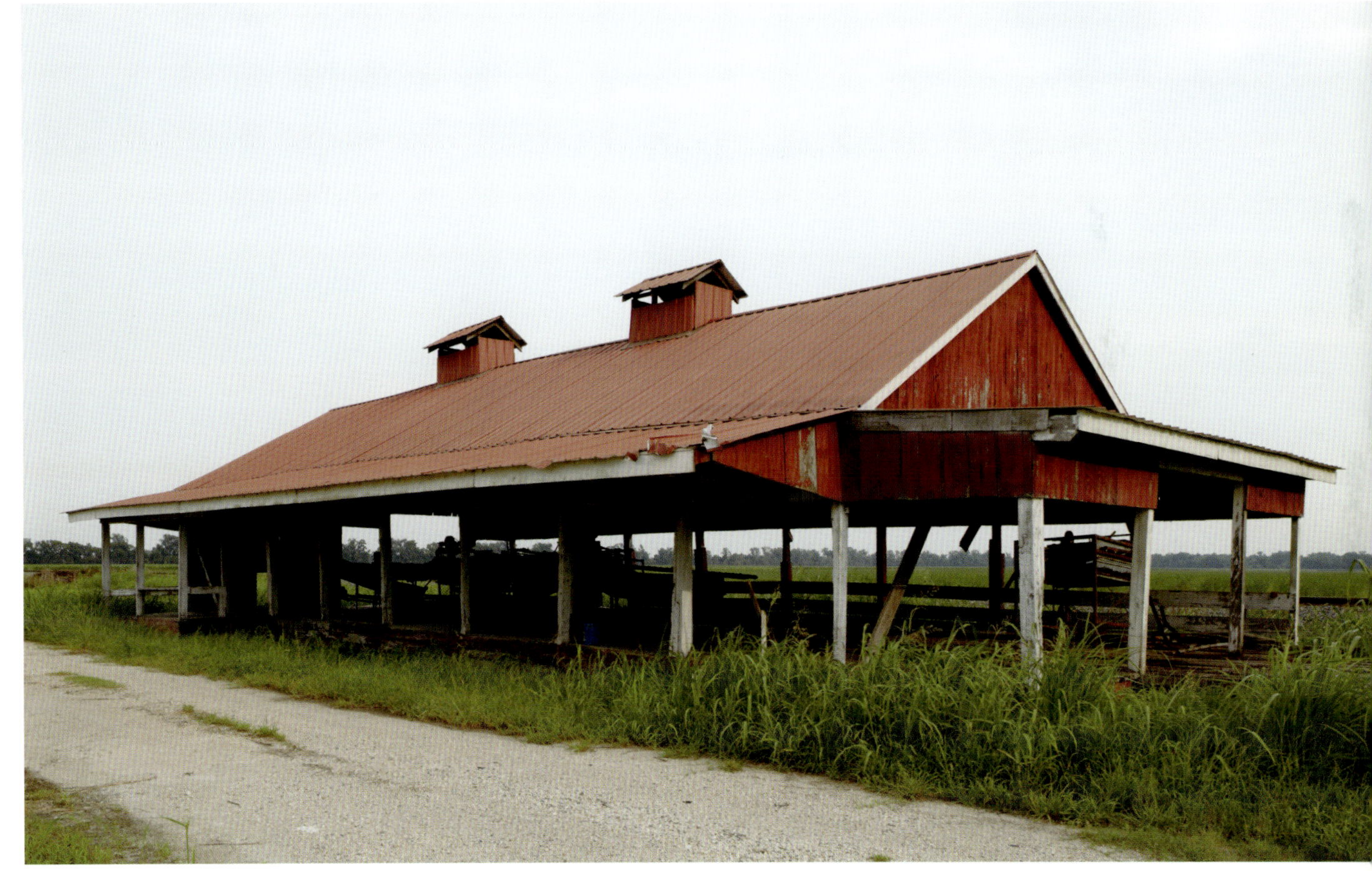

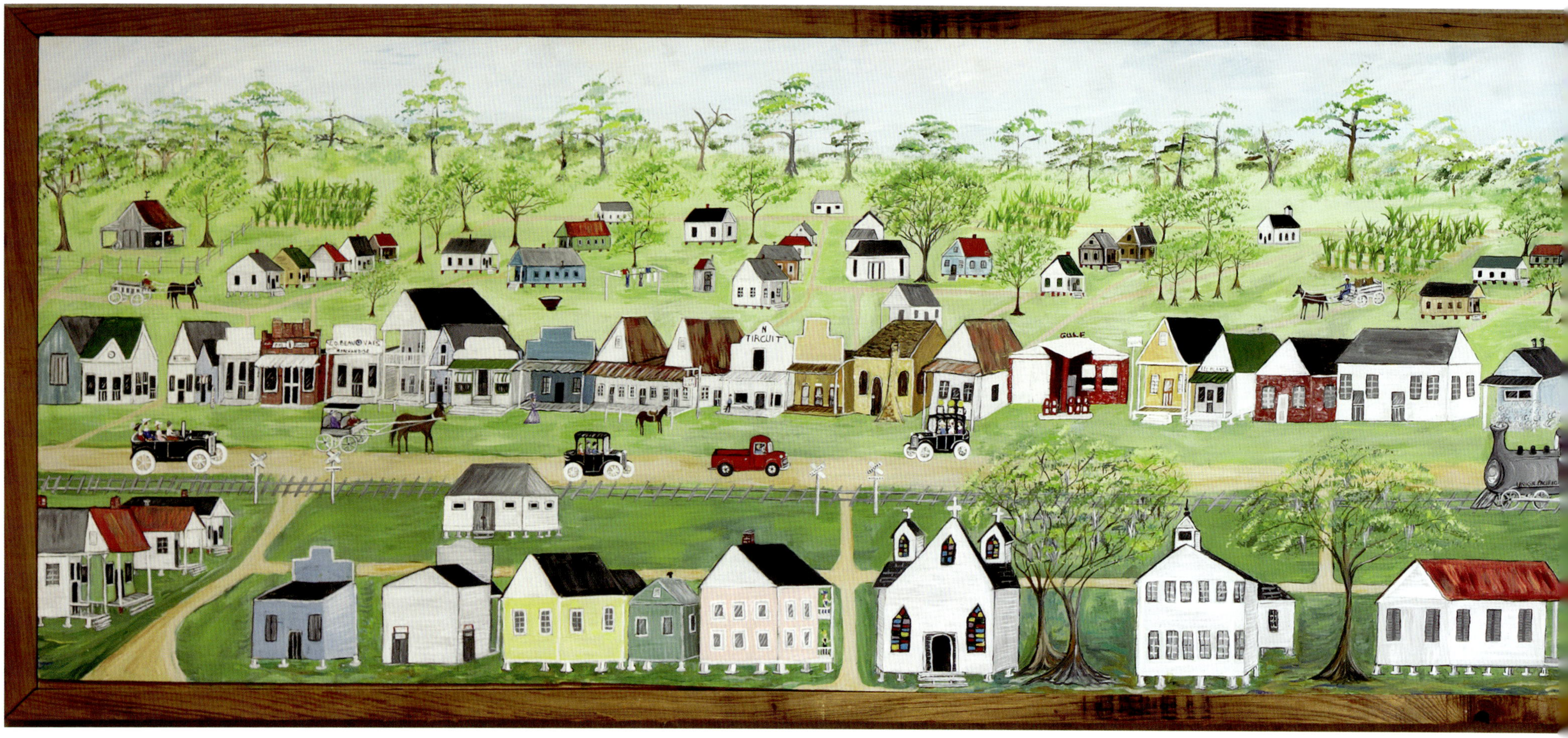

Bikers gather on LA-1, the main street of Morganza, near the former site of Melancon's Café, where a scene from *Easy Rider* was filmed. The *Easy Rider* motorcycle rally held in Morganza attests to the enduring attraction of the 1969 road film and the iconic American motorcycle. The Pointe Coupee Historical Society placed a commemorative marker at the site of the café in 2010.

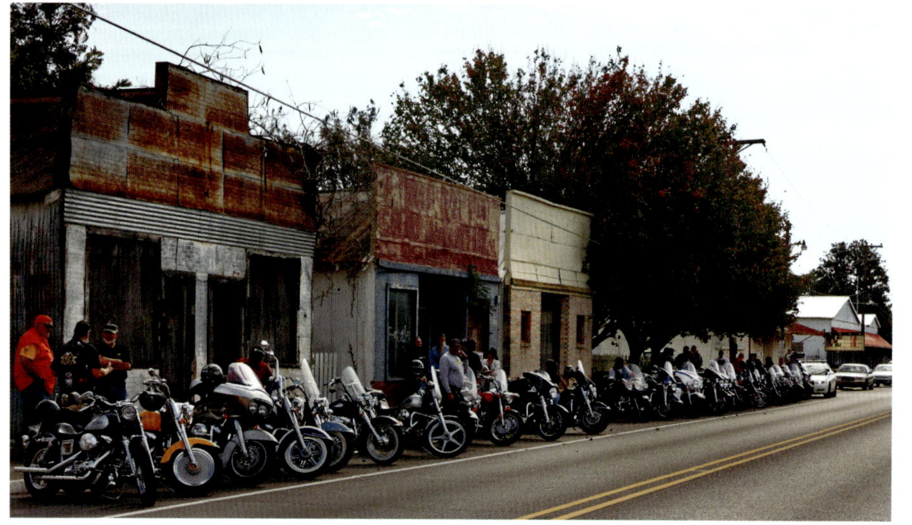

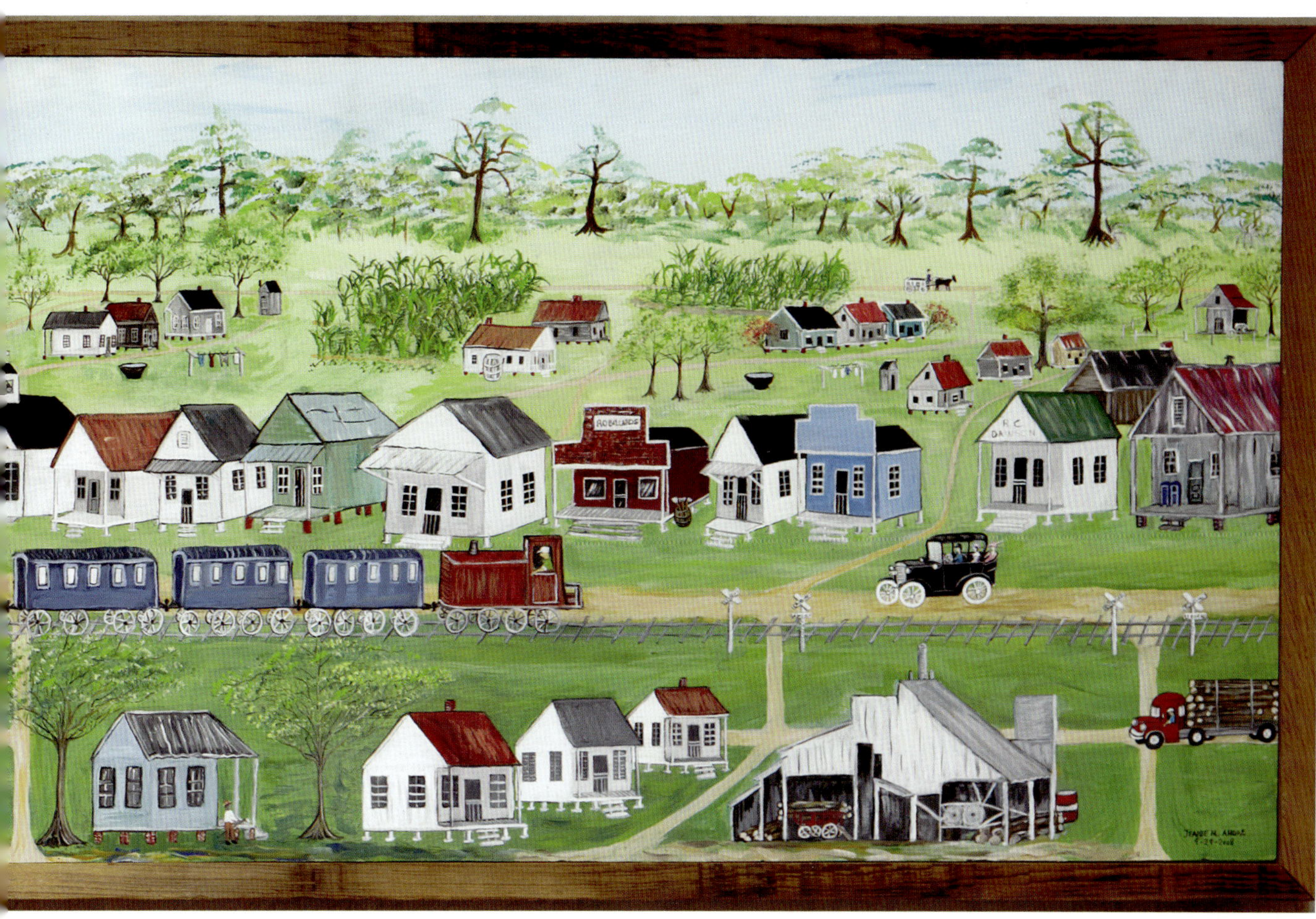

Jeanie Andre painted this idealized portrait of Morganza as a view into the past. Some buildings are still standing in the town: St. Ann Catholic Church, Serio's gas station, and Little Rock Baptist Church (just behind the locomotive). Others, such as Melancon's Café (the brick building with Coca-Cola signs) and Dawson's Sawmill (bottom right), are gone but still clear in people's memory.

Morganza took its name from the plantation of Charles Morgan (ca. 1775–1848), a surveyor from New Jersey who came to Pointe Coupee, married a French woman, and stayed. He became a wealthy landowner and sheriff of Pointe Coupee. The town of Morganza grew up in response to the new Texas & Pacific Railroad, the tracks laid in 1899. The town was incorporated in 1908.

Neal's Salon operates in a building that was once the hub of activity in Morganza, the U.S. Post Office. Today the post office is housed in a modern building across the street. The salon brags, "If your hair isn't becoming to you, you should be coming to us!"

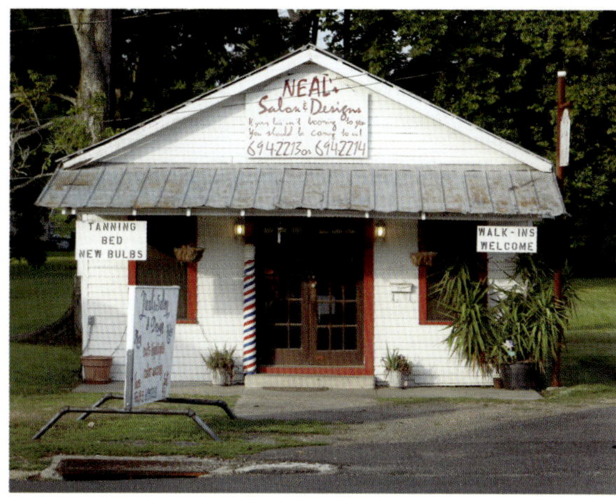

The church building was constructed in 1935, but the church parish dates to 1872 when Our Lady of Seven Dolors was established at Raccourci beside Old River.

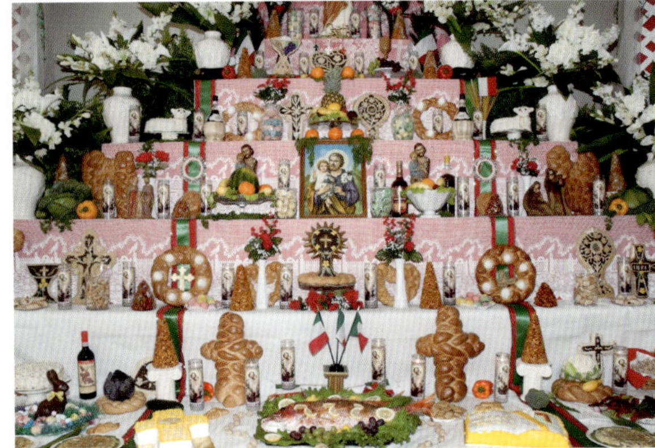

ST. JOSEPH ALTAR

At St. Ann, more than twenty members of the San Giuseppe Altar Ladies have made food and decorated the altar every year for over a quarter-century to mark St. Joseph's feast day, March 19. St. Joseph is the patron saint of Italy and much loved by Italian-Americans. At St. Ann and in many other Catholic church parishes in south Louisiana, his feast is celebrated with a big community dinner of traditional Italian dishes without meat. Huge pots of spaghetti are served with tomato gravy and boiled eggs, symbolizing the rebirth of spring and the coming of Easter.

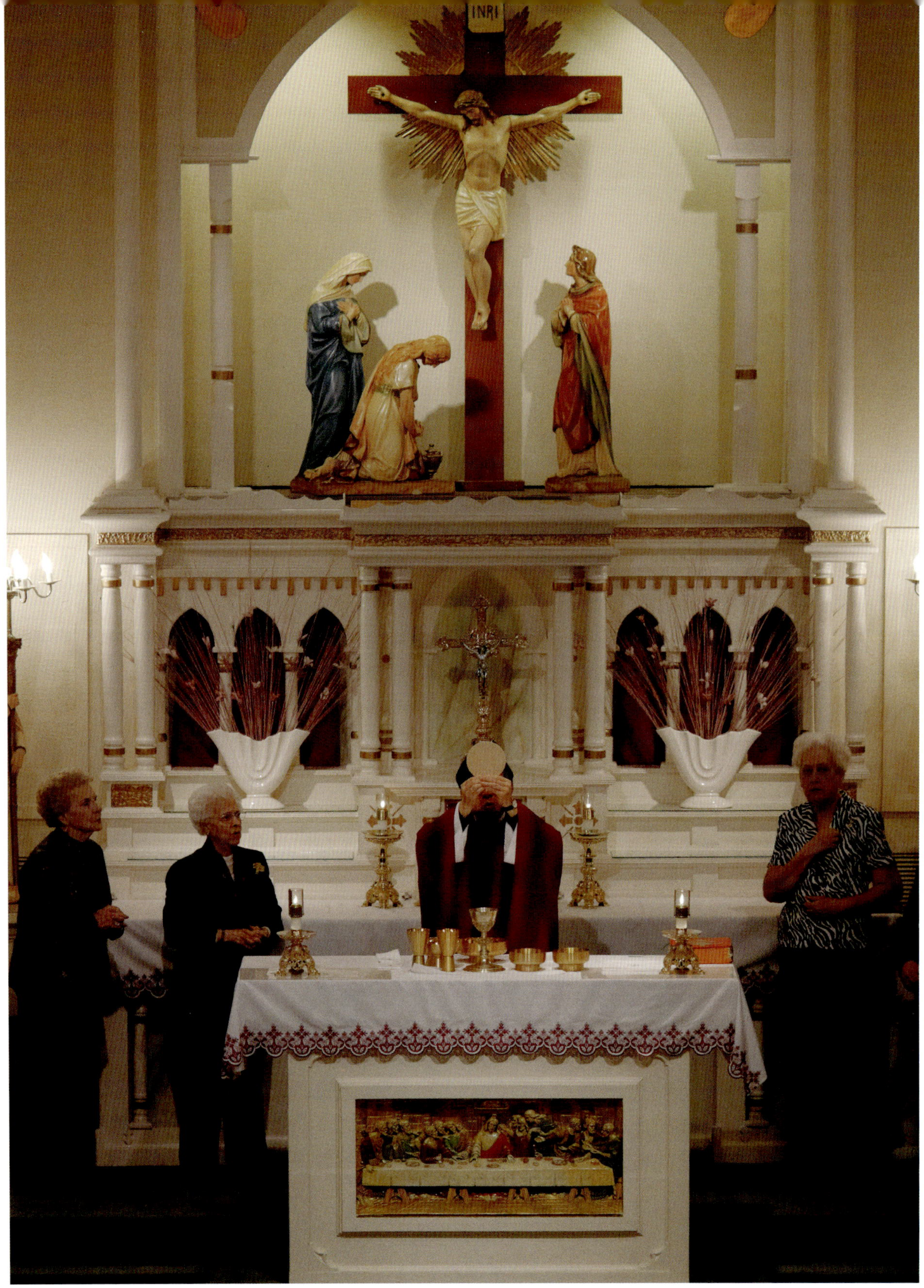

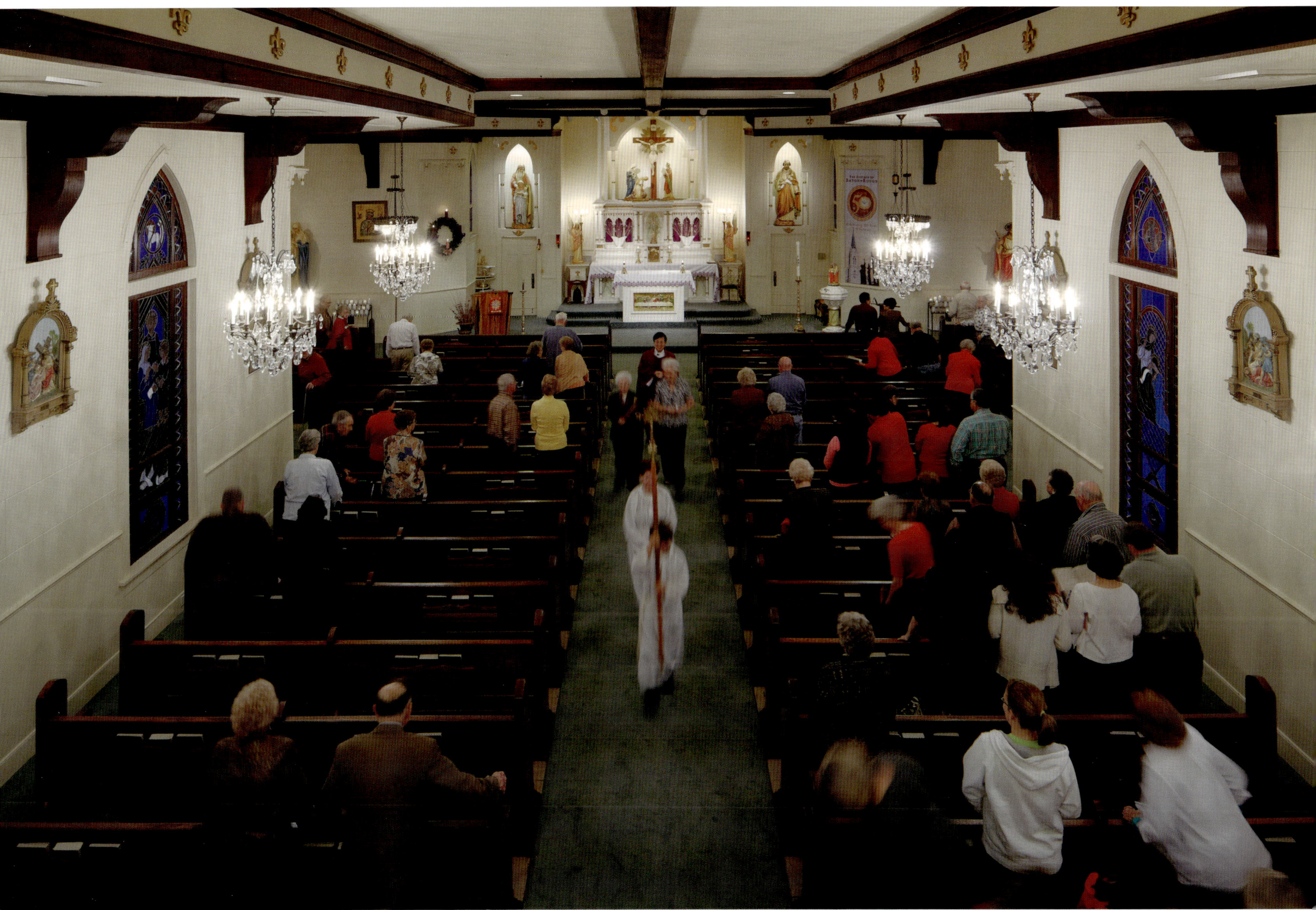

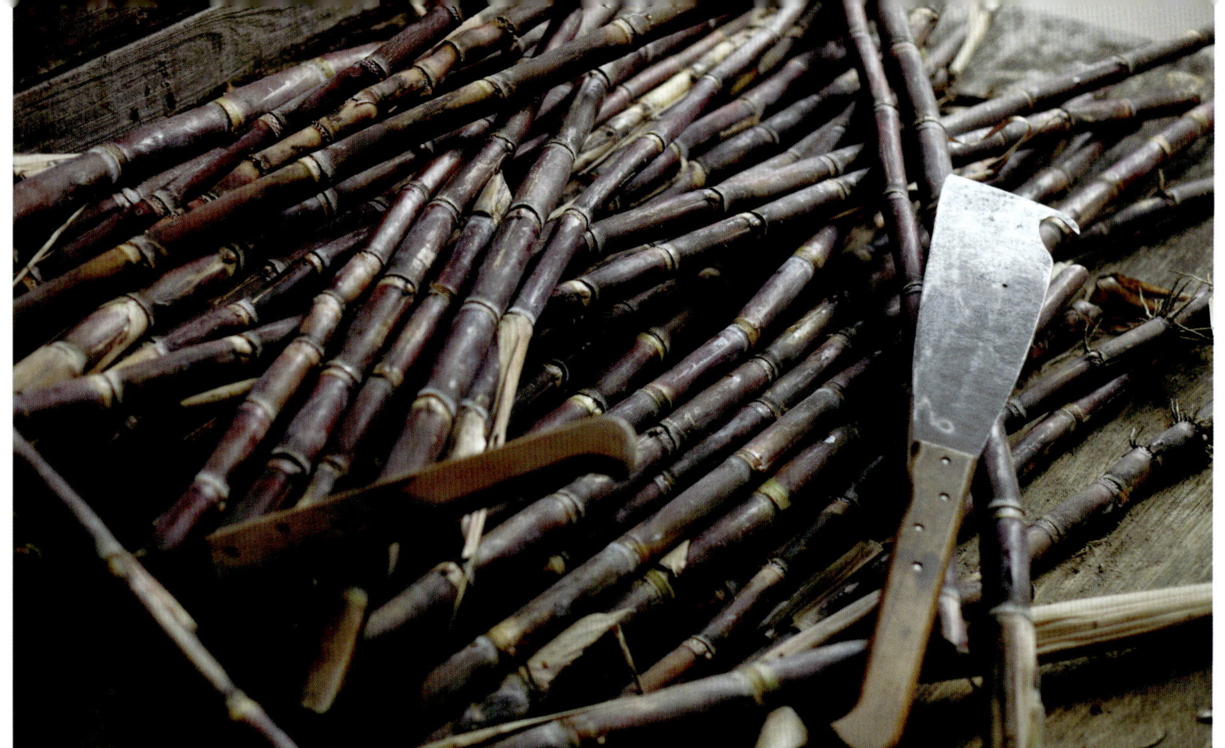

Blue Ribbon cane is not a variety grown on a large scale for making sugar. It is soft, good for chewing, and has lots of juice that is boiled down to make delicious cane syrup.

Donald LeBlanc skims the surface of cane syrup simmering in an open kettle on his Morganza farm.

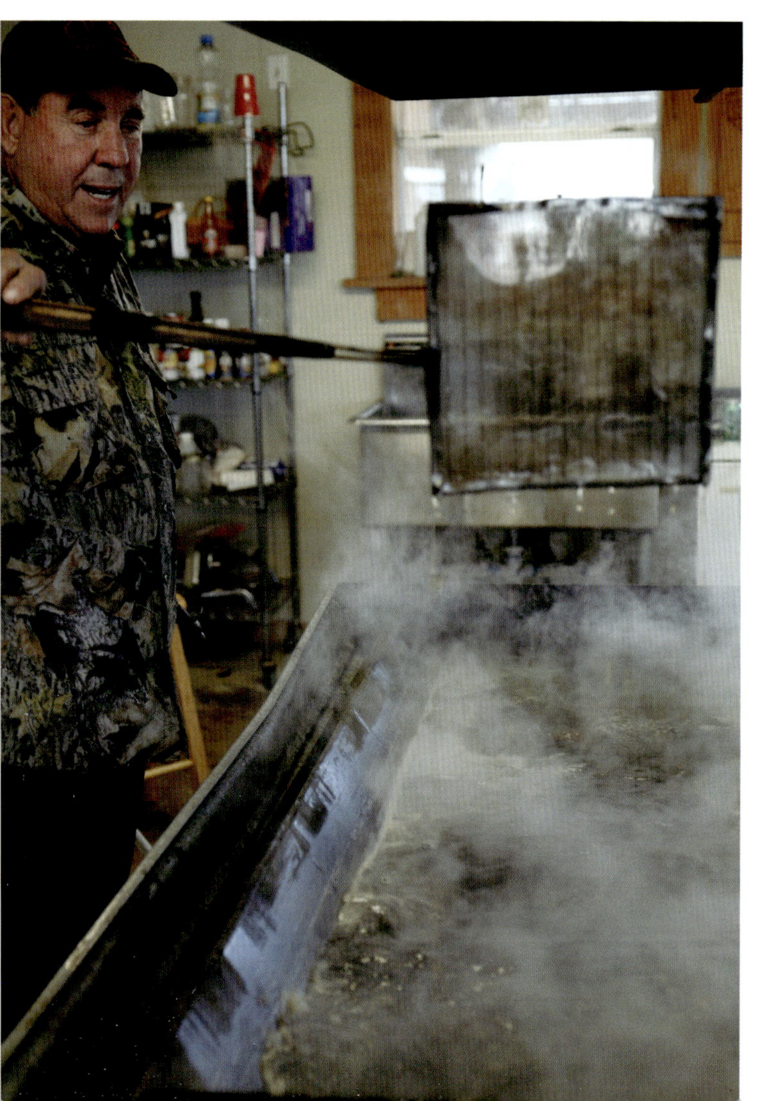

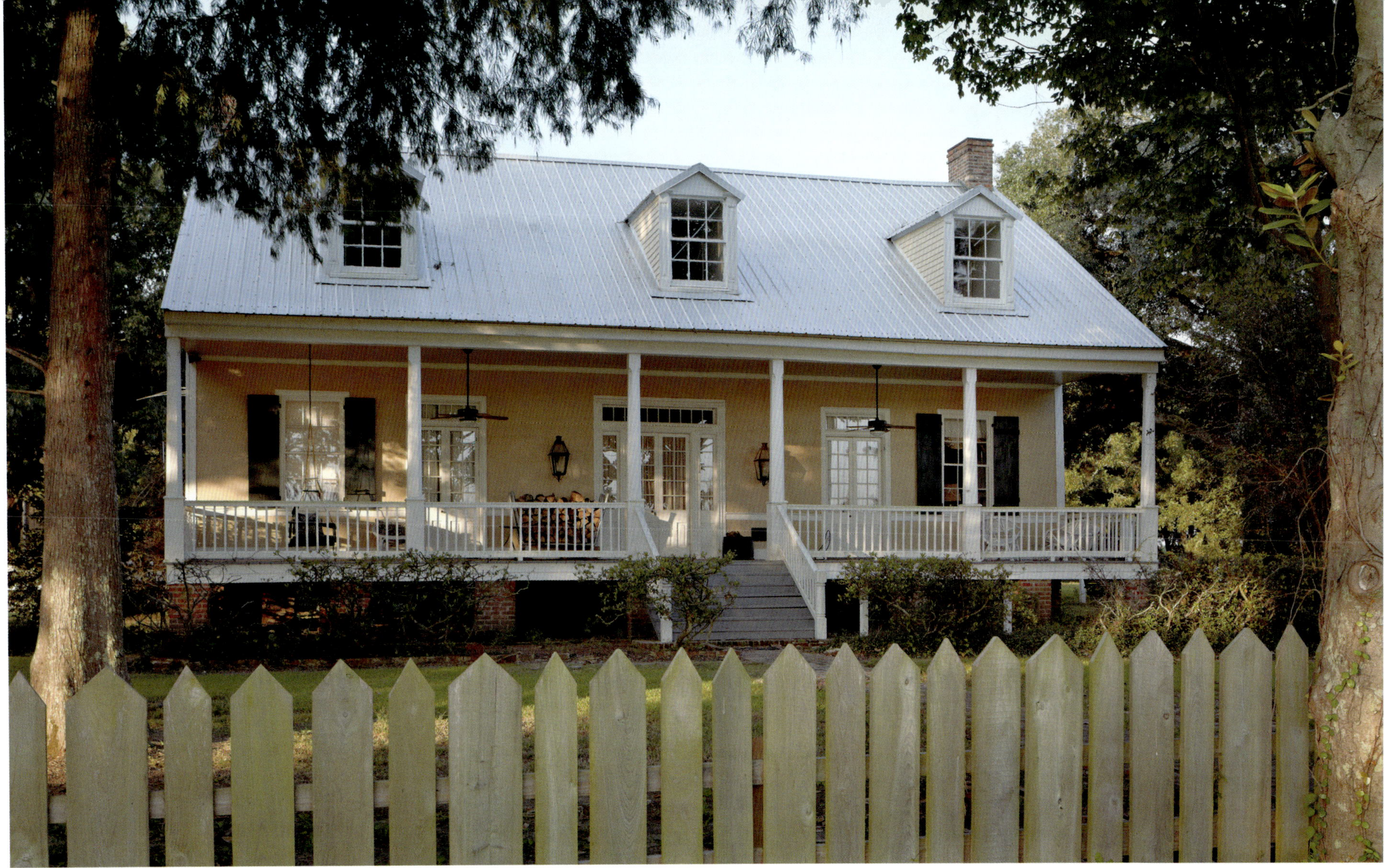

Old Hickory is named in honor of General Andrew Jackson, the hero of the battle of New Orleans at the end of the War of 1812. The original owner of the property was Captain Zenon LeDoux, who fought the British alongside Jackson with his "Company of Volunteers of Pointe Coupee," a local militia of 31 men.

Later the plantation was owned by Confederate captain Ovide Lejeune, father of USMC general John Archer Lejeune. One of Pointe Coupee's most illustrious citizens, John Archer Lejeune was born at Old Hickory in 1867.

For more than twenty years during the mid-twentieth century, the house was used as a public school for African American children.

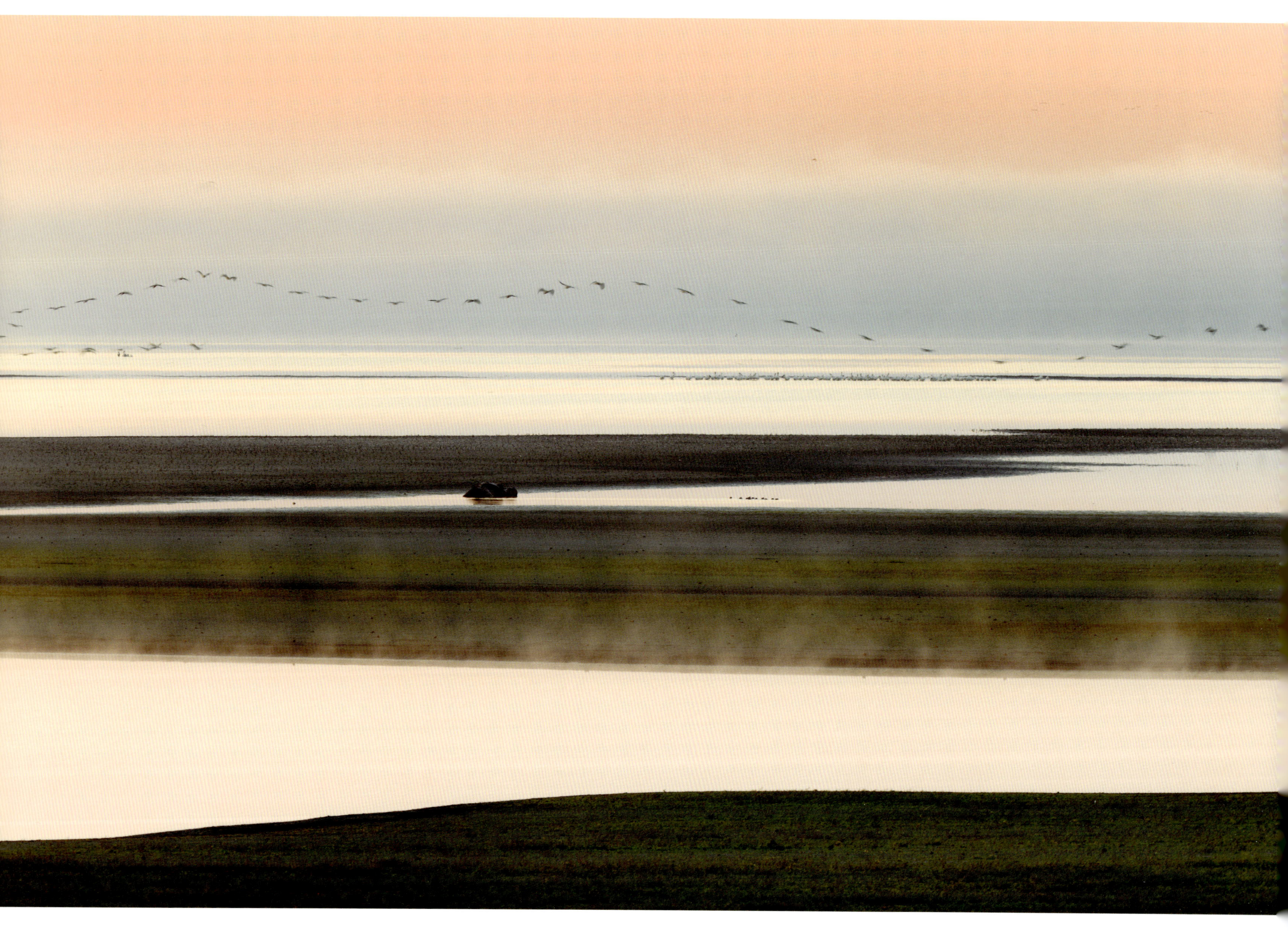

The forebay of the Morganza Spillway fills with river water when the Mississippi River overtops the low levee that separates the waterways. Essentially a manmade wetland, the forebay is one of the best birding sites in Louisiana. In autumn, tens of thousands of white pelicans and roseate spoonbills stop and stay for weeks in the spillway.

The sun rises over the forebay on a crisp October morning. By fall, most of the floodwater has subsided.

Highway LA-1 travels directly over the floodgates of the Morganza Spillway.

After the devastating floods of 1927, the U.S. Army Corps of Engineers began the design and building of the spillway. The structure is designed to allow Mississippi floodwater that might threaten Baton Rouge and New Orleans downriver to flow into the Atchafalaya Basin. Completed in 1954, it has been used only twice: in the Mississippi River floods of 1973 and in 2011.

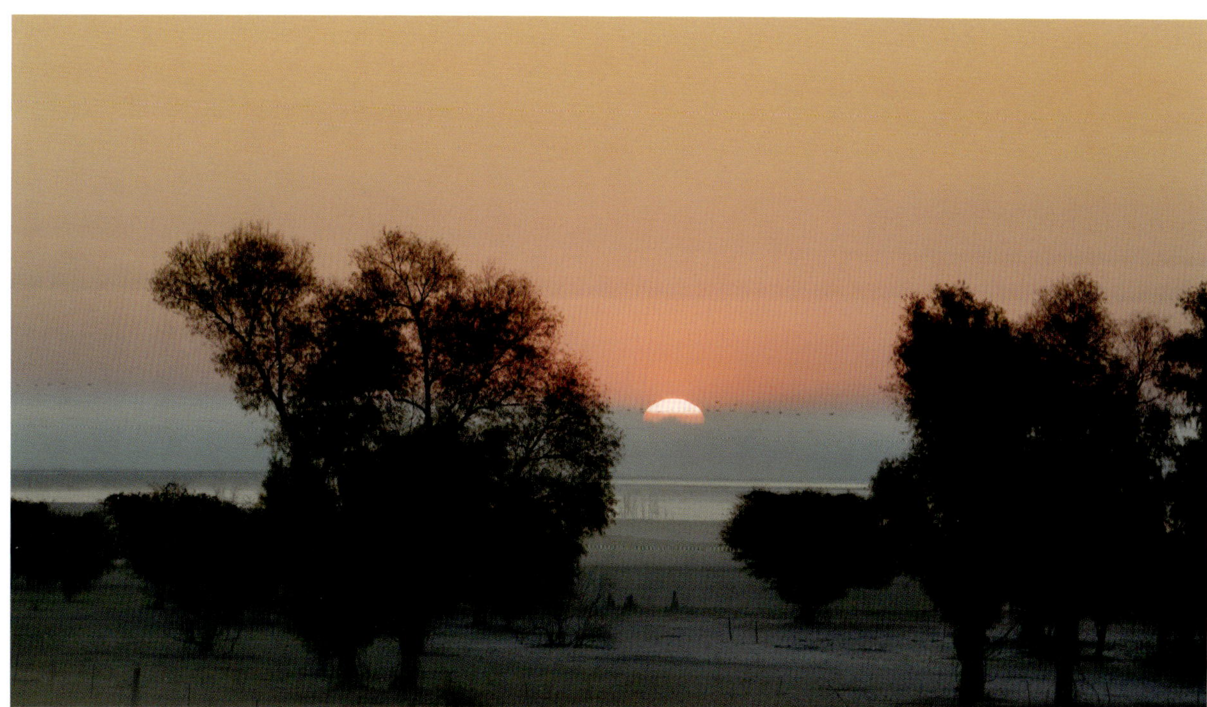

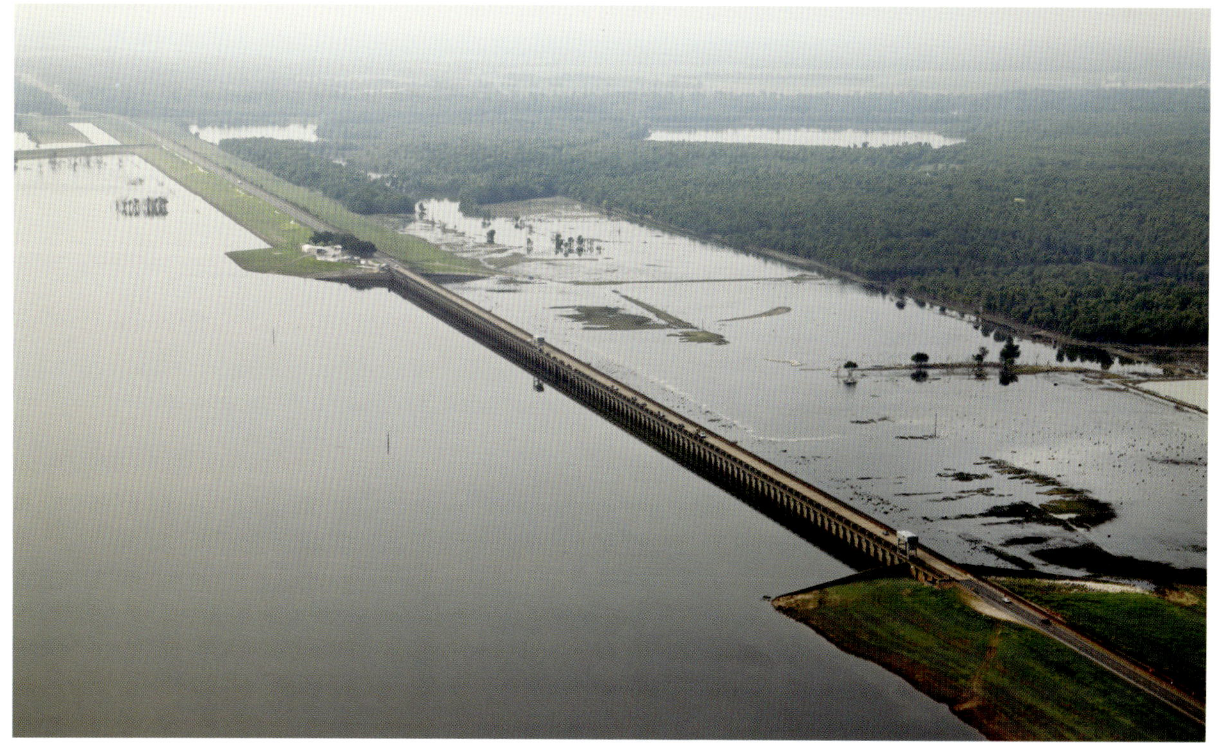

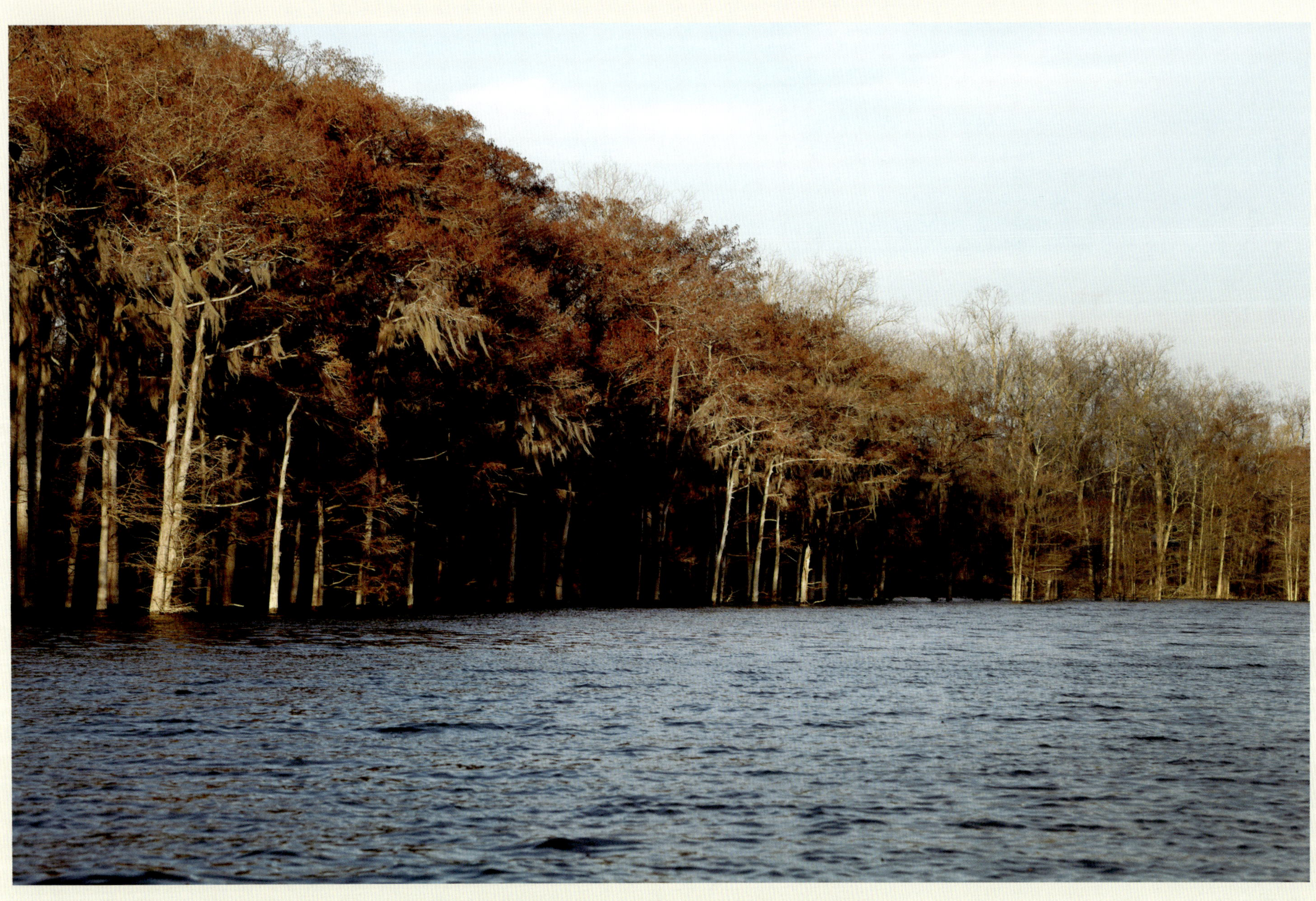

CHAPTER 6

Old River and Upper Pointe Coupee

BAPTIST CHURCHES OF POINTE COUPEE

Mount Zion Baptist Church in LaCour is one of more than forty Baptist churches in Pointe Coupee. Zion refers to Jerusalem. The biblical story of Jews in slavery in Babylon, longing for freedom and comfort in Zion, was deeply felt by African Americans during and after their own slavery in Louisiana and throughout the South.

Two-thirds of the seventy-odd churches in Pointe Coupee are Baptist. Remember, only the Catholic religion was allowed by Louisiana territorial law until the Louisiana Purchase in 1803. The first Protestant minister in southwestern Louisiana was a missionary born in slavery in the Carolinas. Joseph Willis, half-Indian and half-white, first visited Louisiana before 1800. Despite the resistance he met, due to his Protestant religion and his color, Pastor Willis founded Calvary Baptist Church, the first Baptist church in Louisiana, in St. Landry Parish in 1812, and lived on to establish the Baptist church in the state. After legal slavery ended in 1865, many freed blacks found a home and community in the black Baptist churches of the South.

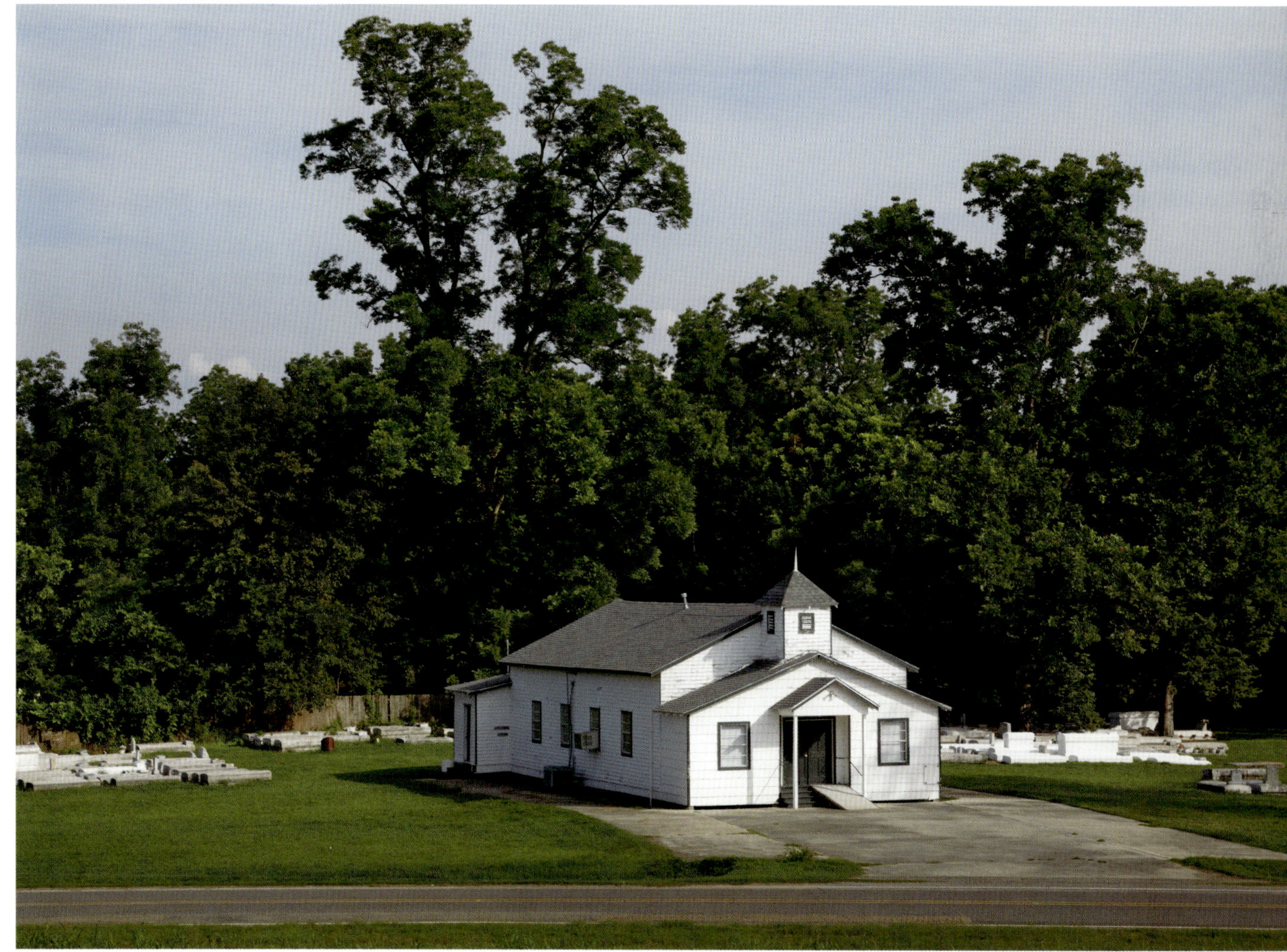

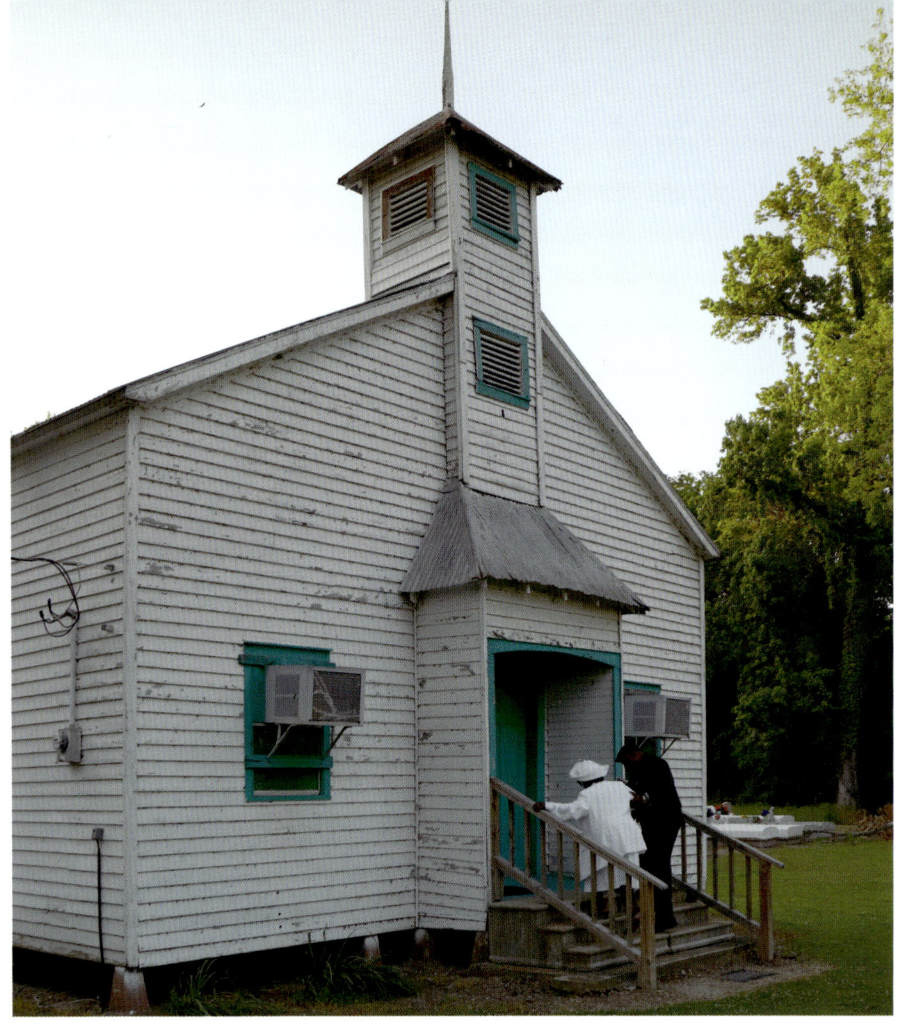

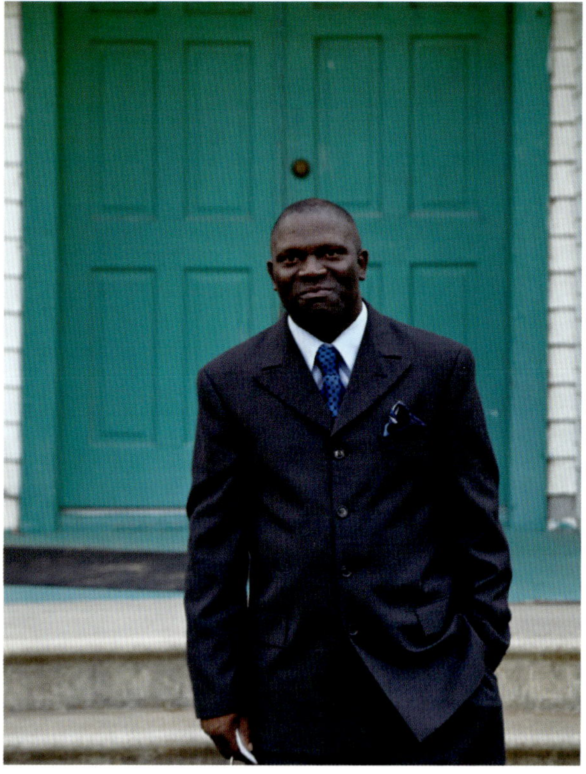

The names of Pointe Coupee's Baptist churches sound like poetry: Cane Brake, Fairland, Faith, Greater St. Peter, True Light, Morning Star, Little Rock, Good Faith, Mount Pilgrim, Mount Olive, New Pilgrim Rest.

Brother Roosevelt Scott helps Sister Minnie Howard up the steps of Old St. Mark Baptist Church in Batchelor.

The Reverend Dr. Lionel Davis is the pastor at Old St. Mark and three other Baptist churches in Pointe Coupee and West Baton Rouge.

A cyclist bikes toward Morning Star Baptist Church, also known as Stonewall Baptist, on the Pointe Coupee Road. Archaeologists have found artifacts dating from the 1740s in this immediate area.

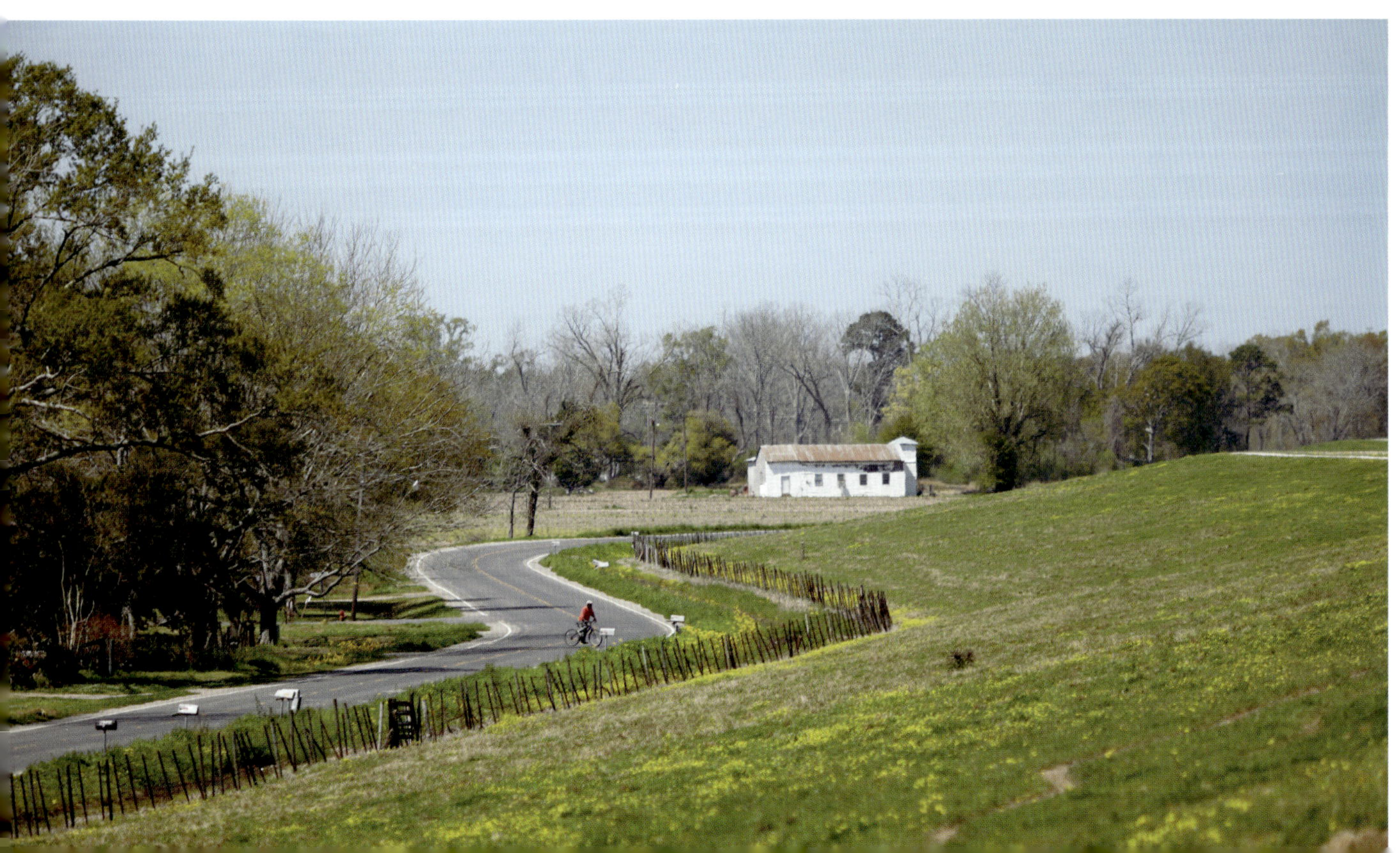

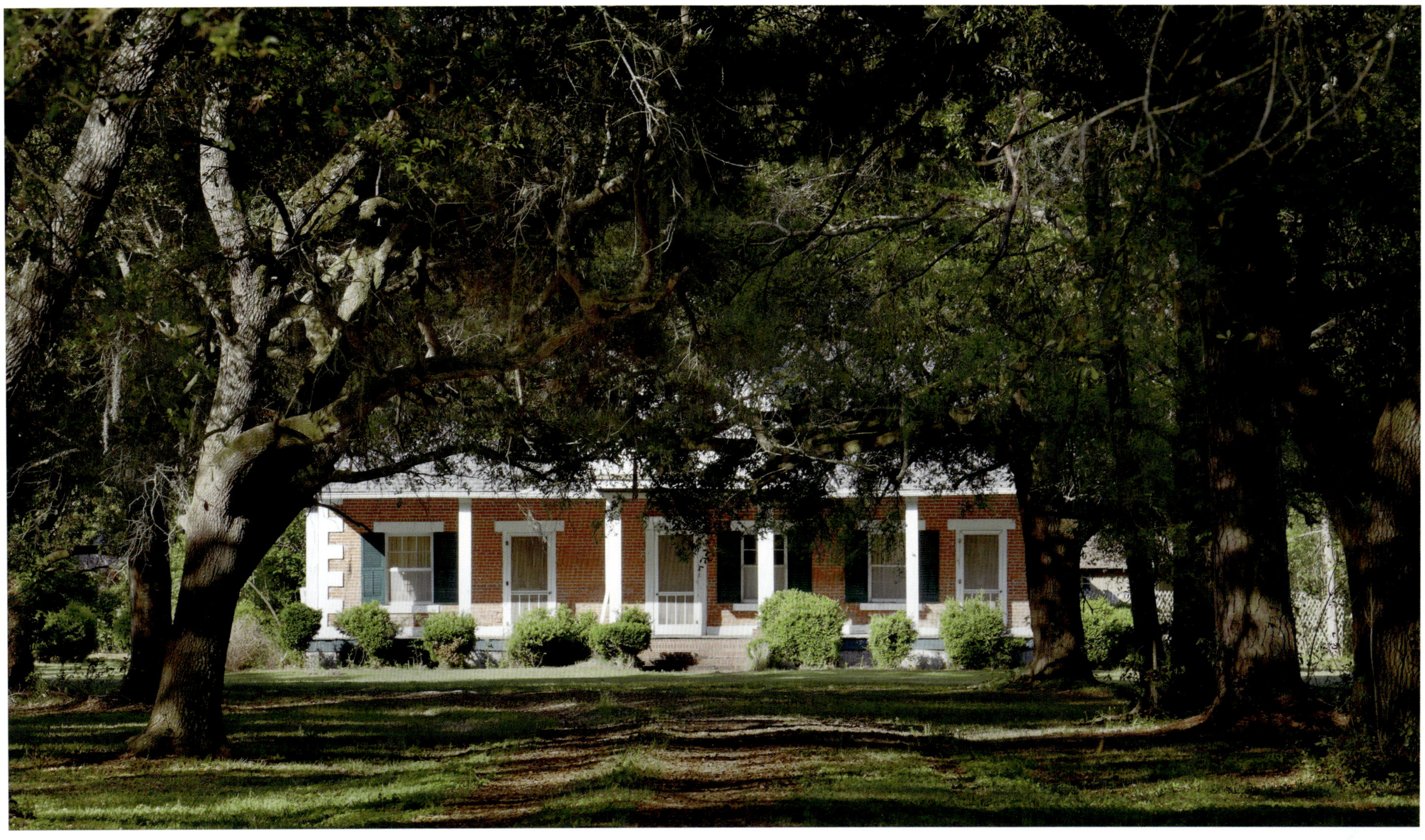

The river road along the levee by Old River is called Claiborne Road for a few miles as it narrows and curves through fields and woods. A narrow gateway off Claiborne Road reveals a long drive with an *allée* of oaks and an old house built in the 1830s or '40s. Originally owned by Charles Stewart, who built nearby Lakeside, this is Bella Vista. Said to have been used as a slave hospital before the Civil War, and known as home to descendants of Louisiana's first governor, William C. C. Claiborne, Bella Vista has the charm and mystery of Old Louisiana.

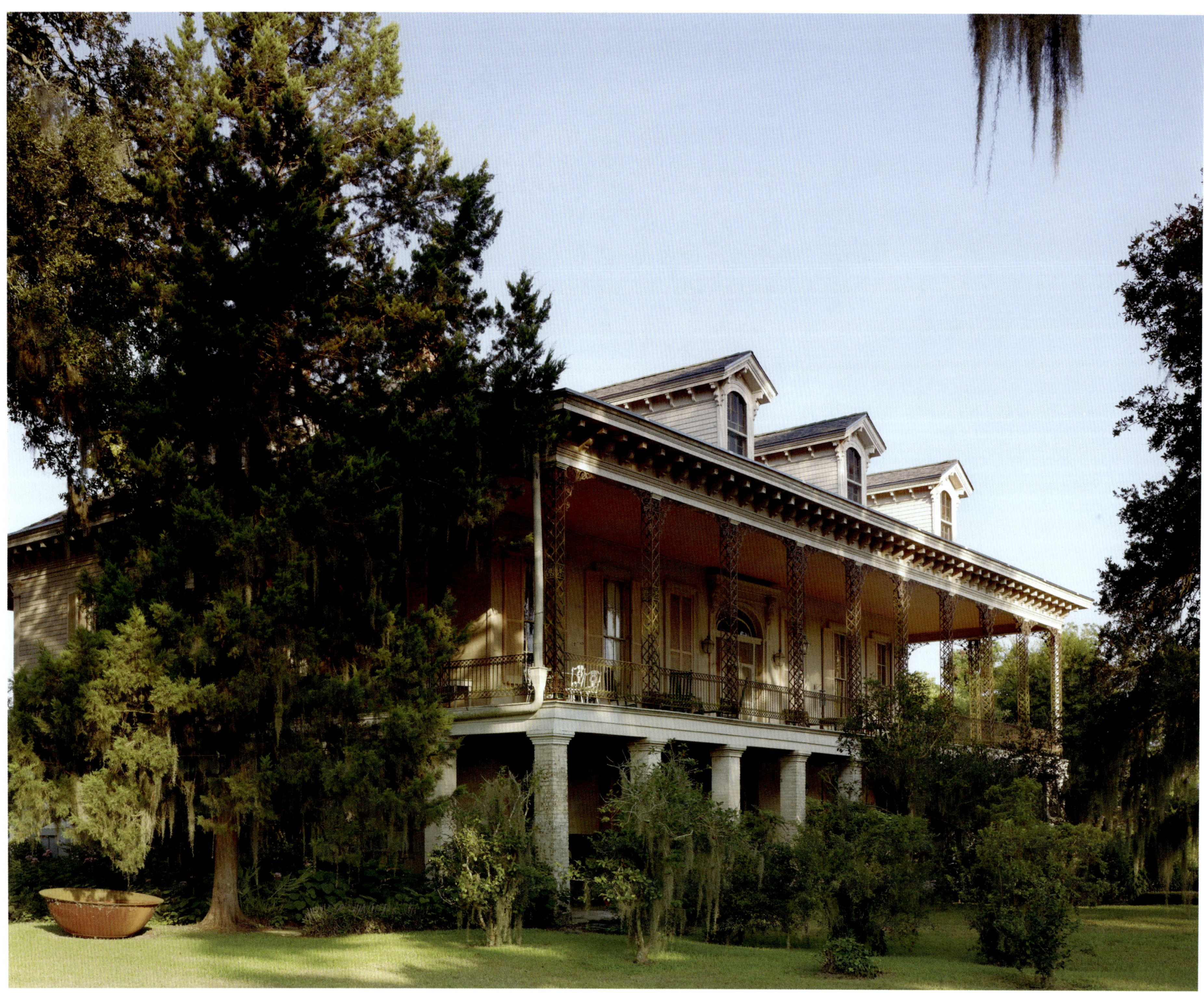

Lakeside is the largest house in Pointe Coupee Parish, built beside Old River, an oxbow lake that was once the main channel of the Mississippi River. Levees stand between the house and the lake, protecting buildings and farmlands from Mississippi floods that still fill Old River to the top of the levees.

Lakeside was the cornerstone of a large plantation established by Charles Stewart in the 1830s. Stewart bought the land from the Marquis de Lafayette, to whom it had been given as a gift by the U.S. government on the recommendation of Thomas Jefferson after the Louisiana Purchase.

The grand house was built in 1830. The iron stairway and upstairs railings were probably added later, and are said to have come from Paris. Hunt Slonem, an artist who has owned the house since 2005, says, "The house has been pink as far back as anyone living can remember. It's just so beautiful. Untouched by time."

A pair of original wooden dovecotes, of Anglo-American form, stand at the rear of Lakeside. The *pigeonniers* of French homes were almost always located at the front of the house, announcing the wealth and status of the owners. First owner Charles Stewart may have felt the house spoke for itself.

The gardens of Lakeside issue an invitation to stop and enjoy the shade of ancient trees. Spanish moss fills the old camellias. The levee beyond protects the house from the whims of the Mississippi by way of Old River.

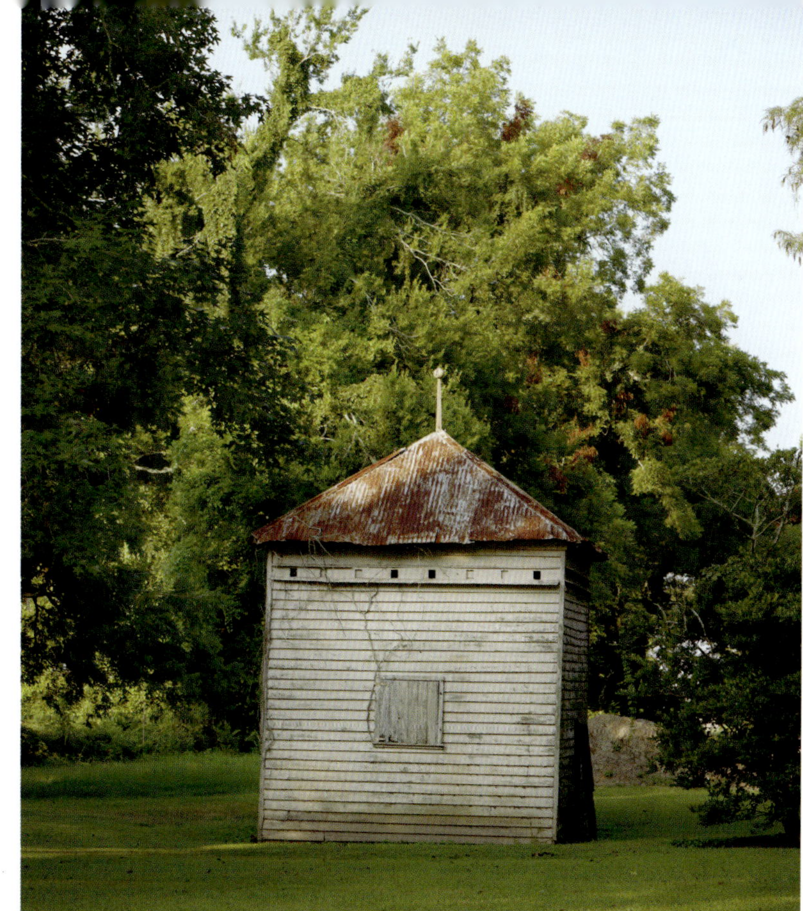

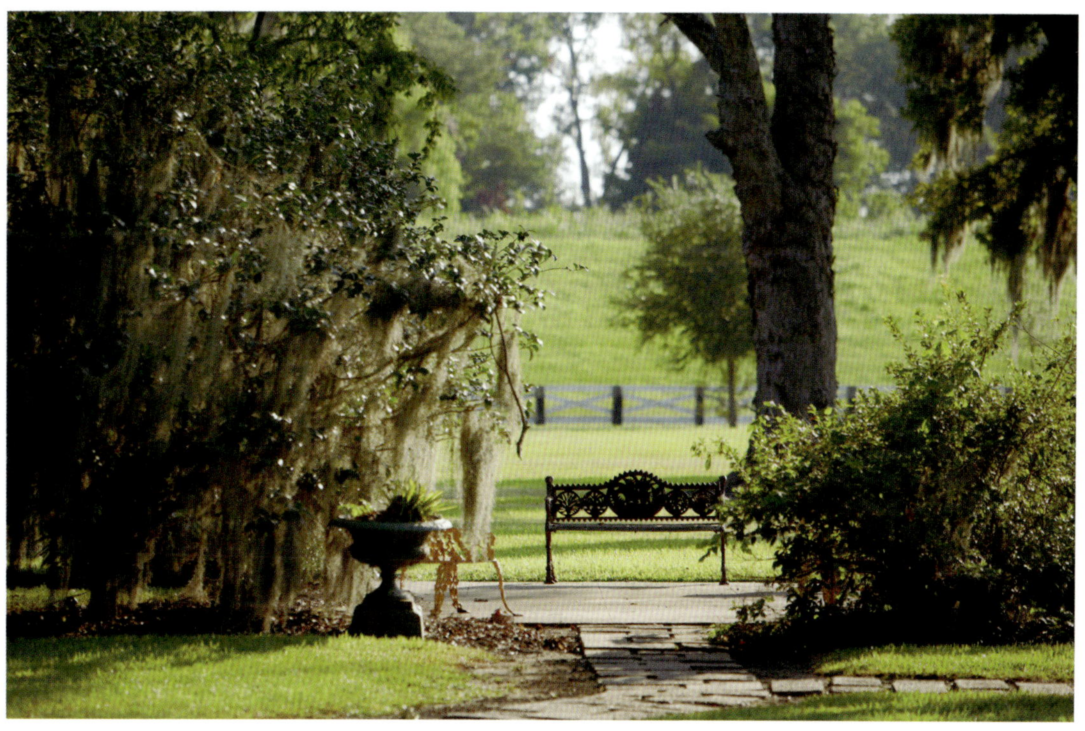

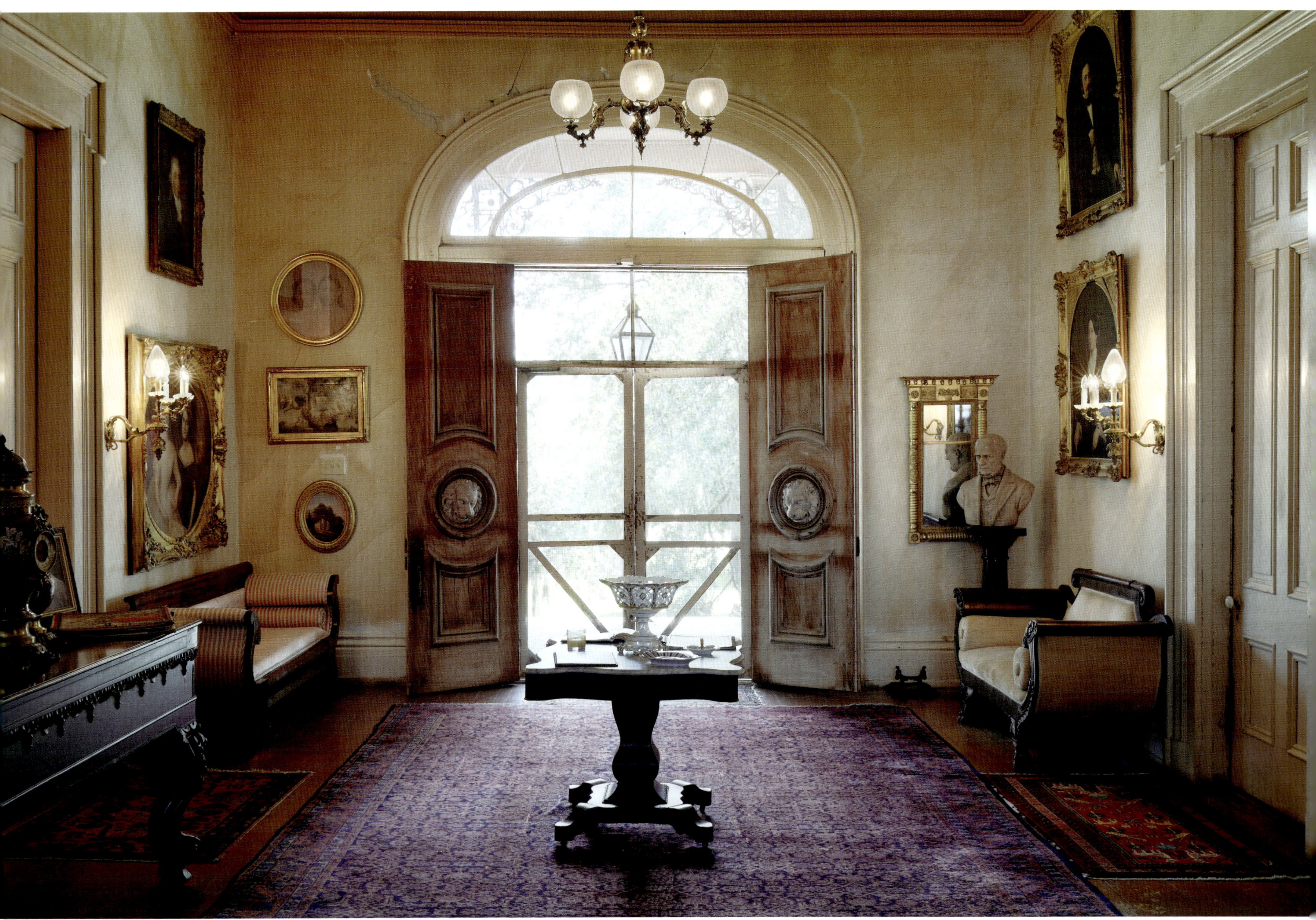

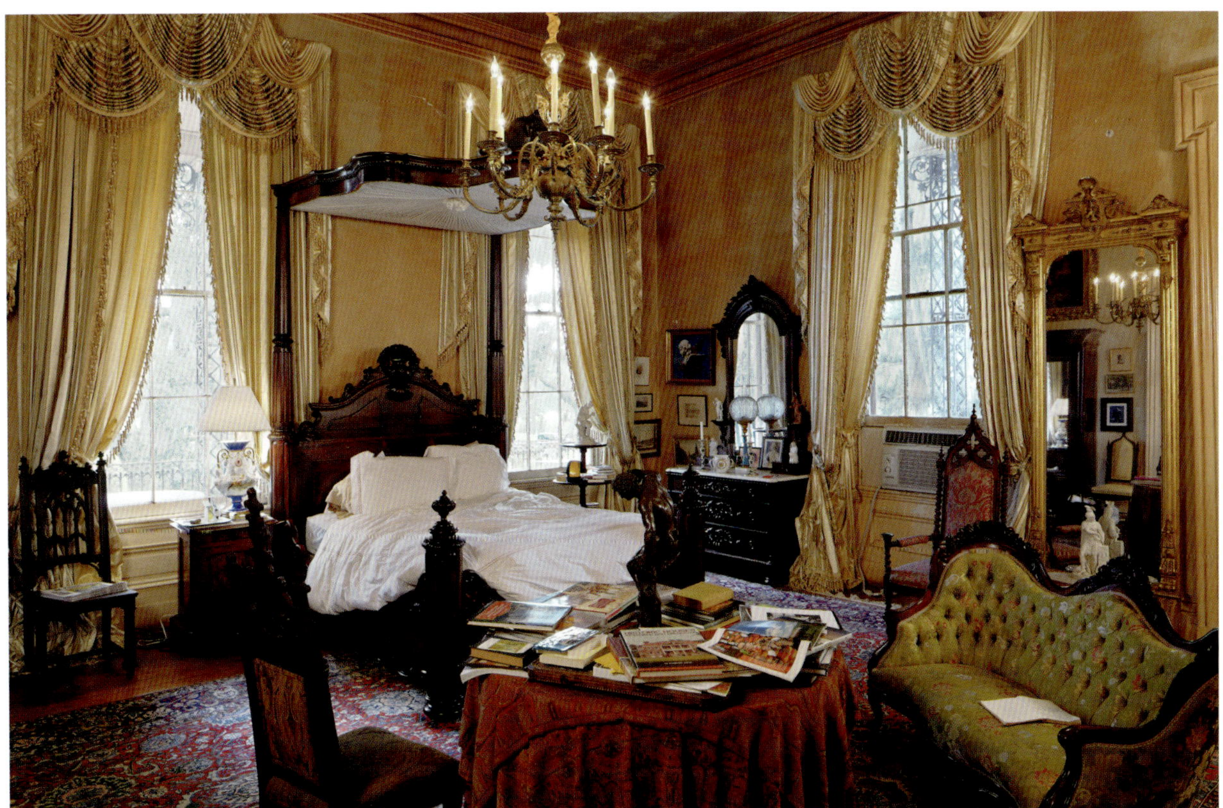

The wide central hall of Lakeside runs the full depth of the house, from front to back galleries. Hunt Slonem left the walls alone, keeping the old paint and antique patina. The piano at the left is original to Lakeside. The rug was purchased at a weekend flea market in New York City, where Slonem keeps his painting studio.

The bed in the master bedroom was made by Prudent Mallard (1809–1879), whose work is prized throughout Louisiana. Slonem found the bed at a shop in nearby Morganza. Gothic chairs, around the room and throughout the house, are favorites of the collector. The drapes were made by the late Buzz Harper and his partner Les Wisinger of New Orleans.

One of Pointe Coupee's most familiar land-marks stands on LA-1 in Batchelor, near the Pointe Coupee Farmers' Elevator. Alone in a broad field, it is the smokestack of an early sugar mill, the rest dismantled and moved to Oakland Plantation in Lakeland in 1890. This was the mill of Torwood Plantation, closely associated with Lakeside and Bella Vista. Nearby, in the same field, is a small graveyard, like an island sur-rounded by crops. The cemetery belongs to the Pilgrim Rest Baptist Church.

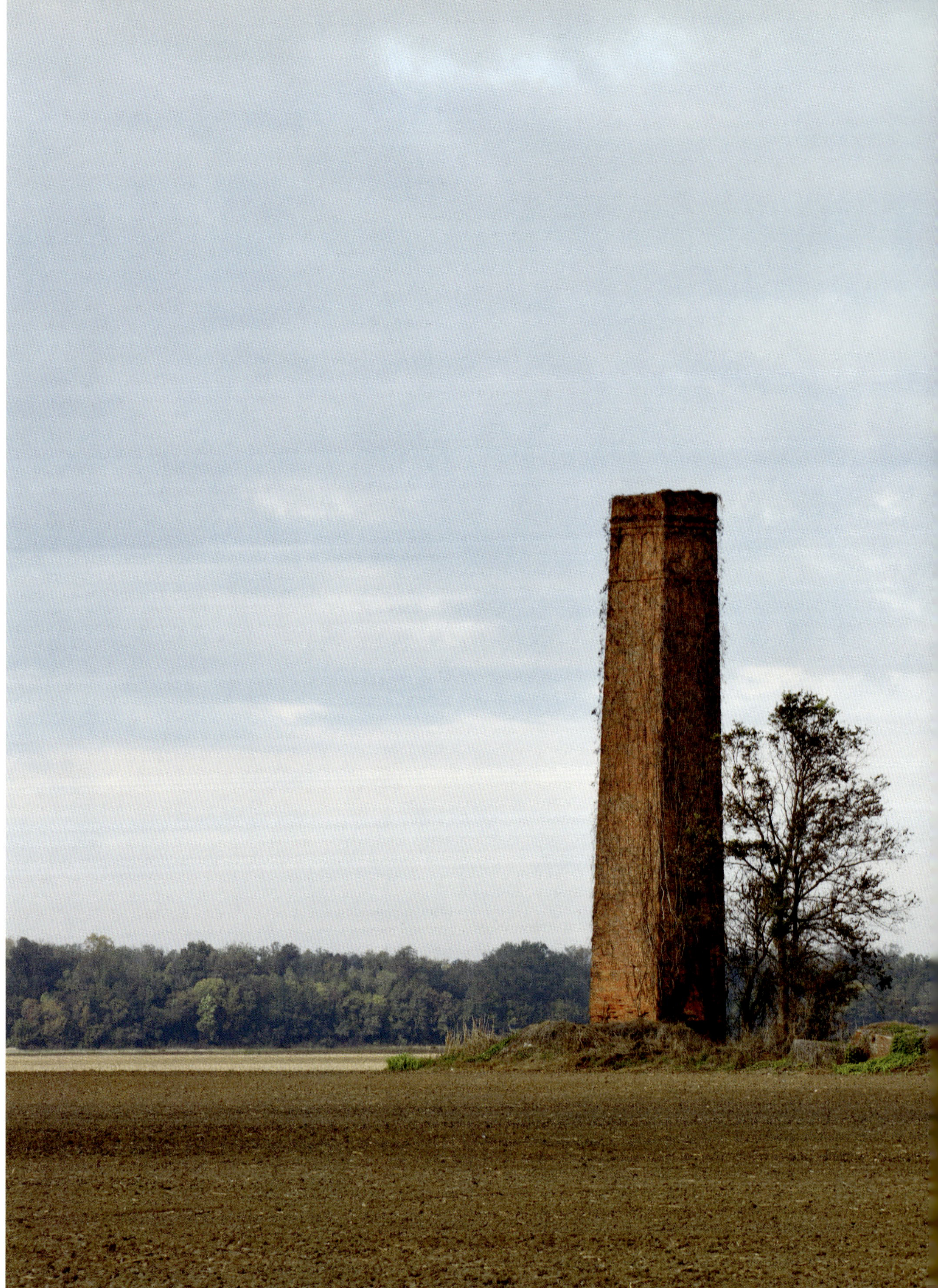

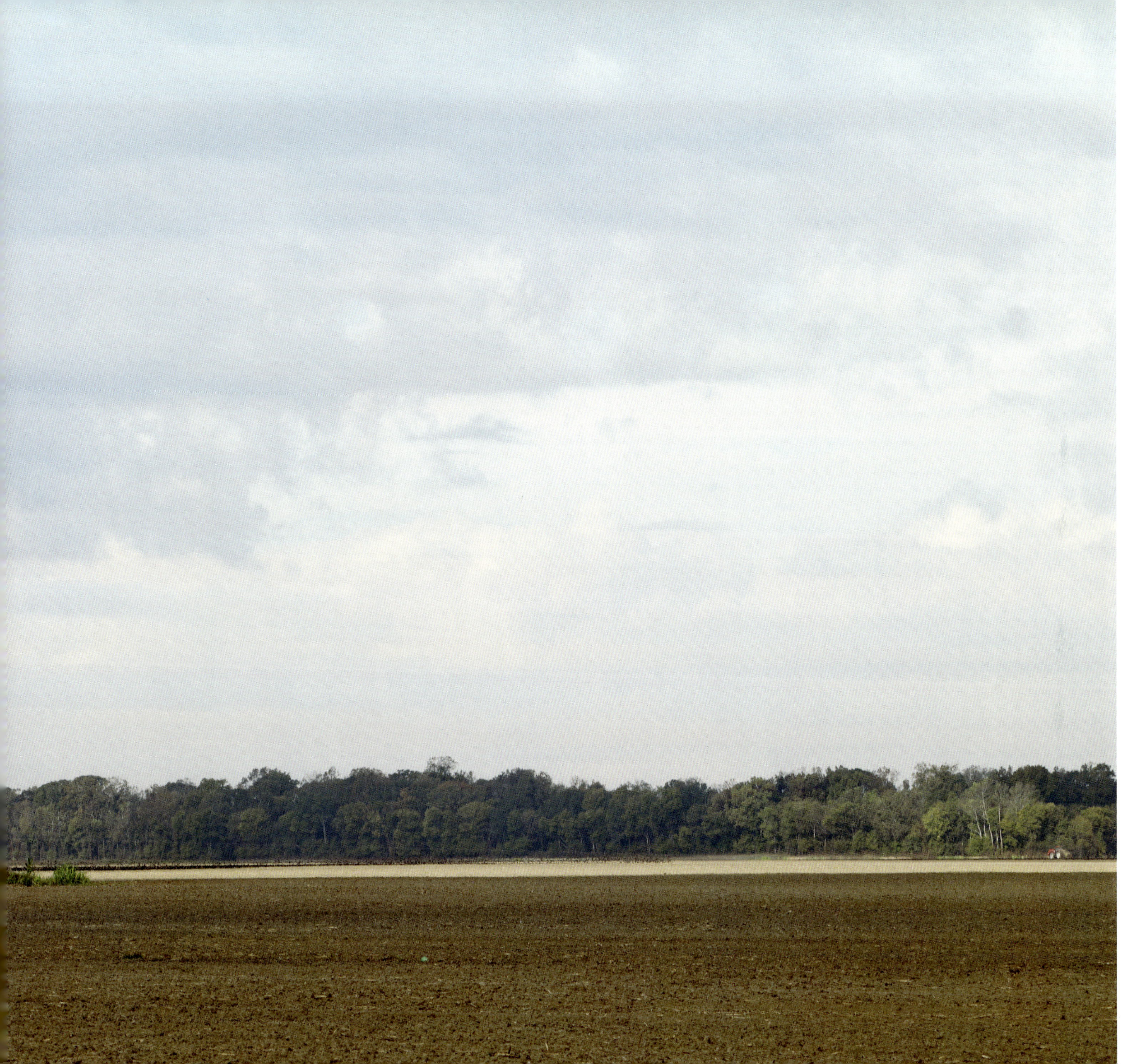

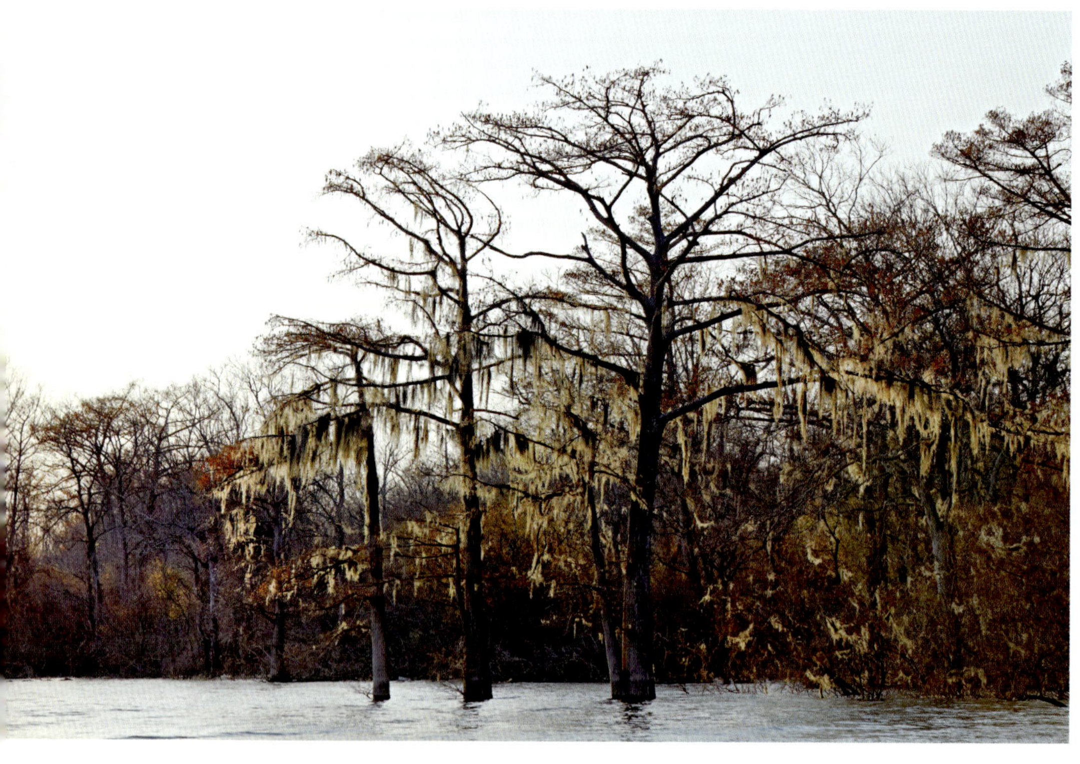

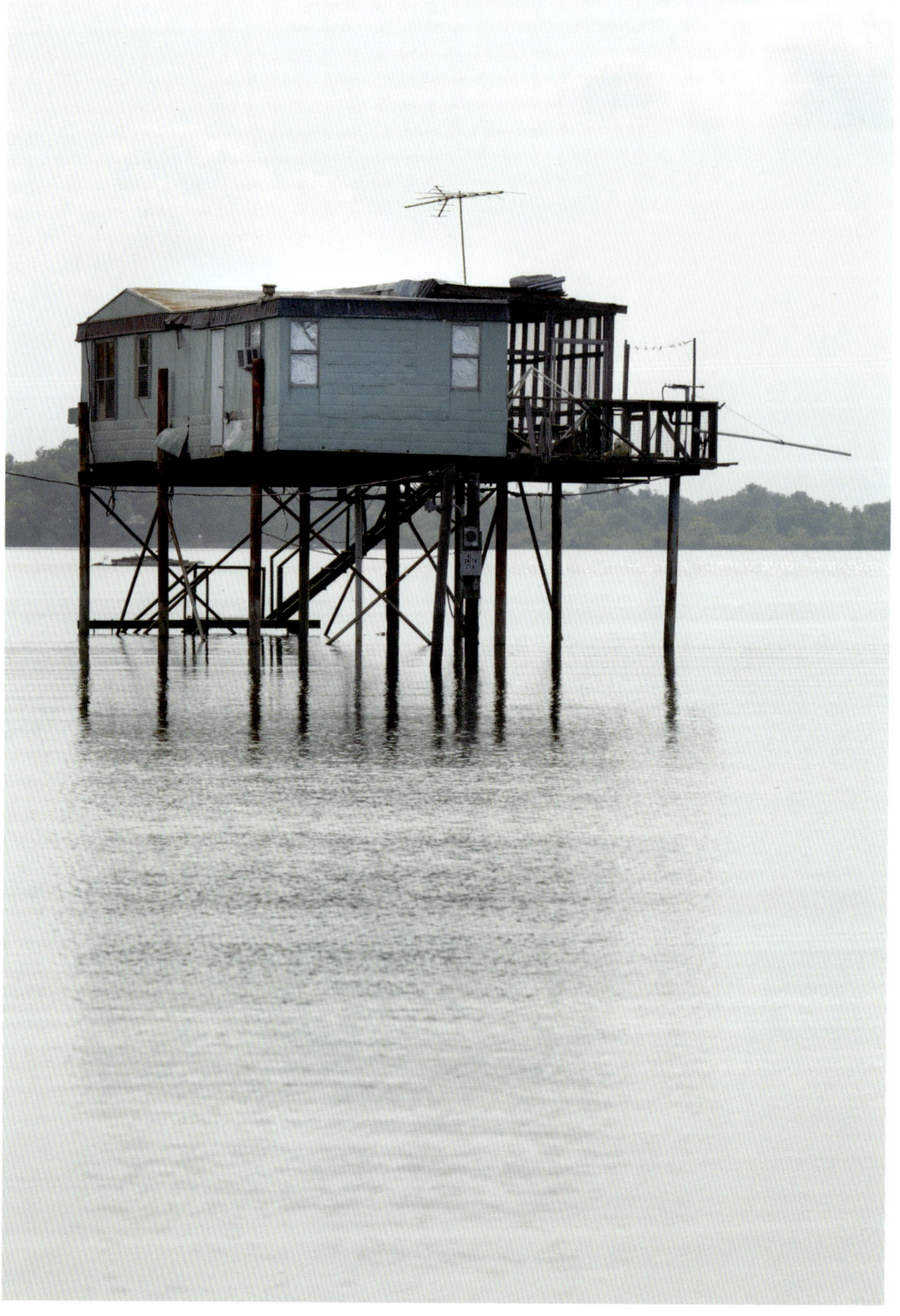

Old River, an oxbow lake of the Mississippi cut off in 1847, still floods with the Mississippi every spring. The lake can rise as much as forty feet, so the trees around its banks must tolerate weeks or even months of inundation. Edged naturally with bald cypress, Old River probably looks today much like the Mississippi looked for thousands of years before levees were constructed.

Raccourci is the island within the oxbow lake Old River. *Raccourci* is French for "short cut."

Camps at Old River must accommodate the annual floods. They are either built on tall pilings or engineered on floats to rise and fall with the river.

At low water, the exposed roots of trees along the banks of Old River present dramatic evidence of their ability to adapt to changing conditions.

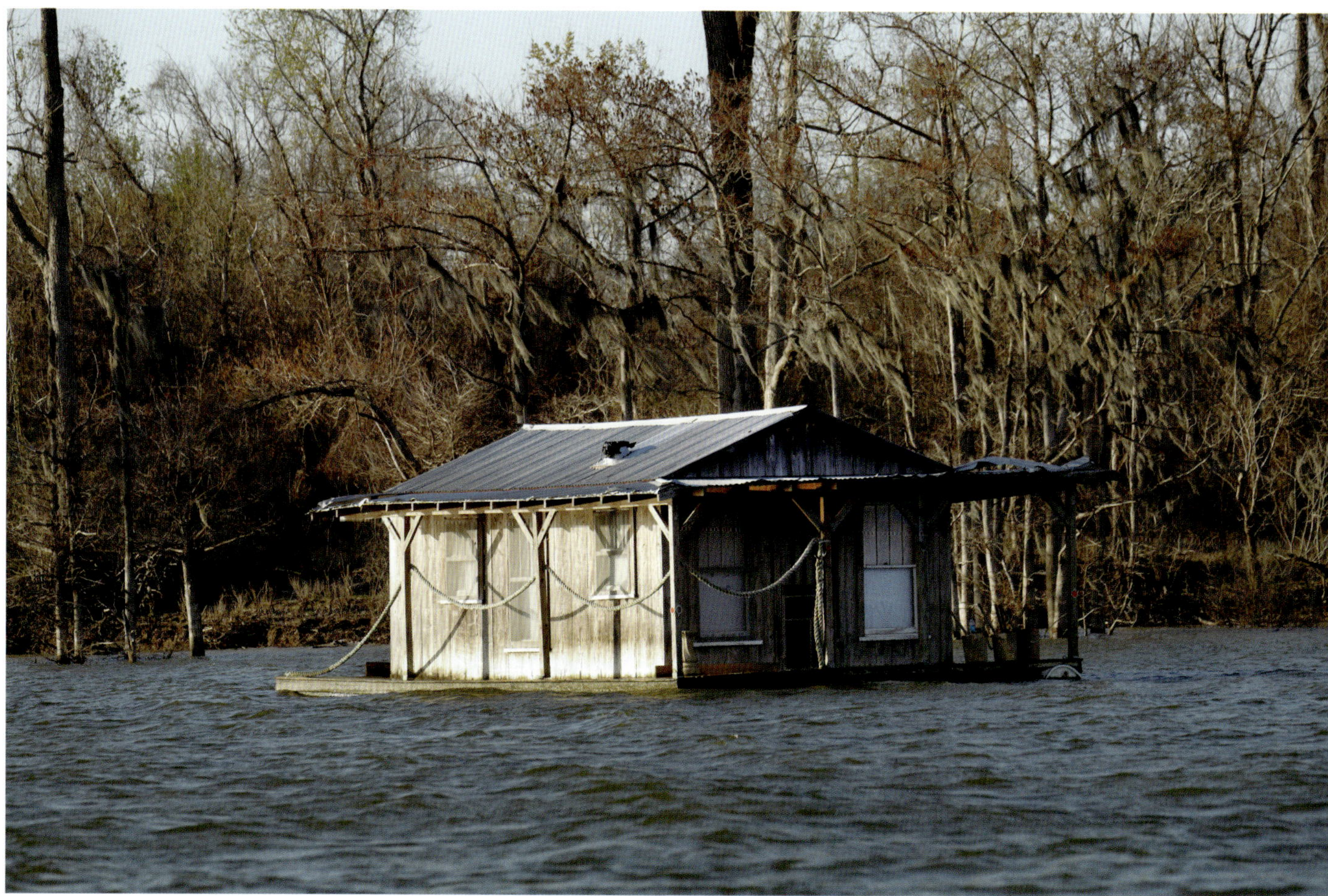

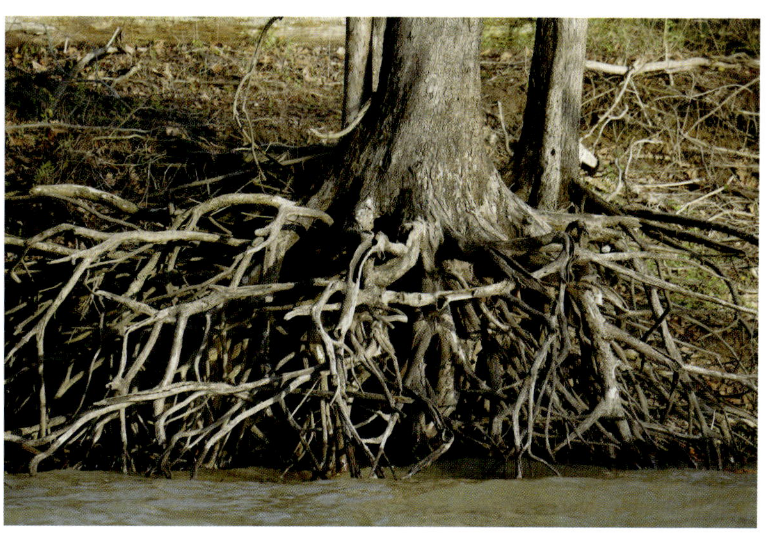

Taylor Plantation bears the name of William Taylor, cousin of the twelfth president of the United States, Zachary Taylor (1784–1850). Mrs. Zachary Taylor is said to have visited this house and attended services at nearby St. Stephen's Episcopal Church. The house looks out on Bayou Latanache, and in the great flood of 1912 water rose all the way to the upper gallery.

Taylor is a short distance from LA-1, which is part of the new scenic Zachary Taylor Parkway that extends from Alexandria, Louisiana, to Poplarville, Mississippi. Zachary Taylor himself owned a plantation in East Baton Rouge Parish, and is the only U.S. president Louisiana may claim as her own.

A Pink Perfection camellia blooms profusely in the garden of Taylor Plantation. The Pink Perfection was made the official flower of the Parish of Pointe Coupee in 1940 by resolution of the police jury.

Taylor's plantation bell is silenced by time's changes and the soft cover of a thornless rose.

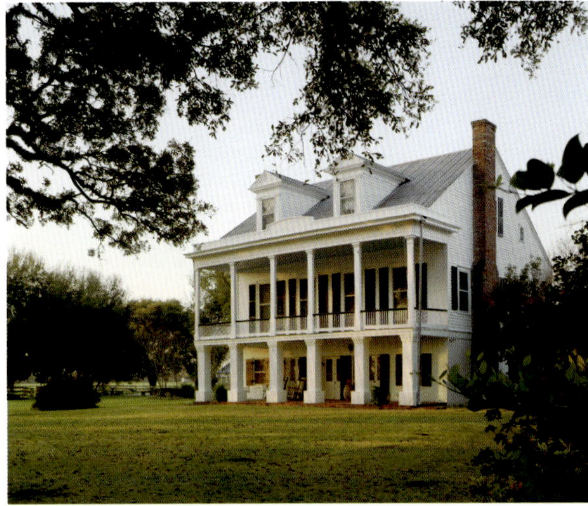

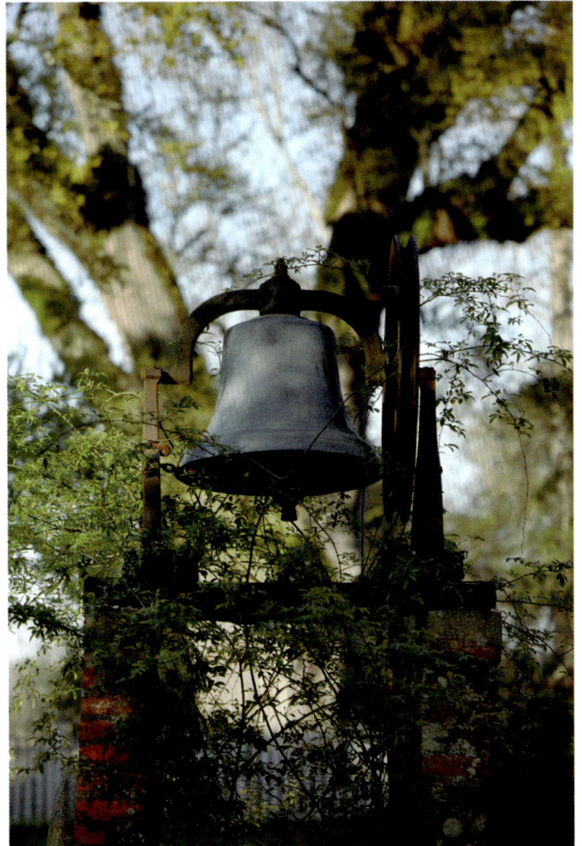

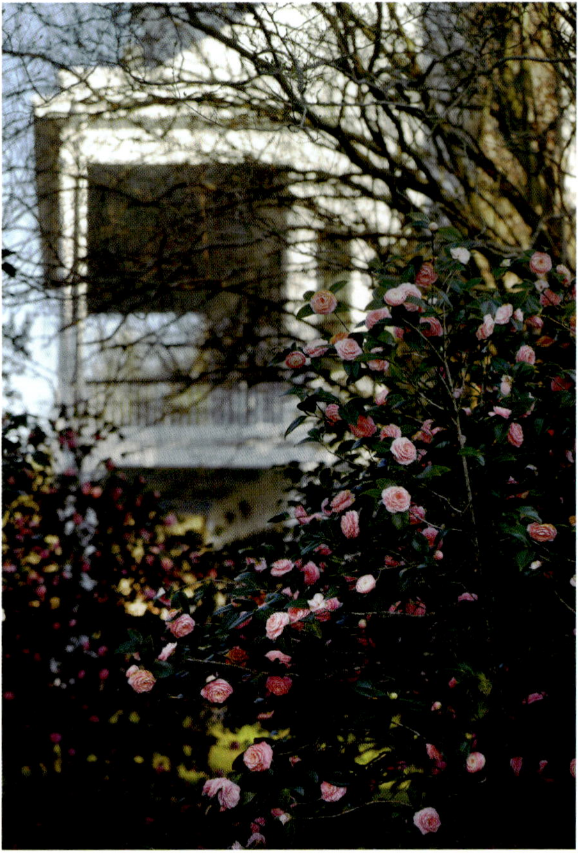

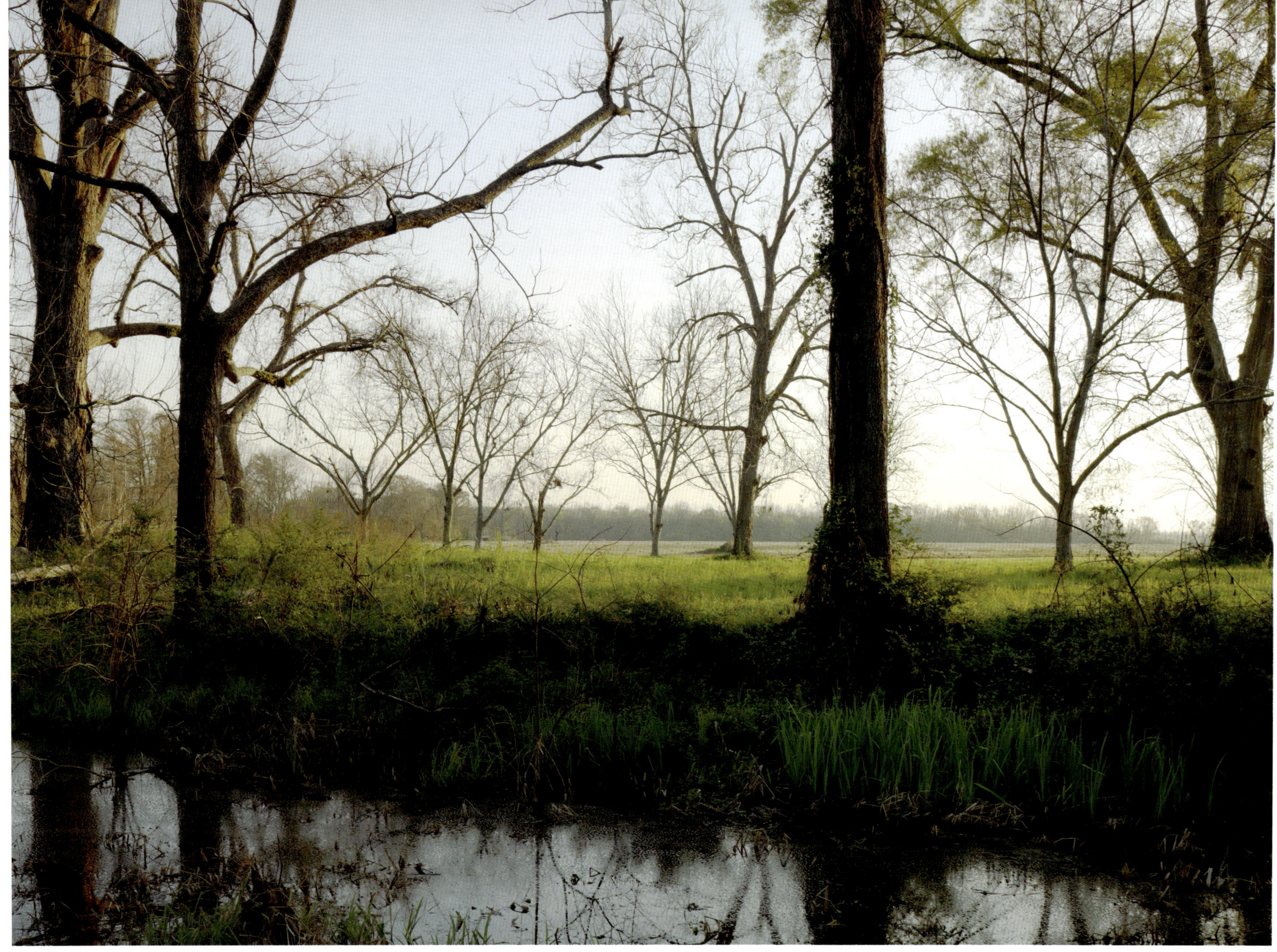

Bayou Latanache, named for an Indian chief, flows along country roads and through fertile fields of Pointe Coupee. "Latanache" means "fan palm," probably the Louisiana palmetto.

St. Stephen's Episcopal Church seems to stand alone in a vast field dotted with graves and trees. Its actual location is Old Williamsport, near Innis. The remarkable Gothic Revival building was completed in 1859, but its congregation started more than ten years earlier as St. James Mission, one of the first Protestant churches in Pointe Coupee.

It was named St. Stephen's and consecrated by the first Episcopal bishop of the diocese of Louisiana, the Right Reverend Leonidas Polk (1806–1864). Polk was later called "the Fighting Bishop" and served as a general in Jefferson Davis's Confederate army. He was killed during the Civil War. The U.S. Army training post Fort Polk, near Leesville, Louisiana, was named for Leonidas Polk.

The church building was designed by Frank Wills, the official architect of the New York Ecclesiological Society. Its stained-glass windows were made in England, shipped via New York to New Orleans, and brought up the Mississippi River to Williamsport. Sunday services in the old church continue today as they have for more than 160 years almost without fail.

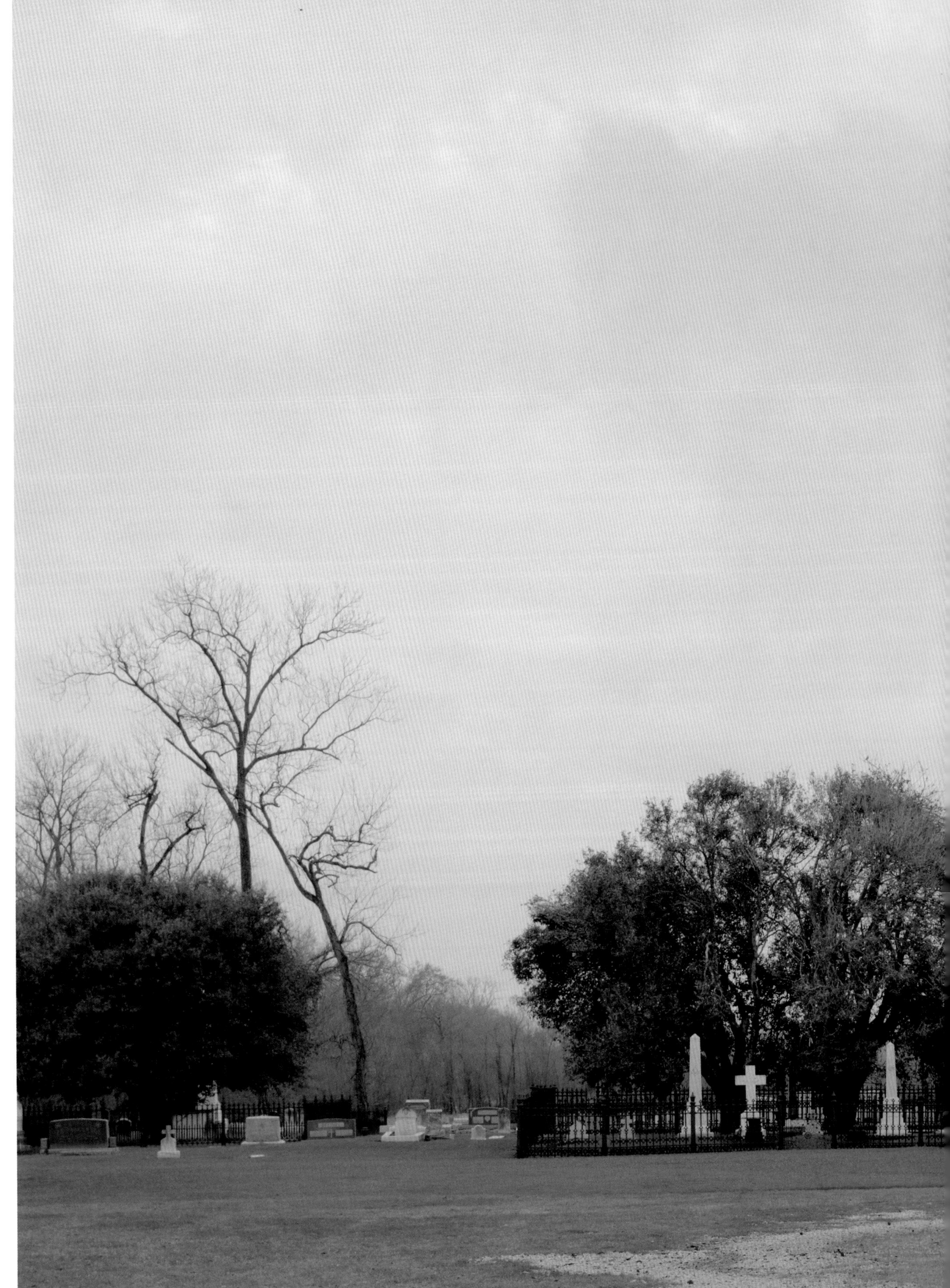

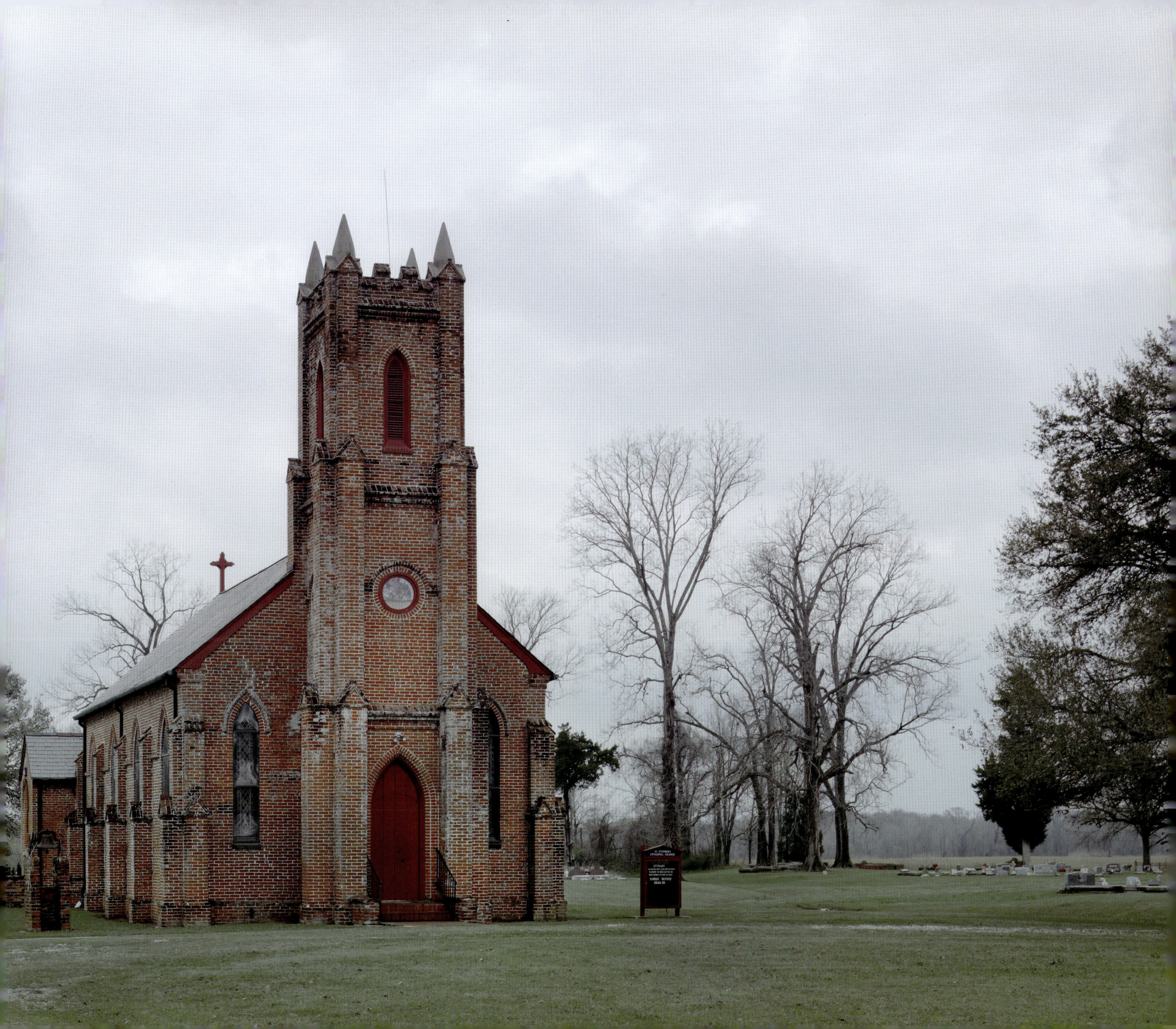

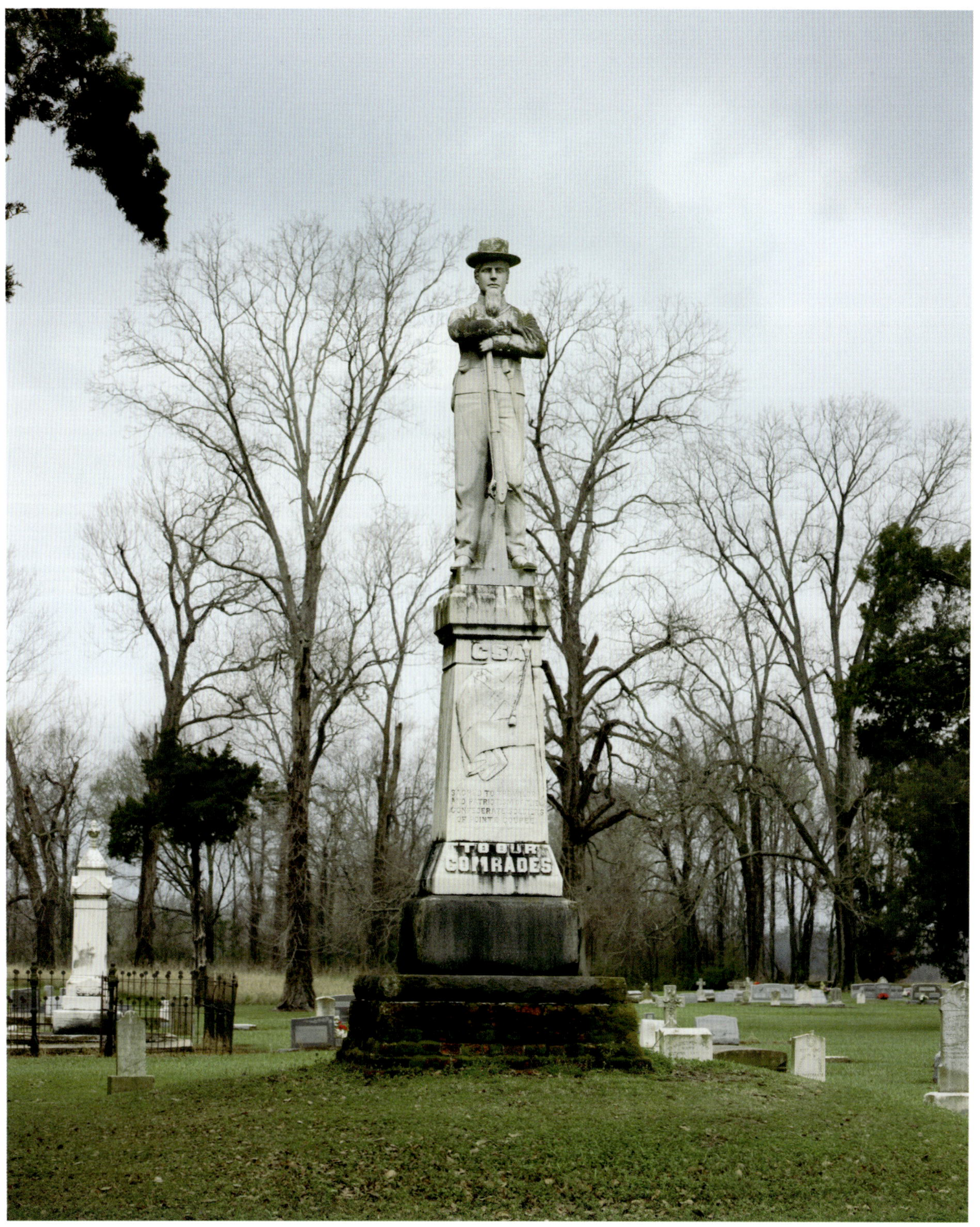

A monument to the memory of Confederate soldiers was placed in the cemetery of St. Stephen's and dedicated on Memorial Day of 1904. Memorial Day was first observed in May 1868 as Decoration Day, a day of reconciliation honoring soldiers, Federal and Confederate, who died in the American Civil War. To this day, more Americans died in the Civil War than in all other wars fought by Americans combined.

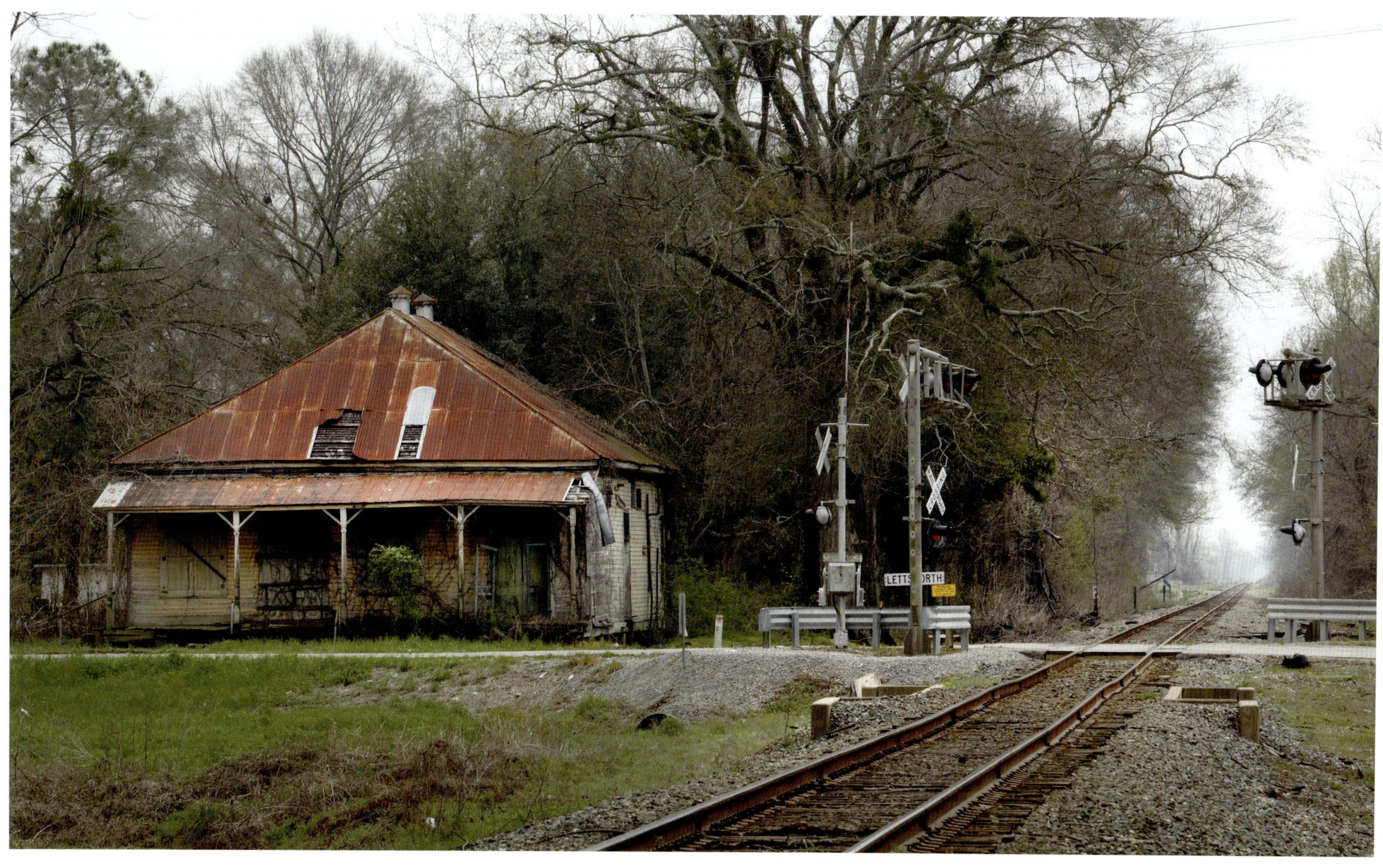

MOUNGER STORE

An old general store sits at the railroad crossing marked "Lettsworth" on LA-1. Trains still rumble by frequently, but without stopping or even slowing down. The Mounger Store closed for business almost fifty years ago.

The tracks were laid in 1899–1901 by the Texas & Pacific Railroad, and ran from Addis in West Baton Rouge Parish through Glynn, New Roads, LaBarre, Morganza, Batchelor, Innis, Lettsworth, and Torras all the way to Ferriday in Concordia Parish.

Bald cypress trees grow freely in Bayou Lettsworth, pushing their odd knees up from root systems underwater. The tiny green plants that live on the water surface are not scum, but duckweed (ducks consider it food), the world's smallest flowering plant. Bayous, meandering slow-moving waterways, create a complex network throughout Pointe Coupee. It is often difficult to tell where one named bayou ends and another begins.

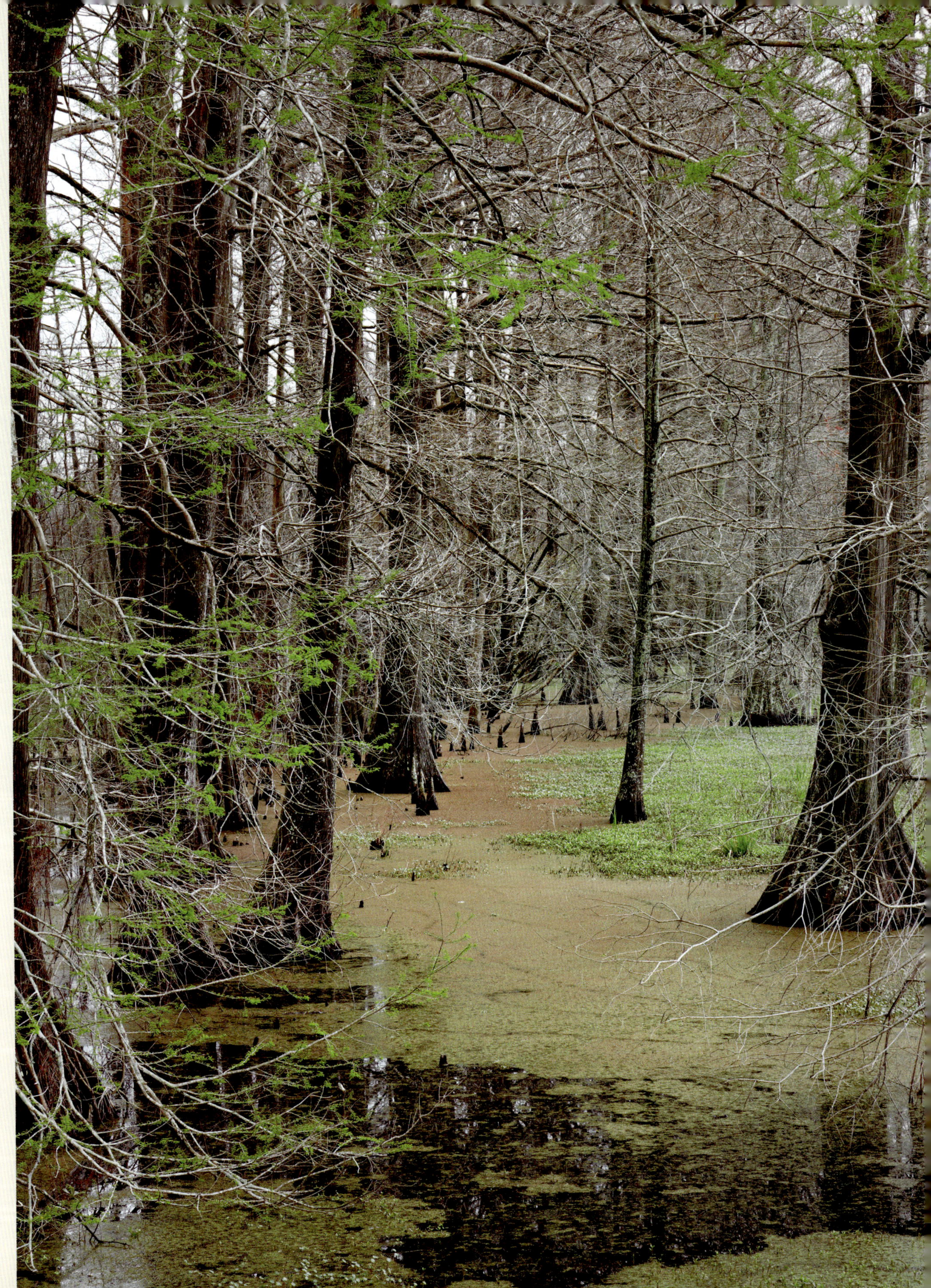

CHAPTER 7

Three Rivers and the Atchafalaya

COTTON

Upland cotton grows near the site of the Battle of Bayou Fordoche. Cotton was king in the South from the 1830s, right through the Civil War, until the arrival of the boll weevil, an insect that devastated southern cotton fields around 1906.

Cotton bolls open, ready for harvest. Long after the Civil War, cotton continued to be picked by hand. Reliable harvesting machinery finally began to take the place of human labor in the 1950s.

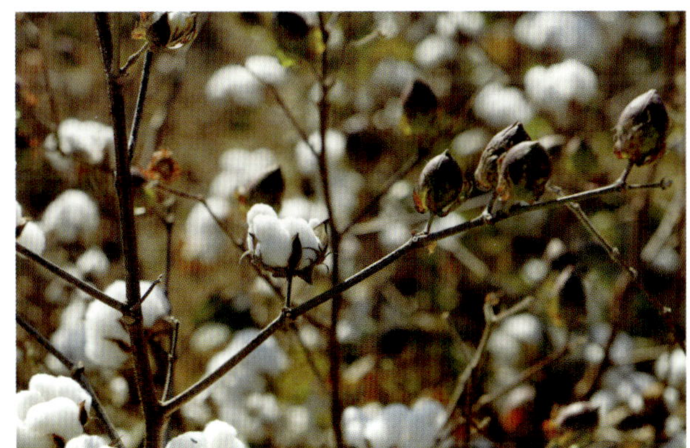

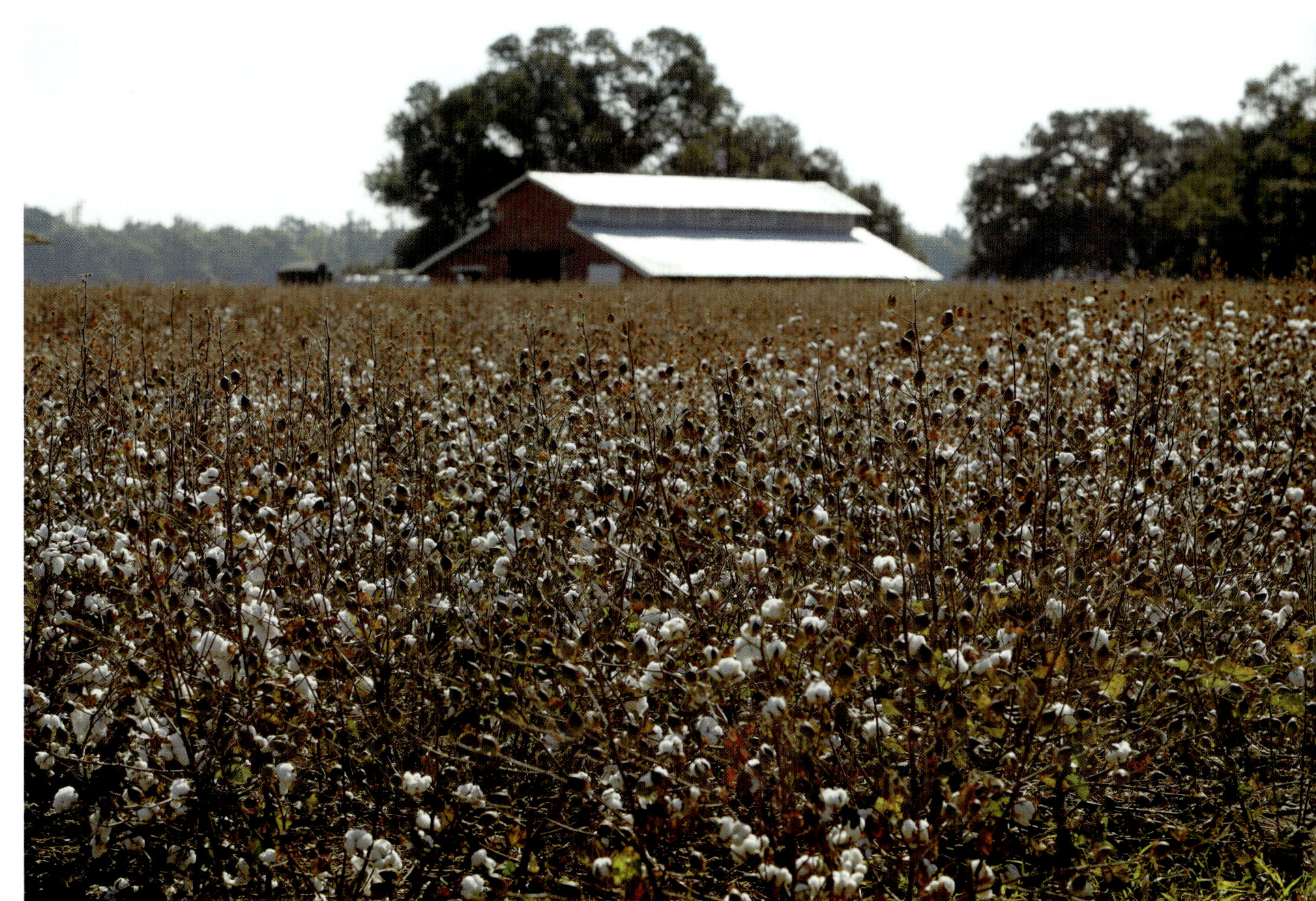

Seed cotton (raw cotton with seeds) brought by truck from the field is moved from the trailer into the machinery of the cotton gin by vacuum.

Lint is one of the by-products of the ginning process, along with seed, mote, and trash.

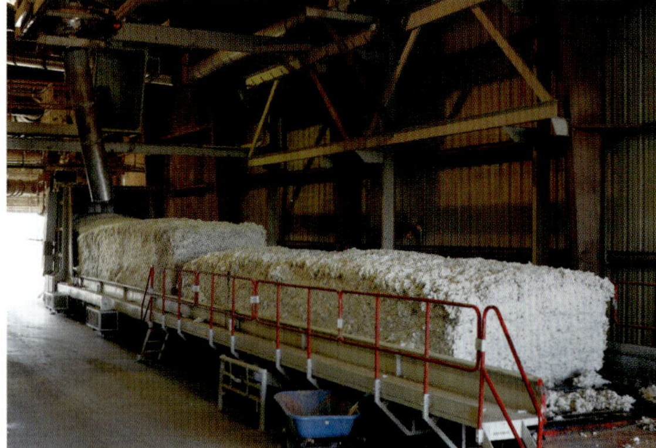

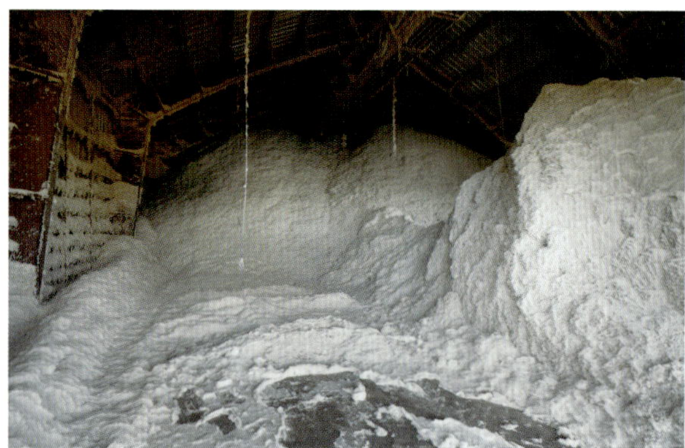

Cotton fiber is separated from the seed in the huge engine of the Tri-Parish Cotton Gin in Lettsworth, built in 1991. "Gin" is short for "engine." This plant has ginned as many as 50,000 bales of cotton in a season. The ginning season runs from September 1 to December 31.

Eli Whitney patented the cotton gin in 1794. The invention revolutionized the cotton industry worldwide as it replaced the painstaking handwork of combing seeds out of cotton with a faster, more automated process. However, picking cotton in the field remained slow and painful labor until the mid-twentieth century.

The modern gin uses essentially the same method Whitney designed more than two hundred years ago: Dryers reduce moisture to make the process more efficient, a series of spiked rollers and cylinders separate cotton from trash, centrifugal force removes the trash, rotating saws and filters pull seed from the cotton, seed is removed by auger, lint cleaners comb out immature seeds and other foreign matter, and finally the clean cotton is baled to be sent to the textile mill.

Today's cotton gin is the latest of many gins in the parish since the nineteenth century. One old gin, no longer operating, is still seen from LA-1 in Lettsworth.

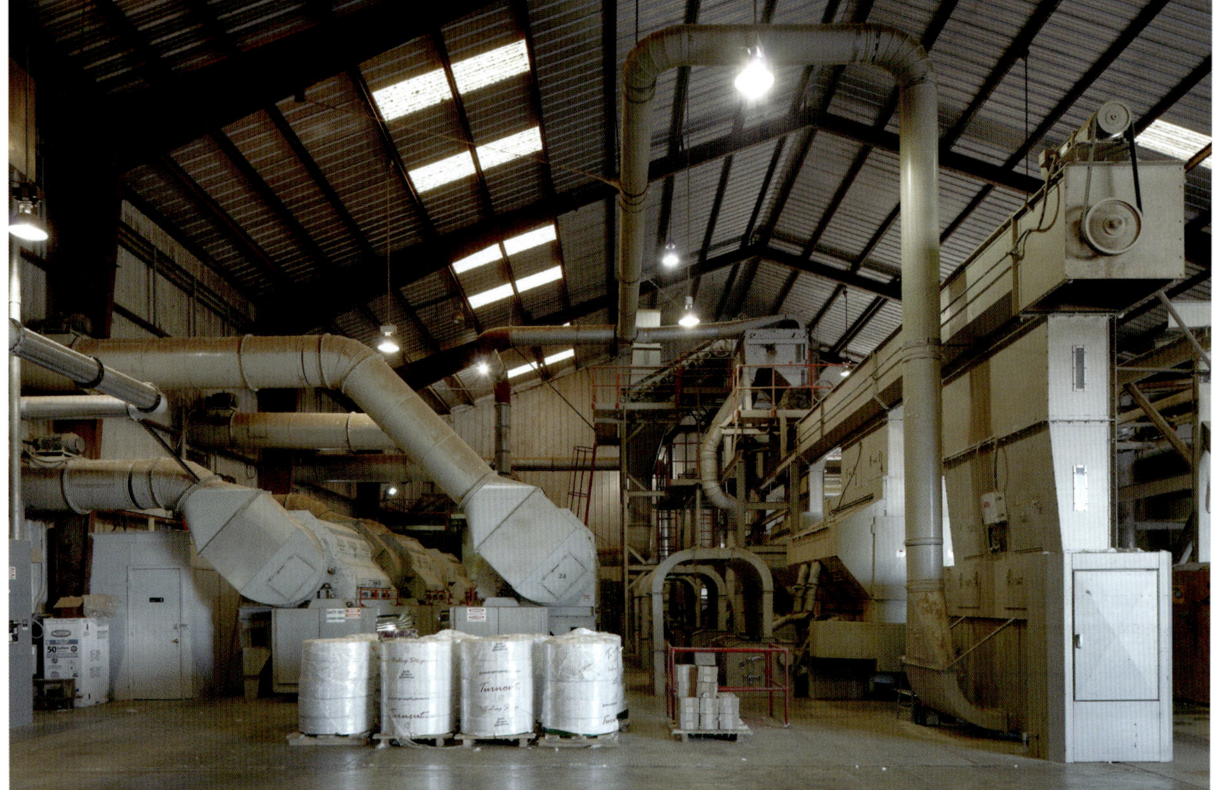

The area of land at the very top of Pointe Coupee is called Three Rivers. From the air the confluence of the rivers is visible, here looking east: The waters of the Red River (*left*) and Lower Old River (*upper right*) join, flowing on to the Gulf of Mexico as the Atchafalaya (*lower right*). Originally Turnbull's Bend in the Mississippi, the course of the river was altered by Captain Henry Shreve in 1831, and was changed again in the twentieth century by the Army Corps of Engineers. Today the Old River Control Structures north of this site divert 40 percent of Mississippi River flow into the Red River just before it pours into the Atchafalaya.

A small bayou, bordered by farm roads on each side, wiggles through a patchwork of agricultural fields in Upper Pointe Coupee.

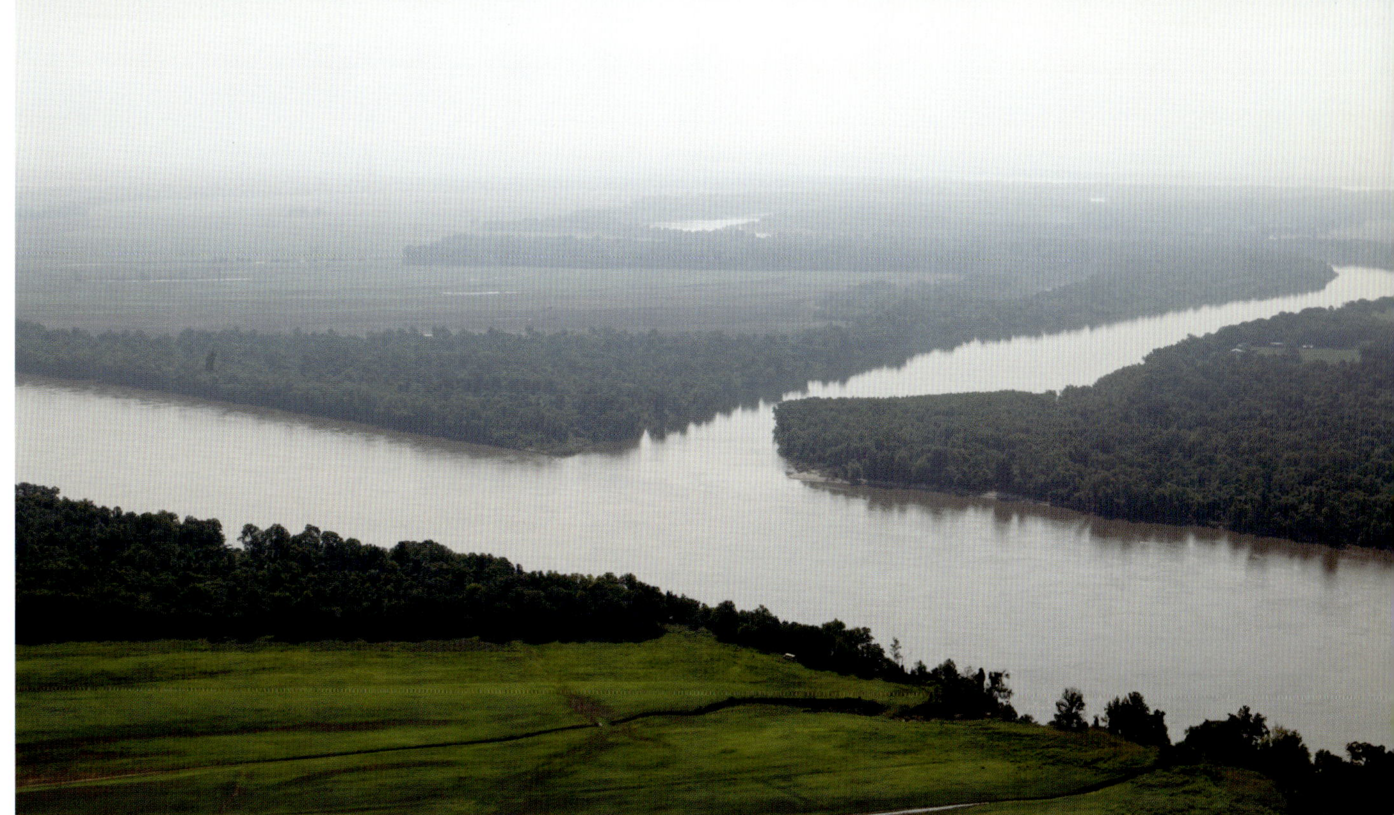

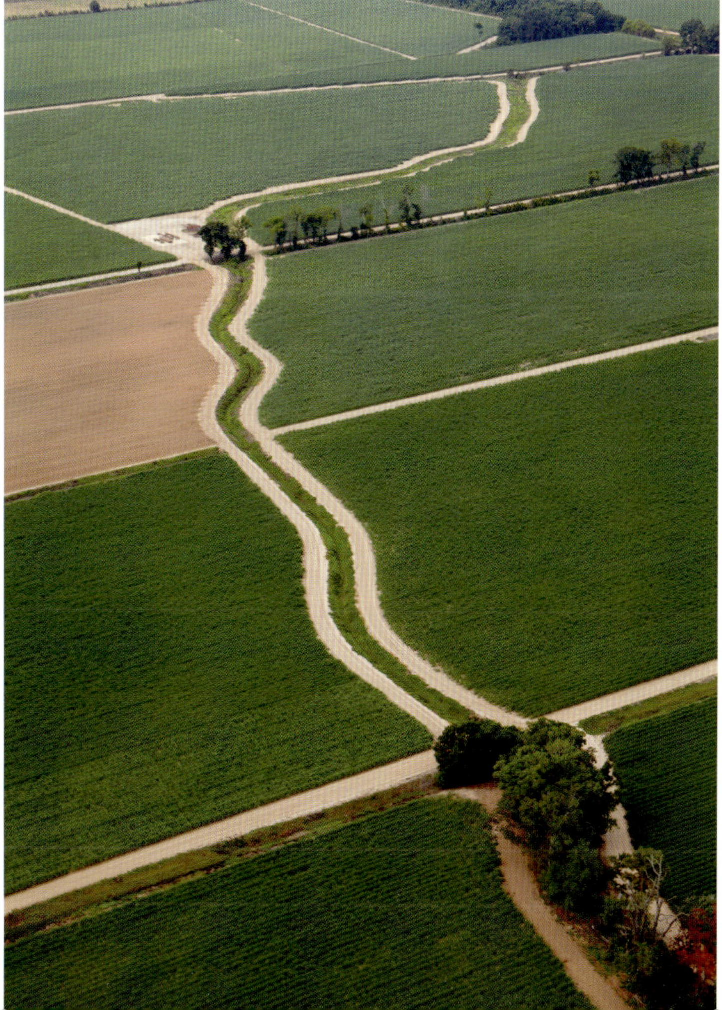

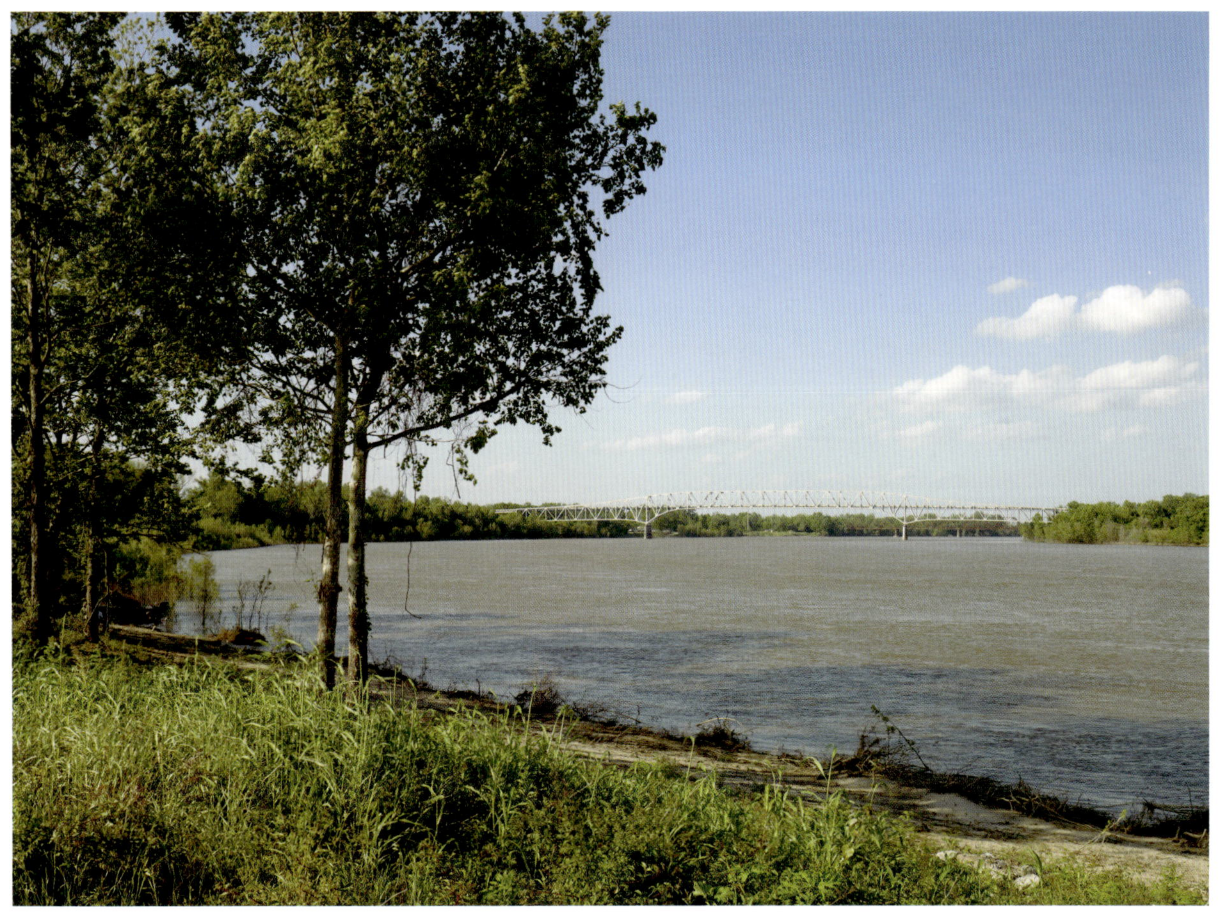

Looking up the Atchafalaya River from the public landing at Simmesport in Avoyelles Parish, one can see the bridges connecting Simmesport to Legonier in Pointe Coupee. By boat the Red River is little more than two miles upstream from here.

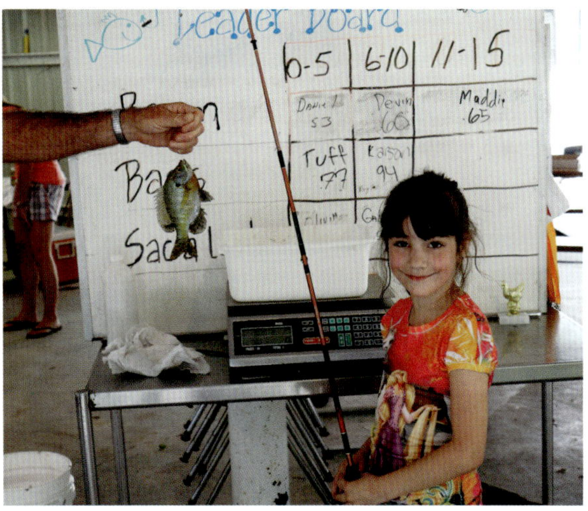

FISHING RODEO

A proud contestant displays her catch in the annual Roland Landry Memorial Fishing Rodeo.

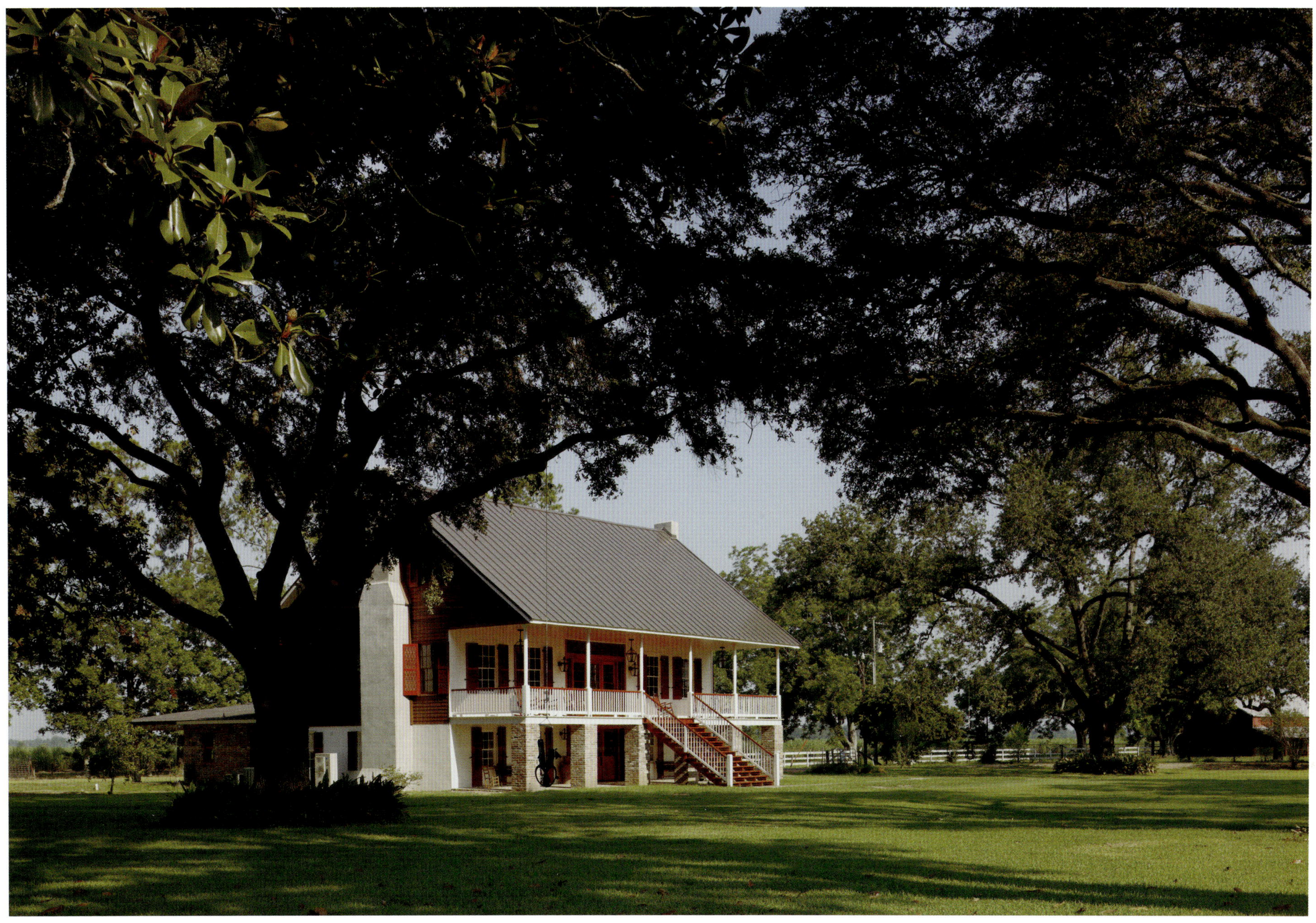

BELVUE

Mary Beth and George Guerin recently restored their Lettsworth home, Belvue, a classic Louisiana raised cottage dating to the 1830s.

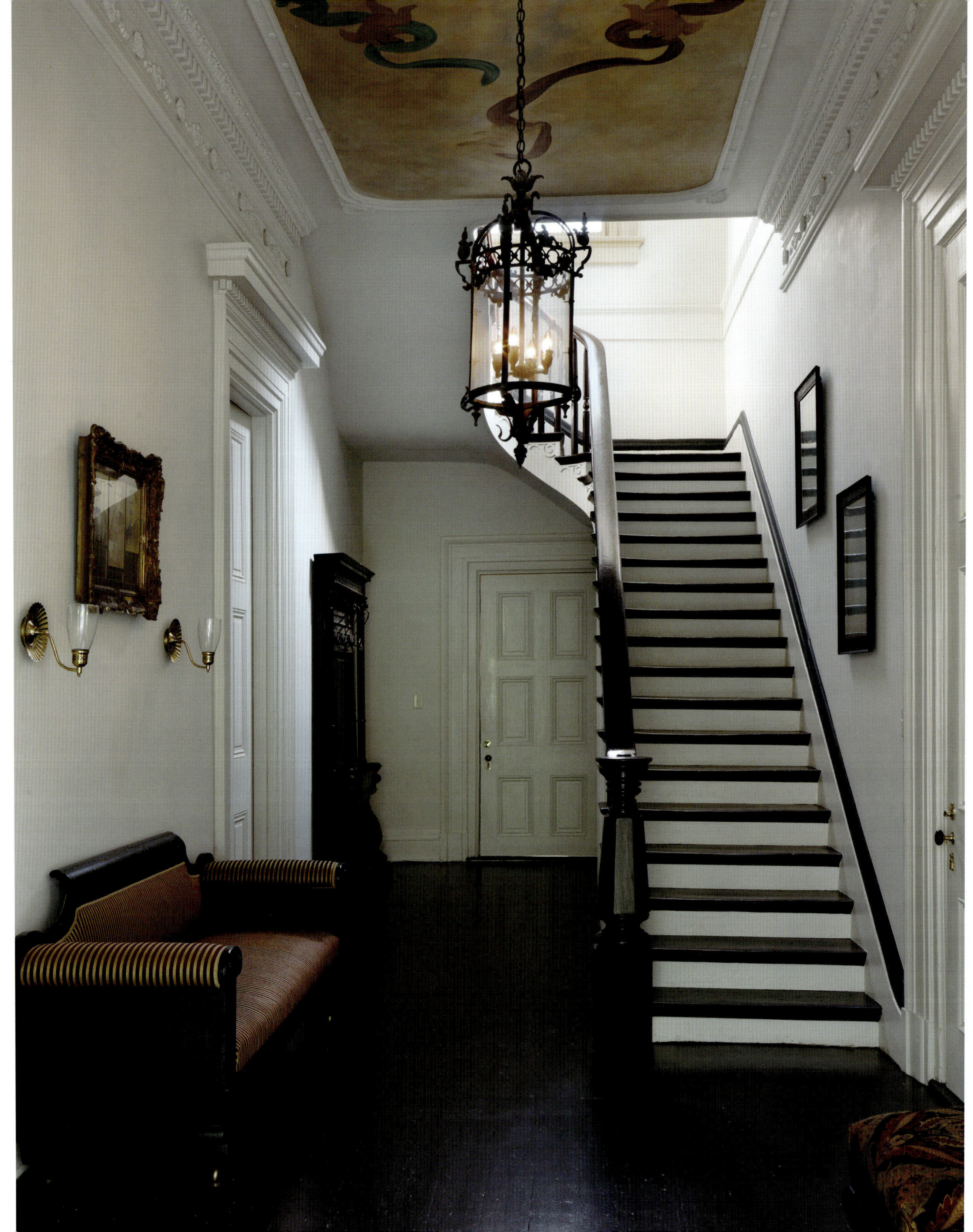

White Hall is believed to have been named for its magnificent entry hall, recently restored and furnished in nineteenth-century fashion.

White Hall is the only antebellum home remaining on the Atchafalaya River in Pointe Coupee. Before the Civil War there were as many as forty-six plantation homes in this parish and across the river in Avoyelles and St. Landry Parishes. Almost all were lost to the economic devastation that followed the Civil War coupled with the ravaging flooding of the rivers.

White Hall was built by Elias Norwood, the owner and builder of Richland in East Feliciana Parish. Two of his sons owned estates on the Atchafalaya. Captain Sam Norwood lived on Norwood Plantation, and Abel John Norwood lived on Kirk, or Kirkwood. Elias began building White Hall on the Pointe Coupee side of the river near his sons, but died before the house was finished.

Captain Bennet B. Simmes operated a ferry across the Atchafalaya near the mouth of Bayou de Glaises in the 1830s and 1840s. Simmes bought White Hall around 1857 after Norwood's death, and finished the house in grand style. Simmesport, across the Atchafalaya, is named for Captain Simmes.

In 1863 White Hall was occupied by Federal soldiers and is said to have been used as headquarters by Union general Nathaniel Banks.

The Glynn family of Glynnwood Plantation in southeastern Pointe Coupee owned White

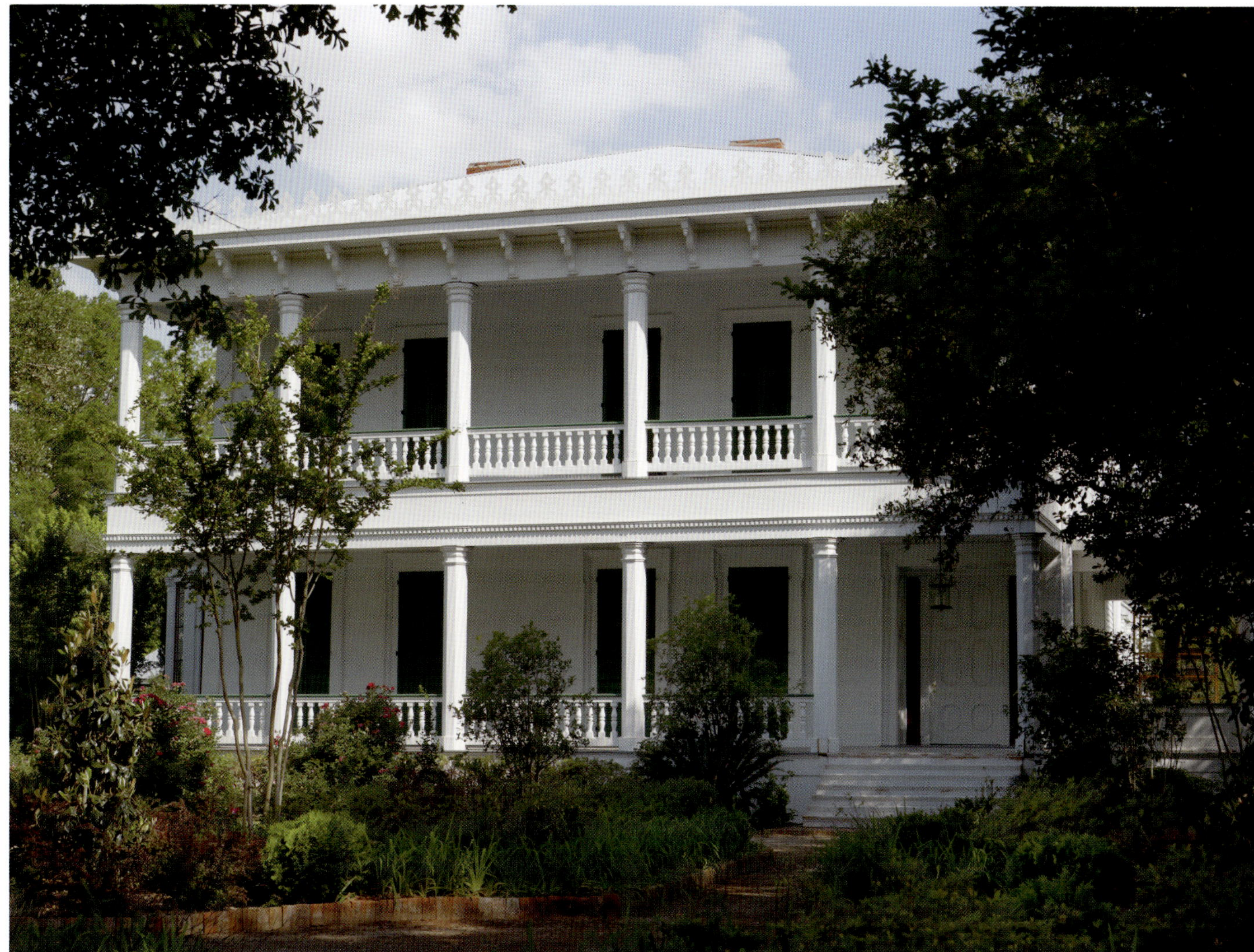

Hall from 1910 until 1975. In the late twentieth century the house was overgrown, barely visible from the levee road. It was rescued from almost certain destruction by current owners and preservationists Marc Becker and Gary Sutton, who have undertaken a careful restoration.

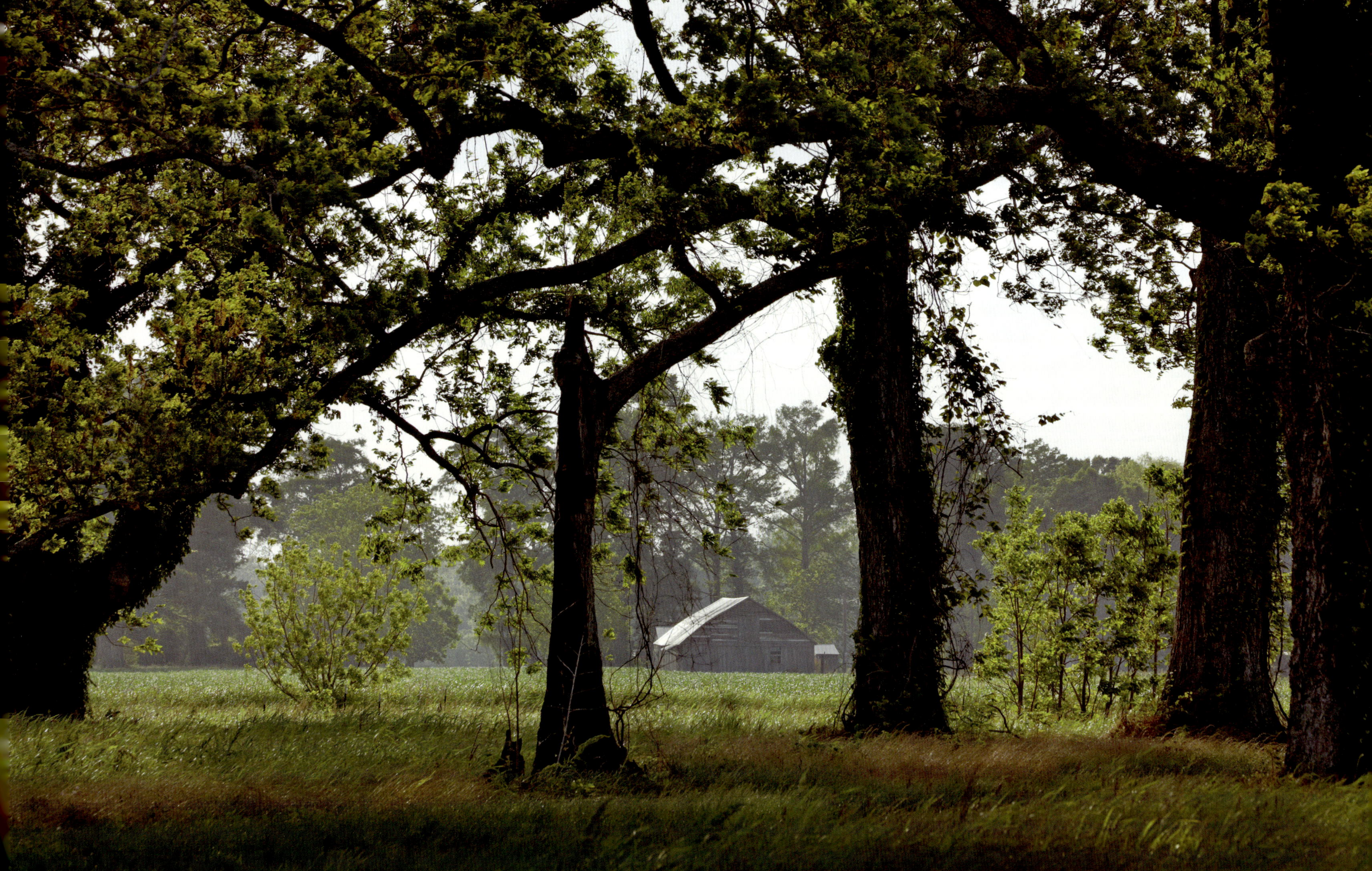

Fields of corn and wheat grow side by side and next to native pecan trees on the Cotten Brothers Farm on Bayou Latanache.

146

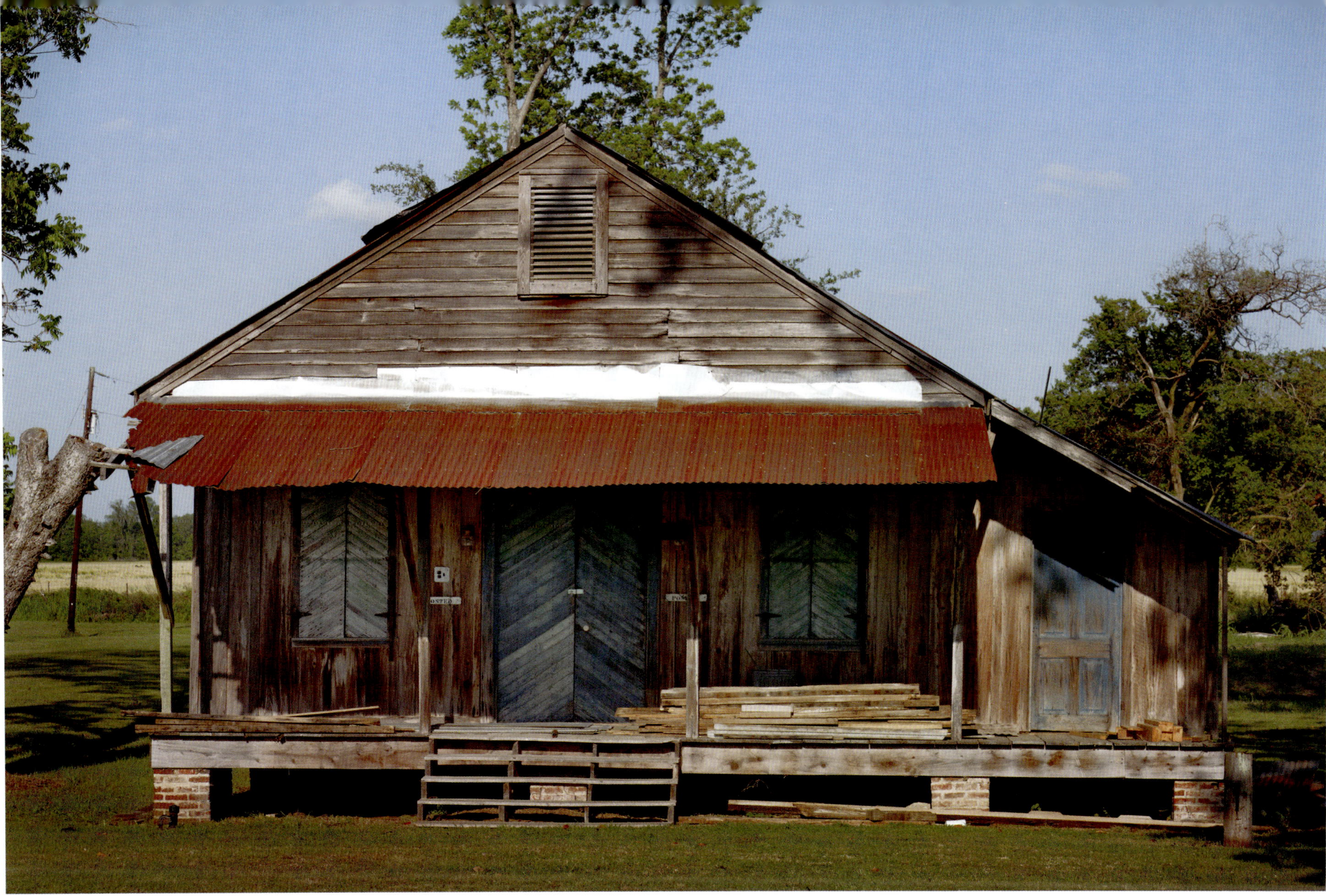

JACOBY STORE

The hundred-year-old Jacoby Store stands on the Atchafalaya river road only a few miles from the Simmesport bridge. The store was run for some years by the Corben family, and Postmaster Robert L. Lindsey ran the post office inside the general store in the early twentieth century.

Small stores or commissaries were located on almost every plantation in antebellum times. Many continued to supply staples to sharecropper families for decades after the Civil War, until the prevalence of the automobile made it possible to travel farther to meet daily shopping needs. Today, only one, Alma Store in Lakeland, still operates in Pointe Coupee. Several old general stores, vacant but in handsome condition like the Jacoby Store, stand as landmarks throughout Pointe Coupee, reminding passersby of changes in the economy and shopping habits of local people over the past century.

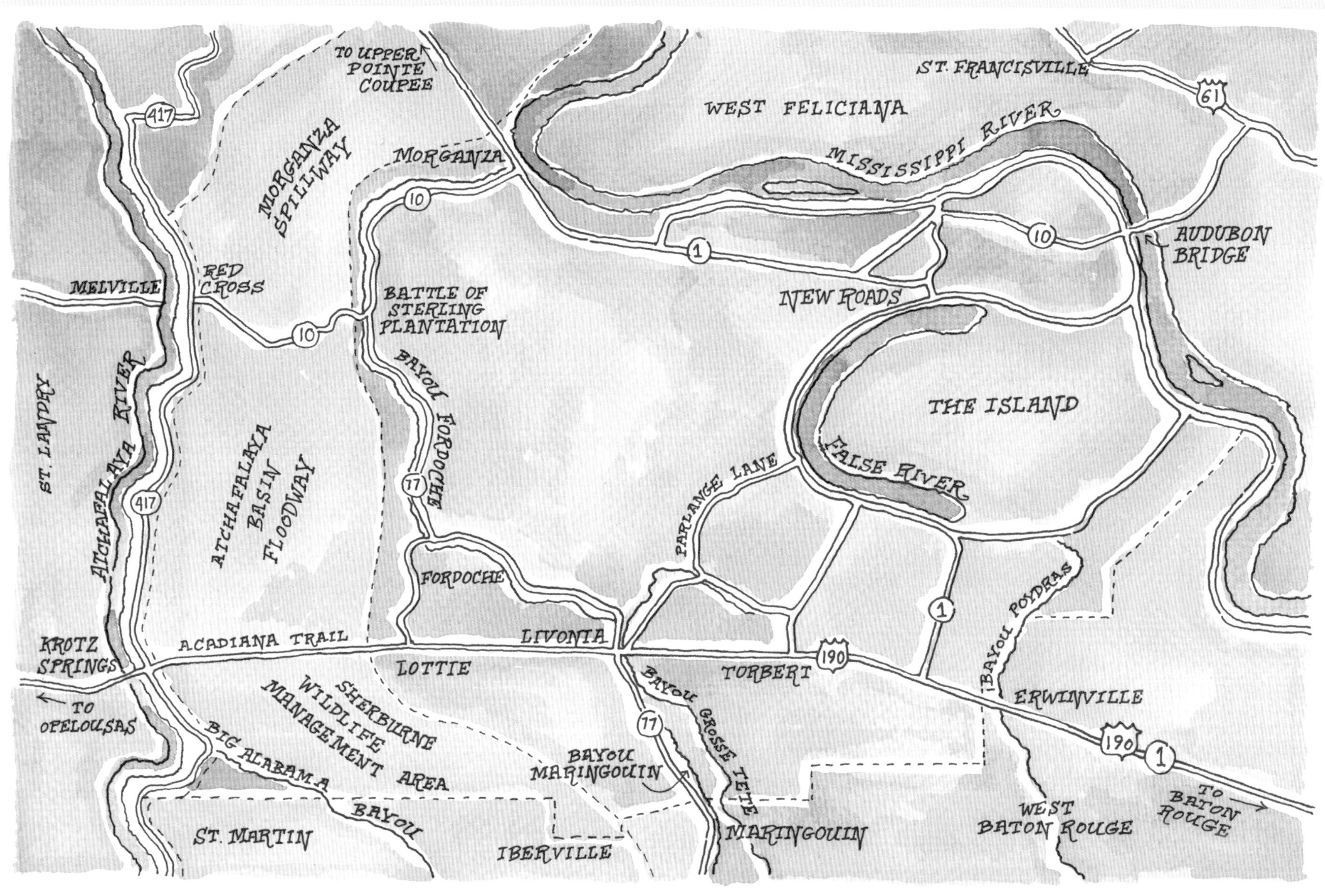

TO UPPER POINTE COUPEE
ST. FRANCISVILLE
WEST FELICIANA
61
417
MORGANZA SPILLWAY
MORGANZA
MISSISSIPPI RIVER
10
10
1
AUDUBON BRIDGE
MELVILLE
RED CROSS
NEW ROADS
BATTLE OF STERLING PLANTATION
10
THE ISLAND
ST. LANDRY
ATCHAFALAYA RIVER
BAYOU FORDOCHE
PARLANGE LANE
FALSE RIVER
17
ATCHAFALAYA BASIN FLOODWAY
417
BAYOU POYDRAS
FORDOCHE
1
KROTZ SPRINGS
ACADIANA TRAIL
LIVONIA
190
ERWINVILLE
TO OPELOUSAS
LOTTIE
TORBERT
SHERBURNE WILDLIFE MANAGEMENT AREA
BAYOU GROSSE TETE
190
1
BIG ALABAMA
77
BAYOU MARINGOUIN
TO BATON ROUGE
BAYOU
WEST BATON ROUGE
ST. MARTIN
IBERVILLE
MARINGOUIN

CHAPTER 8

Fordoche, Livonia, and the Bayous

BAYOU FORDOCHE

Black willow branches gently shade a stand of spider lilies blooming in April along the banks of Bayou Fordoche.

A historical marker is all that tells of a Civil War battle that took the lives of 42 men and wounded another 130. The battlefield is a cane field today.

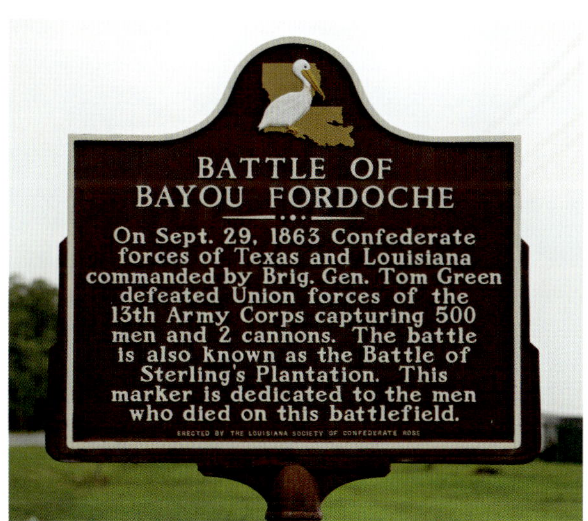

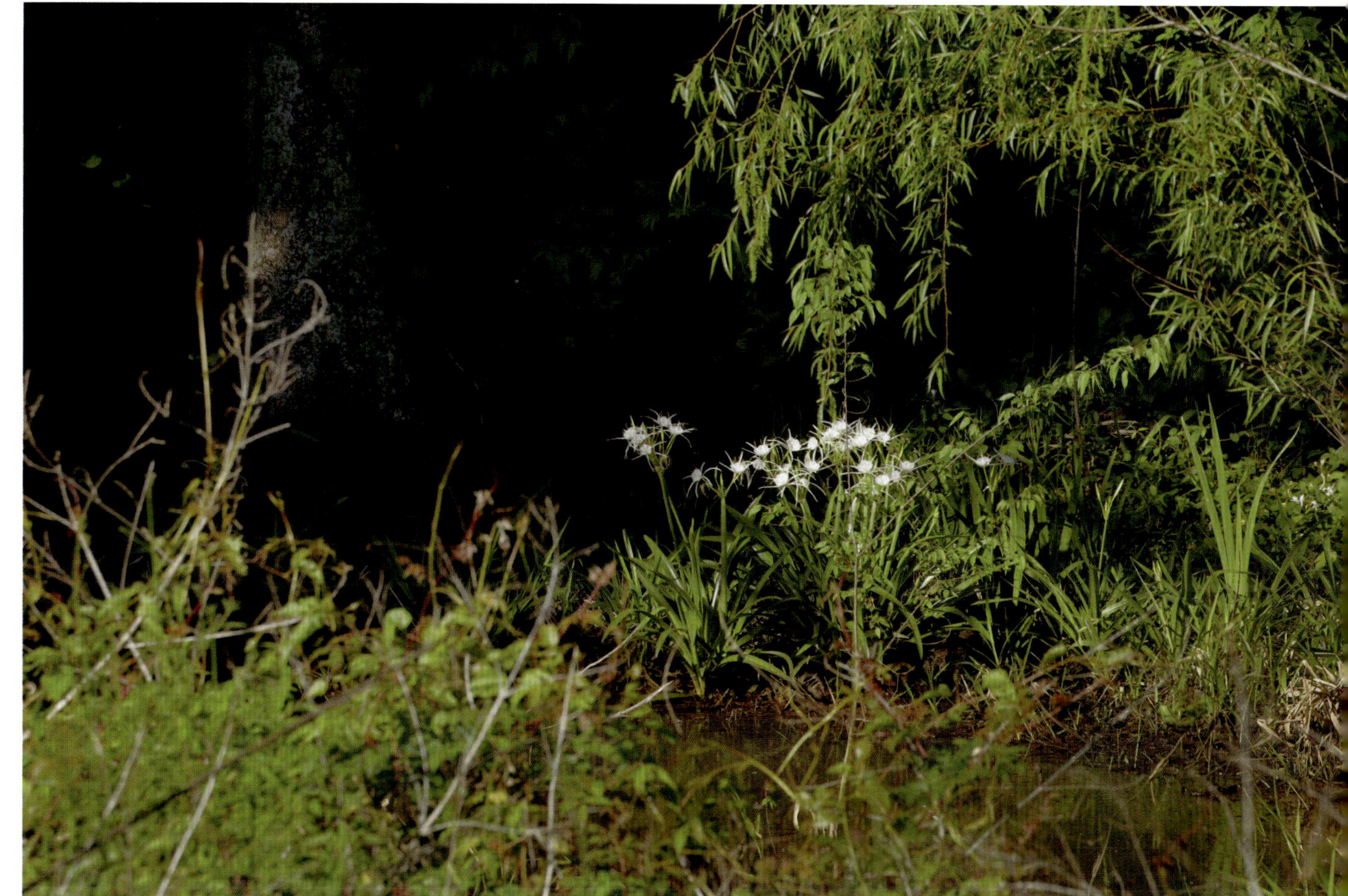

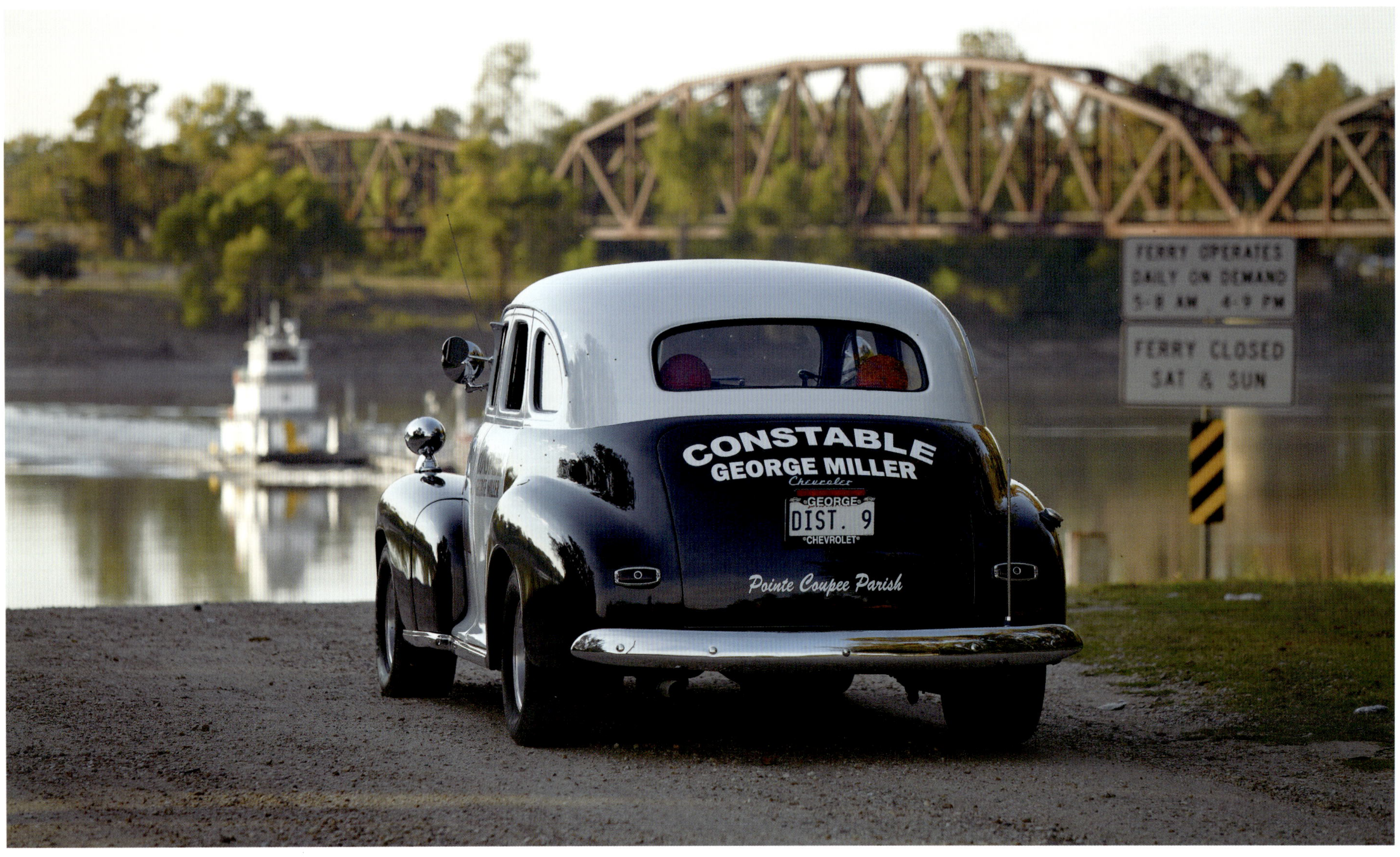

MELVILLE FERRY

Constable George Miller waits to drive his antique Chevrolet onto the Melville Ferry at Red Cross. The small ferry carried passengers and vehicles across the Atchafalaya for more than sixty years before service was discontinued in 2010. The railroad bridge seen here replaced an old bridge built in 1883, lost to the river in the 1927 flood. A railroad bridge built in 1909 at Krotz Springs survives as the oldest bridge in the parish.

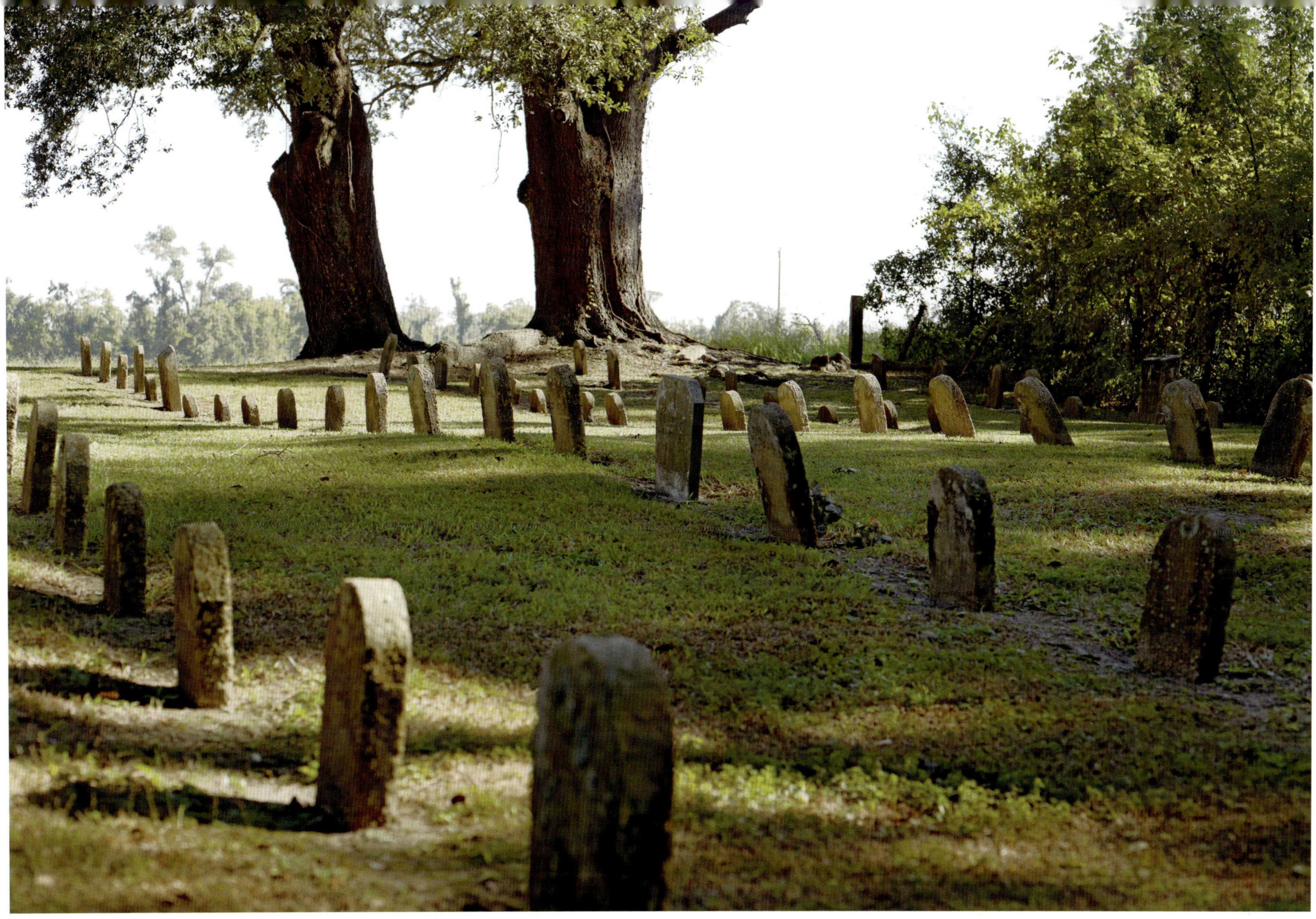

Two live oaks shade the churchyard of the Zion Travelers Baptist Church, organized in 1880 on the banks of Bayou Fordoche. The cemetery lies quietly on a plot of land between fields of corn and beans. Among a number of very old gravestones rest almost seventy that are simply marked UNKNOWN. Most of these graves were relocated in the 1940s as land was cleared of homes, farms, and churches to create the Morganza Spillway.

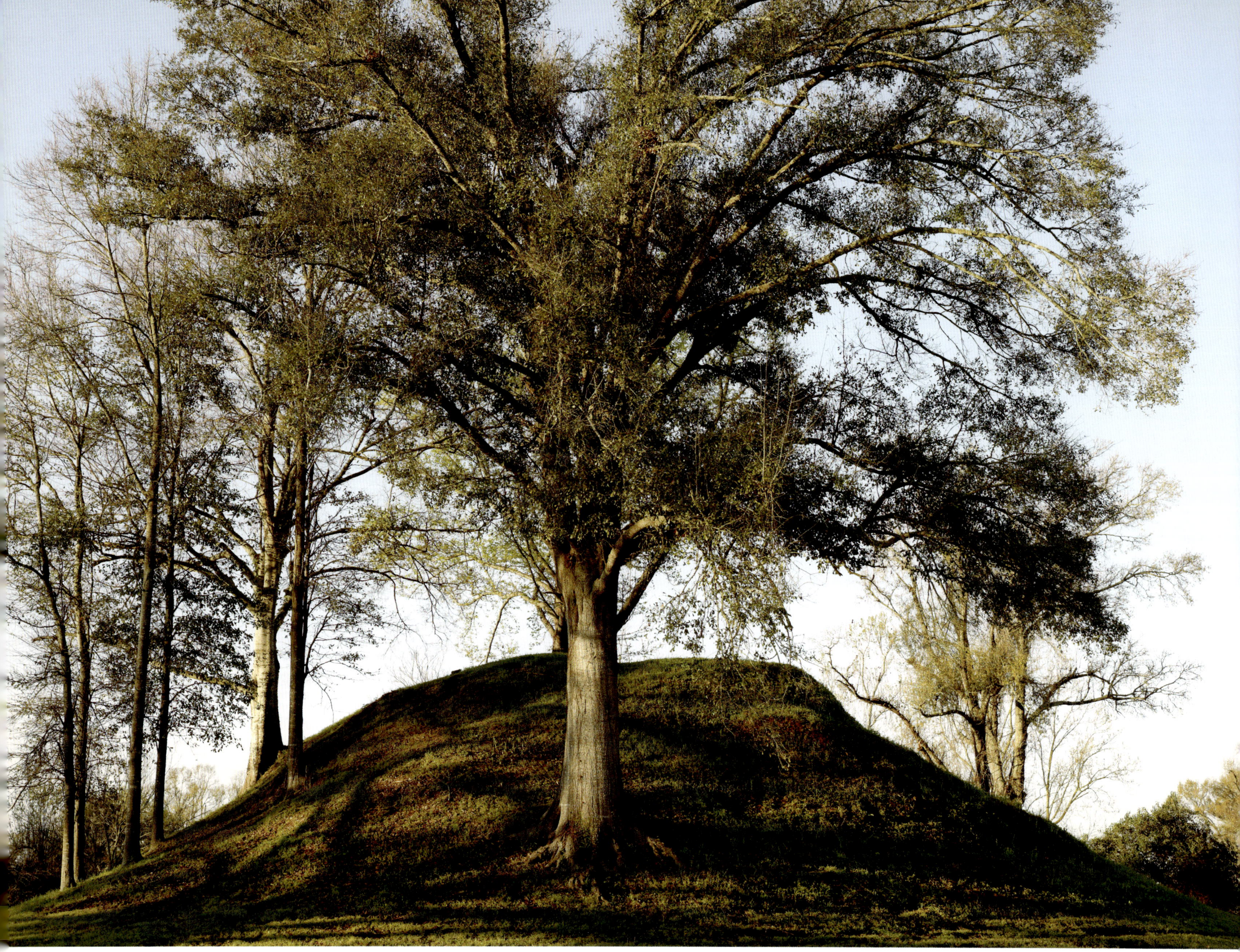

A large Indian mound stands beside Bayou Grosse Tete, near its confluence with Bayou Fordoche and Portage Bayou. The mound is clearly visible from Highway 78, the road that runs from Livonia to Frisco. It is one of several built by Native Americans during the Coles Creek period, between AD 700 and 1200.

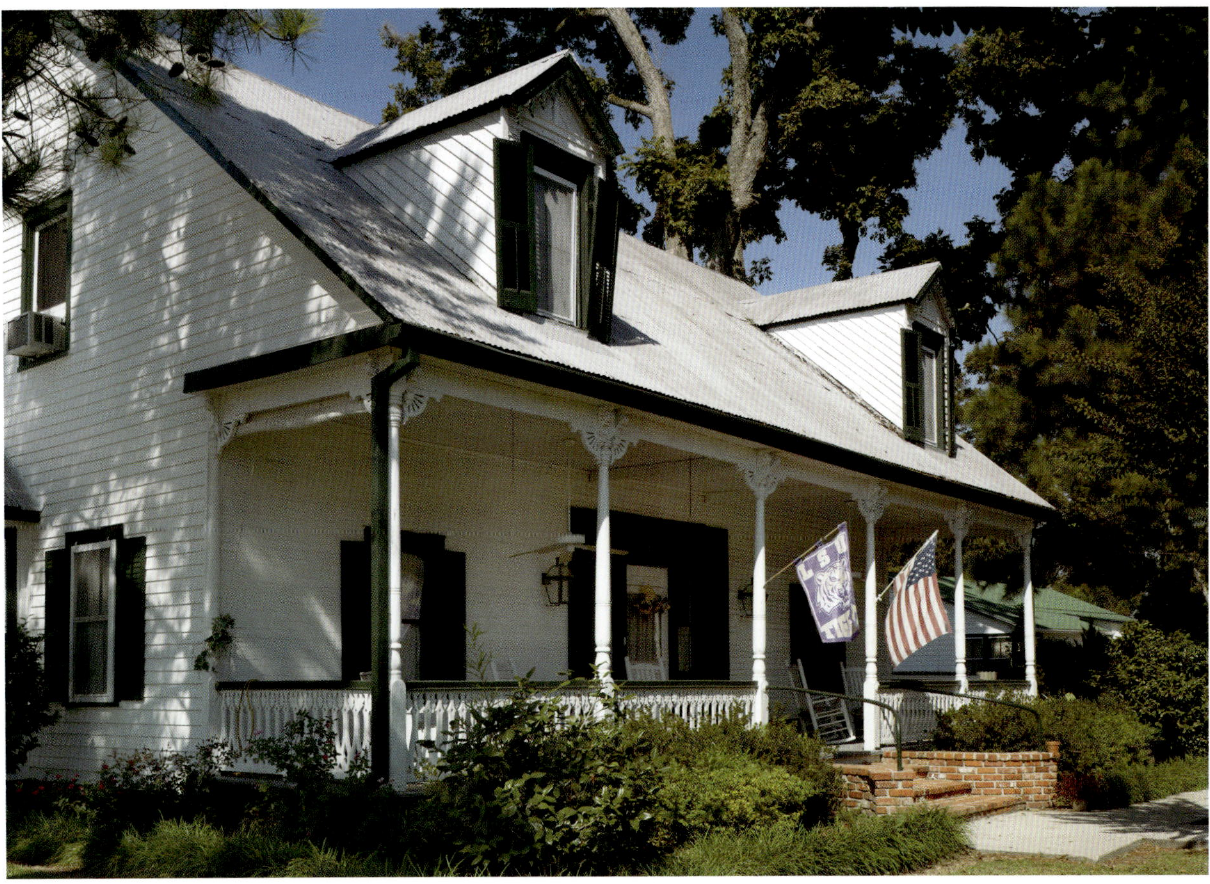

An LSU flag flies alongside the Stars and Stripes at Dreyfus House, built about 1850. A small embankment runs across the front yard between the house and Bayou Grosse Tete, a remnant of the Fordoche–Grosse Tete levee built in 1876 to protect southwestern Pointe Coupee and northern Iberville Parish from frequent flooding.

Dreyfus Store, not seen here but next door to Dreyfus House, was built before 1930. It replaced a previous building that burned in 1925. Both general stores were run by the Dreyfus and Weil families for much of the nineteenth and twentieth centuries. In addition to mercantile products and provisions, the store contained a post office and an apothecary. In 1989 the store was changed over to become a popular restaurant, Joe's Dreyfus Store, that put Livonia on the map as a charming Old Louisiana dining destination. The restaurant carries on today, and Dreyfus House is now operated as a bed-and-breakfast inn.

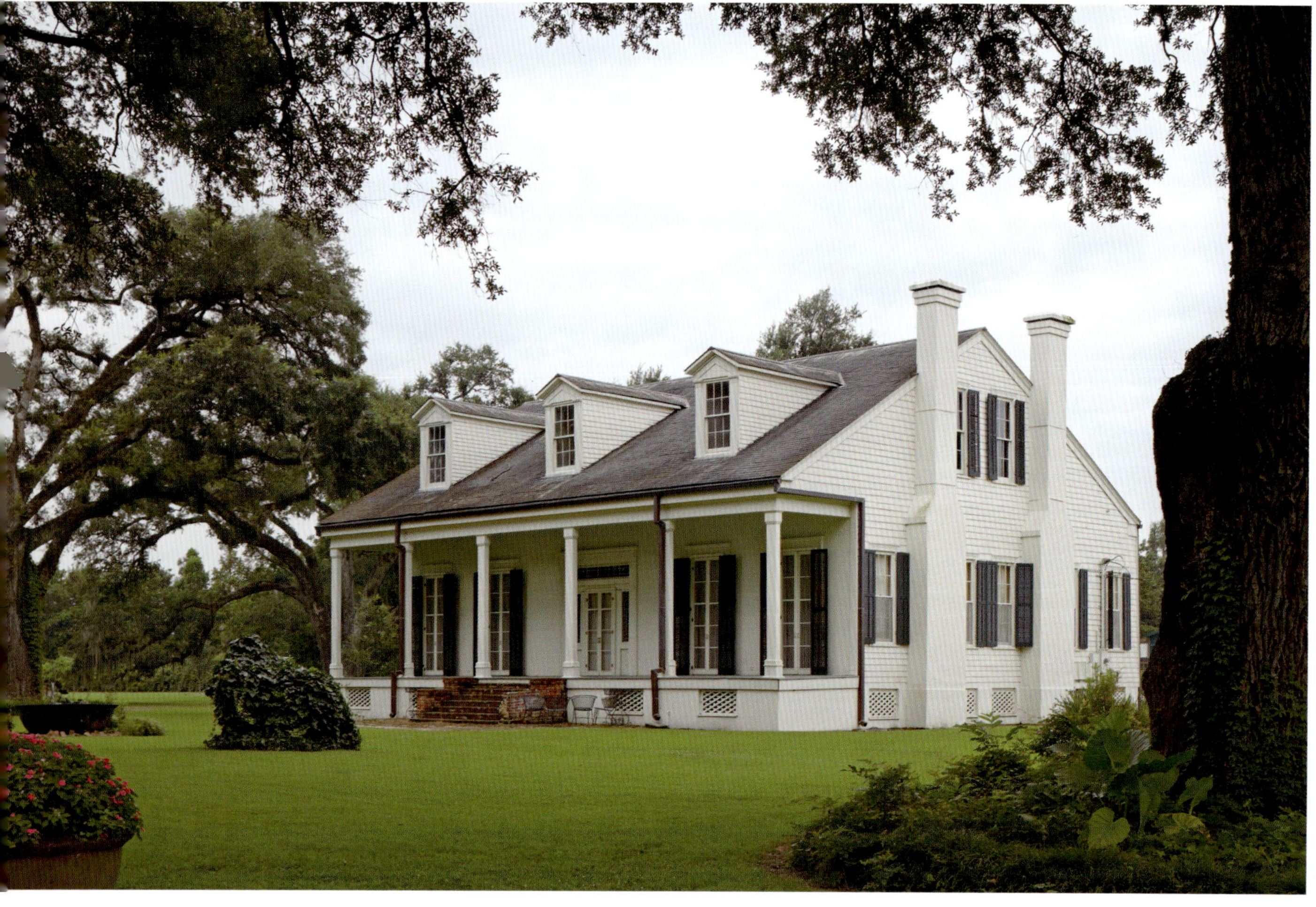

El Dorado was built for David Barrow (1805–1874), who also owned Alma and nearby Kenmore Plantation. The fine interior woodwork is said to be similar in quality to that found at Afton Villa, Barrow's fabulous St. Francisville home (destroyed by fire in 1963). Today El Dorado is the center of a large sugar plantation, long owned by the Nicholson family of New Orleans.

An important event in Civil War history took place at El Dorado. Confederate general Robert E. Lee surrendered at Appomattox on April 9, 1865, officially bringing the war to an end. But Confederate captains William Ratliff and James Collins did not surrender until June 7, almost two months later. They did so at El Dorado, and some call it the last surrender of the Civil War.

A grove of ancient live oaks surrounds the plantation home of El Dorado. Thirty-one of the trees are registered with the Live Oak Society. As old trees succumbed to fierce hurricanes—Andrew in 1992 and Gustav in 2008—El Dorado's caretakers planted young live oaks to ensure the future of the grove.

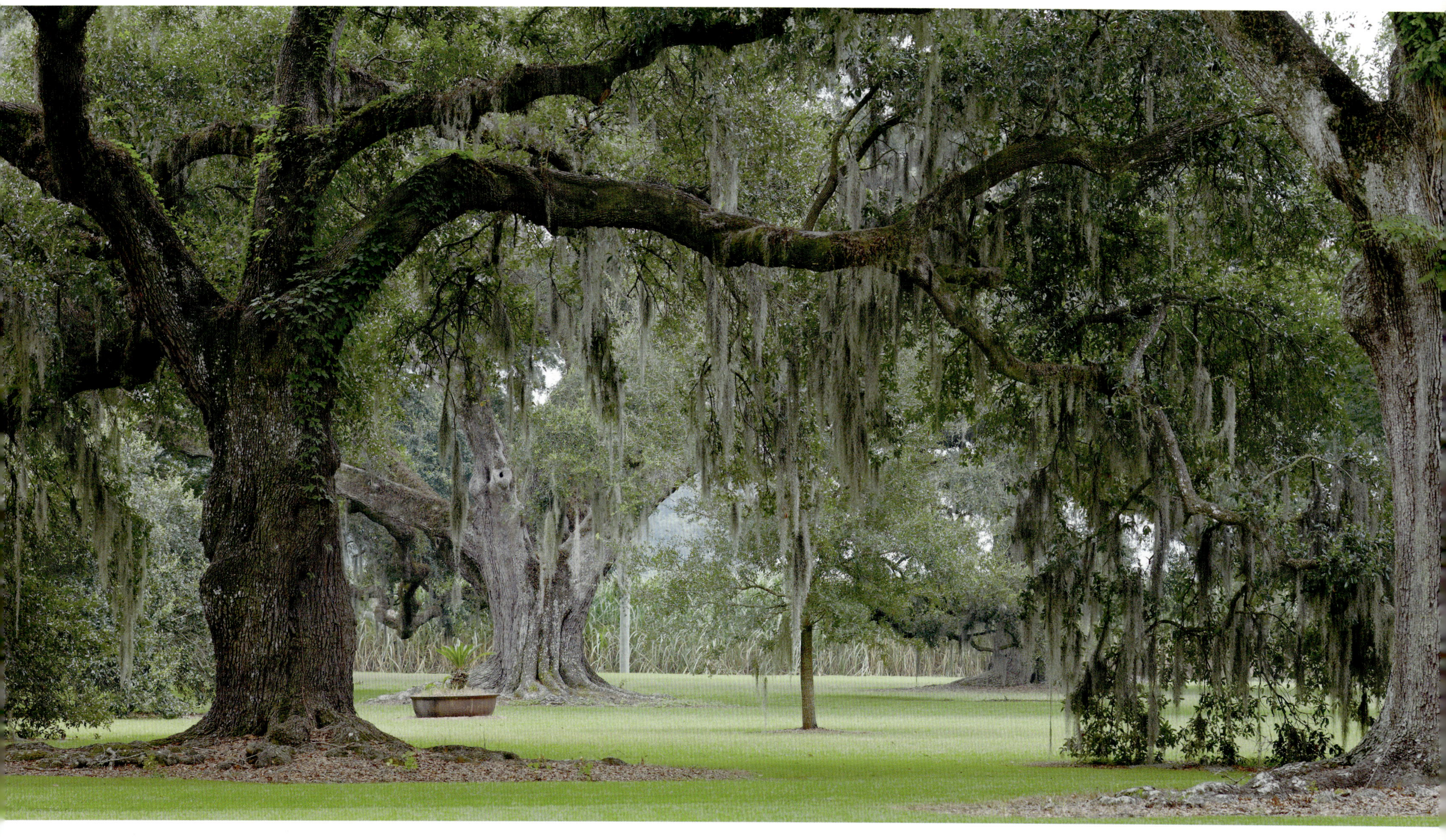

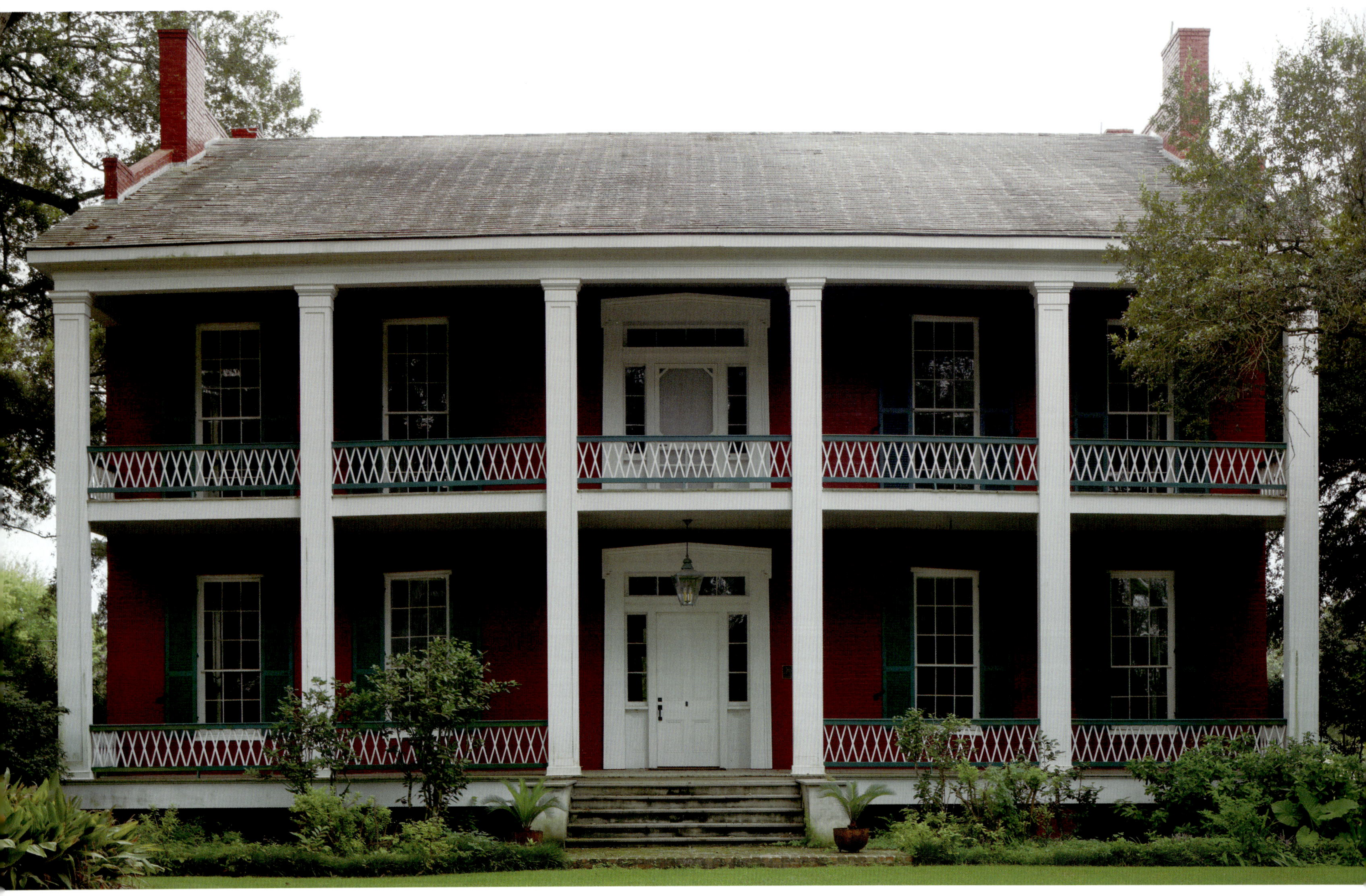

Valverda sits proudly on the bank of Bayou Grosse Tete in the southernmost part of Pointe Coupee Parish. Valverda was home to Henry S. Johnson (1783–1864), the fifth governor of Louisiana. An Episcopalian and a Virginian by birth, Johnson served as governor from 1824 to 1828. Early in his term, Johnson welcomed a visit to Louisiana from the Revolutionary War hero the Marquis de Lafayette, who was spending the better part of a year on a grand tour of America. Johnson benefited greatly from the popularity of his French guest.

Johnson lived at Valverda from 1855 until his death in 1864. His wife, Elizabeth Rousby Key, was a cousin of Francis Scott Key, author of "The Star-Spangled Banner." Johnson was buried on the grounds of Valverda, but the location of his grave has been forgotten.

Valverda's simple Greek Revival floor plan—four rooms on each floor, one in each corner, with wide central halls—is easy to glean from the side view. The house's two-story columns and painted brick are unique among the old houses of Pointe Coupee. This is the first truly American house in the parish, its architectural heritage traced more to Georgia and Virginia than to Louisiana. When the house was renovated in the early 2000s, the owners found what is probably the date of construction written in pencil on the back of a trim board: "Jonnie Cormier Feb 19 1842."

Also in 1842 Parlange Lane was opened, connecting False River with Bayou Grosse Tete. Livonia was the crossroads between French settlement to the north and English to the south.

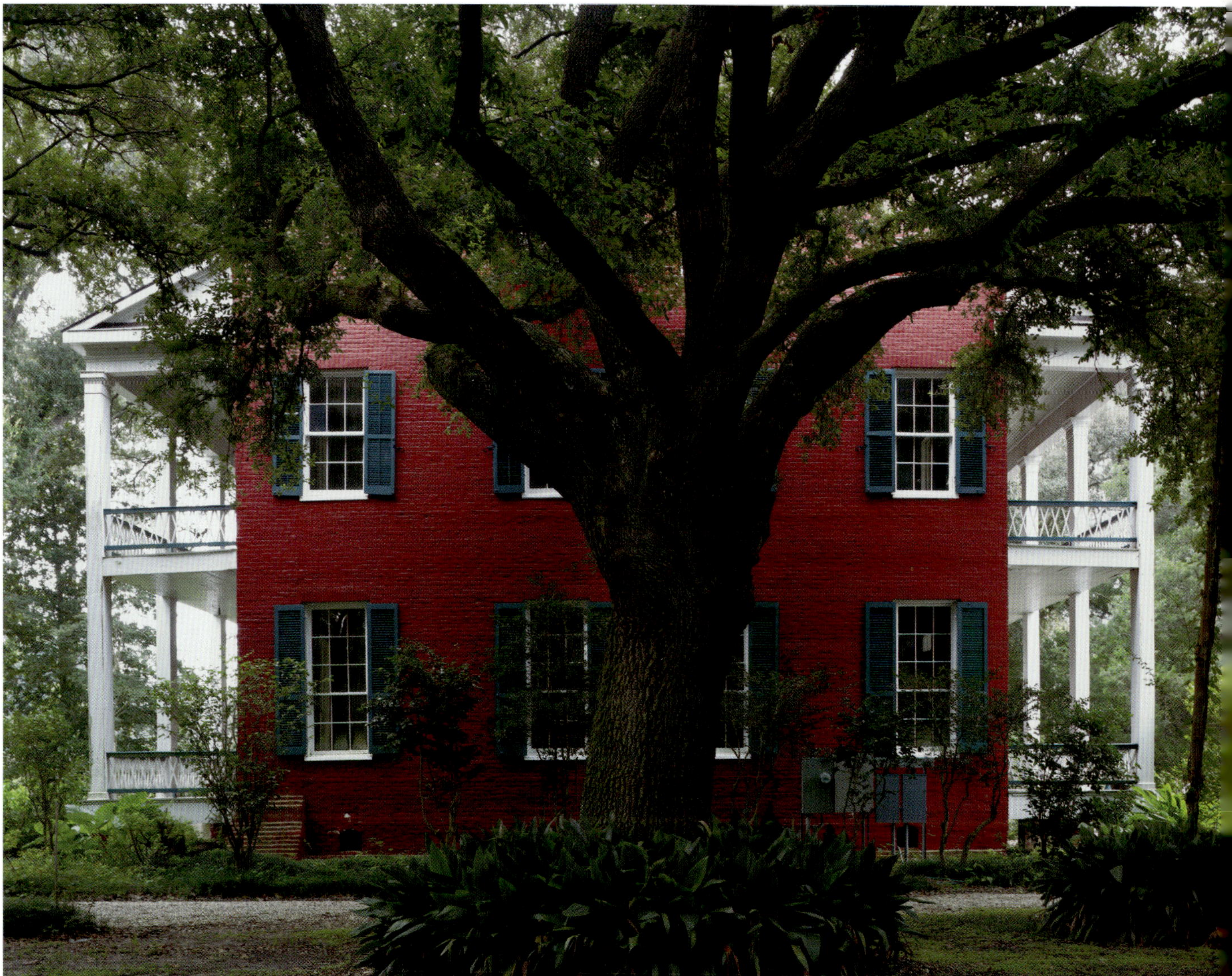

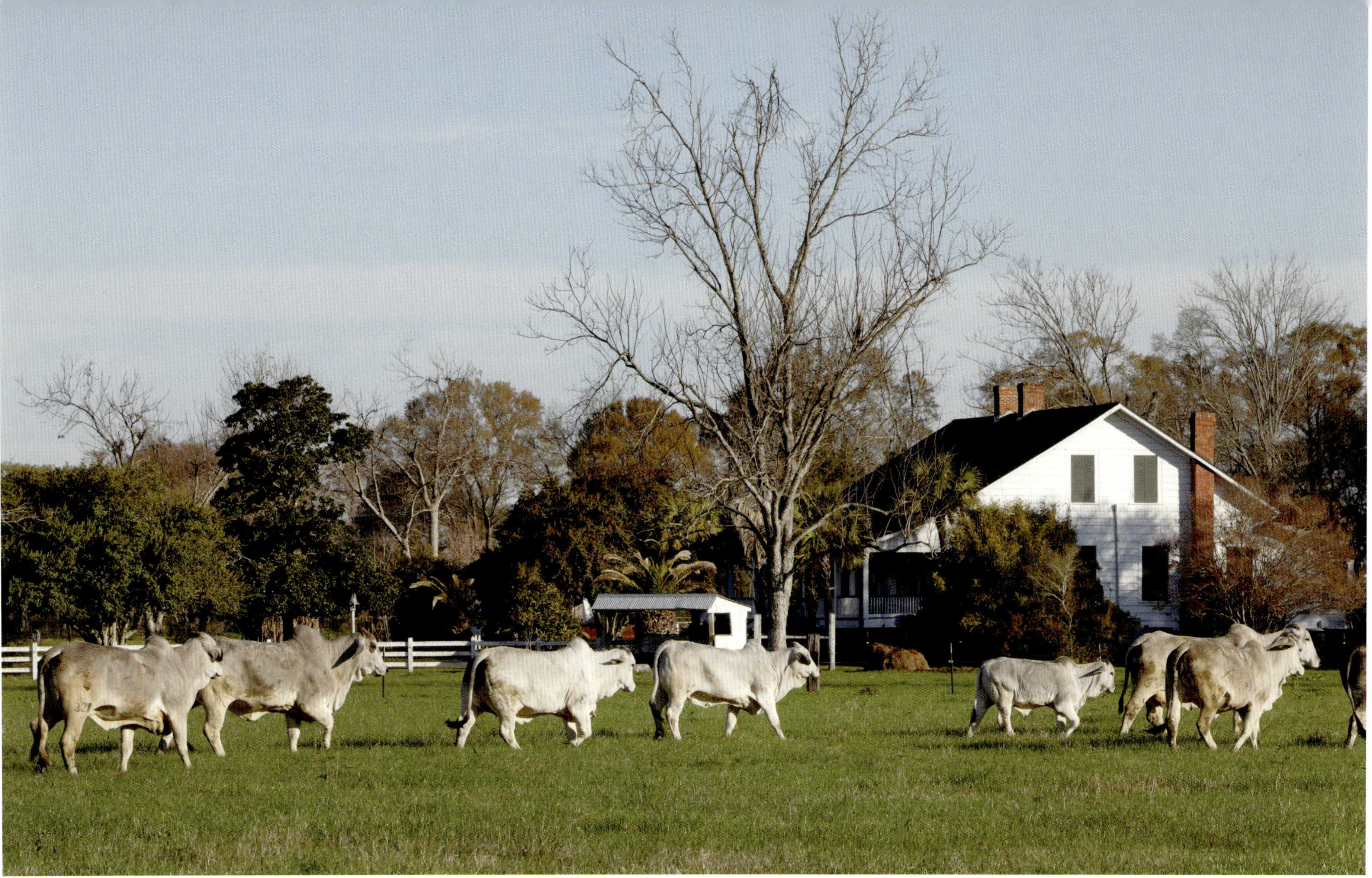

Brahman cattle graze in the fields of Kenmore, recalling one of the plantation's early owners, David Barrow. One of Louisiana's wealthiest planters, Barrow owned three Pointe Coupee plantations in the 1850s. His family received a pair of Brahmans as a gift from the British government in 1854. Brahman cattle originated in India and are extremely heat tolerant. The Bar-rows bred the exotic animals with domestic cattle and found that the crosses resulted in excellent new bloodlines. These animals came to be known as Barrow Grade cattle, a superior breed.

The home is a center-hall raised cottage built on what was a huge cotton plantation in the 1850s. Located on Bayou Maringouin, the house and cattle today belong to Mike and Lisa James.

A plantation home once stood at the end of this magnificent avenue of live oaks. Today the trees stand alone in a great field.

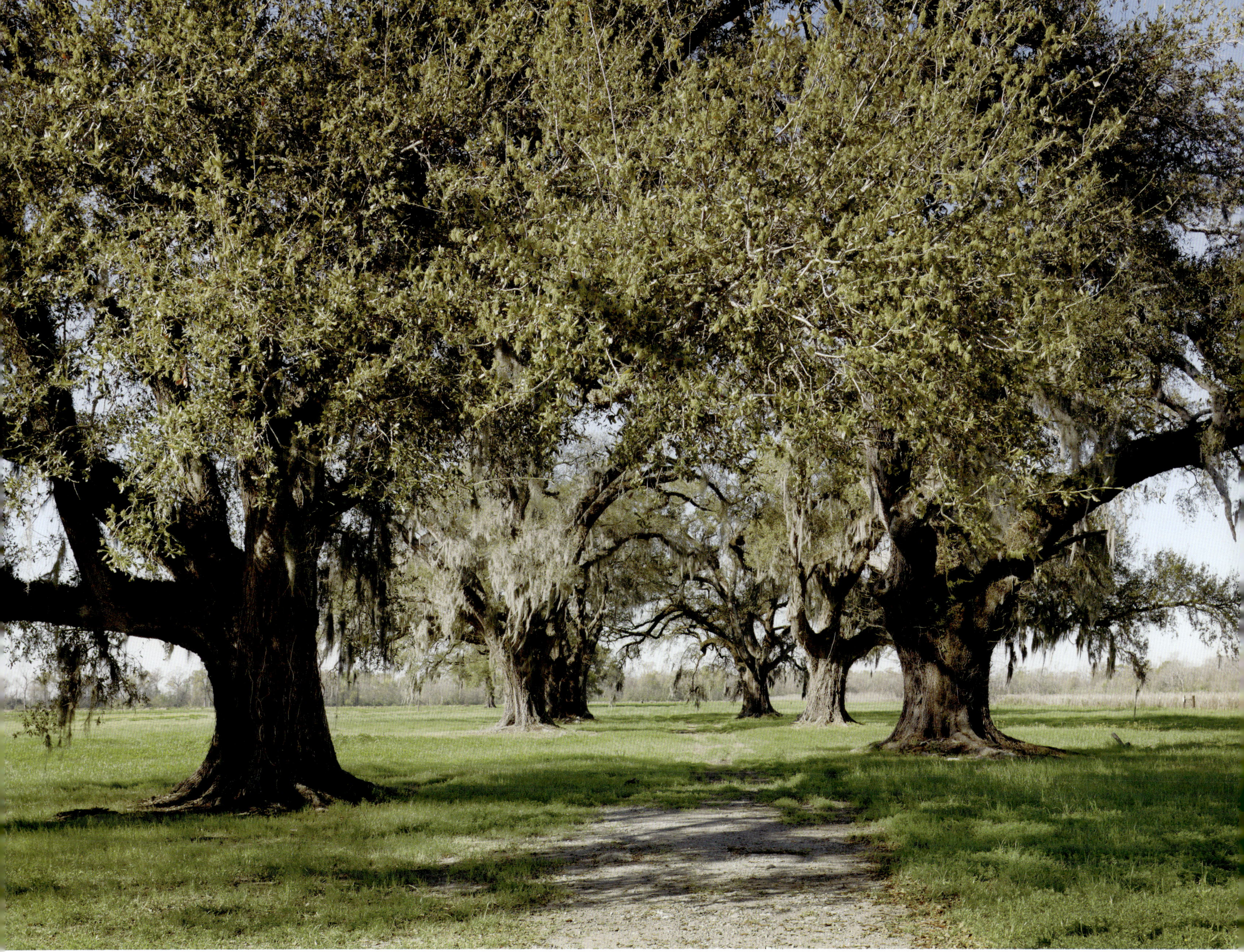

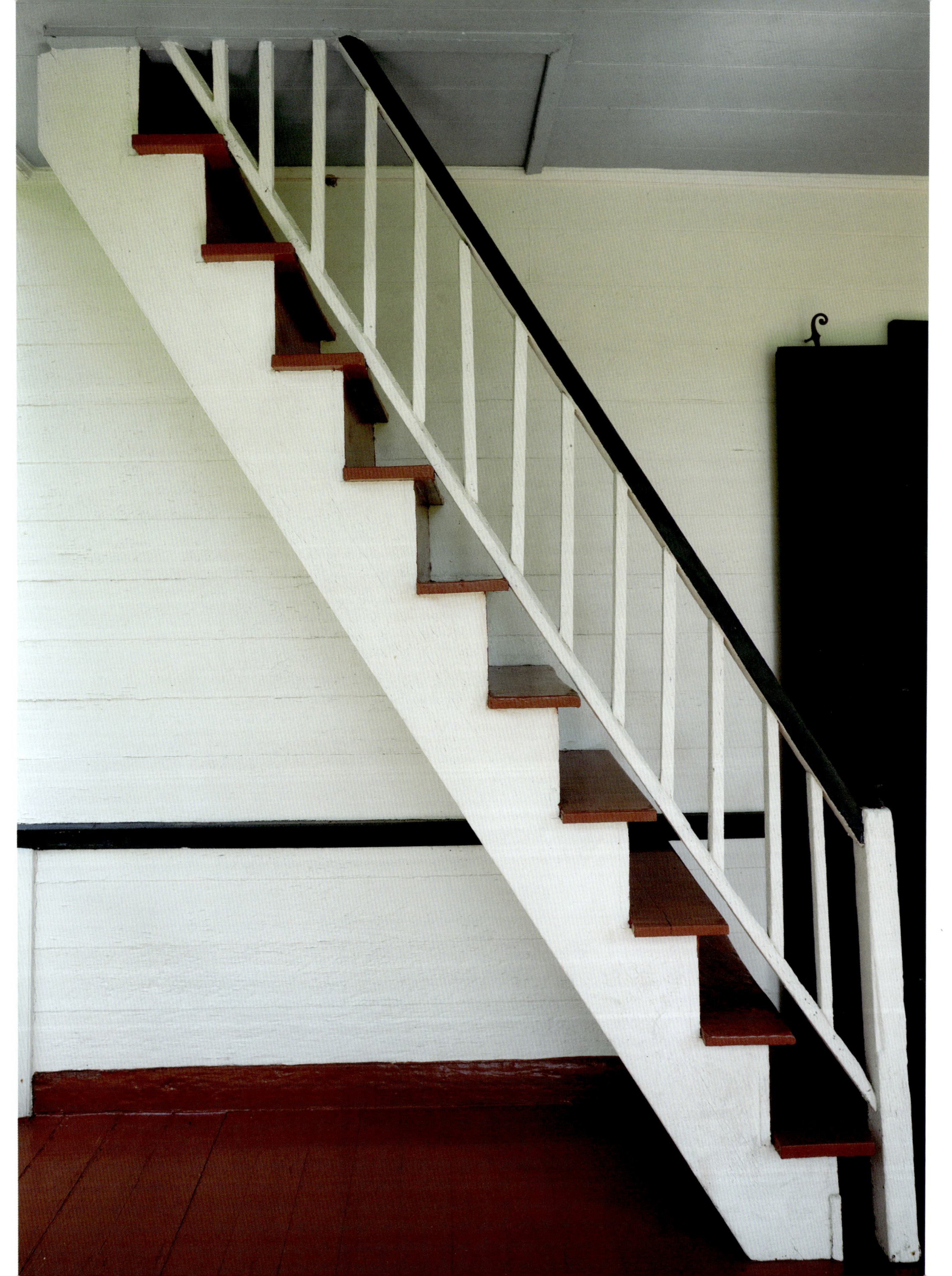

APPENDIX

Historic Trees and Buildings in Pointe Coupee Parish

NATIONAL REGISTER OF HISTORIC PLACES
(www.nps.gov/nr/)

Building	Year Added
Parlange*	1970
St. Stephen's Episcopal Church	1974
White Hall Plantation	1977
LeJeune House	1978
Old Hickory	1979
Ovide Lacour Store**	1979
St. Francis Chapel	1979
Bonnie Glen	1980
Pointe Coupee Parish Museum	1980
Pointe Coupee Parish Courthouse	1981
El Dorado Plantation House	1982
Glynnwood	1982
River Lake	1983
Lakeside	1984
Pleasant View	1984
LeBeau House and Kitchen	1985
Albin Major House	1991
Austerlitz	1991
Fannie Riche House	1991
Labatut House	1991
Saizan House	1991
Wickliffe	1991
North Bend	1992
Valmont Bergeron House	1992
Jean Baptiste Bergeron House	1994
Satterfield Motor Company	1994
Cherie Quarters Cabins	1995
Poydras High School	1996
Samson-Claiborne House	1997
First National Bank	2002
Valverda	2002
Jaques Dupre House	2003

*Also listed as a National Historic Landmark.

**Demolished in the 1980s.

MORE INFORMATION FOR READERS AND VISITORS

Alma Plantation
4612 Alma Road
Lakeland, LA 70752

American Association of State and Local History
1717 Church Street
Nashville, TN 37203

Arts Council of Pointe Coupee
P.O. Box 669
New Roads, LA 70760

Atchafalaya National Heritage Area
Louisiana Office of Tourism
1051 North Third Street
Baton Rouge, LA 70804

Bergeron Pecans
10003 False River Road
New Roads, LA 70760

Center for Acadian and Creole Folklore
University of Louisiana at Lafayette
P.O. Box 40831
313 Dupré Library
Lafayette, LA 70754

Centre for the Arts
P.O. Box 440
1104 West Main Street
New Roads, LA 70760

CODOFIL
Council on the Development of French in Louisiana
217 West Main Street
Lafayette, LA 70501

Creole West Productions
www.creolewest.com

Les Créoles de Pointe Coupée
Father Joseph Conway Rodney Center
812 New Roads Street
New Roads, LA 70760

Department of the Archives
Catholic Diocese of Baton Rouge
1800 South Acadian Thruway
Baton Rouge, LA 70808

Dreyfus House Bed and Breakfast
2741 Maringouin Road W
Livonia, LA 70755

Ernest J. Gaines Award for Literary Excellence
Baton Rouge Area Foundation
402 N. Fourth Street
Baton Rouge, LA 70802

Ernest J. Gaines Center
University of Louisiana at Lafayette
400 East St. Mary Boulevard
Lafayette, LA 70503

Friends of French Studies at LSU
LSU Department of French Studies
416 Hodges Hall
Baton Rouge, LA 70803

Glaser's Produce Farm
8925 False River Road
New Roads, LA 70760

Joe's Dreyfus Store Restaurant
2731 Maringouin Road W
Livonia, LA 70755

Jones and Jones Cypress
6314 Hwy 1
Batchelor, LA 70715

K.C. Stairs and Woodworks
453 East Main Street
New Roads, LA 70760

LeBlanc's Pure Cane Syrup
7721 Morganza Hwy
Morganza, LA 70759

Louisiana Division of Historic Preservation
P.O. Box 44247
Baton Rouge, LA 70804

Louisiana State Archives
Louisiana Secretary of State
P.O. Box 94125
Baton Rouge, LA 70804

Louisiana State Museum
660 North 4th Street
Baton Rouge, LA 70802

LSU AgCenter
Pointe Coupee Co-Op Extension Service
180 East Main Street, 1st floor
New Roads, LA 70760

Louisiana Trust for Historic Preservation
P.O. Box 1587
Baton Rouge, LA 70821

Ma Mama's Kitchen
124 West Main Street
New Roads, LA 70760

Mississippi River Parkway Commission
222 State Street, Suite 400
Madison, WI 53703

Morel's Court and Restaurant
210 Morrison Parkway
New Roads, LA 70760

Mon Rêve Bed and Breakfast
9825 False River Road
New Roads, LA 70760

National Trust for Historic Preservation
1785 Massachusetts Avenue NW
Washington D.C. 20036

The Pointe Coupee Banner
123 St. Mary Street
New Roads, LA 70760

Pointe Coupee Chamber of Commerce
P.O. Box 555
New Roads, LA 70760

Pointe Coupee Farm Bureau
P.O. Box 728
New Roads, LA 70760

Pointe Coupee Gallery
111 New Roads Street
New Roads, LA 70760

Pointe Coupee Historical Society
Julien Poydras Museum and Arts Center
P.O. Box 462
500 West Main Street
New Roads, LA 70760

Pointe Coupee at the Millennium
www.pcatm.org

Pointe Coupee Museum
8348 False River Road
New Roads, LA 70760

Pointe Coupee Office of Tourism
P.O. Box 733
727 Hospital Road, Suite B
New Roads, LA 70760

Pointe Coupee Parish Library
Historical Materials Collection
201 Claiborne Street
New Roads, LA 70760

Pointe Coupee Pecans
P.O. Box 10
Glynn, LA 70736

Pointe Coupee Parish Police Jury
P.O. Box 290
106 East Main Street
New Roads, LA 70760

Pourciau House, A Wayfarer's Retreat
109 Peach Street
New Roads, LA 70760

Purdin Koi Farm
7017 Cline Drive
Glynn, LA 70736

The Riverside Reader
P.O. Box 771
570 N. Jefferson Avenue, Suite A
Port Allen, LA 70767

Samson House Bed and Breakfast
405 Richey Street
New Roads, LA 70760

Satterfield's Restaurant
108 East Main Street
New Roads, LA 70760

Sherburne Wildlife Management Area
La. Department of Wildlife and Fisheries
5652 Hwy 182
Opelousas, LA 70570

Teach for America
501 Government Street, Suite 100
Baton Rouge, LA 70802

Tri-Parish Cotton Gin
20539 La. Hwy 970 N
Lettsworth, LA 70753

Zachary Taylor Parkway
P.O. Box 14265
Baton Rouge, LA 70898

SUGGESTED READING

Barry, John M. *Rising Tide: The Great Mississippi Flood of 1927 and How It Changed America.* New York: Simon and Schuster, 1997.

Brasseaux, Carl A., with photographs by Philip A. Gould. *Acadiana: Louisiana's Historic Cajun Country.* Baton Rouge: Louisiana State University Press, 2011.

Costello, Brian J. *A History of Pointe Coupee Parish, Louisiana.* Murray G. LeBeau Memorial Edition. Margaret Media Inc., 2010.

Cothran, James R. *Gardens and Historic Plants of the Antebellum South.* Columbia: University of South Carolina Press, 2003.

Curet, Bernard. *Our Pride: Pointe Coupee.* Baton Rouge: Moran Publishing, 1981.

Dameron, Wink. *Conversations with My Grandfather.* Xlibris, 2011.

DeHart, Jess, with Melanie Hamlet DeHart. *Plantations of Louisiana.* Gretna, La.: Pelican Publishing, 1982.

Friends of Hill Top Arboretum. *A Pocket Guide to Louisiana Native Trees.* Baton Rouge: Morgan Printing, 1997.

Field, Martha R. *Louisiana Voyages: The Travel Writings of Catharine Cole.* Edited by Joan B. McLaughlin and Jack McLaughlin. Jackson: University Press of Mississippi, 2006.

Fricker, Jonathan, et al. *Louisiana Architecture: A Handbook on Styles.* Lafayette: Center for Louisiana Studies, University of Louisiana at Lafayette, 1998.

Gross, Steve, et al. *Creole Houses: Traditional Homes of Old Louisiana.* New York: Abrams, 2007.

Hall, Gwendolyn Midlo. *Africans in Colonial Louisiana: The Development of Afro-Creole Culture in the Eighteenth Century.* Baton Rouge: Louisiana State University Press, 1992.

Heck, Robert W. *Religious Architecture in Louisiana.* Baton Rouge: Louisiana State University Press, 1995.

Holden, Jack D., et al. *Furnishing Louisiana: Creole and Acadian Furniture, 1735–1835.* New Orleans: The Historic New Orleans Collection, 2010.

Jackson, Mary Alice Victorian. *At Mama's House: A Collection of Poems.* Fort Collins, CO: Creole West Productions, 2006.

Katz, Ron. *French America: French Architecture from Colonialization to the Birth of a Nation.* New York: French Heritage Society, 2004.

Katz, Vincent. *Pleasure Palaces: The Art and Homes of Hunt Slonem.* Brooklyn: powerHouse Books, 2007.

Klingler, Thomas A. *If I Could Turn My Tongue Like That: The Creole Language of Pointe Coupee Parish.* Baton Rouge: Louisiana State University Press, 2003.

Laughlin, Clarence J. *Ghosts along the Mississippi: The Magic of the Old Houses of Louisiana.* New York: Bonanza Books, 1958.

Le Page du Pratz, M. *The History of Louisiana.* Edited by Joseph G. Tregle, Jr. Baton Rouge: Louisiana State University Press, 1975.

Leumas, Emilie G., and Renee B. Richard. *Roots of Faith: History of the Diocese of Baton Rouge.* Strasbourg, France: Editions du Signe, 2009.

Parlange, Angèle. *Creole Thrift: Premium Southern Living without Spending a Mint.* New York: HarperCollins, 2006.

Riffel, Judy, ed. *A History of Pointe Coupee Parish and Its Families.* Baton Rouge: Le Comité des Archives de la Louisiane, 1983.

Robin, C. C.. *Voyage to Louisiana, 1803–1805.* Translated by Stuart O. Landry, Jr. Gretna, La.: Pelican Publishing, 2000.

Sanford, J. I. *Beautiful Pointe Coupee and Her Prominent Citizens.* New Orleans: American Printing Co., 1906. Reprinted by Pointe Coupee Historical Society, 1999.

Seebold, Herman de Bachellé, M.D. *Old Louisiana Plantation Homes and Family Trees (in Two Volumes).* Gretna, La.: Pelican Publishing, 1941, 1971, 2004.

Seibert, Mary Frances. *Zulma: A Story of the Old South.* Natchez: Natchez Printing and Stationery Co., 1897.

Turner, Suzanne, with photographs by A. J. Meek. *The Gardens of Louisiana: Places of Work and Wonder.* Baton Rouge: Louisiana State University Press, 1997.

Twain, Mark. *Life on the Mississippi.* Boston: James R. Osgood and Co., 1883.

Winters, John D. *The Civil War in Louisiana.* Baton Rouge: Louisiana State University Press, 1963.

Young, Reggie Scott, et al. *This Louisiana Thing that Drives Me: The Legacy of Ernest J. Gaines.* Lafayette: University of Louisiana at Lafayette Press, 2009.

Zink, Frances Pirotte. *Julien Poydras: Statesman, Philanthropist, Educator.* Lafayette: University of Southwestern Louisiana, 1968.

BOOKS BY ERNEST J. GAINES

The Autobiography of Miss Jane Pittman, 1971
Bloodline, 1968
Catherine Carmier, 1964
A Gathering of Old Men, 1983
In My Father's House, 1978
A Lesson before Dying, 1993
A Long Day in November, 1971
Mozart and Leadbelly: Stories and Essays, 2005
Of Love and Dust, 1967

BOOKS BY BRIAN J. COSTELLO

Canal Street and Beyond—Louisiana's 20th Century Department Stores, 2003
The Catholic Church in Pointe Coupee, 1996
C'est ça yé dit: Creole Folktales, Superstitions, Remedies, Customs, Nicknames, and Linguistic Peculiarities of Pointe Coupee Parish, Louisiana, 2004
Chronicles of Carnival: A History of the New Roads Mardi Gras, 1993
Creole Pointe Coupee: A Sociological Analysis, 2002
Desolation Unmeasured . . . The Tragic History of Floods in Pointe Coupee Parish, Louisiana, 2007
From Porche to Labatut: Two Centuries on the Pointe Coupee Coast, 2002
From Ternant to Parlange: A Creole Plantation through Seven Generations, 2002
A History of Carnival in Louisiana, 2003
A History of Pointe Coupee Parish, Louisiana, Murray G. LeBeau Memorial Edition, 2010
The House of Lejeune, 2002
The Life, Family, and Legacy of Julien Poydras, 2001
Louisiana Mardi Gras, 1997
New Roads: A Community in Retrospect, 1993
Quintessential Creoles: The Tounoir Family of Pointe Coupee, 2003
Rolling for Charity: A Pictorial History of the New Roads Lions Carnival Parade, 2004

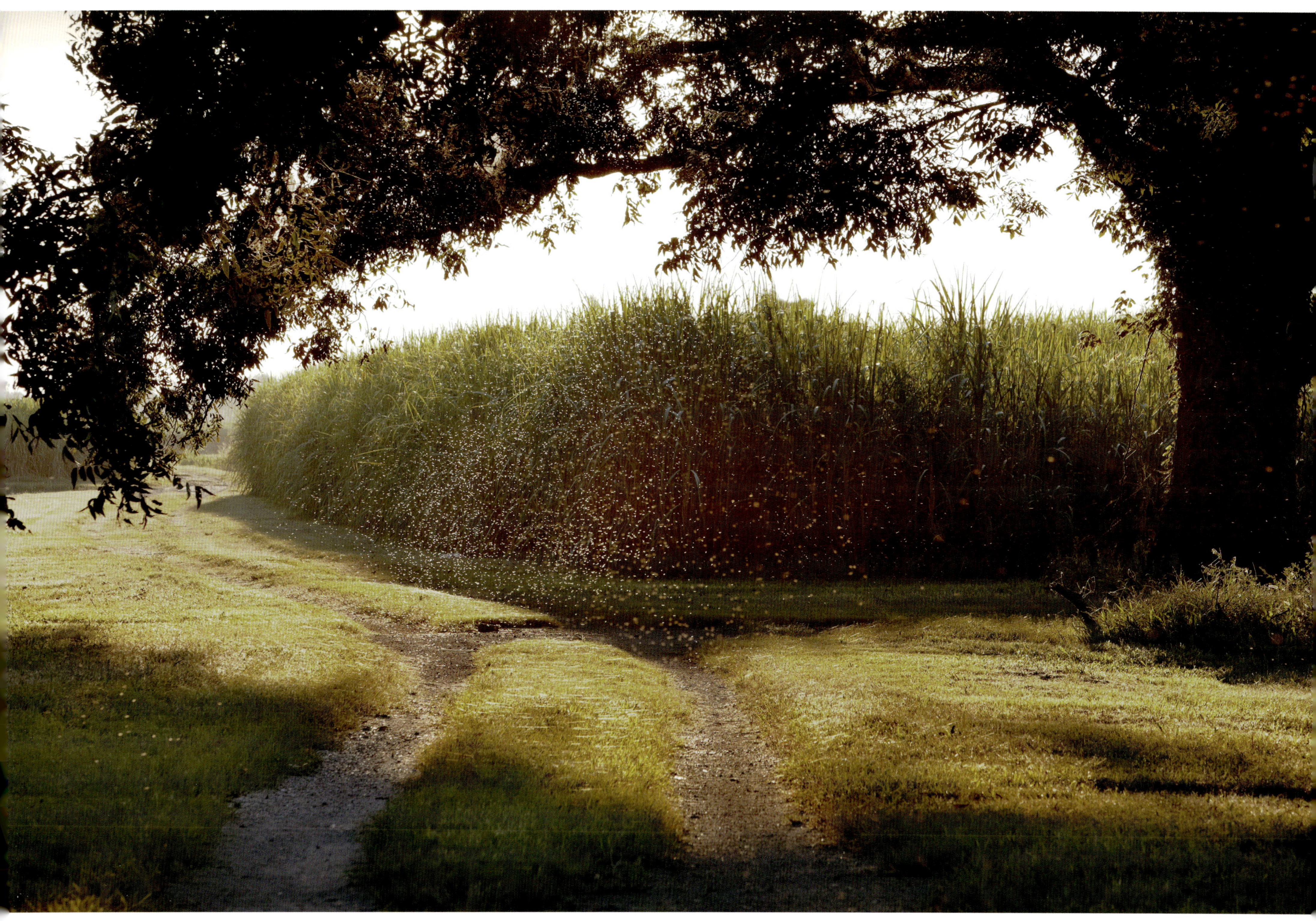

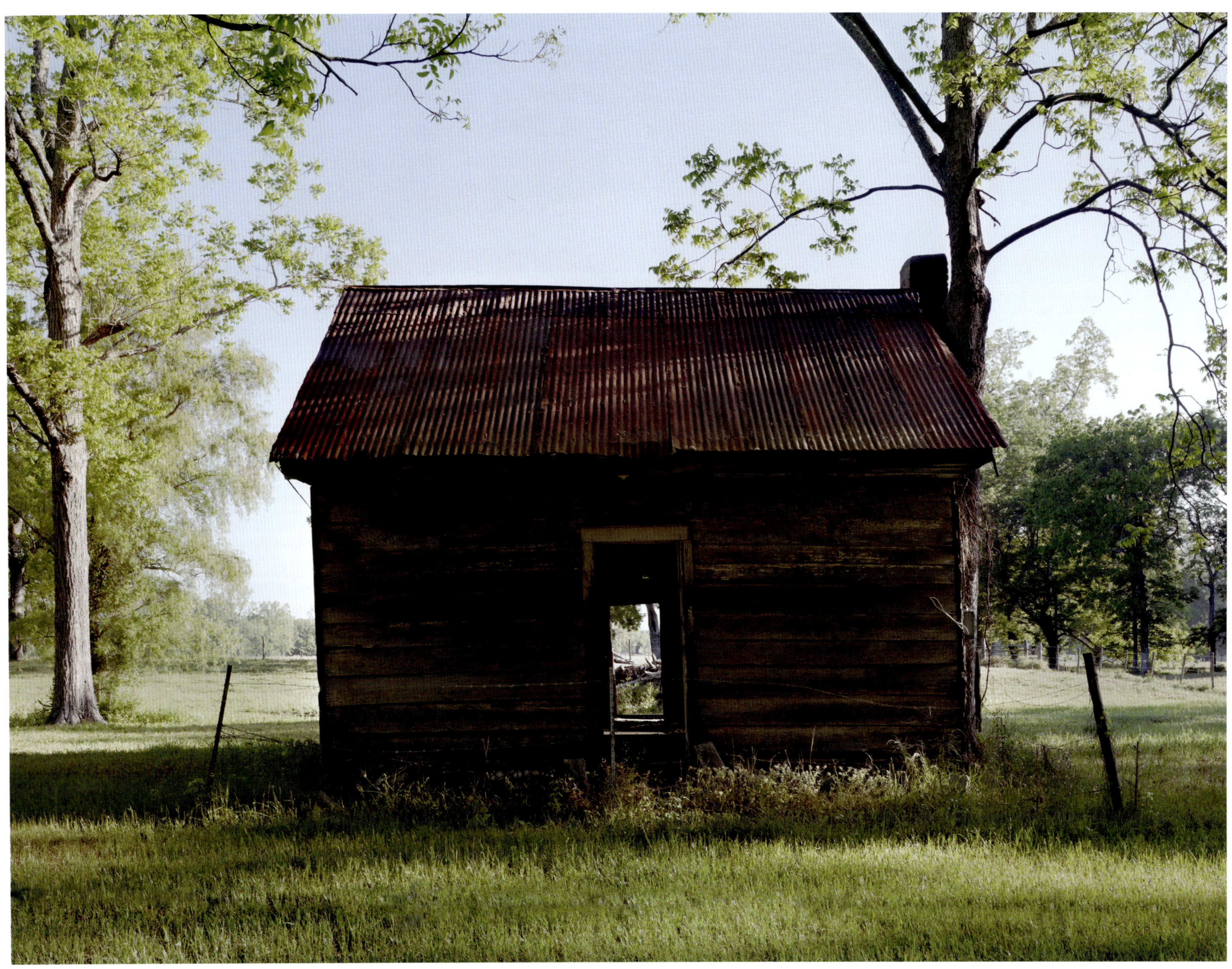

INDEX

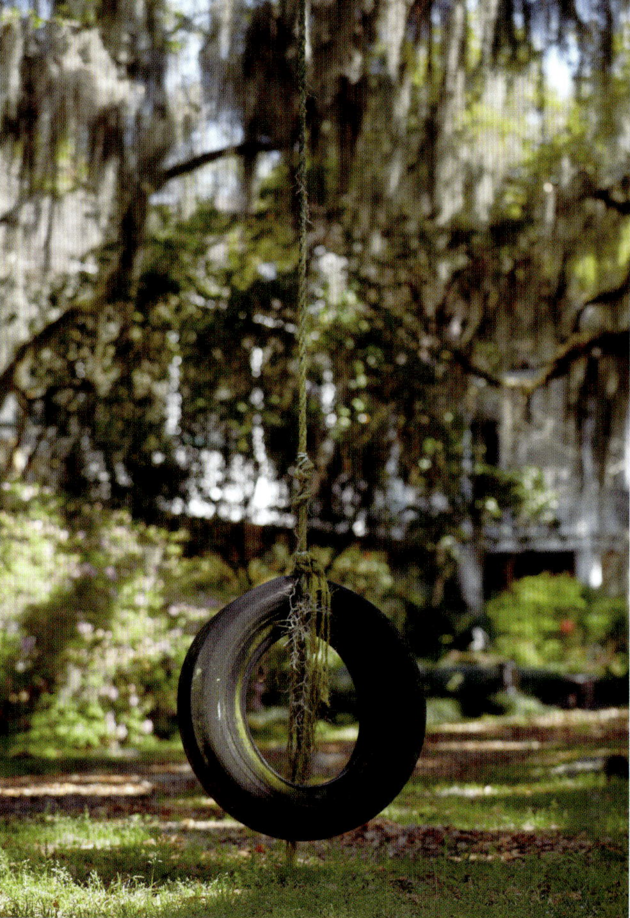

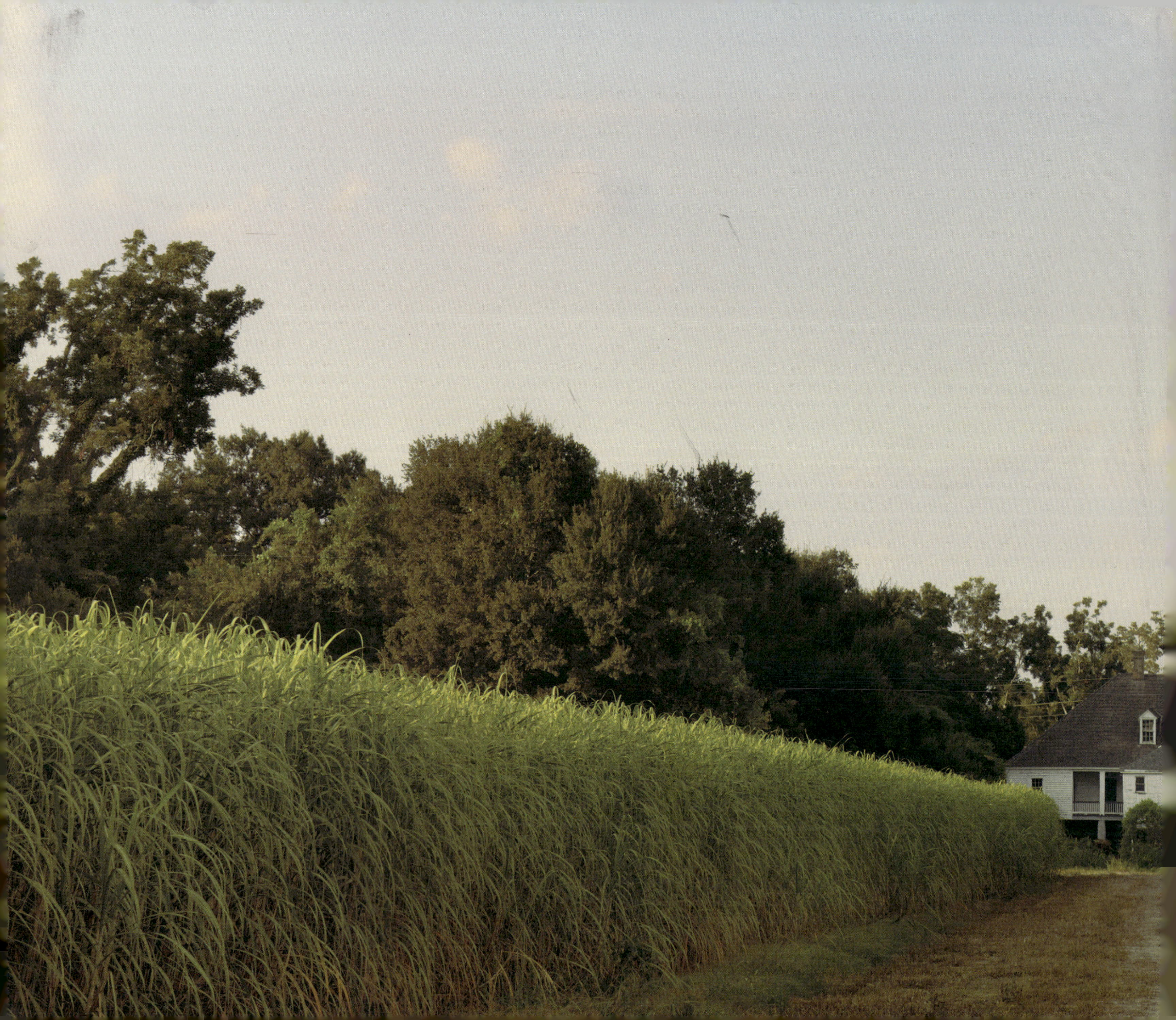